THE ARTS
OF MANKIND

EDITED BY ANDRÉ MALRAUX
AND GEORGES SALLES

Assyria

ANDRE PARROT

THE ARTS OF
ASSYRIA

TRANSLATED BY STUART GILBERT
AND JAMES EMMONS

GOLDEN PRESS · NEW YORK

49542

Library of Congress Catalog Card Number: 61-11170
Printed in France

CONTENTS

Frontispiece: *Assyrian Art*. Lion hunting. *Til Barsce.*
Seventh Century B. C. Wall Painting in the Palace.

For my wife
MARIE-LOUISE

PREFACE

THAT our *SUMER* should be followed by a volume dealing with Nineveh and Babylon was almost a foregone conclusion. But though the Sumerians and Assyrians inhabited the same region, Mesopotamia, they represented very different types of humanity. The Sumerians, those 'mystery men of Near Eastern history,' were essentially inventive and creative, and their artistic achievements vie with the greatest of all time. The Assyrians, who now made their entry on the scene, though perhaps less original in some respects, proved their good judgment by turning to account the discoveries and inventions of their brilliant predecessors.

In *SUMER* we described the dawn of art and civilization. With the present volume we enter on a later period, more comprehensible in many respects but still not fully explored. Year by year new discoveries are bringing home to us the gaps in our knowledge of the period and leading us to revise many hitherto accepted ideas.

True, the comparatively recent discovery of the Sumerian world created a greater sensation, but we must not forget the widespread amazement that greeted the revelation of the Assyrian world over a hundred years ago when, in February 1847, those human-headed bulls 'whose ice-cold eyes had gazed on Nineveh' were unloaded from a Seine barge in Paris. There is a strangely evocative power in the names of certain ancient cities, and Nineveh is one of these. Though less well known, the name of Assur is little less potent, for Assur was the cradle of a great race which has left an indelible mark on history and by methods of the utmost ruthlessness succeeded in establishing Assyrian dominion throughout the

Middle East. For that matter, the Sumerians, too, were far from pacifist-minded and in their cities the doors of the temple of War were rarely closed. But they were more discreet, so to say, about their military exploits and refrained from vaunting them, anyhow on the iconographic plane. Not so, the Assyrians. Congenitally pugnacious, they gloried in their feats of arms and in bloodshed (the blood of the vanquished, needless to say) and did so not merely callously but ostentatiously. And, as was to be expected, their art reflects this attitude.

A few months ago we were once again engaged in excavations in the Euphrates region, at Mari, which is known to have been occupied by an Assyrian garrison for several centuries, and one of our tasks was to distinguish, among the finds made in this area, which pertained to the Sumerians and which to the Assyrians. This proved no easy matter since it was clear that the local population, though thoroughly imbued with Sumerian culture, had long been Semites. The amalgamation of the two cultures could thus take place easily and without conflict: a fact that has been demonstrated ever more convincingly by each of our successive excavations of this site.

The Assyrian world brought to light in the mid-nineteenth century was essentially that of a military civilization. Hundreds of reliefs were uncovered by the workers employed by the pioneer English and French excavators, Layard and Botta, and all related to warfare and Assyrian triumphs on the battlefield. We are spared none of the methods this warrior race employed for achieving an hegemony whose motive seems to have been not so much a desire for 'living room,' as that very human urge which goes by the name of ambition. A pernicious urge, for, once unleashed, nothing can arrest it. And ineluctably it ends in *hubris* and catastrophe: at the height of the conqueror's success comes his downfall.

The Assyrian monarchs were perpetually haunted by the fear of death. That is why, though they had well-trained troops to

ASSYRIAN ART. TIL BARSIP. WINGED GENIUS KNEELING (EIGHTH CENTURY B.C.).

protect them, they also posted at the entrances of their palaces gigantic human-headed bulls whose function it was to keep ceaseless guard over the sovereign, while on the walls of court-yards and corridors winged genii reinforced the human body-guard. There can be no doubt that the monarchs attributed

ASSYRIAN ART. TIL BARSIP. SOLDIER WITH LANCE AND BUCKLER (EIGHTH CENTURY B.C.).

equal efficacy to both classes of defenders, human and superhuman.

Such was the world which we are about to enter and which is revealed under all its aspects in the present volume. For a long while it was accessible only by way of black-and-white reproductions. For though they once were brilliantly painted, the stone reliefs had lost practically all their colour when the archaeologists' spade restored them to the light of day. Yet we now know that the Assyrians called on their artists to carry on the tradition of wall painting, legacy of the Mesopotamian past. In the nineteenth century only insignificant fragments of the murals had been discovered. But in 1929 the expedition led by François Thureau-Dangin (at Til Barsip) had the good fortune to uncover a provincial palace whose decorations had survived almost intact.

ASSYRIAN ART. TIL BARSIP. ARMED SOLDIER ESCOR- →
TING THE ROYAL CHARIOT (EIGHTH CENTURY B.C.).

Unfortunately the delicate technique of reomving paintings from a wall had not then been fully mastered and the discoverers had to confine themselves to making copies on the spot of their successive finds.

After a single exhibition (in 1930), at the Orangerie des Tuileries in Paris, even these copies somehow got mislaid and, despite persistent efforts to trace them, it was only in the present year (1961) that we succeeded in our quest. As originally published, practically all were small reproductions in black-and-white. Today we can present these murals to our readers in all their pristine beauty and with the wealth of colours that delighted those who first set eyes on them, in the seventh or eighth century B.C. They are nothing short of a revelation and, in our opinion, it was well worth delaying slightly the publication of this volume, in order to include these richly detailed scenes, for the first time reproduced in colour, which conjure up so vividly before our eyes the power and the glory of Assyria in her heyday. Looking at the plumed horses galloping towards a lion pierced with arrows, we learn something of the mentality of these born fighters who trained themselves for war by hunting wild beasts on the steppe. Thus the frequent grimness of their art need not surprise us; the men of Nineveh and Assur had lost the art of smiling. Indeed they had no leisure or occasion for light-heartedness; the ancient Land of Eden had ceased, for them, to be a Paradise.

PART ONE

2 - SEAL IMPRESSION. MYTHOLOGICAL SCENE (FIRST HALF, 1st MILLENNIUM). — LOUVRE

I

THE ASSYRIANS AND THE IRON AGE

(1245-606 B.C.)

THE Assyrians, who gained control over Mesopotamia in the thirteenth century B.C. were by no means newcomers to the region. Indeed, of all the peoples that had dominated Meso-potamia during the previous two thousand years, none had an older claim to the country than they. We find them dwelling in the Upper Tigris region at the very dawn of history and an inscribed tablet of the eighth century B.C. lists the names of no less than one hundred and seven Assyrian kings. In all, from the earliest times to the downfall of the Assyrian empire, one hundred and sixteen kings successively occupied the throne of Assur. This continuity is all the more re-markable when we compare it with the eleven kings of Akkad, the five of the Third Dynasty of Ur, the eleven of the First Dynasty of Babylon and even the thirty-six Kassite monarchs. This is not to say that Assyria enjoyed independence, still less hegemony, through-out the period. Several times Assur and Nineveh came under foreign rule; Akkadians and Sumerians occupied both cities for a while. Nevertheless Assyria preserved her racial integrity and lost nothing of that spirit of enterprise which had led her to found trading stations and colonies in far-off Anatolia in the late third and early second millennium B.C.

← 1 - TIL BARSIP (TELL AHMAR). THE GIANT
HEADSMAN (8th-7th CENTURIES B.C.).

I

Assyria took over the culture and art of Mesopotamia without any attempt to modify them and also transmitted them to other lands by way of her colonies. The temple of Ishtar at Assur was adorned with pre-Sargonid statuary indistinguishable from that of Mari, the Diyala region and Lagash, and the headless statue sometimes identified with Zariqum, king of Assur, was quite in the Gudea tradition. This was natural enough; there was no reason why the Northerners should eschew the glamour of the culture that had flowered in the plain watered by the river whose upper reaches lay within their territory.

It was doubtless due to Shamshi-Adad I (Shamshi-Addu) that Assyria became fully conscious both of her native vigour and of her imperial destiny. The Mari tablets have much to tell us of this king who, in a reign of thirty-three years, not only spoke the language of a great leader but enforced his words with deeds. With his occupation o Mari and the appointment of one of his sons, Iasmah-Adad, as his vice-gerent there, Shamshi-Adad I founded an empire which included not only the Tigris and Euphrates valleys but also large areas beyond the rivers. It was probably about this time, the eighteenth century B.C., that the kings of Assur first had the idea of that imperial hegemony which they were to extend to its extreme limits in the following centuries. But this ambitious project was not immediately successful. Its first setback was due to Hammurabi; then the Kassites had to be reckoned with, and finally the Mitanni, even more dangerous opponents, since they had pressed forward to the very banks of the Tigris. However, after yielding for a while to *force majeure*, the Assyrians took advantage of a confused political situation to regain their freedom of action.

This was achieved in the thirteenth century B.C. Within the triangle bounded on two sides by the Tigris and the Great Zab, a new State emerged, toughened by the years of struggle, confident

3 - THE 'ASSYRIAN TRIANGLE'

2

in its mission. The Assyrians were a warlike, virile race. The northern climate, less debilitating than the damp heat of the lowlands, told in their favour, but it was above all to their leaders, who made it a point of honour never to let their advance be checked by any city however strong, that they owed the instrument of their triumphant progress: a disciplined, well-equipped army.

For our present purposes there is no need to describe the successive campaigns which brought the armies of Nineveh and Assur, reign by reign and even year by year, ever further westward. The extreme limits of their advance were marked in different directions by the Persian Gulf and Elam in the

4 - ASSUR. KING ZARIQUM(?)   5 - 'DER CONSISTORIAL-RAT'

east, the Armenian mountains in the north, the Mediterranean and Cyprus in the west, the Arabian desert and Egypt (as far as Thebes) in the south.

Art and civilization marched hand in hand with these military exploits. Two distinct phases emerge: the first lasting from the thirteenth century to about the year 1000 B.C., the second from that date to the downfall of Nineveh (612 B.C.). The former extends from the local and regional emancipation of Assyria herself to the launching of the great expeditions into foreign lands. Its outstanding figures are two kings: Tukulti-Ninurta I (1243-1207 B.C.) who conquered Babylon, and Tiglathpileser (1112-1074 B.C.) who advanced to the Mediterranean. The second period covers the spectacular extension of Assyrian rule, ever harsher and ever gathering speed. A series of kings, from Assurnasirpal II (883-859) to Assurbanipal (668-631) advanced from victory to victory. Unless the historical background is borne in mind, it is impossible to understand Assyrian civilization and art. For the evolution of the former and the inspiration of the latter were closely linked up with the events taking place on the battlefields; this was in the fullest sense of the term an 'Iron Age.' The word 'pity' meant nothing to the Assyrians; their minds were wholly set on victory, victory at all costs and achieved by all means fair or foul.

6 - BABYLON. SEAL IMPRESSION. FIGURE AND ZIGGURAT (LATE 2nd MILL.).

From the first they dipe verything possible to ensure the whole-hearted co-operation of the gods. Tukulti-Ninurta I commissioned several altars with effigies of himself as a worshipper. On one the king is shown standing between two acolytes holding a staff topped by a 'star disk.' On another he is represented twice, first as he approaches the altar of the god Nusku, then as he kneels before it.

Such humility was new; hitherto kings had been shown with their hands clasped, but never kneeling. Another interesting point is that the god never appears in person, he is represented only by his symbols (animals or inert objects). This is confirmed by seal impressions showing a king approaching the gate of a temple. In one we see the dog of the goddess Gula on an altar; on another, Ea's emblem, the goat-fish. This omission of the figures of the gods corresponded to a change in the theological conceptions of the age.

Nevertheless the Assyrians were far from breaking with tradition, and the temples of Assur (which for this period is the city we know best) were dedicated to the old Mesopotamian gods: Ishtar, Sin, Shamash, Anu, Ea, to whom now were added Adad, the storm god, and Assur, who took the place of Enlil. Thus all the leading deities of the ancient pantheon, including the two fundamental triads, were taken over. They were given residences as splendid as the royal palaces and sometimes rendered still more imposing by the addition of a ziggurat. There were three ziggurats in the Assyrian capital and another just across the Tigris at Kar-Tukulti-Ninurta, a town founded by the king of that name to commemorate his victory over Babylon. Ziggurats were by now a familiar feature of the Mesopotamian scene and we may be sure that the Assyrians, true to their 'imperial idea,' spared no expense and energy in erecting theirs.

7 - KAR-TUKULTI-NINURTA. WALL PAINTINGS (13th CENTURY B.C.).

8 - ASSUR. ALTAR OF TUKULTI-NINURTA I (13th CENTURY B.C.). — BERLIN MUSEUM

It is no easy matter reconstructing these sacred edifices; they have been badly damaged and sometimes 'restored.' We have to rely on occasional representations of them in seal designs, giving an idea of their elevation and the general aspect of an architecture that set much store on towers, pilasters and crenellated roofs. Fragments found in excavations reveal that the palace of Tukulti-Ninurta I was also adorned with wall paintings. In them we often find the sacred tree or plant with antithetical animals on each side. This age-old motif was now increasingly stylized, with every trace of naturalism suppressed, but though its purpose was essentially decorative, symbolism was not excluded. Wavy lines, herring-bone patterns and friezes of rosettes must have had a precise meaning for the contemporary beholder.

Agreeing with Andrae, we cannot regard the well-known relief found at Assur in the temple of Assur as Assyrian; probably it is a Kassite work. The central figure is a bearded man, whose cap and garment incised with the scale pattern show him to be a mountain god. But there also are plants sprouting from his body, and goats are feeding on the branches he is holding—proving that he is a vegetation god as well. On each side of him is a small female deity holding the flowing vase from which water is streaming out. All are typically Mesopotamian themes: the figure whose lower portion with its scale pattern represents 'the mountain,' the confronted animals nibbling branches, the goddesses with the flowing vase. But both lay-out and execution are rather clumsy and we hesitate to ascribe them to an Assyrian hand. For all the other works surviving from this period go to show that by now the Assyrian sculptors had thoroughly mastered their craft, and frequently achieved a high standard of elegance.

* * *

The second phase of Assyrian expansion, from about 1000 B.C. on, was one of incessant warfare; Assyria overran the eastern world and drained it of its resources, exterminating or deporting entire populations. But all the time the tide of war rolled westward, towards the one true enemy, sole objective of these far-flung campaigns—Egypt—and one by one the barriers were swept away.

The historical books of the Bible and the annals of the Assyrian kings record the successive stages of this inexorable advance; after the conquest of Damascus and Syria came that of Samaria, capital of Israel, then Philistia, then 'the river of Egypt' which constituted the official frontier. Starting from the banks of the Tigris, the armies of Nineveh came in sight of the lower reaches of the Nile. Under Ramesses III in the twelfth century B.C., Egypt had already had to face a Philistine invasion, but its advance had been halted promptly and effectively. This time the invader was of another calibre and, succeeding where his predecessors had failed, Esarhaddon occupied Memphis. Assurbanipal did even better; following the course of the Nile, his armies forced their way into Upper Egypt and entered Thebes 'of the hundred gates' (663 B.C.). It may well have seemed that the Assyrian empire was due to last for many centuries. Only fifty years later nothing remained of it; Nineveh went up in flames, and its inhabitants paid the penalty of defeat. But before her violent extinction, Assyria had developed an art and architecture measuring up to the military exploits of her years of triumph.

9 - ASSUR. VEGETATION GOD (SECOND HALF, 2nd MILL.). — BERLIN MUSEUM →

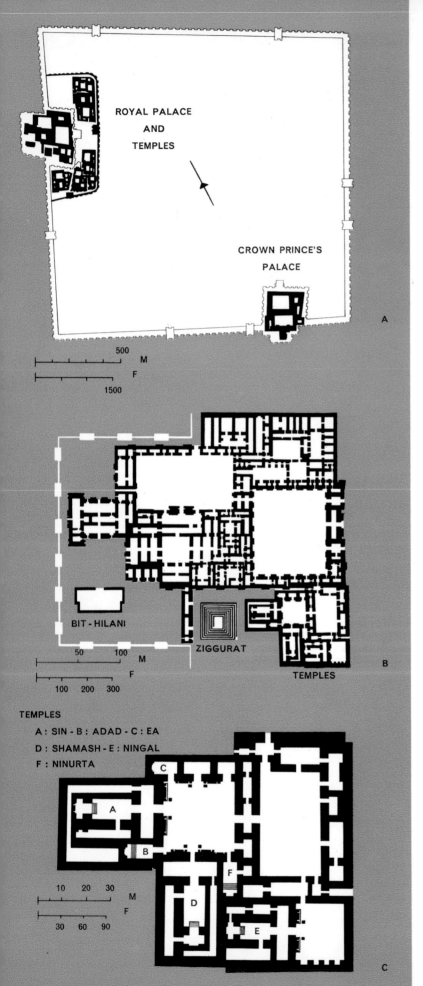

ROYAL PALACE
AND
TEMPLES

CROWN PRINCE'S
PALACE

A

500
M
F
1500

BIT - HILANI

50   100
M
F
100   200   300

ZIGGURAT

B

TEMPLES

TEMPLES

A : SIN - B : ADAD - C : EA
D : SHAMASH - E : NINGAL
F : NINURTA

C

A

B

F

D

E

10   20   30
M
F
30   60   90

C

All, beginning with the palaces, which rank among the most remarkable architectural achievements of all time, is on a gigantic scale. Most systematically investigated has been Sargon's palace at Khorsabad (Dur Sharruduk), unique not only for its size and the regularity of its planning but also for the magnificence of its decorations and appointments. Entirely Sargon's creation, the town in which it stood was built in record time: six years. 'Within this space of time,' the king proudly boasts in an inscription, 'I built a city with [the labours of] the peoples subdued by my hand, whom Assur, Nabu and Marduk had caused to lay themselves at my feet and bear my yoke at the foot of Mount Musri, above Nineveh. In accordance with my god's command and the prompting of my heart, I gave it the name Dur Sharrukin.'

The bricks are inscribed with a text still more eloquent in its brevity: 'Sargon, King of the World, has built a city. Dur Sharrukin he has named it. A peerless palace he has built within it.'

The site of the city covered nearly a square mile, forming an irregular square surrounded by a wall with seven gates. Three of them were decorated with reliefs and friezes in glazed bricks.

Though the city was planned on a large scale the architects prudently began by centring their activities on the enclosing wall and

10 - KHORSABAD (8th CENTURY B.C.)
    (A) OVER-ALL PLAN OF THE CITY
    (B) THE PALACE. (C) THE TEMPLES

8

the citadel located on the north-east and abutting on one of the shorter sides of the ramparts. It contained the palace, a large temple and a number of residences of State officials. At the far end of the city and slightly projecting beyond the enclosing wall was a large building evidently occupied by a person of high rank, which is thought to have been the palace of the Crown Prince.

As the plan shows, only quite a small part of the town had been completed when the king died, after enjoying the amenities of his new capital for only two years. Had he lived longer the inner area would certainly have been filled with private houses, huddled together in the shadow of the ramparts, as was the case with all Assyrian cities. The king's palace testifies to the high ability of both architects and builders. Assurnasirpal had succeeded in building his residential city at Nimrud on an imperial scale, but no other monarch had had Sargon's advantage of working with a free hand on a virgin site. This is why Khorsabad was justly described as 'peerless.'

No less impressive than the mere size of the palace (two hundred and nine rooms and courts, covering some twenty-five acres) is its skilful planning (the size of the open courts diminishes as we move towards the private residential quarter), and the adaptation of the buildings to the lie of the land; several terraces facing north-north-west ensured not only coolness but a fine view of the nearby mountains. We shall speak later of the decorations, so profuse and enormous as to arouse rather admiration of their grandeur than aesthetic pleasure. This ornamental gigantism was a corollary of the architectural lay-out, and its purpose was to bring home to foreigners the king's immense power and his invincibility. Grace and beauty, even religious sentiment, were minor considerations.

Yet all the Assyrian kings, and not least Sargon, while building gorgeous palaces for themselves were not unmindful of the abodes of their gods. There were several temples at Nimrud and Assur, and Dur Sharrukin (Khorsabad) almost from the start had seven. It is significant that six of them formed an architectural complex added, obviously as an afterthought, to the royal palace. Since the gods were given a quarter to themselves, they retained their independence, yet each temple was in fact a palace chapel. Sargon had six deities to cater for: Sin, Shamash, Adad, Ea, Ninurta and Ningal; the moon, the sun, the gods of thunder, of the waters and of war, and a goddess. Outside this precinct, but near by, the temple of Nabu, son of Marduk, proved that, though Khorsabad was his residential city, Sargon bore in mind the claims of Babylon. Nor did he neglect those of Uruk, another of the great cities of his empire, since reliefs of its local hero Gilgamesh figured on the façade of his palace.

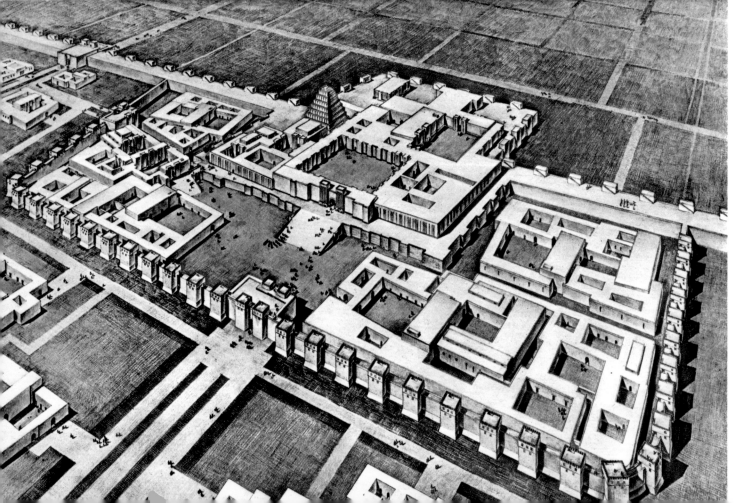

13 - DUR SHARRUKIN (KHORSABAD).   THE ZIGGURAT (8th CENT. B.C.).   (A) ELEVATION ACCORDING TO PLACE.   (B) ELEVATION ACCORDING TO BUSINK

Naturally in addition to these temples a ziggurat was needed, in order to facilitate the gods' descent on earth. For the sacred tower served as a landing stage for the 'boat of heaven.' Excavation has revealed only four stages of the ruined ziggurat of Khorsabad; originally, according to the calculations of Place and his architect Thomas, there were three more; in which case the tower was one hundred and forty feet high and consisted of seven stages. These, it used to be thought, were painted in various 'symbolic' colours: white, black, purple, blue, vermilion, silver and gold. But specialists are not so sure of this today and the Dutch architect T.A. Busink, one of the leading experts in this field, believes that the ziggurat had only five stages and on the summit was a temple dedicated to Assur, known to have been one of the chief gods of Sargon's pantheon, who otherwise would have had no temple at Khorsabad. Access to it was had, not by an ordinary stairway, but by a spiral ramp winding round the core of the tower. This was an innovation, followed to some extent, at a later date, in the famous ziggurat of Babylon, the Biblical 'Tower of Babel.'

Building on a gigantic scale was now to be paralleled by an unprecedented wealth of ornamentation; the sculpture of the Neo-Assyrian period had a sumptuousness greater than any that the East had ever known, or ever was to know. There were two reasons for this: an ample supply of raw materials and the Assyrians' desire to leave their mark on history.

← 11 - DUR SHARRUKIN (KHORSABAD).   VIEW OF THE CITY FROM THE ZIGGURAT (8th CENTURY B.C.)

← 12 - DUR SHARRUKIN (KHORSABAD).   BIRD'S-EYE VIEW OF SARGON'S PALACE (8th CENTURY B.C.)

Differing from the stoneless plains of central and southern Mesopotamia, the region of the Upper Tigris was rich in a gypseous alabaster which was easily extracted from local quarries and, being a relatively soft stone, was equally easy to carve.

But there was a drawback; these slabs were too fragile to resist atmospheric conditions (high winds and winter rains) and fire (when, for example, palaces were burnt down by enemies). Also, the very facility of execution sometimes, it seems, detracted from the quality of the sculpture, though, given the salutary fear the kings inspired, there can have been little danger of the sculptors' wilfully scamping their work.

It is clear that one of the reasons for this enormous output of works of art was the Assyrians' wish to proclaim, iconographically, their pre-eminence, and these picture chronicles supplemented the written records. A king who saw to it that his exploits were narrated, down to the least detail, on stone or clay tablets in their official (i.e. censored) version, also saw to it that these representations served as propaganda and conformed to state requirements. Under this dictatorial régime both scribes and sculptors were docile executants, and a certain constraint makes itself felt in their productions. Here we have one of the reasons why Assyrian art never moves us; it is too persistently

14 - KALAKH (NIMRUD). STELE OF ASSURNASIRPAL
(9th CENTURY B.C.). — BRITISH MUSEUM

'directed', dutifully stereotyped. We feel it is committed to the task of enhancing the king's prestige and representing him as a superman all of whose deeds were prodigies of valour and statesmanship.

Hence the elaboration—and the petrification—of the royal iconography. The king ended up as a mere type form and the living model was so thoroughly merged into the function as to lose all personality. Indeed all Assyrian kings look so much alike that, failing inscriptions, it is almost impossible to distinguish them. They always cut imposing figures, stately and hieratic. It is hard to believe that nature was so sadly uninventive as to reproduce time after time almost exactly the same monarch, or that these sculptured effigies should be regarded as in any way faithful portraits.

This is borne out by the examples given on later pages; in statues and reliefs alike, Shalmaneser III, Assurnasirpal II and Sargon II are to all intents and purposes indistinguishable from each other.

Similarly the scenes represented conform to cut-and-dried formulas. Not that they are devoid of interest; but we cannot help regretting the exclusion of all those small topical details which would have told us something of the climate and mores of the age.

In studying both the content and the formal qualities of this art,

15 - DUR SHARRUKIN (KHORSABAD). KING SARGON II (8th CENTURY B.C.). — TURIN MUSEUM

16 - KALAKH. THE SACRED TREE (9th CENT. B.C.). — BRITISH MUSEUM

17 - KALAKH. CAPTURE OF A TOWN (8th CENT. B.C.). — BRITISH MUSEUM

18 - KALAKH. ASSURNASIRPAL WAGING WAR (9th CENT. B.C.) — BRITISH MUSEUM

we cannot fail to see the large part played by convention. In the reliefs everything is represented on the same plane, without the least hint of depth. As Gadd has observed, it is as if all were visualized on an opaque screen, with nothing in front of or behind it. The artists' chief concern was symmetry, orderly arrangement. Their compositions are so rigorously balanced that they often reproduce, in reverse, a scene already represented.

An example is the relief showing the king with a genius in front of the 'sacred tree' with a winged disk above it, in which the same theme is repeated with only trifling differences: on the left the king is holding the battle-mace, with his arm stretched towards the ground; on the right he clasps it with his arm bent.

Spatial recession is suggested by placing figures not behind, but above or below the main scene, on the same plane. Examples are the battlepieces in which figure Assurnasirpal's or Tiglathpileser's officers. The Assyrian sculptor was equally baffled by the problem of perspective when it came to representing the human figure, whether in profile or full face. In the former case he arrived at an uneasy compromise by giving a twist to the figure's torso and an unnatural elevation to one of the shoulders, the result being a more or less three-quarter view. When rendering figures full-face, he divided the body into two parts, head and bust shown in front view, and the lower part of the body from the waist down in profile. On close inspection of some works we notice anatomical anomalies, such as five-legged bulls; yet these effigies are masterpieces of free fancy combined with no little ingenuity.

14

19 - ASSUR. KING SHALMANESER III (9th CENTURY B.C.). — BRITISH MUSEUM

Assyrian art was remarkably prolific and it took several forms. A great abundance of works of sculpture has come down to us; this was in fact the major art of the Assyrians. But we must begin by noting the extreme paucity of figures in the round. Out of a hundred and sixteen Assyrian kings, statues of two only, Shalmaneser III and Assurnasirpal II, have been discovered. The former was represented twice at Assur, seated on a cubic throne without a back; the head is missing in both cases. A third statue of this monarch (with the head this time) is

15

preserved in the Istanbul Museum. A fourth was found in pieces by a peasant, in 1956, at the foot of the acropolis of Nimrud. It was stored away pending the arrival of the expedition led by Mallowan, who promptly took steps to have it reconstructed. The restoration was carried out with much care in the workrooms of the Iraq Museum at Baghdad. The inscription leaves no doubt that it represents Shalmaneser III (858-824 B.C.) who, after listing on it his various exploits, recounts the campaigns of the twenty-first and twenty-fourth years of his reign. The king, who is standing with his hands clasped, wearing a pointed cylindrical tiara and fringed robe, seems to be awaiting with quiet confidence the verdict of posterity. Placed, it appears, in the temple of Ninurta (in 827 or 826 B.C.), the statue was deliberately shattered, probably by the Medes in 612 B.C. A statue of the king's son Assurnasirpal was also found, intact, at Nimrud. He is represented standing, bare-headed, holding the attributes of sovereignty, a battle-mace and a sickle-sword. In both cases the sculptor has schematized, indeed dehumanized, his model. For the wavy bands traversing Assurnasirpal's robe fail to give any illusion of vibrant life beneath. The general impression is that of a ruthless tyrant, devoid of human feeling, an impression heightened by the tight-set lips and bleakly staring eyes.

20 - KALAKH (NIMRUD). KING SHALMANESER III (SIDE VIEW). — ISTANBUL MUSEUM

21 - KING SHALMANESER III (FRONT VIEW) →

23 - KALAKH (NIMRUD). ASSURNASIRPAL II, DETAIL (9th CENTURY B.C.). — BRITISH MUSEUM

24 - KALAKH. 'THE GOD NABU' (9th-8th CENTURIES B.C.).   25 - DUR SHARRUKIN. CARYATID FIGURE (8th CENTURY B.C.).

Indeed there is more gentleness in the face of the bearded genius (the so-called 'God Nabu') four effigies of which were presented to the god by Bel-tarsi-iluma, governor of Kalakh (Nimrud), 'on behalf of the life of King Adadnirari III and of Sammu-ramat, Lady of the Palace.' Here the lower half of the body is rendered schematically as a cylinder spreading out a little at its base.

The statues of gods with the flowing vase, found in the temple complex of Sargon's palace at Khorsabad, have the same air of dignified repose, and also the same strictly geometrical composition. So it is all the more surprising to light on this statue (unhappily much mutilated) of a naked woman found at Nineveh. Here for once the human body, disdained one would think by Assyrian sculptors, is modelled with loving care. But this figure is an exception, and it had no progeny.

26 - NINEVEH.   STATUE OF A WOMAN (11th CENTURY B.C.). — BRITISH MUSEUM →

27 - HADATU (ARSLAN TASH). GENIUS HOLDIND A BOX (8th CENTURY B.C.). — ALEPPO MUSEUM

With four provincial statues commissioned by Tiglathpileser III for a temple of Ishtar at Arslan Tash (Hadatu) we return to the 'official' style. Each depicts a bearded genius wearing a long fringed robe and holding a stone box. They copy a style dating back to the reign of Adad-nirari III, and already known thanks to Rassam's discoveries at Nimrud. In 1955 Mallowan found another statue of this type, greatly mutilated, also at Nimrud. These figures have some of the traditional qualities of ancient Sumerian statuary: gravity, serenity, hieratic formalism. Here, however, the hands are not clasped in prayer but hold out an open box—perhaps a receptacle for offerings; for the practice of placing collecting-boxes at the doors of sanctuaries is nothing new. And the worshippers at Arslan Tash and Nimrud had good reasons for being generous with their alms, since a god was watching them.

28 - HADATU (ARSLAN TASH). - HEAD OF THE GENIUS HOLDING A BOX (8th CENTURY B.C.). — ALEPPO MUSEUM →

29 - KALAKH (NIMRUD). WINGED HUMAN-HEADED LION (9th CENTURY B.C.). — BRITISH MUSEUM

While sculpture in the round is extremely rare, there is a great abundance of reliefs. The disproportion is hard to account for. Obviously these Assyrian sculptors had thoroughly mastered their craft—why then did they confine themselves to reliefs? Often they carried them to a point where only a few strokes of the chisel would have sufficed to free the figures from the slabs on which they were carved. Yet something held them back. The spirited renderings of Assurbanipal's lion-hunts make the sculptors' evident reluctance to carry their art to its logical conclusion all the more intriguing.

The illustrations speak for themselves and we need do no more than briefly recapitulate some of the leading themes. To begin with, then,

31 - KALAKH (NIMRUD). GUARDIAN LION (9th CENTURY B.C.). — BRITISH MUSEUM

we have the stone animals placed in pairs at the entrances of temples and palaces as 'guardians of the gate.' Their purpose was obviously to ward off potential evil. In the texts they are described as *shedu* and *lamassu*, but while the former could be either a good or a bad genius, the *lamassu* was invariably a good one.

Assyrian sculptors displayed a singularly fertile imagination in their renderings on a huge scale of the hybrid animals bequeathed by an age-old Oriental tradition. Only once do we find a group of guardian lions treated naturalistically. Winged human-headed lions, centaur-lions, and winged human-headed bulls (all of which figured at Nimrud) were the favourite motifs.

← 30 - DUR SHARRUKIN (KHORSABAD). 'GATE A' OF THE CITADEL (8th CENTURY B.C.). — IN SITU

32 - KALAKH (NIMRUD). WINGED HUMAN-HEADED BULL (9th CENTURY B.C.)

33 - HADATU (ARSLAN TASH). GUARDIAN LION (8th CENTURY B.C.). — ALEPPO MUSEUM

34 - KHORSABAD. WINGED HUMAN-HEADED BULLS. (A) LOUVRE (B) ORIENTAL INSTITUTE, CHICAGO

The same types of animals figured at Nineveh as well, where they were made by the sculptors employed by Sargon's son Sennacherib. The curious fact that the sculptors often gave these animals five legs has been interpreted in various ways, but there can be no question of the purport of the forms in which the qualities of four distinct types of living beings are so boldly synthesized: man, the lord of creation; the eagle, monarch of the skies; the lion, king of beasts; and the bull, fecundator of the herds.

At Khorsabad, however, Sargon's gate guardians were invariably bulls, sometimes facing towards the approaching visitor, sometimes with their bodies in side view but slewing round their heads towards him.

35 - KHORSABAD. WINGED HUMAN-HEADED BULL, DETAIL (8th CENTURY B.C.). — LOUVRE →

36 - KHORSABAD. GILGAMESH HOLDING A LION CUB (8th CENT. B.C.)   37 - KHORSABAD. HUMAN-HEADED GENIUS (8th CENT. B.C.)

At Khorsabad, too, and only there, a figure of Gilgamesh, full face, holding a lion cub, stood between two large slabs adorned with bulls. At Khorsabad again, inside the palace gates, was a winged, human-headed genius in high relief holding a pine-cone sprinkler with which to purify those who, after passing the guardian bulls of the gate, were admitted to the interior of the palace.

These Assyrian bulls were in the Sumerian tradition; reproductions on a colossal scale (with wings added) of the small steatite bulls of Lagash. They may well have been the source of Ezekiel's vision of composite creatures, having the fourfold aspects of a man, a lion, an eagle and a bull, which 'went every one straight forward' (Ezekiel i. 9).

38 - KHORSABAD. GILGAMESH HOLDING A LION CUB, DETAIL (8TH CENTURY B.C.). — LOUVRE →

39 - STELAE: (A) NIMRUD. ASSURNASIRPAL II. — MOSUL. (B) KURKH. SHALMANESER III. — BRITISH MUSEUM. (C) ZINJIRLI. ESARHADDON

Guardian animals and human-headed genii with situlae of holy water were carved on slabs in such high relief that very little would have been needed to convert them into sculpture in the round. One of the reasons why the sculptors did not free these figures from the slab on which they were carved was that free-standing figures would have been more vulnerable and the stone ground assured a far greater stability. Another reason was that the slabs were essentially architectural elements: orthostats lining and protecting the lower parts of walls. Functionally speaking, the carvings were superfluous; they were added both for the reasons we have already suggested and for others which will be discussed at a later page.

Before describing the themes most frequently employed in these reliefs, mention may be made of the isolated monuments which were intended to impress visitors to the palace and inspire them with a salutary dread of its august occupant.

First, we have a series of stelae on which the king alone is represented. Of these the most recently discovered is the one Mallowan unearthed in 1951, when excavating Nimrud. In the upper and middle portion of a large rectangular slab inscribed with a long historical text (one hundred and fifty-five lines), a space was reserved for an effigy in low relief of King Assurnasirpal II. He is shown side-face, bedecked with jewels, pendants and bracelets, and wearing a tiara. In his right hand

34

40 - (A) BABYLON. ASSURBANIPAL   (B) NIMRUD. 'OBELISK' OF SHALMANESER III   (C) NINEVEH. 'OBELISK' OF TIGLATHPILESER

he holds a staff; in his left a battle-mace.   Above him are the divine
symbols of Sin, Assur, Enlil, Adad and the seven globes of the *sibitti*,
keeping watch and ward over their vice-gerent on earth.

This 'official' prototype was reproduced, with little change, in subsequent portrayals of Assyrian kings.   We find the same accoutrement in
effigies of Assurnasirpal II, Shalmaneser III, Shamshi-Adad V (who
is wearing on his breast a handsome Maltese cross) and Adad-nirari III.
On the two monuments found at Zinjirli and Tell Ahmar, however,
Esarhaddon is shown holding in leash his enemies: Abdimilkutti, King
of Sidon, and Ushanahura, son of Taharqa, King of Egypt and Nubia.
At Babylon, breaking with a century-old iconographical convention,
Assurbanipal had himself represented full face in the humble posture
of a basket-bearer.   This was a reversion to a very ancient precedent,
notably the representation of the Sumerian Ur-Nanshe, Patesi of Lagash,
who also had had himself depicted with a basket on his head.

On a second type of monument, topped with a ziggurat, we find
reliefs commemorating the king's victories.   The oldest, erected by
Tiglathpileser I and found at Nineveh, shows captives doing homage
to the king.   That he owed his success to the gods' help is indicated by a
winged sun-disk with two hands issuing from it: one in the act of blessing,
the other drawing a bow, symbol of victory.   An identical work recounts
the victories of Assurnasirpal I, and another more famous one, those of

41 - KALAKH. ASSURNASIRPAL SEATED (9th CENTURY B.C.). — BRITISH MUSEUM

Shalmaneser III before whom Jehu, King of Israel, is doing obeisance, his head bowed to the ground. Here we have a detailed pictorial chronicle, with explanatory texts, of Shalmaneser's campaigns. But once again the divine assistance given the victor is duly acknowledged, for the ziggurat at the top of this stele makes it clear not only that the god dominates all the king's exploits but also that it is to the god that the booty and captives are handed over.

But the carved stelae were only a prelude to the vast series of 'pageant pictures' lining the courtyards and walls in the rooms and corridors of the royal palace. Never before had any civilization celebrated its pomp and power to such spectacular effect. And since the king was not merely the figurehead but the very embodiment of the régime, his personal exploits were given special emphasis. But only one side of his life, its official side, was represented: his activities in the palace and in the 'noble sport' of big-game hunting (regarded as training for war), and his prowess on the battlefield. There is no denying that this restricted range of themes often produces a monotonous effect.

A welcome exception is the scene, illustrated here, which gives us a glimpse of the king's personal life in the palace. For once he is seated, taking his ease, cup in hand. Wearing the peaked tiara, his hair and beard exquisitely

42 - KALAKH (NIMRUD). ASSURNASIRPAL HOLDING A BOW (9th CENTURY B.C.). — BRITISH MUSEUM

36

groomed, Assurnasirpal is lavishly bedecked with jewellery: earrings, a necklet, and bracelets at his wrists and elbows. The cup from which he is going to drink has been filled by his cup-bearer, a high-ranking court official chosen with especial care since, given the frequency with which unpopular monarchs were dispatched by poison to another world, he held the king's life in his hands. The king's safety is well provided for; not only are two armed guards in attendance but, furthermore, celestial protection is ensured by winged, human-headed genii making the gesture of purification.

Elsewhere the king is shown in the role of worshipper. He has doffed his tiara and holds in his left hand the 'sacred plant' while his right is raised in homage. At Khorsabad we see Sargon carrying a sacrificial ibex and his gaze has a remarkable intentness, an air of firm resolve. Obviously the sculptor wished both to stress the monarch's regal mien and to render every detail of hair and beard with meticulous precision. Though the model's muscular development is less exaggerated than in the Nimrud figures, the general effect is dry and static, the only lively note being struck by the animal's head, with its alert eyes and pricked-up ears. Yet even the little ibex seems unnaturally rigid, all its muscles tensed; perhaps because it has seen the sacrificer's knife and scented danger.

43 - DUR SHARRUKIN (KHORSABAD). SARGON II CARRYING THE SACRIFICIAL IBEX (8th CENTURY B.C.). — LOUVRE

37

44 - DUR SHARRUKIN (KHORSABAD). CARRIERS OF 'TOWNS' (8th CENTURY B.C.). — LOUVRE

46 - NINEVEH. SACK OF THE CITY OF HAMAAN (1st MILL.). — BRITISH MUSEUM

Again at Khorsabad the king is represented as he comes out of the
Throne Room and stands complacently watching processions advancing
towards him from all sides: soldiers, servants and tributaries—tokens
of his victories and the steady expansion of his empire. All is disciplined, strictly regulated; only the horses adorned with plumes show
signs of restiveness and the grooms leading them have all they can
do to keep them in hand.

← 45 - DUR SHARRUKIN (KHORSABAD). PLUMED HORSES' HEADS
     (8th CENTURY B.C.). — ORIENTAL INSTITUTE, CHICAGO

47 - KALAKH (NIMRUD). FUGITIVES SWIMMING WITH WATER-SKINS (9th CENTURY B.C.). — BRITISH MUSEUM

But actual warfare is by far the most frequent theme and in it the king always has the leading role. He personally takes part in every campaign and figures in the forefront of the battle. Needless to say, only successful campaigns are represented and, of these, only carefully selected scenes.

48 - KHORSABAD. 'SEASCAPE.' FLOATING TIMBER (8th CENTURY B.C.). — LOUVRE

49 - NINEVEH. SENNACHERIB AT THE SIEGE OF LACHISH (690 B.C.). — BRITISH MUSEUM

50 - NINEVEH. DEFEAT OF THE ELAMITES (7th CENTURY B.C.). — BRITISH MUSEUM

There are some marked changes in the style of Assyrian narrative imagery between the reigns of Assurnasirpal and Assurbanipal, a period of about two hundred years. In the ninth century only a few representative figures are employed; that is to say, two or three soldiers do duty for an army. There is not the slightest attempt to render perspective or relative dimensions. Thus sometimes the king in his chariot stands higher than the town he is besieging and defenders of fortresses are as tall as the towers they are manning. Depth is suggested by placing figures or accessories in the open space above the scene represented. At first sight we may be startled by this procedure, but soon we realize that as a convention it is as acceptable as another, and that the sculptors could thereby conjure up a scene more vividly than was possible with a system of narrow superimposed registers. Actually Assyrian art never succeeded in choosing between these two

51 - NINEVEH. WILD SOW AND ITS YOUNG IN THE MARSHES (7th CENTURY B.C.). — BRITISH MUSEUM

52 - NINEVEH. WARFARE IN THE MARSHES (7th CENTURY B.C.). — BRITISH MUSEUM

methods, static and dynamic, and sometimes we find them employed simultaneously in the same work, as in the depiction of Assurbanipal's victories over Elam. But by then a notable change of style had intervened; no confusion is possible between ninth-century reliefs and those of the seventh. After a series of transitional phases, illustrated by the Khorsabad 'seascape,' the scenes of Sennacherib's siege of Lachish and his campaign in the marshes, the relief became much lower, scenes were incised far more than modelled. Also dimensions were scaled down so that more and more figures could be included in each frieze. Thus the representation of the defeat of the Elamites contains a vast number of bodies and accessories. Scenery, too, was rendered in much greater detail: the reeds and copses of the marshlands, rivers, canals teeming with fish, palm groves and fig-trees—everything, in short, that helped the spectator to visualize the landscape setting of each incident.

53 - NINEVEH.   TOWNSFOLK LED INTO CAPTIVITY, DETAIL (7th CENTURY B.C.). — LOUVRE

However, the fact that narrative had ceased to be a matter of stereo-typed formulas and that artists had more scope for personal initiative did not put an end to repetitions of such hackneyed subjects as the triumphal progress of the king in his chariot, or the long processions of captives, leading their livestock and followed by cartloads of children. But captivity was not the only penalty of defeat; it was accompanied by executions, massacres and torture. The remarkable proliferation of such motifs shows that Assyrian artists, or rather their patrons, took pride and pleasure in representations not only of actual warfare but of its often cruel aftermath. The purpose of such scenes was to impress beholders with the invincibility of the conqueror and the folly of resistance. The palace of Khorsabad was filled with depictions of savagery and carnage, grim reminders, for visitors and courtiers alike, of the ruthless efficacy of the royal war-machine.

54 - NINEVEH.   TOWNSFOLK LED INTO CAPTIVITY, DETAIL (7th CENTURY B.C.). — LOUVRE

55 - NINEVEH. CAPTIVES, DETAIL OF THE SIEGE OF LACHISH (7th CENTURY B.C.). — BRITISH MUSEUM

How, indeed, could any other nation hope to stand up against so well equipped and trained an army as that of Assyria in the early first millennium B.C.? Not only its organization and equipment but its tactics in the field are illustrated in the reliefs. It contained all the basic elements of a modern army corps: cavalry, infantry, engineers, armoured vehicles—the only thing lacking was an air force!

56 - NINEVEH. TOWNSFOLK LED INTO CAPTIVITY, DETAIL (7th CENTURY B.C.). — LOUVRE

57 - NINEVEH. HORSEMAN SHOUTING, DETAIL (7th CENTURY B.C.). — LOUVRE

58 - NINEVEH. CAMP SCENE: ORDERLY IN A TENT (7th CENTURY B.C.). — BERLIN MUSEUM

We even have glimpses of the life of the troops in camp behind the fighting line, as in the topical detail illustrated, a welcome change from the conventional battlepieces. We see an orderly busy in a tent, making his officer's bed, and about to place a jug of water ready to hand in case the officer should feel thirsty in the night. Unfortunately, such glimpses of daily life 'behind the scenes' are all too rare, and their almost total absence is yet another reason for the curious impersonality and lack of 'human interest' which characterize so much Assyrian art.

59 - NINEVEH. CAPTIVES RESTING AND EATING (7th CENTURY B.C.). — LOUVRE →

60 - NINEVEH. 'THE FEAST IN A GARDEN' (7th CENTURY B.C.). — BRITISH MUSEUM

The famous relief showing Assurbanipal and the queen taking refresh-
ment in a garden illustrates one of the brief interludes in a life spent for
the most part on active service. The king is back in Nineveh, reclining
on a couch, cup in hand, narrating his exploits to the queen, who is
seated on a chair in front of him. (This is one of the very few scenes in
which a woman figures.) A harpist is playing in the background, servants are plying fly-whisks and birds are twittering in the trees. But
even in this idyllic scene there is a jarring note; on a tree beside the
harpist hangs the severed head of Teuman, King of Elam.

61 - NINEVEH. MUSICIANS, DETAIL
(7th CENTURY B.C.). — LOUVRE →

62 - KALAKH (NIMRUD). ASSURNASIRPAL HUNTING BULLS (9th CENTURY B.C.). — BRITISH MUSEUM

Hunting, as we have said, was regarded not only as a sport of kings but also as the best training for the field of battle. The earliest Assyrian hunting scenes show Assurnasirpal, armed with bow and arrows and riding in a chariot, hunting bulls and lions. There are few figures: only the king, the driver and some soldiers, on foot or mounted. The scene is treated with forcible directness and a rare feeling for plasticity. Stress is laid on the king's athletic prowess (with a single hand he dispatches a bull that has rashly flung itself on the chariot) and on his skilful marksmanship; the animals are riddled with arrows. It seems that after every hunt a libation was poured on the bodies of the slain animals, but the reasons for this have never been elucidated.

63 - NINEVEH. ASSURBANIPAL DISPATCHING A LION (7th CENTURY B.C.). — BRITISH MUSEUM

5

64 - KALAKH (NIMRUD). ASSURNASIRPAL LION-HUNTING (9th CENTURY B.C.). — BRITISH MUSEUM

When the king of Nineveh bade his sculptors commemorate his
prowess as a hunter, the shortcomings to which we have referred were
brilliantly eliminated, and this form of art took on a new lease of life.
Not only do these later sculptors display a better grasp of animal anatomy,
a greater mastery of their medium and a much improved technique,
but the whole handling of forms undergoes a drastic change.   Hitherto

The form of sport practised by Sennacherib during the lifetime of
Sargon, his father, and illustrated in the hunting reliefs from Khorsabad,
was less dangerous. We see the crown prince tracking down small
game—hares, gazelles and birds—in the woodlands or on the edge of a
lake. But, compared with the great hunting scenes of Assurbanipal's
reign, these seem hardly more than hastily executed sketches.

59

65 - NINEVEH. ASSURBANIPAL LION-HUNTING (7th CENTURY B.C.). — BRITISH MUSEUM

these had tended to be static, not to say inert. Now the sculptors
bring them vividly to life, as in those incomparable masterpieces of
animal sculpture: the 'Dying Lioness' and the 'Lion and Lioness'.

Each of these reliefs merits close study; taken together they form one
of the most remarkable 'frescoes' in stone ever devoted to the celebration
of the god of hunting.

67 - DUR SHARRUKIN (KHORSABAD). HUNTING AND HAWKING, DETAIL (8th CENTURY B.C.). — LOUVRE

The sportsmen are seen setting out at daybreak. The big hunting dogs are straining at their leashes, fretting at the delay. The lions, too, are restless after being penned up for days in wooden cages, eager for the moment when the trap-door is opened. The king is ready for the fray whatever form it may take, whether he is to fight on horseback, from his chariot or—at greater risk—on foot. His weapons are a hunting spear, a bow and arrows, and sometimes he dispatches an animal with his sword. The lions put up a stiff resistance, flinging themselves furiously on their attackers. One is represented clawing at the belly of the king's horse, but the monarch keeps his head and drives his spear home with a mighty thrust. In the hunting field as on the field of battle, the monarch's tactics are unerring.

68 - NINEVEH. HUNTSMAN HOLDING A DOG IN LEASH (7th CENTURY B.C.). — BRITISH MUSEUM

69 - NINEVEH. LION RELEASED FROM ITS CAGE (7th CENTURY B.C.). — BRITISH MUSEUM →

70 - NINEVEH. THE DYING LIONESS (7th CENTURY B.C.). — BRITISH MUSEUM

The carnage is prodigious, the whole arena is strewn with dead or
dying lions riddled with arrows, while others are wheeling round, about
to launch themselves into a last desperate attack on their assailants.
Even when mortally wounded, the animals can still be dangerous.
Pierced by three arrows, the Dying Lioness still has strength enough
left to raise herself on her forefeet, though her hindquarters are paralysed,
trailing on the ground. She is obviously *in extremis* but her fangs are
bared—if she must die, she will sell her life dearly. Meanwhile in the
offing, in the shade of trees whose trunks are wreathed with creepers,

71 - NINEVEH. LION AND LIONESS (7th CENTURY B.C.). — BRITISH MUSEUM

72 - NINEVEH. HUNTING WILD ASSES (7th CENTURY B.C.). — BRITISH MUSEUM

we see a Lion and Lioness still outside the danger zone.   The lion has
heard the roars of the hunted animals and is rising to its feet; the lioness,
still stretched on the ground, is clearly on the alert.

But now the hunt is moving on, in pursuit of a new quarry, a herd
of wild asses.   Arrows are whizzing through the air, hunting dogs
race forward.   In the distance gazelles with their young are moving
away, slowly as yet, for the danger does not seem imminent, but the buck
bringing up the rear has scented trouble, is looking round and soon no
doubt will give the signal for a general stampede.

73 - NINEVEH. GAZELLES IN FLIGHT (7th CENTURY B.C.). — BRITISH MUSEUM

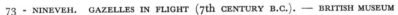

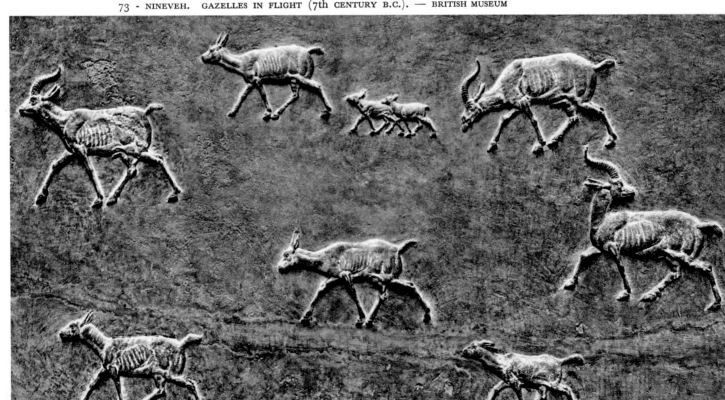

74 - NINEVEH. GROOMS BRINGING IN A DEAD LION (7th CENTURY B.C.). — LOUVRE

Finally we see the return of the hunt. Servants, bending under the weight, are carrying back to the palace the day's bag and aligning the bodies at the foot of a fire altar, while the king, holding a cup in his right and, walks forward to render thanks to the gods and pours a libation over the dead lions.

75 - NINEVEH. GROOMS BRINGING IN A DEAD LION 76 - NINEVEH. ASSURBANIPAL MAKING A LIBATION (7th CENT. B.C.). — BRITISH MUSEUM

77 · DUR SHARRUKIN (KHORSABAD). GENIUS (8th CENT. B.C.). — LOUVRE   78 - KALAKH (NIMRUD). GENIUS (9th CENT. B.C.). — LOUVRE

Besides the gigantic lions, centaurs and human-headed bulls acting as wardens of the palace, there are effigies of beings who may be identified with genii, belonging to the personnel of the celestial courts (for, like kings, the gods too had their retinues). Sometimes they assume the form of human beings equipped with wings; sometimes that of winged hybrids with human bodies and animal heads. Their functions, it would seem, were always beneficent. Often they are associated with an extremely stylized tree, evidently an object of veneration. The purport of the scene of a genius touching the tree with a pine-cone and holding in his left hand a small pail (situla) is a moot point. Some think it represents the fructification of the palm-tree. We are, however, more inclined to think that the genius is collecting the sacred fluid exuding from the trunk and leaves and that when he plunges the pine-cone into the situla the liquid it contains will be transmuted into holy water. With this water the genius will proceed to sprinkle the king so as, no doubt, to purify him, but above all to immunize him against the influences of evil powers. (The same rite of purification was enjoined on members of the royal household and on visitors to the palace.)

This proliferation of genii tends to mask the curious fact that major deities are practically never represented. Exceptions are some stone slabs, dating to the reign of Assurnasirpal, which show Assur or Shamash borne on a winged disk hovering above the battle-field and assisting the king who is standing in a chariot below. A panel of glazed bricks from Assur represents a man, presum-ably the king, worshipping a god on a pedestal, and from the same city comes a limestone slab showing Adad standing on a winged bull and Ninurta bow in hand.

But though absent from the palaces on the banks of the Tigris, the major gods were often repre-sented in the provinces; for exam-ple in the rock sculptures at Maltai, Bavian and Hines. Here the rock face provided settings vast enough to do justice to great processions and majestic effigies of the gods. At Maltai Sennacherib is shown rendering homage to a whole pan-theon of gods, amongst them Assur, Ninlil, Sin, Shamash, Adad and Ishtar. At Hines Sennacherib wor-ships Assur and Ninlil only but, as at Khorsabad, there are effigies of Gilgamesh and a lion flanked by winged, human-headed bulls.

79 - ASSUR. SCENE OF WORSHIP (1st MILL.). — BERLIN MUSEUM

80 - HINES REGION. ROCK SCULPTURES OF SENNACHERIB (7th CENTURY B.C.).

81 - GOMEL GORGE, HINES REGION. RELIEF OF SENNACHERIB (7th CENTURY B.C.).

82 - ASSUR. RITUAL BASIN WITH GODS AND GENII (8th-7th CENTURIES B.C.). — BERLIN MUSEUM

An object that Andrae found, in fragments, in a well in the great temple of Assur is of a quite exceptional nature. This was a large rectangular tank decorated in the centre of each side and at the corners with a god clasping to his breast the flowing vase. The water issuing from them either streams into vases which seem poised in air, above, or sinks to the ground. Here, again, we find the motif of four streams pouring from the same container. Beside each god is a man clad in a fish-skin and holding a situla.

It would have been hard to assign a date to this monument, were it not that fragmentary inscriptions on two sides prove that it was made in the time of Sennacherib (704-681 B.C.). Though easy enough to describe, it is far from easy to interpret. For one thing, it is not absolutely certain that the gods with the flowing vase should be identified with Ea. Their attendants clad in fish-skins, however, are almost certainly priests. The most that can safely be said is that the purpose here was to associate the 'god of the sweet waters' with their natural denizens, i.e. fish, and that basic to this curious composition is a set of themes deriving, if at a long remove, from Sumerian times.

83 - ASSUR. RITUAL BASIN, DETAIL: A GOD (8th-7th CENTURIES B.C.). — BERLIN MUSEUM →

84 - HADATU (ARSLAN TASH). THE GOD ADAD (8th CENTURY B.C.).   85 - TIL BARSIP (TELL AHMAR). ISHTAR OF ARBELA (8th CENTURY B.C.).

Usually the gods are mounted on their animal attributes; an iconography to which Isaiah alludes (probably without understanding it) when he exults over the fall of the idols of Babylon: 'Bel boweth down, Nebo stoopeth, their idols were upon the beasts, and upon the cattle' (xlvi. 1). In the same tradition are two stelae in the Louvre which were found in Assyrian provincial residences in North Syria. One of them comes from Arslan Tash (Hadatu) and shows Adad, with a lightning-flash in each hand, standing on a bull; on the other, found at Til Barsip (Tell Ahmar), Ishtar of Arbela, goddess of war, is advancing, mounted on a lion.

However, the themes were not exclusively of a religious order. Hadatu has yielded carved slabs featuring such 'classical' Assyrian motifs as the royal chariot, processions of soldiers and horsemen. And

76

86 - TIL BARSIP. KING ESARHADDON (669 B.C.). — ALEPPO MUSEUM   87 - TIL BARSIP. THE GOD TESHUB (LATE 2nd - EARLY 1st MILL.). — LOUVRE

at Til Barsip two stelae were found commemorating Esarhaddon's victories over Egypt and Phoenicia. Moreover both cities followed the Assyrian practice of setting up at the gates of palaces huge guardian animals, bulls and lions, but rendered under their natural aspects. The function of the gate lions at Til Barsip was clearly indicated by their names: 'The rushing storm, irresistible in attack, laying rebels low, procuring that which satisfies the heart,' and 'He who pounces on rebellion, sweeps away the enemy, drives out evil men and lets the good men enter.'

The large stelae of a Hittite type, also found at Til Barsip, which show Teshub, supreme god of the elements, standing on his animal attribute, the bull, with an axe in his right hand and the lightning-fork in his left, and with the winged disk above him, belong to a very different world. That these works are essentially Hittite, not Mesopo-

88 - HADATU (ARSLAN TASH). BULL PASSANT (8th CENTURY B.C.). — LOUVRE

tamian in conception is borne out by the inscriptions in Hittite hieroglyphics. Garments and headdresses have nothing in common with
those of the Tigris and Euphrates valleys. Only the animal bearing
the god was common to the two cultures. (This accounts for the fact
that in the Til Barsip relief Esarhaddon places himself under the protection of this 'alien' god.) Bull of Teshub, bull of Adad, bull of the
Canaanite god Baal—all go to show that, though the local religions
differed, their iconography was always drawn from a common source.

89 - TIL BARSIP (TELL AHMAR). THE GOD TESHUB
(LATE 2nd - EARLY 1st MILL.). — ALEPPO MUSEUM →

CHAPTER I

THE ASSYRIANS
AND THE IRON AGE

(1245-606 B.C.)

Despite the emergence of Assyrian art and culture at an earlier period, it is not until nearly the end of the second millennium that they display any real originality. The political and military successes of the Assyrians and the steady growth of their empire lead to intensified productivity in the field of art. For their rulers, congenitally authoritarian, see to it that their orders are carried out to the letter. It is an 'Iron Age' in the fullest meaning of the term. From the Tigris to the Nile, from Nineveh to 'hundredgated' Thebes, the Assyrian armies roll westward, like a tidal wave, sweeping all before them. Then suddenly, at the very time when the edifice of Assyrian power seems destined to last for centuries, it collapses under the onslaughts of Medes and Neo-Babylonians.

Despite the wanton damage inflicted by the conquerors, enough remains of the palaces and their sculpture, planned on the same gigantic scale, to make us realize the magnificence of the Assyrian achievement. True, all this magnificence has a propagandist purpose—to impress the world at large with the greatness and invincibility of the ruling race—and the over-all effect of the sculptured chronicles displayed in the royal residences at Nineveh, Nimrud, Khorsabad and Assur, with their stereotyped effigies of the monarchs, is apt to be monotonous. Stress is invariably laid on military exploits; we are spared none of the horrors of the battlefield. Yet some of the great hunting scenes in which Assurbanipal, one of the most cultivated kings of this Iron Age, plays a leading part, are noble works in their own right and justly rank among the masterpieces of world art.

KINGS	SITES
Tukulti-Ninurta I (1243-1207)	ASSUR
	KAR-TUKULTI-NINURTA
Tiglathpileser I (1112-1074)	NINEVEH
Assurbelkala (1071-1054)	NINEVEH
Assurnasirpal I (1047-1029)	
Assurdan II (932-910)	
Tukulti-Ninurta II (890-884)	ASSUR
Assurnasirpal II (883-859)	NIMRUD
Shalmaneser III (858-824)	ASSUR
	NIMRUD
	BALAWAT
Shamshi-Adad V (823-810)	NIMRUD
Adad-Nirari III (810-782)	NIMRUD TIL BARSIP
Tiglathpileser III (745-727)	NIMRUD
	HADATU (ARSLAN TASH)
Bel-Harran-Bel-usur	
Shamash-resh-usur	MARI-BABYLON
Sargon II (721-705)	DUR SHARRUKIN (KHORSABAD)
	ASSUR
Sennacherib (704-681)	ASSUR NINEVEH BAVIAN MALTAI-HINES
Esarhaddon (680-669)	ZINJIRLI NINEVEH TIL BARSIP
Assurbanipal (668-631)	NINEVEH TIL BARSIP
Fall of Nineveh (612)	
Assurballit II (611-606)	

ARCHITECTURE	SCULPTURE	TERRACOTTA	EGYPT	AEGEAN
	Altars Mountain-god of the Temple of Assur		New Kingdom Tuthmosis III (1504-1450) Ramesses II (1301-1235)	Late Minoan I (1550-1450) Late Minoan II and III (1450-1180)
Palace, Ziggurat		Assur in the 'Aura'		Coming of the Dorians
	Obelisk in the British Museum Woman's Torso		Late Period Psusennes I (1054-1009)	End of the Dorian Invasions (1050)
	Obelisk			
	Stele A		Sheshonk I (950-929)	
Palace Ziggurat	Statue Stelae Reliefs Statues		Osorkon II (870-847)	Composition of the Homeric Poems (850)
	Statues Stele Black Obelisk			
	Stele			
Palace	Stele Statues of 'Nabu' Statue with a 'Box'			
	Reliefs			
Palace	Statues with a 'Box' Stele			
	Stele			
Palace Ziggurat	Reliefs	King List Enamelled Panel	Shabaka (716-701)	
Palace	Ritual Basin			
Palace	Reliefs Rock-face Reliefs Rock-face Reliefs		Taharqa (689-663)	
Palace	Stele Stelae			
Palace Palace	Reliefs	Library	Psammetichus (663-609)	

91 - TELL HALAF. SCORPION-MAN (EARLY 1st MILL.). — ALEPPO MUSEUM

II

FROM THE KHABUR TO THE TIGRIS

THE Assyrian imprint, as we have seen, is unmistakable at Arslan
Tash and Tell Ahmar on the Middle Euphrates; it reappears,
somewhat modified at Tell Halaf, the ancient Guzana of the
Neo-Assyrian period. Located near the sources of the Khabur river,
the site was settled as early as the beginning of the fourth millennium
B.C. By reason of its painted pottery, Tell Halaf has given its name to
one of the protohistoric phases of Mesopotamian culture, between the
Samarra and al 'Ubaid periods . Then the site was abandoned for over
two thousand years. On the ruins of the ancient settlement a new town,
Guzana, sprang up in about the eleventh century B.C., on which an
enterprising monarch, Kapara, son of Hadianu, conferred the lustre of
a capital by erecting stately buildings adorned with hundreds of reliefs.
The acropolis overlooking the Khabur river was crowded with temples
and palaces. One of these buildings, described by the excavators as a
'Temple Palace,' contained what was certainly the strangest assortment
of sculpture ever brought together, and intended, one would think, to
plunge the spectator into a mysterious, dread-inspiring world.

The terrace on which the building stood could only be reached
through a gateway guarded by two winged human-headed, scorpion-
bodied monsters. A winding stone-paved approach rose gradually to the

92 - TELL HALAF. PALACE OF KAPARA. RECONSTRUCTION OF THE 'SCORPION GATE' (EARLY 1st MILL.).

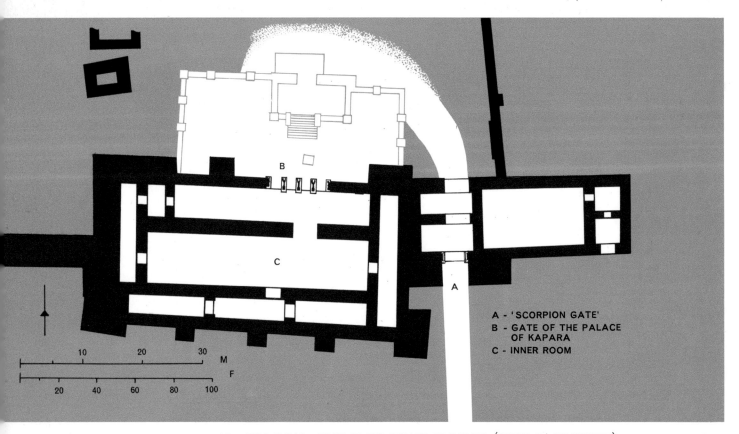

A - 'SCORPION GATE'
B - GATE OF THE PALACE
    OF KAPARA
C - INNER ROOM

93 - TELL HALAF. PLAN OF THE PALACE OF KAPARA (EARLY 1st MILLENNIUM).

94 - TELL HALAF. SCORPION-MAN, DETAIL
(EARLY 1st MILL.). — ALEPPO MUSEUM

95 - TELL HALAF. PALACE OF KAPARA. RECONSTRUCTION OF THE PORTICO (EARLY 1st MILL.). — TELL HALAF MUSEUM, BERLIN

foot of a stairway leading up to a terrace where the visitor was confronted by a huge portico framed by two winged sphinxes and divided into four bays by three tall column-figures, two male, one female, standing on three animals of a menacing aspect, a lioness, a lion and a bull. Under the bellies of the animals were various scenes: a stag lying on its back, a hunted gazelle galloping towards a small palm-tree, and a lioness suckling her cub.

Seen against the dark mass of the basalt building towering above them, with their eyes of white stone inlaid with a pellet of black schist, these animals surmounted by the three tall statues must have struck awe into the heart of the contemporary beholder, whose fears were certainly not allayed by the two winged griffins posted on either side of the portico. The main room of which this was the entrance was found empty, devoid of any furnishings which might have enabled

96 - PALACE OF KAPARA. THE PORTICO, DETAIL (EARLY FIRST MILLENNIUM). — TELL HALAF MUSEUM, BERLIN

(A) BULL HUNT — ALEPPO MUSEUM

(B) GENII AND WINGED DISK — ALEPPO MUSEUM

us to identify the building and associate it with a god or a prince.

Nor is any clue to its function or attribution to be found in the great orthostats of the façade; their arrangement defies explanation. First, on the left, came a bull hunt, followed by a slab carved with a scene we shall meet with elsewhere: three genii together holding up a winged disk; then a lion passant with gaping jaws and its fangs bared. On the right was another lion in the same style, a Teshub brandishing a mace and a boomerang, a stag hunt and a magnificent winged human-headed-bull.

All these reliefs in coarse-grained basalt are carved in the flat, sometimes rather carelessly; thus in the hunting scenes, the sculptor at times fails to show the bowstring and the base of the arrow which ought to be seen above the archer's face. But these works nevertheless convey an impression of power and even majesty that is far to seek in the hundreds of smaller reliefs lining the bottom of the wall.

Obviously mere artisans, often little skilled, were employed on carving these slabs, which the architects could well have left bare but preferred to decorate as cheaply as possible. Several museums own specimens of these blocks of basalt or pink limestone, with their more or less hastily executed figures shown in profile: foot soldiers and mounted warriors,

97 - TELL HALAF (EARLY 1st MILLENNIUM)
(C) STAG HUNT — ALEPPO MUSEUM

88

98 - TELL HALAF (EARLY 1st MILL.). (A) LION PASSANT (B) THE GOD TESHUB (C) WINGED BULL. — TELL HALAF MUSEUM, BERLIN

A

B

C

D

100 - TELL HALAF. ANIMAL ORCHESTRA (EARLY 1st MILLENNIUM).

hunters in chariots, camel drivers, various animals alone or locked in combat, winged genii, hybrid beings, scenes of religious rites, boats, etc. This local or at best provincial art has undeniable reminiscences of the Mesopotamian iconography, such as animals confronted on either side of a palmette and two men killing a giant, seemingly a restatement of the slaying of Humbaba, 'guardian of the cedar forest,' by Gilgamesh and Enkidu. Even more surprising is a scene of music-making animals, the only known precedent for which is the similar scene on the soundbox of a lyre from Ur, pre-dating it by nearly two thousand years.

← 99 - TELL HALAF (EARLY 1st MILLENNIUM). (A) ARCHER — LOUVRE
(B) LION ERECT — ALEPPO MUSEUM. (C) WINGED GENIUS — LOUVRE
(D) SLAYING OF A GIANT — WALTERS ART GALLERY, BALTIMORE

101 - TELL HALAF. DIVINE OR ROYAL COUPLE (EARLY 1st MILL.). — ALEPPO MUSEUM

This strange art also found expression in several statues in the round, like the couple shown above, god and goddess or king and queen, seated side by side on a low bench, the left hand of each figure clasping the knee, the right hand clenched, the bare feet splayed out on the ground. This ponderous geometric style reappears, slightly modified, in two other figures: a king or god armed with boomerang and dagger, and a queen or goddess with many necklaces and bracelets, holding a small receptacle.

102 - TELL HALAF. (EARLY 1st MILL.).
(A) KING OR GOD — ADANA MUSEUM
(B) QUEEN OR GODDESS — ALEPPO →

A   B

104 - TELL HALAF. GODDESS WITH HANGING BRAIDS, DETAIL (EARLY 1st MILL.) TELL HALAF MUSEUM, BERLIN

Most striking of all, however, is the large statue of a woman from Tell Halaf, found immured in a solid mass of crude bricks in the wall of the acropolis, which we have called the Goddess with Hanging Braids. The huge block of basalt, transported from the banks of the Khabur to those of the Spree, was completely destroyed in an air raid in 1943. Seated on a bench, holding a cup with her right hand, this goddess had a curiously forbidding air, due largely to the geometrical treatment of the volumes, the haggard face and the impenetrable eyes framed by two long braids. Tight-lipped, supercilious, proud of her unloveliness, she kept intact the secret of her identity to the very end.

← 103 - TELL HALAF. GODDESS WITH HANGING BRAIDS (EARLY 1st MILL.). — TELL HALAF MUSEUM, BERLIN

Sculpture in the round was less plentiful than reliefs but the goddess with the braids was not an isolated find. A few yards away, also walled up in the masonry, another smaller statue of a goddess appeared, a ponderous figure seated on a throne, wearing a low crown, with her feet resting on a stool. Whatever the sculptor's intention may have been, for us today there is something peculiarly repulsive about this burly goddess with her bloated face and triple chin.

Here in fact we meet at every turn with the phantasmagoric. Mention has already been made of the scorpion-men. Even more intriguing is this huge bird of prey carved in basalt, perched on a small capital adorned with eight acanthus leaves which originally belonged to a column reposing on a stone base.

The bird is treated in a compact, schematic style, here particularly effective. The over-size head with its great beak and eyes, framed by a bandeau on each side ending in a spiral, befits a savage monarch of the skies, serving here perhaps as a solar symbol. Nowhere do we find a more telling and expressive elaboration of the symbolic birds on a smaller scale that had sometimes figured on Kassite boundary stones and the Tell Halaf sculptors may well have deliberately imitated the work of the Kassite craftsmen, whose priority is unquestionable.

105 - TELL HALAF. BIRD OF PREY ON A CAPITAL
(EARLY 1st MILL.). — TELL HALAF MUSEUM, BERLIN

9

106 - TELL HALAF. GODDESS (EARLY 1st MILL.). — ALEPPO MUSEU

107 - DUR SHARRUKIN (KHORSABAD). THE 'HAREM.' RECONSTRUCTION OF GATE Z (8th CENTURY B.C.).

While stone reliefs form the standard ornamentation of Assyrian palaces, they sometimes give place to other works composed of glazed bricks, moulded in more or less salient relief. Fine examples were found at Khorsabad, notably on the so-called 'decorated' gates of the city and above all on the façades of several temples.

The most complete ensemble of glazed brickwork was the one decorating the doorway of the temple of Sin, excavated by Victor Place (who thought the building was a harem). On either side of the entrance a curious procession was to be seen, headed by the king, with a lion, an eagle, a bull, a fig-tree and a plough behind him; last of all came the prime minister. The portrayal of the two men conforms to the traditional iconography. It is not easy, however, to explain the *raison d'être* of the other elements. Perhaps the lion, king of beasts, symbolizes the suzerainty of the Assyrian empire. The eagle reigns supreme in the skies; the bull evokes the fecundity of the flocks, the fig-tree the fertility of the orchards; the plough stands for agriculture. But the idea behind the *combination* of these elements remains something of a riddle.

The same motifs (with a few variants) figure before the temples of Shamash and Ningal and in the temple of Nabu. So it must have been a standard combination of symbols.

There were no such enigmas at Khorsabad where, in one of the rooms of Residence K, it has been possible to reconstitute a mural decoration some forty feet high. Above a double frieze of kneeling winged genii, framing a row of confronted bulls, a semicircular arch was decorated with the customary scene of worship: the god (perhaps Assur) receiving homage from a king followed by a high-ranking official, presumably the owner of the house. The colors employed were blue, red, black, green and white, with blue, red and white predominating.

108 - DUR SHARRUKIN (KHORSABAD). DECORATION OF RESIDENCE K

109 - TIL BARSIP (TELL AHMAR). WALL PAINTING IN THE PALACE. WINGED GENIUS LEADING A BULL (8th CENTURY B.C.).

The Assyrians made an extensive use of wall paintings. The accounts of them given by nineteenth-century excavators were inadequate, and not until the recent explorations of Assur, Khorsabad and Nimrud could this new chapter in the history of art be written.

The ensemble brought to light at Til Barsip (Tell Ahmar), however, by the Thureau-Dangin expedition in 1930-31, is by far the most extensive. The length of wall space decorated with paintings measures well over four hundred feet. It is a matter of regret that, except for a few fragments, it proved impracticable to detach and preserve these works. Nevertheless, the scrupulously accurate copies of them made by Lucien Cavro convey some idea of an ornamentation which was in many respects highly original and certainly the work of experienced artists.

In this provincial residence whose final form bears the mark of Assurbanipal, throne room, reception rooms, corridors and bathrooms were decorated with brightly coloured compositions, celebrating the king's achievements as monarch, warrior and big-game hunter. It came as a surprise to uncover under the intonaco some sketches strangely out of keeping with the rest: for example, in the throne room, a group of women, three of them portrayed full face in the nude.

110 - TIL BARSIP (TELL AHMAR). WALL PAINTING IN THE PALACE. WINGED HUMAN-HEADED BULL AND MAN WITH LOTUS (8th CENTURY B.C.).

These nudes, however, were an exception. The rest of the work conforms to well-established traditions, though often with variants of form which seem to indicate that these decorators were allowed a freer hand and showed more initiative than was usual. This is immediately apparent from a comparison with the stone reliefs of Nimrud, Nineveh and Khorsabad, where we find nothing quite like this winged eagle-headed genius stepping forward with both hands tightly gripping the neck of a bull presumably being led to the sacrifice. Though the combination of a winged human-headed bull and a winged human-headed genius occurs at Khorsabad, the latter there always follows the animal, and is invariably represented in front view with a pine-cone in one hand and a situla in the other. At Til Barsip the bull is moving forward, but the figure accompanying it has neither wings nor the divine tiara and holds a lotus in his right hand and a poppy (?) in his left. In this instance both man and animal are moving at a brisk pace which brings to mind a passage in Ezekiel referring to the animals he saw in his vision: 'And they went every one straight forward . . . and they turned not when they went' (i. 12). Though they were heightened with colours, the reliefs had none of the brilliance of these paintings.

III - TIL BARSIP (TELL AHMAR). WALL PAINTING IN THE PALACE, DETAIL OF PLATE 113. TWO SERVANTS BEHIND THE THRONE (8th CENTURY B.C.).

10

112 - TIL BARSIP (TELL AHMAR). WALL PAINTING IN THE PALACE. KING TIGLATHPILESER III GIVING AUDIENCE (8th CENTURY B.C.).

At Til Barsip, moreover, the king was in familiar surroundings. The wall paintings there teem with dignitaries, officials and servants shown performing their appointed duties, just as the king was accustomed to see them in his usual residences on the Tigris. Among them are beardless youths with their carefully groomed curls held in place by a red head-band, just such young men, fat and sleek, as Daniel was later to refer to in his description of Nebuchadnezzar's court at Babylon (i. 15). But there are also bearded men of maturer years, with earrings, approaching the throne two by two.

For even when travelling the king continued to mete out justice, to give audience and hear petitions, to receive the homage and tribute of subject peoples. The largest composition in the palace at Til Barsip, over seventy feet long, shows him seated on the throne holding a long sceptre. He is receiving a group of foreigners, presented to him by the *tartan*. Behind the latter stand two officials and an 'usher's' uplifted hand indicates that the visitors may approach the king.

A similar scene figures in another room. Seated on the throne, with the staff of authority in his hand, the sovereign is giving audience to a

113 - TIL BARSIP (TELL AHMAR). WALL PAINTING IN THE PALACE. KING TIGLATHPILESER III GIVING AUDIENCE (8th CENTURY B.C.).

114 - TIL BARSIP (TELL AHMAR). WALL PAINTING IN THE PALACE, DETAIL OF PLATE 113. TWO ROYAL OFFICIALS (8th CENTURY B.C.)

group of tributaries, whose leader has prostrated himself and in fact lies face down, flat on the ground, beside the high court official, the *tartan*, behind whom stand several dignitaries in the order prescribed by protocol. Immediately behind him is the grand eunuch, followed by two bearded men and the 'usher.' On the far left are servants and soldiers back from a victorious expedition, judging by the presents they have brought to the king: daggers, cups, rings of precious metal and elephant tusks.

115 - TIL BARSIP (TELL AHMAR). WALL PAINTING IN THE PALACE, DETAIL OF PLATE 116. SOLDIER EXECUTING A PRISONER (8th CENTURY B.C.). →

116 - TIL BARSIP (TELL AHMAR). WALL PAINTING IN THE PALACE. EXECUTION OF AN ENEMY (8th CENTURY B.C.).

The Assyrians often wantonly slaughtered their prisoners. Here, deaf to the appeals of one of his comrades, a soldier has seized a prisoner by the hair and is about to cut off his head with a short sabre. Elsewhere we see prisoners harnessed to a chariot like oxen.

117 - TIL BARSIP (TELL AHMAR). WALL PAINTING IN THE PALACE. PRISONERS HARNESSED TO A CHARIOT (8th CENTURY B.C.).

118 - TIL BARSIP (TELL AHMAR). WALL PAINTING IN THE PALACE, THE 'WHITE HORSES' (8th CENTURY B.C.).

The usual mounts and draught animals of the Assyrians were horses, and they were particularly fond of teams of swift, mettlesome coursers. Horses often figure on the stone reliefs; sometimes ridden by the king, who is evidently quite at ease in the saddle; sometimes drawing the royal chariot at the slow pace prescribed for ceremonial occasions; sometimes galloping across the steppe in hunting expeditions. Horses also formed part of the tribute paid by subject peoples.

The royal stables consisted entirely of thoroughbreds, which figure prominently in the paintings in the throne room at Til Barsip. Several saddle horses, standing two by two with plumed heads, seem on the point of bolting; soldiers are holding them back and trying to keep them under control.

119 - TIL BARSIP (TELL AHMAR). WALL PAINTING IN THE PALACE, THE 'BROWN HORSES' AND 'BLACK HORSES' (8th OR 7th CENTURY B.C.).

In addition to wall paintings, the Assyrians also decorated their buildings with revetments of thin strips of bronze nailed to doors, some of them patterned with scenes that have yielded a wealth of historical information, at once detailed and factually precise.

Such are the 'bronze doors' of Balawat, (the ancient Imgur Bel, between Nineveh and Nimrud), which figured on an edifice built by Shalmaneser III. Measuring several yards in length, each plaque was decorated on two registers; these were divided into narrow zones by lines in relief and each zone was stamped with rosettes disposed round a central stud. These decorative elements were first engraved, then hammered into shape; the inscriptions were added after the bronze plaques had been nailed to the door. The incidents illustrated relate to the campaigns on which the king embarked between 860 and 849 B.C., and which led the Assyrian armies from southern Babylonia to Armenia and even as far afield as western Syria and the Phoenician coast. While certain scenes are repeated with little variation, others introduce a topical note that greatly enhances their interest. Often enough, to be sure, we find the stock themes of processions of warriors or tributaries, the siege of a fortress, or an occupied city being put to fire and sword. But there are also many details that never figure in reliefs.

On the shores of Lake Van, for instance, soldiers are seen flinging sacrificial animals into the water, while sculptors are busy carving a stele with the king's likeness. On another strip we see a Syrian king, evidently an invalid, lying on his bed on the terrace of his palace and notifying his surrender to an attacking force of archers supported by war chariots. On still another, relating to the Phœnician campaign, the engraver shows the King of Tyre, accompanied by his wife or daughter, standing on a promontory of his island city and gazing at two boats which are conveying to the mainland the offerings intended to appease the Assyrian invaders. The boat on the right has come to a stop a few yards from the shore, and one of the men who are unloading it can be seen standing in the shallow water.

Another fragment represents the arrival of an embassy bringing tribute from Sangar, King of Carchemish. Standing in front of the royal pavilion, King Shalmaneser receives the delegation. In order to curry favour and make his offerings more acceptable, the conquered monarch has apparently included his own daughter. Elsewhere Shalmaneser is seen receiving news of current military operations, which seem to have been successful, judging by the number of heads, each row or heap of which no doubt stands for a captured city. Another successful campaign is evoked by the customary atrocities and reprisals: enemies impaled and fruit trees cut down.

← 120 - TIL BARSIP (TELL AHMAR). WALL
PAINTING IN THE PALACE. THE 'PINK
HORSE' (8th OR 7th CENTURY B.C.).

112

IMGUR BEL (BALAWAT). BRONZES, 9th CENTURY B.C. — BRITISH MUSEUM.
121 - THE INVALID KING OF HAMA SURRENDERING TO THE ASSYRIANS.
122 - PHOENICIAN CAMPAIGN: BOATS WITH TRIBUTE FROM TYRE.
123 - THE CAPTURE OF ASHTAMAKU: THE ASSYRIAN CAMP. →

IMGUR BEL (BALAWAT). 124 - SYRIAN CAMPAIGN : THE CAPTURE OF ASHTAMAKU (849 B.C.). — BRITISH MUSEUM

IMGUR BEL (BALAWAT). 125 - PRISONERS IMPALED. 126 - THE KING OF HAMA MAKING HIS SUBMISSION TO SHALMANESER — BRITISH MUSEUM

IMGUR BEL (BALAWAT). 127 - THE SIEGE OF DABIGU (9th CENTURY B.C.). — BRITISH MUSEUM

IMGUR BEL (BALAWAT). 128 - ARCHERS ATTACKING DABIGU. 129 - SURRENDER OF HAMA (9th CENTURY B.C.). — BRITISH MUSEUM

A   B

130 - LABARTU PLAQUE (EARLY 1st MILL.). — PRIVATE COLLECTION

We find the same technique employed in other Assyrian cities, at Assur in the temple of Adad, at Khorsabad in the 'Harem' and the temple of Nabu.

Bronze-work was in fact a flourishing industry. Here, needless to say, we can only deal with such pieces as have intrinsic artistic merit. First may be mentioned a series of bronze lions fitted with dorsal rings, many examples of which have been found. Crouching, their jaws wide open and hindquarters tensed, the animals are poised as if about to spring at some intruder. It matters little whether these bronzes served as weights (as is suggested by the inscriptions and marks engraved on some of those discovered at Nimrud); or whether, in view of the rings, they were used to tether horses or to secure the ropes of tents or perhaps of the banners that were flown above the palace on special occasions. Whatever they were used for, the craftsmen who made them imbued them with a nervous energy which, though combined with a marked sobriety of line and even a certain schematism, conveys the ferocity of a wild animal at bay no less effectively than the reliefs illustrating Assurbanipal's hunting exploits or those of Gilgamesh. The work of the Assyrian animal carvers is seen to advantage when we compare the Khorsabad lion with that of Susa, a cold and lifeless replica turned out by copyists who may have been conscientious

131 - THE DEMON PAZUZU (FIRST HALF, FIRST MILLENNIUM). — LOUVRE

132 - DUR SHARRUKIN (KHORSABAD). CROUCHING LION (8th CENTURY B.C.). — LOUVRE

but were certainly uninspired. We reach the same conclusion if we compare the Susa lion with some loose pieces found at Khorsabad: heads of bulls, heifers and antelopes, all admirably adapted to their function of decorating the arm-rest of a chair or throne.

The bronze statuette of Pazuzu, of unknown provenance, introduces us into the fantastic world of hybrid monsters. A leering face surmounts the gaunt body of a man, equipped with two pairs of outspread wings, whose feet are the talons of a bird of prey. Claw-like hands add to the weirdness of this demonic figure, described in an inscription as 'king of the evil spirits of the air.' A personification of the scorching wind of Mesopotamia that blows from the south and brings both storms and fever, he is the ruthless adversary of all good genii. True, by means of exorcism his baneful influence could be counteracted, but the iconography of these evil spirits reveals the awe that they inspired in men whose whole lives were torn between irrational fears and a precarious sense of security. Despite the good offices of the beneficent genii with situla and pine-cone, such demons as Pazuzu and Labartu continued to wreak havoc among men, and it took the combined resources of medicine and magic to break their stranglehold on the body of the victim and force the demon to take flight to the west where the gates of the underworld opened to receive him.

117

133 - KING ESARHADDON AND HIS MOTHER NAQIA (7th CENTURY B.C.). — LOUVRE

The Louvre has recently acquired a large bronze plaque which, though fragmentary, is of considerable importance both historically and iconographically. It must have served originally as the revetment of an altar or throne. Represented on it are two figures identifiable from inscriptions as King Esarhaddon followed (and this is unique in Mesopotamian iconography) by a woman, Naqia, the king's mother and wife of Sennacherib. Both are walking to the right and—a curious gesture—pressing a short rod to their nose. This was the act of humility appropriate to persons of royal blood, who were thereby exempted from bowing down in the dust. The size and weight (thirty lbs.) of this plaque says much for the skill and versatility of the Assyrian bronze-founders, equally proficient in small- and large-scale works.

134 - URARTU. KING ASSURDAN (10th CENTURY B.C.). — LOUVRE   135 - ERZERUM. GOD ON A LION (1st MILL.). — LOUVRE

Assyrian influence made itself felt well beyond the banks of the
Tigris. Thus the art of the Lake Van region (called Urartu in the
ancient texts), while it has an originality and an imprint of its own, is
nevertheless steeped in Assyrian reminiscences. An English specialist,
R.D. Barnett, has carefully regrouped all the works found thereabouts,
now scattered in various museums, and thus enabled us to see and study
hem in something like their original unity. Several of them are in the
Louvre, for example the statuette of King Assurdan (tenth century B.C.)
and notably a horned lion supporting on its back the figure of a god, of
which only the lower part of the robe remains. Barnett's findings have
made it clear that this latter statuette was not an isolated work, and that
along with other animals and hybrids it formed part of a throne.

119

136 - SUSA. CAPITAL (5th-4th CENTURIES B.C.). — LOUVRE

From the same region comes a magnificent series of bulls' heads, which once decorated large receptacles. The Louvre has one example of this truly impressive art, which seems to be an aftermath of traditions going back some two millennia or more. These Urartu bulls are remarkably like the Sumerian bulls of Ur, and they later reappear on Achaemenian capitals. Akin to them—but with essential differences—is that unique group of works known today as the 'Luristan bronzes.'

137 - URARTU. BULL'S HEAD (1st MILLENNIUM B.C.). — LOUVRE

138-146 - BRONZE DOORS OF
BALAWAT, DETAILS. CAMPAIGNS
OF SHALMANESER III (NINTH
CENT. B.C.). — BRITISH MUSEUM

A - DEDICATION OF A ROYAL STELE
B - CARRYING OFF WAR BOOTY
C - FELLING TREES IN A CONQUERED CITY
D - SETTING FIRE TO THE CITY OF KHAZANU
E - MASSACRE OF PRISONERS
F - SACRIFICES AND ERECTION OF A STELE
G - ROYAL PAVILION — BAKING BREAD
H - CONVOY OF PRISONERS AND ANIMALS
I - PRISONERS LED OUT OF SUGUNIA

CHAPTER II

FROM THE KHABUR
TO THE TIGRIS

On the fringe of the Assyrian kingdom, near the sources of the river Khabur, Guzana (Tell Halaf) becomes a flourishing centre of provincial art. The sculpture found there introduces us to a mysterious, phantasmal world whose atmosphere is still unmistakably Assyrian, though less markedly than that of works from Arslan Tash and Tell Ahmar. Particularly arresting is a series of statues and reliefs from the time of Kapara (eleventh-tenth centuries B.C.), which may fly in the face of present-day notions of beauty but certainly command attention for the sheer driving power and systematic distortions of their realistic style.

In addition to sculpture, the Assyrians made extensive use of wall painting, and though the surviving works are badly damaged and disfigured, it is now clear that painting was a more highly developed art than hitherto supposed. The compositions uncovered at Tell Ahmar and Khorsabad leave no room for doubt: the palaces of the Assyrian kings were not only decorated with stone reliefs but also with large-scale wall paintings.

This delight in all forms of figure composition is further evidenced by the bronze relief plaques on the doors of certain buildings. Particularly impressive are the famous 'bronze doors' of Balawat (the ancient Imgur Bel), illustrating the military campaigns of Shalmaneser III.

Bronze-work was a flourishing industry throughout the Assyrian period. Besides reliefs, we find statuettes and figurines of gods, kings and hybrid beings. It is much to be regretted that war and pillage have swept away so many works. The surviving remnants, all the more precious for their rarity, are but a fraction of what once existed.

KINGS	SITES
Tukulti-Ninurta I (1243-1207)	KAR-TUKULTI-NINURTA
Kapara (11th-10th century)	TELL HALAF
Assurdan II (932-910)	
Assurnasirpal II (883-859)	NIMRUD
Shalmaneser III (858-824)	BALAWAT (IMGUR BEL)
Adad-Nirari III (810-782)	TIL BARSIP
Sargon II (721-705)	KHORSABAD
Esarhaddon (680-669)	
Assurbanipal (668-631)	TIL BARSIP

ARCHITECTURE	SCULPTURE	METAL	PAINTING	EGYPT	AEGEAN
				Ramesses II (1301-1235)	Late Minoan II and III (1450-1180) Coming of the Dorians (1250)
Palace			Wall Paintings		
Palace	Statues Reliefs				
		Headless Statuette (Horned Lion)		Sheshonk I (950-929)	
Palace		Bronze Lions	Wall Paintings	Osorkon II (870-847)	
			Wall Paintings		
					Institution of the Olympic Games (776 ?)
Palace Ziggurat		Bronze Lions Bronze Plaques	Wall Paintings	Shabaka (716-701)	
		Bronze Reliefs : Naqia, Bull's Heads (Urartu)		Taharqa (689-663)	
			Wall Paintings	Psammetichus (663-609)	

148 - LURISTAN. CHEEK-PIECE (FIRST HALF, 1st MILLENNIUM). — TEHERAN MUSEUM

III

ECLIPSE OF THE ASSYRIANS

A quarter of a century ago, the market in antiquities was suddenly flooded with *objets d'art* of a quite unusual kind, said to come from Luristan, a mountainous region of western Iran. The unsettled state of the country was a godsend to clandestine diggers, but practically ruled out any scientific research work conducted by qualified archaeologists. Exceptionally, Erich Schmidt, in 1938, succeeded in making excavations at Surkh Dum, where in the ruins of a temple he uncovered a large quantity of objects, obviously votive offerings. They formed an homogeneous group markedly different from the miscellaneous objects previously unearthed by treasure-hunters. This explains the chronological uncertainty which still prevails, some dating these Luristan finds as early as the beginning of the second millennium, others as late as the Achaemenian period (sixth century B.C.).

This wide gap in time can, however, be considerably reduced, provided care is taken not to assign to the art of Luristan the Mesopotamian objects discovered in this area, which had found their way there as the result of the hazards of war or in the form of more or less voluntary offerings. A case in point is the large dagger in the Louvre, inscribed with the name of Marduk-nadin-akhe, King of

Babylon (twelfth century B.C.). But even if objects of this sort are disregarded for our present purposes, there remain enough to demonstrate the brilliant originality of the local craftsmen, who developed a style quite unlike that of contemporary Assyrian and Hittite art.

The most fruitful phase of the art of Luristan seems to have synchronized with the Neo-Assyrian period and may thus be dated to the early first millennium. Its beginnings can be assigned to about the twelfth and eleventh centuries B.C., and its final phase to the time when the Achaemenians came on the scene.

As has often been pointed out, the productions of this art were easily portable objects, suited to the requirements of such nomad races as the Scythians and Cimmerians. This would also account for the great number of horses' bits and headstalls, many of which seem to have been actually used. These nomadic horsemen were exceedingly warlike (hence the abundance of weapons), and also great hunters (hence the frequency of hunting scenes on their metal belts). They wore a type of garment that entailed the use of a great many pins, and the pin-heads are notable for an intricate ornamentation that testifies both to the vanity of their owners and to a belief in the talismani powers of certain figurations.

149 - LURISTAN. BIT WITH MOUFFLONS (FIRST HALF, 1st MILLENNIUM). — LOUVRE

150 - LURISTAN. CHEEK-PIECE WITH WINGED MOUFFLON (FIRST HALF, 1st MILL.). — DAVID-WEILL COLLECTION

The themes stem from the animal kingdom and while the representations are naturalistic up to a point, there is always something added : a
touch of fantasy, associating them with that occult, symbolic world
which has always meant so much to Asiatics. The animals on the
cheek-pieces of the bits are mostly winged sphinxes and moufflons or
human-headed beasts, their bodies studded with peculiar excrescences.

151-152 - LURISTAN. PIN-HEADS. HEROES AND ANIMALS (FIRST HALF, 1st MILL.). — DAVID-WEILL COLLECTION

The designs on the pin-heads are even more intriguing. Schmidt discovered a whole group of pins whose decorative patterns defy any systematic interpretation. On a flat metal disk, around a large central face in relief, the artist has engraved, then embossed, a number of more or less symmetrically disposed motifs: men, animals, palmettes, rosettes and other elements apparently devoid of any precise significance, though vaguely reminiscent of certain Mesopotamian vases of the third millennium. Also the faces in the centre of the pin-heads have equivalents in some cylinder seals, while the lion-masks with their flattened cheeks have a curious resemblance to pre-Sargonid renderings of animal heads.

We get the same impression of a Mesopotamian repertory drawn on and exploited by the Luristan bronze-workers, from a number of oval or rectangular pin-heads (always, however, executed in open-work) and above all from the figurines affixed, it would seem, to the tops of poles or staffs. These reproduced the typically Babylonian motif of pairs of antithetical animals with twisted or inordinately elongated bodies. Confronted beasts of prey are always shown with snapping jaws, and even the slender ibexes have a truculent air; the effect these craftsmen seem to aim at is one of stark ferocity. But the figurines do not go to the lengths of the stylistic distortions we find in the idols and some carved pin-heads. The stock theme of the latter—the hero vanquishing wild beasts—serves as a pretext for compositions of a quite remarkable boldness. Forms are drastically schematized and abbreviated with an eye to decorative effect and it is often hard to distinguish the initial motif from the successive modifications it has undergone.

Not all the Luristan bronzes, however, are so intricate. For example the figure of the hero holding two dogs by their hind legs has a fine linear simplicity and the three elements are elegantly fitted into an oval

having the appearance of a torque.
It is less easy to decipher an open-
work rectangular plaque with a
cruciform design whose leading
motif is a man with curly hair,
a bare chest and a quadruple belt.
With his raised hands he is holding up two huge horns rising from
his forehead, and two dogs are
biting their tips. Transversely, at
right angles, two smaller figures
of the same type but without the
horns repeat the central figure's
gesture. With a view to structural
symmetry, the horns and dogs are
reproduced in the lower segment,
but the face and torso of the
protagonist are omitted.

Still bolder is this idol in whose
upper part we again see a 'hero'
gripping two animals, their bodies
curved to form a loop. The lower
part has a curious ambivalence;
there is no knowing if we have here
a man's hips and legs or the feet
and hindquarters of the animals
fused into a single mass.

These works have been variously interpreted, but this much is
certain: that, allowance made for
modifications in the intervening
period, they owe much to the
ancient themes of Mesopotamia
and, in particular, of Sumer, but
nothing at all to Assyrian iconography. It is impossible to say
why these themes persisted and by
what channels they were transmitted. There is nothing like them
in either Kassite or Elamite art.

The prototype of the above-
mentioned composite idol can be

153 - LURISTAN. IDOL (FIRST HALF,
        1st MILLENNIUM). — LOUVRE

154 - SUMERIAN SEAL IMPRESSION, DETAIL
        (MID-3rd MILLENNIUM). — LOUVRE

traced to Sumerian seal designs of the third millennium. And it is as inexplicable in the earlier period (c. 2500 B.C.) as it is in this later age when the Luristan bronze-workers took it over, adding the 'ferocity' which is the hall-mark of their art.

A similar use of Mesopotamian prototypes is apparent in certain weapons, in particular the halberds with iron blades mounted on bronze shafts. The juncture between the two metals is decorated with a curious zoomorphic motif that evidently derives from the lion-headed eagle. Though forms are drastically curtailed, the flattened lion-mask and the tail feathers, closely welded together, are easily identifiable. Here too we have an obvious borrowing from Sumer, but, once again, there has been a break of continuity and nothing is known of the intermediate phases.

The same can be said of this 'standard,' formerly dated to the Parthian period, but which we are more inclined to associate with Luristan. Four men holding hands are enclosed in a perfect circle resting on the backs of two bulls. Gyrating in an endless dance they symbolize, presumably, the cyclical movement of all life; also perhaps that of the sun. This was nothing new; as far back as the second millennium B.C. a mould (found at Mari) represented four men with their hands linked in just the same manner.

155-156 - LURISTAN. AXE-HEAD AND 'STANDARD' (1st MILL.). — DAVID-WEILL COLLECTION AND LOUVRE 132

157 - (A) BABYLONIAN MOULD (B) SYRO-CAPPADOCIAN SEAL IMPRESSION (2nd MILL.). — ALEPPO AND NEWELL COLL.

158 - LURISTAN. SITULAE. (A) WINGED SPHINXES (B) BANQUET SCENE (FIRST HALF, 1st MILL.). — LOUVRE

The reminiscences found in another group of objects, very different from those described above, and relatively homogeneous, were less remote.   First we have the bronze pails or *situlae* used for ritual purposes; they have the form of cylinders with a rounded base adorned with a rosette.   The designs along the sides were first chiselled, then lightly hammered out.   The themes are simple, often concerned with hunting.

Hunting scenes also figure on the engraved bronze plaques, originally sewn on leather belts, a fine example of which can be seen in the Louvre. Here archers are represented along with a variety of animals: a buck, a lion, a bull, a fox, a boar attacked by hunting dogs, antelopes, and a hare carried off by a bird of prey.   The costumes and attitudes of the huntsmen on the belt are identical with those on the *situlae* and justify us in dating these objects to the same period, the middle of the Assyrian epoch, i.e. the ninth and eighth centuries B.C.

159 - LURISTAN.   BELT PLAQUE.   HUNTING SCENE (FIRST HALF, 1st MILLENNIUM). — LOUVRE

160 - HAN ART. THE 'RED BIRD' (2nd CENTURY A.D.).

161 - SHANG ART. RITUAL VASE — MUSÉE ROYAL, BRUSSELS

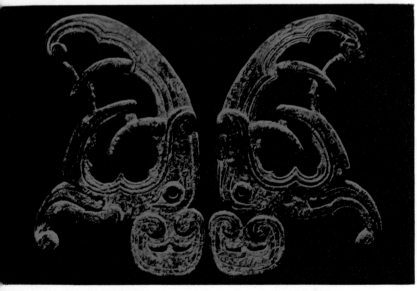

162 - CHINESE 'T'AO-T'IEH' HEADS — MUSÉE GUIMET, PARIS

The hilts of swords and daggers were often richly ornamented. In a handsome sword, recently acquired by the Louvre, the blade emerges from a crescent affixed to an open-work socket representing a scene which we believe to be unique: a procession of four short-skirted figures with their arms uplifted, like atlantes.

The ceremonial dignity of the battle-axes does not preclude touches of free fancy. Thus the prongs projecting from the socket are sometimes changed into animals' heads, or the blade issues from a monster's gaping mouth. Here, too, traditions of the north or west have been adapted to the local taste. For Luristan, while borrowing freely, never contented itself with servile imitation. The influence of this art was remarkably widespread; some have detected traces of it as far afield as China. Indeed there is no question that the amazing dynamism of some Luristan ibexes foreshadows that of the famous Red Bird of the Han period and the face of the 'hero' with his eyes framed by two volutes calls to mind certain ritual vases of the Shang dynasty. By the same token many Luristan schematizations have striking analogies with the *t'ao-t'ieh* heads of Chinese art. Have we here direct influences, pointing to contacts between the two cultures, or similar stylistic developments arrived at independently? The point is one which remains to be looked into.

163 - LURISTAN. CEREMONIAL AXE (EARLY 1st MILL.). — DAVID-WEILL COLLECTION

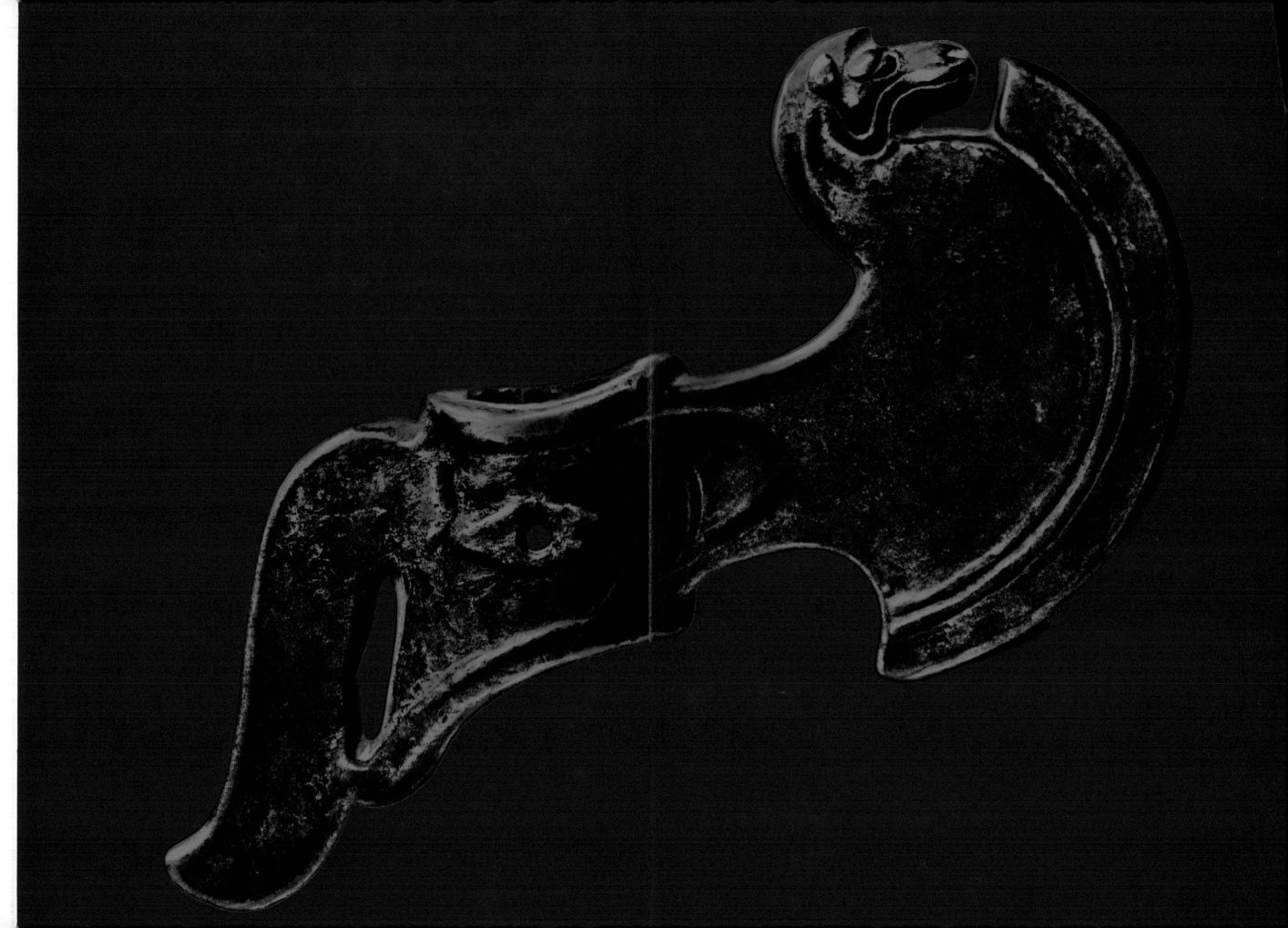

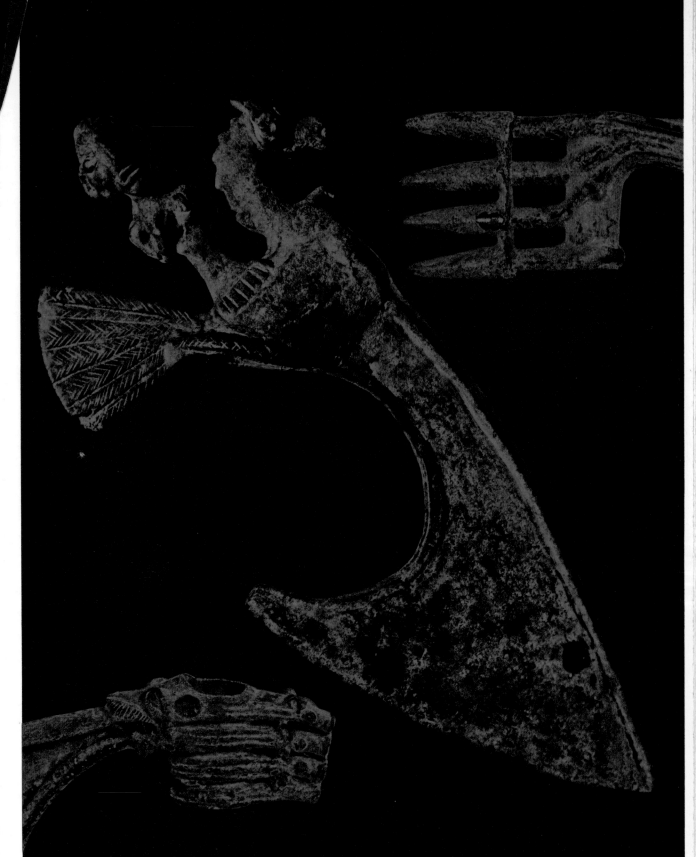

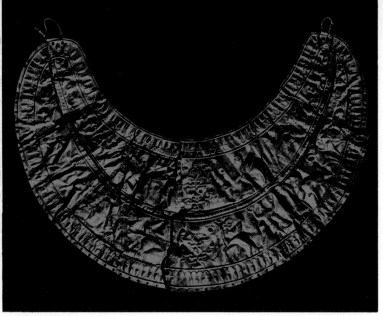

164 - LURISTAN. AXE WITH TOOTHED SOCKET (FIRST HALF, 1st MILL.). — LOUVRE
165 - LURISTAN. CEREMONIAL AXE (FIRST MILLENNIUM).
166 - LURISTAN. BATTLE-AXE WITH ANIMAL MUZZLES (1st MILL.). — LOUVRE

167 - ZIWIYEH. PECTORAL (FIRST HALF, 1st MILL.). — TEHERAN

168 - ZIWIYEH. PECTORAL, DETAIL (FIRST HALF, 1st MILL.).

Had the Assyrian cities not been so systematically pillaged, archaeologists would certainly have unearthed great quantities of jewellery. As it is, few articles of personal adornment figure today in national or private collections. It is evident from the reliefs that the monarchs delighted in jewellery: earrings, bead necklaces, open bangles worn above the elbow, bracelets with large rosettes worn on the wrist—a great change from the time of Gudea whom we can hardly picture thus bedecked with ornaments. True, the kings of Mari —anyhow in official ceremonies—did not disdain bracelets and Hammurabi wore a necklet when confronting the god Shamash. But in this respect all alike practised a discretion far to seek at Assur or Nineveh.

The finest collection of jewellery comes from Assur where it was discovered in a tomb, happily unplundered, dating to the middle of the Assyrian period, i.e. the close of the second millennium B.C. The pendants illustrate the technique employed for mounting precious stones on gold. Very often the setting consisted of gold filigree-work, with rosettes made of gold wire looped to imitate the petals of a flower. In the Assyrian necropolis at Mari numerous examples of these techniques were found; also of certain motifs such as double spirals like those of Mycenae and reproducing once again, long afterwards, a theme that figured in the royal Anatolian tombs of Alaja Hüyük.

It was not, however, in Assyria that the most remarkable find of jewellery of this period was made, but in the Iranian province of Kurdistan, at Ziwiyeh, south-east of Lake Urmya. This buried treasure hoard was discovered in 1947 by peasants, with the result that its contents were rapidly dispersed and passed into the hands of private

169 - ZIWIYEH. HEAD OF A GRIFFIN (FIRST HALF, 1st MILL.). — TEHERAN MUSEUM

collectors. It seems probable, however, that the most characteristic pieces have now been traced and classified. They are in gold, silver and ivory. One of the gold objects is a large pectoral ornamented on two registers with animals and fabulous creatures (a winged sphinx, a winged human-headed bull, a winged lion, a winged griffin, a winged ram, a winged atlas, wild beasts of the Scythian repertory, an ibex, a hare and a dog), converging on a highly stylized 'sacred tree.' The design was first hammered out, then finished with a graving tool. Next we have some revetment plaques, executed in the same technique, with scenes on several registers of antithetical processions of animals advancing to the tree, or of curiously stylized fights between a man and a lion.

Besides these pieces, undoubtedly Assyrian in inspiration, there are others executed in a much more forceful style, remarkably akin to that of the so-called 'art of the steppes.' Among these are some bracelets decorated with lions' heads, and one with a griffin's head and neck (delineated with quite amazing vigour), a fragment of a scabbard, a

139

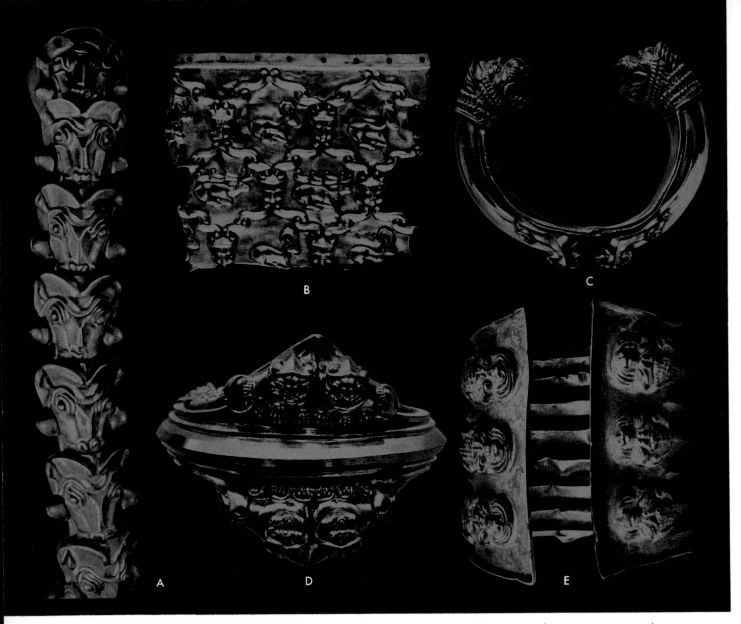

170 - ZIWIYEH AND ZAGROS. (A) FRAGMENT OF A TORQUE (B) OF A BELT PLAQUE (C, D, E) BRACELETS (FIRST HALF, 1st MILL.).

torque, some frontlets, and a decorative ensemble in much higher relief consisting of ibex heads, sometimes placed side by side, sometimes one above the other. Occasionally other animals are profiled against a network of scrolls interspersed with lion-masks, or confront each other across a hole inset in which was a precious stone, now lost.

To the art of the Zagros mountains belongs a handsome bracelet in electrum, the style of which somewhat resembles that of Ziwiyeh. It has no clasp and the thick band of embossed metal has been opened out in such a way as to slip easily over the wrist. The plaque is made in two sections, the gap between them spanned by triangular ribs; the edges are turned up laterally and vertically, and six lions' heads face each other across the opening, three by three. Each is rendered in high relief and no two heads are exactly alike. The eyes are globular, stressed by beetling eyebrows, and the nostrils quivering with life. Though the jaws, being level with the plaque, are not indicated, their presence can be sensed and the general effect of the six massed heads is one of concentrated ferocity. For these lions were meant to act as guardians of their owner and to warn off anyone rash enough to think of molesting him. Slightly different though it is from the Ziwiyeh bracelets, the Louvre bracelet is the work of a closely affiliated school of craftsmen; it may be dated a little earlier—to the beginning of the first millennium.

To about the same period can be assigned two gold objects found at Kalar Dasht in the Mazandaran province of Persia: a dagger whose blade and haft are in one piece, and a bowl decorated with three lions, their heads, carved in the round, attached to it with rivets, These pieces testify to the artistry of the regional craftsmen who, despite foreign influences (in this case Hittite), produced highly original work.

Included in the Ziwiyeh treasure hoard were silver rosettes and pendants used to decorate chariots and harness. The motifs belong to the Assyrian repertory: human-headed bulls, winged disks, lotus-bud friezes, tresses and animals of the Zagros highlands: lions, ibexes and bulls.

171 - ZIWIYEH. IBEX (EARLY 1st MILL.). — TEHERAN MUSEUM

172 - KALAR DASHT. BOWL (EARLY 1st MILL.). — TEHERAN MUSEUM

173 - ZIWIYEH. (A) DECORATIVE PLAQUE (B) DETAIL, BOUNDING LION (EARLY 1st MILL.). — TEHERAN MUSEUM

In the centre of a plaque that had served to adorn a chariot is a bounding lion treated in a style quite out of keeping with both place and period: a remarkable anticipation of Sassanian art. As with so many clandestine finds, the dating of these Ziwiyeh objects cannot be positively established but most specialists agree that they were made between the ninth and seventh centuries B.C., and in any case prior to the Achaemenian age. While there can be no certainty that all belong to the same period, our own view is that the earliest pieces go back to the mid-ninth, the latest to the early seventh century B.C. Agreeing with Godard, we regard them as products of a local Mannaean school directly influenced by Assyrian art. The 'apron' of griffins or rams, sometimes held to suggest a Phoenician origin for these pieces, can be accounted for quite differently. For the Mannaean craftsmen may well have seen Syro-Phoenician ivories that had been imported into Assyria, and copied this detail from them without troubling about its provenance and associations.

When we study the elements of the decorative design we find the stylized 'tree of life,' winged sphinxes, the human-headed bull, the winged genius with the head of a bird of prey holding the pail of holy water, ibexes which seem to have been copied from the Nimrud reliefs or from the embroidery on the robe of Assurnasirpal II. Equally Assyrian is the motif of the hero stabbing a lion, treated here however in a manner

142

174 - ZIWIYEH. LIONESS AND RABBIT, DETAIL OF A PECTORAL (EARLY 1st MILL.). — TEHERAN MUSEUM

recalling that of the hunters on some ceremonial vases. But though the sources of this repertory are unmistakable, there are other elements —e.g. unnaturally plump, thick-set animals—that have nothing Assyrian about them and seem to prefigure Scythian art. In short these Mannaean artists did more than copy or adapt; they created a style in which their native genius could express itself; hence these heads of lions, griffins, ibexes, these animal masks done surely from the life. For whom were these objects originally made? There is no knowing.

175 - SCYTHIAN ART, KELERMES. LIONESS (EARLY 1st MILLENNIUM). — HERMITAGE, LENINGRAD

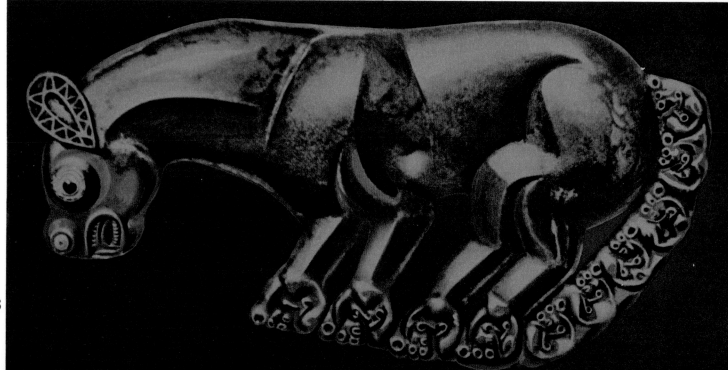

The bronze tub which, according to the peasants, had contained the treasure, bore a design on its outer surface representing a procession of tributaries exactly like the one on the obelisk of Shalmaneser III. Evidently, strange as this may seem in view of the military supremacy of the kings of Nineveh, certain objects made in Assyria had been imported into the land of the Mannai. This certainly holds good orf the numerous ivories which, along with gold and silver, formed part of the Ziwiyeh treasure hoard.

The Assyrians set much store on ivories; not only were these used for the decoration of furniture (chairs, thrones, beds), but a number of toilet articles and knick-knacks were made of ivory. Quantities of them have been found in the capital cities; notably at Nimrud, Khorsabad and Assur. But here we come up against a much-debated problem; are these ivories truly Assyrian, that is to say were they made on the spot by Assyrian craftsmen, or were they imported? For some of them strikingly resemble pieces found on foreign sites, for example at Arslan Tash on the Upper Euphrates and at Samaria, capital of Israel; and the ivories from both these cities are clearly the products of Phoenician or Syrian workshops. Care must therefore be taken to distinguish authentically Assyrian works from these Syro-Phoenician pieces.

Specifically Assyrian ivories were relatively few in number until Mallowan began his excavations at Nimrud in 1949; they could be recognized with some certainty in view of their style and treatment, patently akin to those of the reliefs. It is not too much to say that the remarkable discoveries at Nimrud which began in 1949 and have continued up to 1960 have not only greatly increased our stock of these objects but have opened up a whole new world of art. We will begin, however, by considering the earlier discoveries.

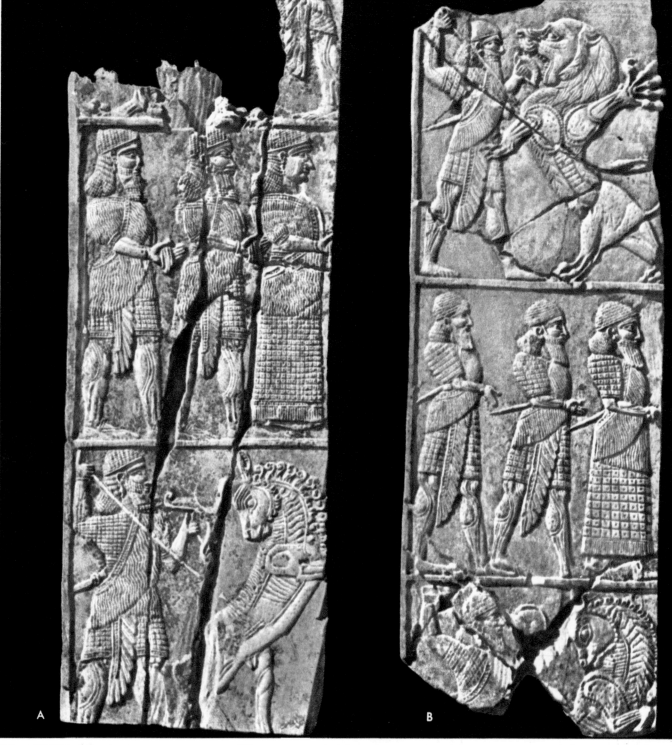

177 - ZIWIYEH. (A) DIGNITARIES AND BULL-HUNT (8th CENTURY B.C.). (B) LION-HUNT AND PROCESSION OF DIGNITARIES (9th CENTURY B.C.).

The ivories found at Ziwiyeh are Assyrian in inspiration and the men who made them were Assyrians. Here, too, we have confronted animals on either side of a palmette, winged sphinxes, winged human-headed genii, processions of officers and nobles, lion and bull-hunts— these latter treated in a style not yet that of Assurbanipal, but no

178 - ZIWIYEH. BANQUET SCENE (8th CENTURY B.C.).

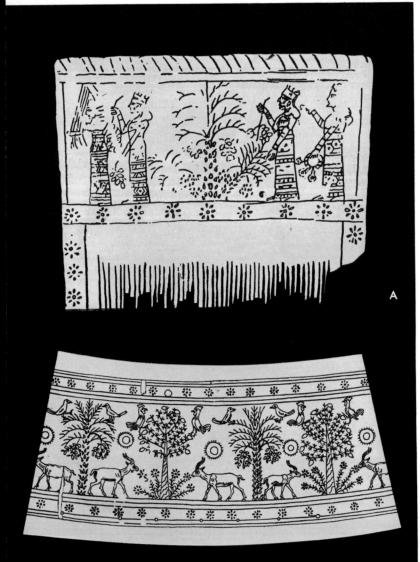

A

B

longer that of Assurnasirpal. Fighting often takes place on foot, but sometimes too in chariots, and certain stylistic traits suggest a dating to about the middle of the seventh century B.C. This is borne out by fragments of banquet scenes with certain resemblances to the stele of Barrekub, from Zinjirli, an eighth-century work.

There is no question that the ivories found at Assur, also, are distinctively Assyrian. For example, the comb engraved with a religious scene, of a goddess (Ishtar?) and officiants, which probably relates to the rites of fertilization of the palm-trees. A pyx (found undamaged) is decorated with a scene which, though naturalistic in conception, has certainly a hidden symbolic significance; gazelles are nibbling flowering shrubs planted at the foot of cedars that alternate with palm-trees. Birds are perched on the branches: cocks on the cedars, crows on the palms. In the background are sun disks. Though this scene is at a far remove from the familiar themes of hunting and warfare, it keeps to the symbolic naturalism of the mid-Assyrian period, when the Kassite tradition still lingered on. The birds on the upper branches of the palm trees might well have been copied from those of the Mari wall paintings. Thus some themes of the ancient Mesopotamian repertory persisted, though reinterpreted by the newcomers.

179 - ASSUR (LATE 2nd - EARLY 1st MILL.)
(A) COMB WITH A RITUAL SCENE
(B) PYX WITH A SYMBOLIC SCENE

180 - DUR SHARRUKIN (KHORSABAD), 8th CENTURY B.C. (A) WOMAN AT THE WINDOW (B) GENIUS PROTECTING HORUS (C) SPHINX

There are two other sets of ivories whose provenance has given rise to discussion: those from Khorsabad and those from Nimrud. The former compose a uniform group inasmuch as all were certainly made by the foreign craftsmen, either Syrian or Phoenician, who reproduced in great numbers, with only very slight variations, such standard themes

181 - HADATU (ARSLAN TASH). COW SUCKLING HER CALF (8th CENTURY B.C.). — ALEPPO MUSEUM

47

as the 'woman at the window,' the female divinities guarding with their wings the sacred tree or the infant Horus, and the winged sphinxes. These last two clearly derive from Egypt, or may more accurately be described as free renderings of Egyptian themes, and it is generally agreed that all these plaques must have been imported from the west either by traders in such wares or as war booty.

The second group of ivories, discovered at Nimrud a century ago by Layard and Loftus, is much more complex and diversified. They utilize some of the themes of the Khorsabad group: the 'woman at the window,' the female divinities guarding Horus, and sphinxes (treated however in a very different manner). But there are other themes—e.g. a cow suckling her calf, genii binding papyrus stems—which are identical with those of small plaques found at Arslan Tash, but imported from Damascus. Then again we find elements of an Egyptianizing style and others in which specialists detect specifically Syrian or, more accurately, North Syrian elements. Here the ivory is carved in high relief, sometimes even in the round. There are figures of women with hanging braids and a cylindrical crown, which in some cases seems to have supported an entablature. The resemblances to certain Tell Halaf sculptures are unmistakable and reveal influences

182 - KALAKH (NIMRUD). WOMAN WITH A CROWN
(1st MILLENNIUM). — BRITISH MUSEUM

deriving from the north-west, from the land of the Mitanni, then under Assyrian rule.

But, as we have said, a whole new world has been opened up by Mallowan's recent excavations at Nimrud. For one thing, the group of specifically 'Assyrian' works has been much enlarged. Following the chronological order of the finds, we begin with an exquisitely carved plaquette discovered in 1951, which shows King Assurnasirpal wearing a crown and a long fringed robe with tassels, and raising a drinking-cup to his lips.

Of Assyrian provenance, too, are the figures of winged genii with human heads or the heads of birds of prey, who, carrying a pail in one hand and a pine-cone in the other, are making the ritual gesture of purification with 'holy water.' The palmettes and braided frame are borrowed from the stock repertory of sculpture. The same is true of a long strip on which the carver has employed to fine effect the familiar motif of antithetical animals—here gazelles—on either side of the palmette.

On another fragment we see a king (doubtless Esarhaddon) who has alighted from his chariot to welcome Medes bringing him tribute. Both theme and treatment are distinctively Assyrian; indeed one might almost visualize this scene as a detail of the obelisk of Shalmaneser.

183 - KALAKH (NIMRUD). KING ASSURNASIRPAL
(9th CENTURY B.C.)

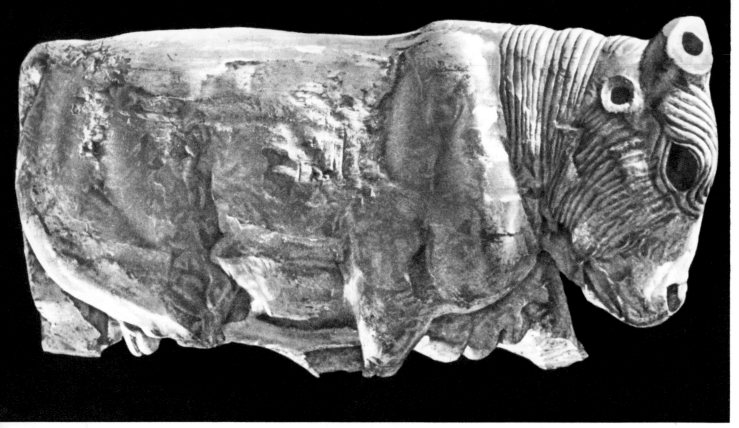

184 - KALAKH (NIMRUD). BULL PASSANT (9th-8th CENTURIES B.C.).

Next we have a group of bulls carved in high relief whose execution
has striking resemblances to that of the animal on the large panel described at a later page. These bulls are rendered with compelling power,
now advancing with a heavy, resolute tread, now lowering their heads,
preparatory to goring their victims. Here the Assyrians reverted to the
great Sumerian tradition of animal sculpture. For in our opinion there
can be no doubt that these ivories were made in Assyria, by Assyrians.

Was this amazing head of a crowned woman from Nimrud, her eyes
sparkling with life, her lips curved in a gracious smile, also the work
of local craftsmen? Despite its affinities with many ivory heads of a
Syrian type belonging to the 'Loftus group,' we believe this to be the
head of an Assyrian lady, in all probability a queen. It would seem
that women, rarely represented in major Assyrian art (the only known
examples are the likenesses of Assursharrat, Assurbanipal's wife, and
Naqia, Sennacherib's wife), figured fairly often in the minor arts.
But who, one wonders, was the model of this 'Monna Lisa' of two and a
half millennia ago, which Mallowan discovered in 1952, buried in mud
at the bottom of a well, nearly seventy feet below the ground level of
the courtyard of Assurnasirpal's palace?

There also existed a more complex technique combining ivory, gold,
coloured glass-paste and inlays of semi-precious stones. Among several

185 - KALAKH (NIMRUD). 'MONNA LISA'
(8th CENTURY B.C.). — BAGHDAD MUSEUM →

186 - KALAKH (NIMRUD). LIONESS MAULING AN ETHIOPIAN(?), DETAIL

such works from Nimrud, all of flawless execution, two small plaques call for special mention. Each illustrates the same curious scene, a lioness savaging a man—an Ethiopian or Nubian, judging by his crisp, curly hair and his features—in a lotus brake. Though the form of the animal is rather perfunctorily rendered, the artist has depicted the victim (who strangely enough seems lost in ecstasy despite his grim predicament) with delicate precision.

Ivory carvers and goldsmiths evidently collaborated in these pieces, but we have no clue to their nationality or where they worked. Indeed everything about these two plaques is a mystery, nor has any satisfactory explanation been given of their symbolism. All we know is that, like that famous ivory, the so-called 'Monna Lisa,' they were thrown into a well, probably to safeguard them in the troubled period following Sargon's death (705 B.C.).

To this wealth of valuable finds can now be added hundreds of interesting pieces stored in the so-called Fort Shalmaneser, an extensive architectural complex discovered in 1957, whose clearance is still in

187 - KALAKH (NIMRUD). LIONESS MAULING
AN ETHIOPIAN (?) (8th CENTURY B.C.).

progress. This is by far the largest collection of ivories ever yielded by an Oriental site. True, much research work will be needed before the various objects can be classified and their provenance determined; but it is already evident that there must have existed at Nimrud a number of workshops of very different types, employing Phoenician, Syrian, North Syrian and possibly imported Egyptian craftsmen. For in some ivories Egyptian inspiration is so marked that the last-named possibility cannot be ruled out. We have particularly in mind the superb winged youth, sole survivor of a pair of figures watching over the birth of Horus, and also the winged sphinx wearing the high Egyptian crown, a pectoral and an uraeus. Possibly these splendid ivories formed part of the tribute paid (prior to 740 B.C.) by Taharqa to King Esarhaddon after the latter's invasion of Egypt.

To Phoenician or Syrian craftsmen can safely be attributed various works of the 'woman in the window' type; also a handsome open-work plaque representing the familiar theme of a cow suckling her calf, against a background of lotus flowers and buds. Of the same provenance are several fragments of winged sphinxes, effigies of the child Horus standing or kneeling, and also perhaps a certain number of plaques depicting an animal (either an antelope or a stag) gambolling in a woodland setting.

The very unusual object illustrated on the following page is believed to have served to decorate a horse's trappings. It represents a winged sphinx crouching on its hind-quarters and facing to the left. Above its head is a large disk or globe inset in the body of a serpent, an obvious replica of the Egyptian uraeus. The right-hand section, or handle, of this singular object is adorned with a lotus-flower whose petals clasp an oval cartouche terminating in two elegantly stylized ostrich-feathers. The inscription within the cartouche appears to read 'Janen' or 'Jejanen.' So far no works of undoubted Egyptian manufacture have been found in this region. So it is safer to presume that the man who carved it did not hail from the Nile valley and we are therefore inclined to assign this object to a Syro-Phoenician atelier.

But the most remarkable group comes from another workshop which, agreeing with Mallowan, we believe to be North Syrian or South Anatolian, for it has affinities with reliefs found at Zinjirli and Carchemish. These ivories constitute a group apart, having nothing in common with any so far discovered at Khorsabad, Arslan Tash, Ras Shamra, Samaria or Megiddo. They show seated or standing figures, carved in light relief, on relatively large rectangles of ivory, of a height varying from about four to nearly ten inches. Identifications of the figures are conjectural; they may equally well be

188 - KALAKH (NIMRUD). HARNESS ORNAMENT (8th CENTURY B.C.).

kings and queens, or gods and goddesses not wearing the horned tiara. The men are standing, bearded, wearing a long woollen (?) robe, drawn in at the waist and leaving one limb free, below which can be seen an undergarment stopping just above the knee. They always clutch with both hands a snakelike plant, as though they had to master it before plucking its fruit.

The gestures of the women, who are sometimes standing but oftener seated on a more or less richly decorated throne, vary considerably. Some are reaching out towards a laid table; one holds a lotus in her left hand and in her right a ring, and a winged disk is hovering above.

All these plaques, dated by Mallowan to the eighth century (730-720 B.C.), had served for ornamenting furniture (beds, chairs, thrones, etc.). The head of one bed was decorated with six

189 - KALAKH (NIMRUD). WOMAN SEATED ON A THRONE (8th CENTURY B.C.). — IRAQ MUSEUM, BAGHDAD

elements; four figures, each with a pail of holy water and holding up a pine-cone, and on either side of them palmettes. The execution of this typically Assyrian theme can hardly have been carried out at Nimrud. Nor that of this prototype of 'St George and the Dragon,' showing a winged, crowned genius thrusting a long sword into a monster's mouth.

The theme of another plaque serving to decorate a bed is no less curious: a seated man with his feet on a bull's back is lifting a cup in the shadow of a lotus. He is guarded on each side by a winged genius with a human body and the head of a bird of prey, attended by a young servant bearing on his shoulders an antelope and a deer.

Outstanding in this group of ivories is a large hunting scene (over eighteen inches long) essentially Assyrian in inspiration, though probably executed by a foreign hand: a work combining fine sobriety with violent movement and compelling power. Four men are standing in a chariot drawn by galloping horses. A huge bull pierced by a spear is sinking to the ground and another, seeking to escape, will soon be brought down by the arrow that one of the hunters is letting fly.

Seal engravers might have been expected to follow in the steps of the ivory carvers. In practice, however, the two minor arts were kept quite distinct; even when the themes were basically the same

190 - KALAKH (NIMRUD). GENIUS VANQUISHING A MONSTER (8th CENTURY B.C.).

191 - KALAKH (NIMRUD). (EIGHTH CENTURY B.C.). (A) DECORATION OF A BED. (B) DECORATION OF A BED. METROPOLITAN MUSEUM, NEW YORK →

A

B

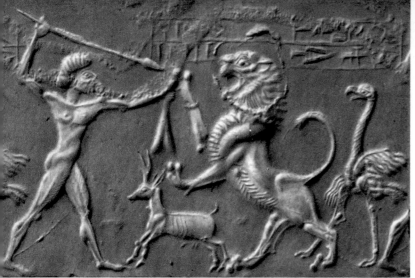

192 - SEAL IMPRESSION. HUNTER SPEARING A LION (1st MILL.). — BRITISH MUSEUM

193 - SEAL IMPRESSION. ARCHER HUNTING (1st MILL.). — MORGAN COLL.

194 - SEAL IMPRESSION. MYTHOLOGICAL SCENE (1st MILL.). — BRITISH MUSEUM

they were handled in a very different manner. Also we find in the glyptic art a curious intermingling of realism and mythological fantasy. Scenes of hunting are often represented but viewed from a new angle. Thus the lion is always represented as a beast of prey that has to be destroyed as being a constant danger to the flocks and herds. The technique of fighting lions was somewhat curious, judging by this seal design representing a completely naked man, armed however with a lance, striking at a lion in front of him. Elsewhere we see a kneeling archer aiming an arrow at his quarry.

Such scenes may well have been done 'from the life.' Oftener, however, the artist indulged in fantasy and showed the hunter pitting himself against fabulous animals: sphinxes, dragons, winged bulls. Here the nature of the quarry makes it clear that these combats between men and beasts had a symbolic significance, which, if not so conspicuous, was probably implicit even in the seemingnaturalistic scenes, judging by the crescents and stars in their fields. Sometimes we see a humanheaded genius with two pairs of wings making play with two winged bulls standing on their hind legs. Elsewhere a tiara'd hunter in a long robe is vanquishing two dragons. One of them, crouching on the ground, seems cowed; the other is trying to evade the hunter's arrow and spitting venom.

195 - SEAL IMPRESSION. MYTHOLOGICAL COMBAT (1st MILL.). — PIERPONT MORGAN COLLECTION

197-200 - SEAL IMPRESSIONS (FIRST HALF, 1st MILLENNIUM). —

196 - SEAL IMPRESSION. ARCHER AND SPHINX (FIRST HALF, 1st MILL.). — PIERPONT MORGAN COLLECTION

The scenic accessories—palmettes, fishes, a winged disk, star and crescent—suggest that the 'hunt' is taking place on a cosmic level, and the destiny of all creation hangs on the issue of the combat, which represents perhaps the conflict between Marduk and Tiamat at the beginning of Time.

Less spectacular although again very probably endowed with inner significance are the scenes of combat between a kneeling archer and a winged human-headed sphinx and of a 'hero' in grappling with winged sphinxes or ibexes.

197

198

199

200

201 - SEAL IMPRESSION. LION ATTACKING A BULL (FIRST HALF, 1st MILLENNIUM). — LOUVRE

In the decoration of some cylinder seals we see animals elegantly disporting themselves in a smiling countryside. Here (and this need not surprise us) are reminiscences of the Kassite repertory. Indeed it is sometimes difficult in the case of certain pieces, even those discovered in the Upper Tigris region, to determine whether their provenance is Assyrian or Kassite.

202 - SEAL IMPRESSION. GAZELLE (EARLY 1st MILL.). — PIERPONT MORGAN COLLECTION

203 - SEAL IMPRESSION. ADORATION OF THE GODDESS ISHTAR (EARLY 1st MILLENNIUM). — BRITISH MUSEUM

In two cylinder seals we find reminiscences of the earliest Mesopotamian iconography, adapted however to the spirit of the age and place. On one a worshipper is paying homage to Ishtar who is standing on a lioness beside a palm-tree with two crossed ibexes near by. On the other, a kneeling man holds up with both arms a deity issuing from a winged disk; he is assisted by two composite creatures, half man, half bull, who share his burden. There are three other participants in this scene: a griffin, a cock and a figure standing beside a bull's hind leg (used perhaps as an altar). What all this means is hard to determine. Possibly we have here an allusion to a solar cult; the rising sun is being lifted above the horizon by the kneeling man and the two acolytes are helping its ascent. The cock is heralding the dawn, which the griffin, genius of the night, is unable to retard. Ishtar, goddess of war; crossed animals; gods opening the gate of heaven; bull-men—all stem from a very ancient tradition, but are given here an Assyrian garb. They have been summoned back into a world that needs their aid in the eternal struggle against the powers of evil, incarnated in the snarling monsters that the beneficent genii put to flight.

204 - KALAKH (NIMRUD). SEAL IMPRESSION. MYTHOLOGICAL SCENE (8th CENTURY B.C.). — BRITISH MUSEUM

205 - SEAL IMPRESSION. ADORATION OF THE SACRED TREE (1st MILL.).   206 - MARI. SEAL IMPRESSION. BANQUET SCENE (1st MILL.).— LOUVRE

Thus, now that the spiritual well-being of his kingdom was assured, the king could devote himself to his ritual functions, such as the adoration of the 'tree of life' and, in the intervals of warfare, to luxurious banquets in the palace. A host of servants were at his beck and call; some plied fly-whisks of woven reeds while the king sat at table, others busied themselves setting out tables, chairs and couches—always without a sound since the floors were covered with mats or, sometimes, carpets. These latter have perished but we can get an idea of their appearance from the paved floors patterned with rosettes surrounded by concentric bands of marguerites, palmettes, garlands and lotus buds. Thus all that was most beautiful in the natural world—the stars in heaven and, on earth, flowers and foliage, the rich verdure of the river banks— was placed at the all-powerful monarch's feet. Perhaps to help him to forget that all in life is not idyllic and that already enemy forces were mustering at his gates, soon to overwhelm Nineveh like a tidal wave.

207 - DUR SHARRUKIN (KHORSABAD). THRESHOLD OF THE PALACE, WITH FLOWER PATTERNS (8th CENTURY B.C.). — LOUVRE

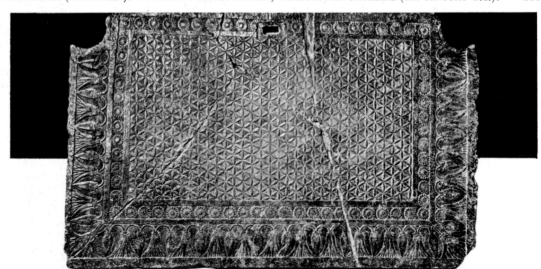

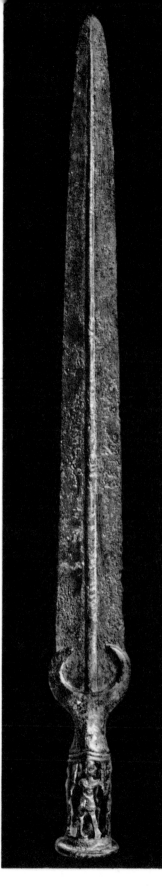

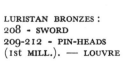

LURISTAN BRONZES :
208 - SWORD
209-212 - PIN-HEADS
(1st MILL.). — LOUVRE

63

CHAPTER III

ECLIPSE OF THE ASSYRIANS

The Luristan bronzes rank among the most intriguing productions of Oriental art. Almost all were found by clandestine diggers, and have given rise to endless controversies, turning largely on the period to which they are to be assigned. The singular appeal of the art of Luristan is due not only to its schematism and bold originality, but to the glimpses it gives us of a strange, uncharted world, a culture unlike any other. Weapons, bits and bridles, objects of personal adornment and utensils—all are richly ornamented and bear the imprint of what is now known as 'the art of the steppes,' combined with reminiscences of the early Mesopotamian period.

The Ziwiyeh treasure was likewise an accidental discovery. It is now dispersed in Europe, the United States and the East. This buried hoard of gold, silver and ivory objects contained some of the finest examples of Iranian craftsmanship. They are of Assyrian inspiration, tinctured with 'the art of the steppes.'

That the Assyrians were not only excellent sculptors and metal-workers but very fine ivory carvers was demonstrated by the early discoveries made by Layard and Loftus at Nimrud, and has been confirmed by the more recent finds of German excavators at Assur and Americans at Khorsabad, and particularly by those made during the last few years by Mallowan at Nimrud. The hundreds of ivories found by Mallowan have filled many gaps in our knowledge and led to an entirely new conception of the influences behind this art, its repertory of themes and the technique employed.

Assyrian glyptic art displays considerable originality, with a stress on symbolism and mythology (whose purport is frequently incomprehensible to us), and in it we find a bold departure from all previous styles.

KINGS	SITES
Tukulti-Ninurta I (1243-1207)	ASSUR
Marduk-nadin-akhe (12th century)	ASSUR LURISTAN
Assurnasirpal II (883-859)	NIMRUD ZIWIYEH LURISTAN ASSUR
Sargon II (721-705)	KHORSABAD LURISTAN
Esarhaddon (680-669)	NIMRUD
Fall of Nineveh (612)	

METAL	IVORIES	GLYPTICS	EGYPT	AEGEAN
				Late Minoan II and III (1450-1180)
			Ramesses II (1301-1235)	
	Ivories	Cylinder Seals		
Inscribed Dagger				
Jewellery				
Bronzes Situlae				
	Ivories	Cylinder Seals	Osorkon II (870-847)	
Hoard of Gold and Silver	Ivories			
Bronzes				
	Ivories			
	Ivories	Cylinder Seals	Shabaka (716-701)	
Bronzes				
			Taharqa (689-663)	
	Ivories			
			Psammetichus (661-609)	

214 - SEAL IMPRESSION. MYTHOLOGICAL SCENE (FIRST HALF, IST MILLENNIUM). — LOUVRE

IV

BABYLONIANS AND NEO-BABYLONIANS
THE RETURN TO THE SOURCES
(990-538 B.C.)

ABYLON had never resigned itself to the hegemony of Assur.
The fall of the Kassite dynasty in the twelfth century B.C. had
left a void in the heart of Mesopotamia and the question now
was: who was to reign in Babylon? The warlike Elamites, whose raids
had wrought such havoc in the past, held aloof, and it was left to the
Assyrians and the Sea-land peoples to vie for supremacy. A merciless
struggle ensued, lasting over half a millennium and broken by periods
of uneasy peace, during which each side made ready for a fresh effort.
The constant aim of the Assyrian kings seems to have been to set up
a local dynasty in Babylon, not as independent rulers but as obedient
instruments of their will. With other opponents the Assyrians might
have succeeded; as it was, they failed completely.

Not only were the Sea-land peoples factious by nature, but the
feeling that they were defending their ancestral heritage inspired them
with pride and grim determination. Rather than give up the struggle
they always preferred to retreat to the 'maquis' of the marshlands,
forcing the Assyrian armies to track them down in costly expeditions
which, though declared successful, had no lasting results. Finally the
Assyrian kings decided to unite Nineveh and Babylon under their own
sceptre. Babylon, which had been laid waste by Sennacherib, now

215 - ABU HABBA. SIPPAR TABLET. NABU-APAL-IDDIN 'PRESENTED' TO THE GOD SHAMASH (9th CENTURY B.C.). — BRITISH MUSEUM

was governed either directly or through viceroys. The last of these, however, Kandalanu, played into the hands of the anti-Assyrian party, to such effect that in 625 it succeeded in seizing the reins of power and installed an independent dynasty founded by an upstart, Nabopolassar, first of a line of six kings. Nineveh was too weak to interfere; thirteen years later, in 612, it was captured by a coalition of Babylonians, Medes and Scythians. The Ninevitic government fled to Harran, held out there for three years, then was swept away for good. Thus once again Babylon held undisputed sway throughout Mesopotamia.

Before dealing with Neo-Babylonian art, it may be well to look into its antecedents and briefly to review the works assignable to this transition period of half a millennium. First we have the foundation tablet from Sippar, in which King Nabu-apal-iddin commemorated the building of the temple of Shamash. No more striking example could be found of a return to the early iconographic traditions. The god Shamash is seated in exactly the same position as on Hammurabi's Code stele, wearing the same crown with four rows of horns, the same long beard, the same chignon, the same long robe, and holding the ring and staff. Only the throne is different, decorated on the side with two bull-men standing on 'the mountain' rendered by the conventional scale pattern which, on the Code stele, figured underneath the god's feet.

168

The three figures advancing towards Shamash might have been taken directly from a 'presentation scene' of the type figuring on Neo-Sumerian seals. Despite the conservatism of this art there are a few innovations, notably the large rayed disk emitting flames, standing on a low table, which is held in place by ropes manipulated by two divine acolytes whose heads and torsos emerge from the top of the canopy. The wavy lines below ground level are a reminder that the earth reposes on the *apsu*, the underground body of fresh water on which all life depends. The Sippar tablet sums up the Babylonian (and Biblical) cosmogony, with its distinct tripartite division of firmament, land and water.

Of Nabu-apal-iddin's successor, Marduk-zakir-shumi, we have a small plaque in lapis lazuli dedicated to Marduk, formerly the god of Hammurabi.

The boundary stone of Marduk-apal-iddin (Berlin Museum) brings us back to the Kassites. By having himself portrayed alone facing a minister who is doing homage to him, this king, the stubborn adversary of Sargon of

216 - BOUNDARY STONE OF MARDUK-APAL-IDDIN (8th CENT. B.C.). — BERLIN

Assyria, proclaims, dramatically and unequivocally, the sturdy independence of his race. The two figures are rather fleshy, and the closely fitting robes tend to emphasize a corpulence which may well have answered to the canon of masculine beauty at that time. King and minister are shown exactly in profile, with no distortion of shoulders or torso; this is unusual enough to be worth mentioning.

Even more striking is the representation at the top, in the purest Kassite style, of the divine emblems of Nabu, Ninhursag(?), Ea and Marduk.

169

This scene is paralleled by another on the boundary stone of Marduk-zakir-shumi in the Louvre, where the inscribed text is dominated by a relief grouping on the same register the king, his scribe and the symbols of Marduk, Nabu, Ea, Shuqamuna, Adad and Nusku. Thus at the height of the Assyrian ascendancy a thematic repertory a full millennium older reappears unchanged. This was more than a reversion to an ancient symbolism; it was also a challenge by the Babylonian rulers to their rivals at Nineveh.

Such were the men in whose steps the Neo-Babylonians followed (626-538 B.C.). While keeping to time-honoured traditions with absolute fidelity, they aimed above all at celebrating the grandeur of the new régime and giving it spectacular expression in the magnificence of their capital city, Babylon. But of the six kings only two measured up to the mighty task they had set themselves: Nabopolassar, founder of the dynasty, and his son Nebuchadnezzar. Less than a century —eighty-eight years all told—was but a short time to repair the wanton damage done by Sennacherib, who deflected the course of the Euphrates into the heart of the city, where it undermined the brick walls and brought them down in ruins. Yet repair it they did, and enough of their work has survived to demonstrate the high ambition and tremendous energy of these master-builder kings.

217 - BOUNDARY STONE OF MARDUK-ZAKIR-SHUMI (9th CENT. B.C.). — LOUVRE

218 - BABYLON. VIEW OF THE CITY AND THE →
ZIGGURAT (7th-6th CENTURIES B.C.).

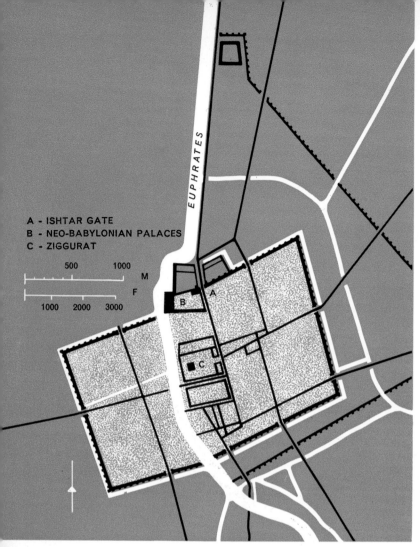

A - ISHTAR GATE
B - NEO-BABYLONIAN PALACES
C - ZIGGURAT

500   1000

1000   2000   3000

219 - BABYLON. PLAN OF THE CITY (7th-6th CENTURIES B.C.).

They began by girdling the city with a double ring of walls. The outer wall, some twelve miles long, enclosed a vast area extending well beyond the city proper; here, in time of danger, fugitives from the outlying villages could take refuge and pitch their tents in safety. The inner wall enclosed the city itself, which was built on both sides of the river, though the residential district, together with the principal temples, lay entirely on the left bank. We can well imagine how Babylon, rising in the midst of the Mesopotamian plain beside a luxuriant oasis——even today the palm grove of Hilleh is the loveliest in Iraq after that of Basra—must have dazzled the eyes of approaching travellers. The far-flung vista of white terraces, lofty walls and towers would have sufficed to produce a spectacular effect, but there was an even greater wonder. The city was dominated by a seven-storey ziggurat and on its summit, some three hundred feet above street level, stood the temple called *E-temen-an-ki* (house of the foundation of heaven and earth), its blue revetment of glazed bricks glittering in the sun. This, the temple of Marduk, was the most impressive of the many monuments representative of this heaven-aspiring Mesopotamian architecture.

Built of sun-dried bricks with a facing of baked bricks, the great ziggurat must have seemed to hold out 'the promise of eternity'—to use the expression of Nebuchadnezzar himself, who completed it. Today the glory has departed; only a water-logged hole marks the site. But we can form an idea of the original structure by reading the description given by Herodotus and by cross-checking it with the data recorded on a cuneiform tablet written in the third century B.C., which supplies us with the exact dimensions.

The whole life and architectural lay-out of Babylon centred on the ziggurat and the temple of Marduk, permanent residence of the city god.

220 - BABYLON.   THE ISHTAR GATE AND THE →
PROCESSIONAL WAY (7th-6th CENTURIES B.C.).

221 - BABYLON (A) LION ON THE SACRED WAY — LOUVRE

221 - BABYLON (B) DRAGON ON THE ISHTAR GATE — BERLIN MUSEUM

Processions approached it along the Sacred Way *(Ai-ubur-shabu)*, whose starting point was a triumphal arch, the Ishtar Gate, through which the worshippers had to pass before beginning the ritual march. After mustering outside the city, in an avenue lined with glazed brick panels figuring a series of lions passant, the processions filed through the gateway. Built entirely of baked brick and reinforced with gigantic pilasters, it was decorated with the animal attributes of Marduk and Adad, dragons and bulls alternating on thirteen superimposed tiers. The figure of each animal stood out against a uniform background tinted blue with powdered lapis lazuli. The dragons were white, with their horns, forked tongues, arched backs and claws picked out with yellow. The bulls were blackish-brown, their horns and hoofs green, the hide and tips of the tails blue. The lions again were white, with yellow highlights on the manes, fangs, claws and the tuft of hair at the end of the tail. Architecture and ornamentation were skilfully adapted to each other, the animals were carved to scale, and despite their multitude (575 dragons and bulls, 120 lions) the arrangement was orderly and harmonious. To the band of marguerites on the plinth corresponded an upper frieze of the same flowers, but larger. Along the top of the gate ran crenellated battlements.

221 - BABYLON (C) BULL ON THE ISHTAR GATE. (7th-6th CENTURIES B.C.). — BERLIN MUSEUM

222 - BABYLON. THE ISHTAR GATE (7th-6th CENTURIES B.C.). — BERLIN MUSEUM →

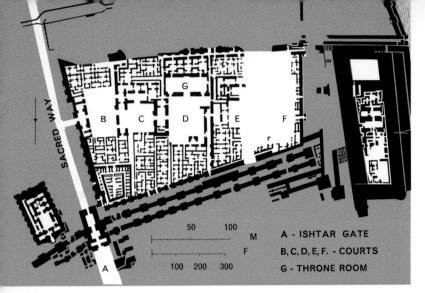

50   100
M
100   200   300
F

A - ISHTAR GATE
B, C, D, E, F. - COURTS
G - THRONE ROOM

223 - BABYLON.   PLAN OF THE PALACES (7th-6th CENTURIES B.C.).

Though the Ishtar Gate is still an impressive sight, the palaces, which formed one of the most grandiose architectural complexes of the capital, are now no more than a mass of rubble. Trapezoidal in shape, with its entrance on the Processional Way, the royal residence was composed of five interlocking units, each with a large courtyard giving access to the living quarters and reception rooms around it.   Opening on the third court was the so-called Throne Room, whose importance was stressed by its triple gateway and richly decorated façade of glazed bricks.   Here again was the familiar procession of lions, but the decorative designs above it were brilliantly original. Set off by a blue ground was a row of yellow columns whose superimposed Ionic capitals were crowned by palmettes and linked to each other by a garland of lotus buds.   Above this, bordered by a thin moulding divided into alternate segments of yellow, black and white, ran a frieze of double palmettes with white petals and yellow centres and rings. While the rose and palm ornaments may have derived from the Assyrian repertory, it was not so with the Ionic capitals, such as the Babylonians must have seen on the Phoenician coast, or possibly at Cyprus.

The famous Hanging Gardens of Babylon ranked among the seven wonders of the world.   Tradition attributed them to Semiramis, but it now seems that they were the work of Nebuchadnezzar.   To strengthen his alliance with the Medes, this king had married Amyitis, daughter of Astyages.   To please his wife, who was pining for the hills and forests of her native Persia, he had a series of terraced gardens built up beside the palace, and a hoist was installed to water them from the irrigation canals in the plain below.   Thus a huge exotic garden overlooking the white roofs of the city was artificially created to remind the homesick queen of her native land.

Something has already been said of religious architecture in connection with the ziggurat of Babylon.   The temple of Marduk *(Esagila)* stood in an enclave near by.   It housed a whole pantheon but the chapel dedicated to Marduk himself was the most lavishly decorated. Nebuchadnezzar claimed to have gilded the entire chapel; even the cedarwood beams of the ceiling were plated with gold and silver. According to Herodotus, the seated statue of the god was a solid mass of precious metal weighing nearly forty tons.

224 - BABYLON.   DECORATED FAÇADE OF THE THRONE ROOM OF THE PALACE (7th-6th CENTURIES B.C.). — BERLIN MUSEUM →

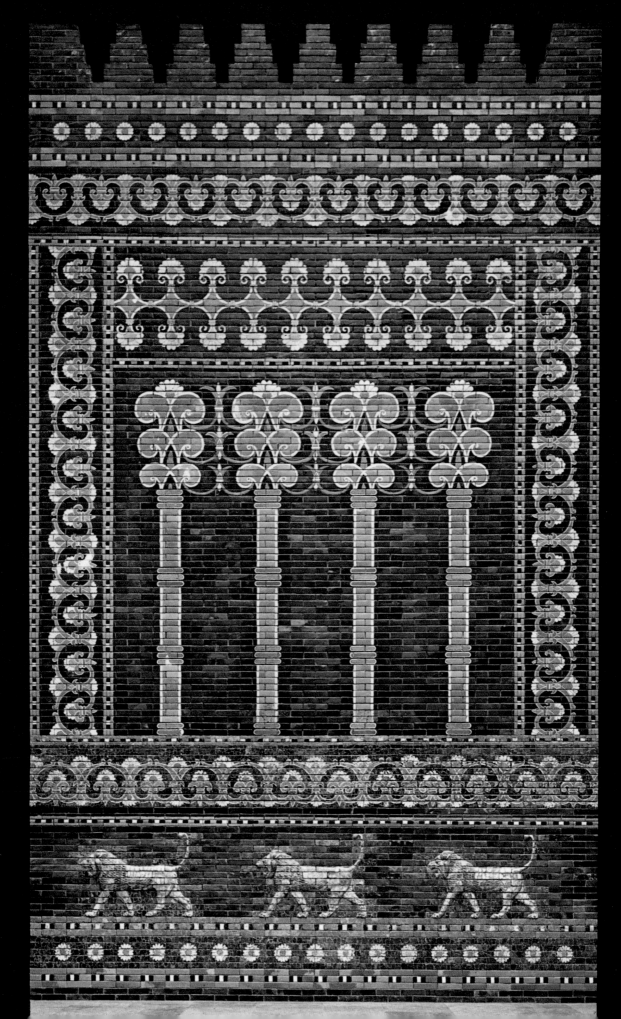

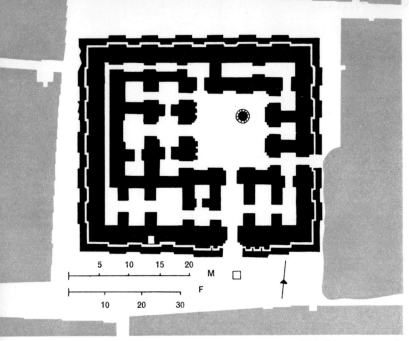

225 - BABYLON. — PLAN OF THE TEMPLE OF ISHTAR (7th-6th CENT. B.C.).

Even allowing for a good deal of exaggeration, it seems that the full technical resources of the time and the finest materials available must have been lavished on the furnishings and cult objects. Of all this nothing has survived; our direct knowledge of it is entirely derived from the magniloquent annals of the Babylonian kings, and descriptions given by early travellers.

In the surviving ruins of less famous temples we have a more rewarding and reliable source of information. Their ground-plans make it clear that the dwelling of the god was built on the lines of a human habitation. It consisted of an inner court, open to the sky and surrounded by a number of rooms; the one selected as the divine abode was invariably a rectangular room entered by a door exactly facing the pedestal on which the god himself was supposed to stand. He could thus be seen from the court, and the approaching worshipper could draw near the 'mercy seat' without turning to either side, and have direct access to the unseen presence signified by the statue. After crossing the court and the outer room he penetrated into the temple cella, the Holy of Holies. By clearly marked stages, then, he passed from the profane to the sacred, just as the present-day Christian can enter the choir only after crossing the preparatory zones of narthex and nave, having the altar facing him all the while.

Both Nabopolassar and Nebuchadnezzar, as we have said, were great builders. To these names it would be unfair not to add that of Nabonidus, last king of the dynasty, whose life and policy alike were guided by his religious zeal. In the old Sumerian capital of Ur, dedicated from time immemorial to the cult of the moon god, the king carried on the work of reconstruction inaugurated by his predecessors, and it was he who completed the rebuilding of the ziggurat. Moreover, to the three stages of the tower that had dominated the plain in the days of the Third Dynasty (late third millennium) Nabonidus certainly added two, possibly four more. Like Babylon and Borsippa, Ur, thanks to him, could now boast of an architecture worthy of its glorious past. For the Neo-Babylonians did more than repair ruined buildings: they restored to Mesopotamia much of its bygone splendour.

Turning from architecture to other art forms, however, we find an almost complete blank. Whereas likenesses exist of every great Assyrian monarch (Tiglathpileser, Shalmaneser, Assurnasirpal, Sargon, Sennacherib, Esarhaddon, Assurbanipal), none has been found of Nabopolassar, Nebuchadnezzar or Nabonidus. Yet it seems hardly credible that the Neo-Babylonian sculptors and bronze-founders should have failed to record the features of these all-powerful rulers, for the edification of their subjects.

It must be confessed that the excavations at Babylon have yielded disappointing results. The pieces of sculpture found in the *Hauptburg*, for example, are not Babylonian at all; they belonged to a kind of museum where the kings displayed their trophies of war—a Hittite stele, Assyrian stelae, statues and a relief from Mari. These works therefore have no place in the present study.

Until recently specialists were reluctant to accept the basalt lion trampling a prostrate man as a Babylonian work. But since the discovery in 1952 of the two Nimrud ivories illustrating a similar theme, there are grounds for holding that this sculpture, so often catalogued as Hittite, may well have originated in Babylon itself. To date it with any plausibility, however, seems out of the question; for quite possibly it preceded the Neo-Babylonian period.

226 - BABYLON. LION TRAMPLING A MAN
(FIRST MILLENNIUM B.C.).

227 - SEAL IMPRESSION. HERO FIGHTING WILD ANIMALS

228 - SEAL IMPRESSION. HERO CAPTURING BIRDS

229 - ADORATION OF THE GOAT-FISH
(7th-6th CENTURIES B.C.). —
PIERPONT MORGAN COLLECTION

There can be no doubt, on the other hand, as to the activity of the engravers, for a great many cylinder and stamp seals can safely be assigned to this period. Specialists make no secret of their quandary, however, when it comes to distinguishing between Assyrian and Neo-Babylonian seals. For the themes are identical: either we have a hero (winged or not) fighting animals, or scenes of worship (a celebrant standing before a religious symbol). For a time figures and accessories were lavishly represented; then their number was reduced, so drastically at times as to impair the composition and lay-out. Notable is the total absence of gods in human form. They are now represented solely by their symbols: crescent, star, stylus, goat-fish, dragon with thunderbolt, and (very often) the *marru* or triangular spade of Marduk.

For the great god of Babylon could be symbolized either by this agricultural implement *(marru)* or by a dragon *(mushrusshu)*. In the Louvre is a boldly schematized bronze representing Marduk's animal attribute with sharply pointed horns and flattened muzzle (the decorative inlays have been lost); presumably this dragon figured on a sceptre or a staff held by a god.

Although generations of kings had dutifully prayed their gods to keep watch and ward over the city, Babylon's days were numbered. Daniel, in his interpretation of Nebuchadnezzar's dream,

likened the kingdom to a great image whose head was of pure gold, the body of silver and brass, the feet of iron and clay. 'A stone. . . smote the image upon his feet. Then was the iron, the clay, the brass, the silver, and the gold, broken to pieces together' (Daniel ii. 34-35). It was Cyrus who flung that stone. Betrayed and deserted by his ministers, Nabonidus shut himself up in the doomed city, surrounded by the images of his gods, while his armies were being routed in the plain of Sippar. Further resistance was useless. Gobryas, former governor of Gutium, went over to the enemy and himself opened the gates of the capital. A few days later, on October 29, 539 B.C., Cyrus entered Babylon and was welcomed as a liberator by the priests of Marduk. To his title of King of Anzan he now added that of 'sovereign of Babylon, Sumer, Akkad and the four quarters of the world.' The greatest capital of the Ancient East had collapsed at a blow, and the Babylonian régime gave place to the Achaemenid dynasty. Almost overnight a new order was imposed on the whole of Western Asia. The exiled Jews were permitted to return to Jerusalem, and Isaiah (xlv. 1), rejoicing in the deliverance of his people, went so far as to hail Cyrus the Persian as the Lord's Anointed.

The downfall, first of Nineveh, then of Babylon, made an end once for all of the political power of Mesopotamia, but its cultural influence survived the disappearance of its empires. The fruit of three thousand years' civilization, Mesopotamian art was too deeply rooted, too vital an expression of the human spirit unconfined by any specific time or place, for it to be obliterated by these successive changes of government, however widespread the violence attending them. And this art continued to flourish under the Achaemenians for the next two centuries. Its survival need not surprise us; this is not the only time in history that a conquered race has taken its conquerors captive. The endless processions of tributaries, warriors and dignitaries in the palace of Persepolis reiterated those of Khorsabad. The great panels of lions in glazed bricks at Susa are faithful copies of those at Babylon on the Processional Way and in Nabopolassar's palace. Times had changed, nevertheless, and Achaemenian architecture and ornamentation have an atmosphere of their own, corresponding to the radical change of the political system and to the new spirit governing the structure of the empire. All this necessarily affected art and, despite these reminiscences of an immemorial tradition, gave it a 'new look.'

230 - DRAGON HEAD: ATTRIBUTE OF MARDUK
(7th-6th CENTURIES B.C.). — LOUVRE →

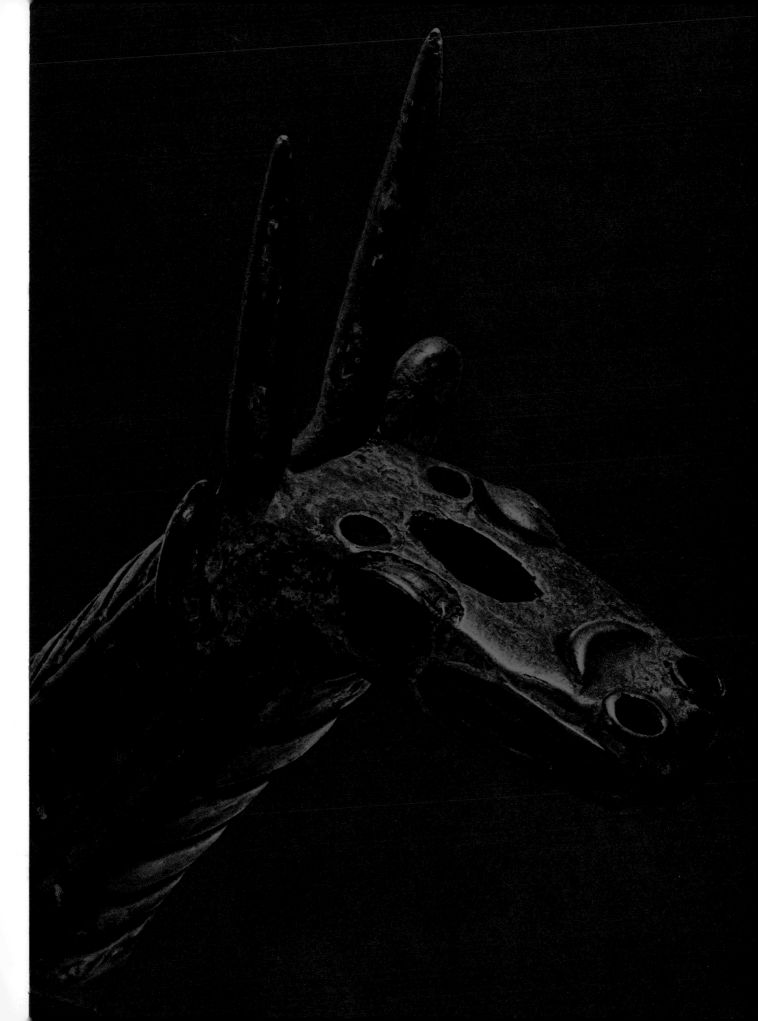

A

B

C

D

E

18

236 - SEAL IMPRESSION. DETAIL, FLEEING OSTRICH (1st MILL.). — PIERPONT MORGAN COLLECTION

KINGS AND DYNASTIES	SITES	
Dynasty 'H' (990-732)		
Nabu-apal-iddin (885-852)	SIPPAR	
Marduk-zakir-shumi I (851-828)	BABYLON	
Dynasty 'J' (732-626)		
Mardu-kapal-iddina II (722-711)		
Neo-Babylonians (626-538)		
Nabopolassar (626-605)	BABYLON	
Fall of Nineveh (612)	BORSIPPA	
Nebuchadnezzar II (604-562)	BABYLON	
	BORSIPPA	
	KISH	
	UR	
	URUK	
Amil-Marduk (561-560)		
Nergal-sarra-usur (559-556)		
Labasi-Marduk (556)		
Nabonidus (555-539)	BABYLON	
	HARRAN	
	SIPPAR	
	UR	

BABYLONIANS AND NEO-BABYLONIANS THE RETURN TO THE SOURCES (990-538 B.C.)

Despite the military might and political supremacy of Assyria, Babylon had never accepted its inferior status, and the history of Nineveh and Babylon in this period is one of continual strife and rivalry between the two capitals. Finally, in the seventh century B.C., an independent dynasty assumes power in Babylon, the so-called Neo-Babylonian dynasty founded by Nabopolassar, first of a line of six kings. Allying himself with the Medes and the Scythians, he succeeds in capturing Nineveh in 612 B.C. and destroying its power.

Neo-Babylonian art takes over the legacy of the past and keeps to the great Mesopotamian tradition. The kings make it their policy to celebrate the grandeur of the new régime, not only by sending military expeditions into neighbouring lands (Nebuchadnezzar captures Jerusalem in 586 B.C.) but by carrying out an ambitious building programme both in Babylon itself and throughout the kingdom. They concentrate their efforts, however, on embellishing the capital, and no expense is spared in making Babylon, with its great walls, its majestic gates, its ziggurat, temples, palaces and hanging gardens, one of the wonders of the world.

Temples, palaces and private houses undoubtedly contained many works of art, but war and pillage have taken so heavy a toll as to leave very meagre pickings for the archaeologist. While the supreme god of Babylon, Marduk, still stands today on the polychrome revetment of the Ishtar Gate, nothing remains of the ziggurat and its temple *E-temen-an-ki*, which once towered some three hundred feet above the plain.

ARCHITECTURE	SCULPTURE	TERRACOTTA	METAL	EGYPT	AEGEAN
				Late Period (1085-332)	
				Osorkon II (870-847)	
Temple of Shamash	Tablet			Takelothis II (847-823)	
	Plaque of Marduk Kudurru in the Louvre				Institution of the Olympic Games (776?)
	Kudurru at Berlin				
			Horned Dragon's Head		
Ziggurat Palace	Cylinder Seals	'Papsukkal' Figurines		Necho (609-594)	
Ziggurat Ezida Temple		Glazed and enamelled Ceramics			
Ziggurat Palace		Lions in Glazed Bricks			
Temples		Bulls and Dragons in Glazed Bricks			
Ishtar Gate		Lions in Glazed Bricks			
Hanging Gardens					
Processional Way					
Ziggurat Ezida Temple					
				Amasis (568-526)	
Temple of Sin Temple of Shamash Ziggurat					

238 - PERSEPOLIS. BABYLONIAN TRIBUTARIES BRINGING GIFTS (6th-5th CENTURIES B.C.).

V

FROM THE ACHAEMENIANS TO THE DEATH OF ALEXANDER THE GREAT
(558-323 B.C.)

The triumph of Cyrus the Persian and the fall of Babylon were a signal for general rejoicings throughout the Near East. Nations that had suffered for centuries from the depredations of the kings of Nineveh and Babylon saw in the downfall of those two well-hated cities an end of their troubles and the beginning of an age of independence. The Medes, who had taken part in the destruction of Nineveh, were compelled to recognize the hegemony of Cyrus, once their vassal, and of the family of the Achaemenidae to which he belonged. After defeating Croesus of Lydia (546) and Nabonidus of Babylon (539), and occupying the whole of Western Asia, Cyrus was about to invade Egypt when he died (530). It was left to his son and successor Cambyses to conquer Egypt (525). In the troubled period following the death of Cambyses (522) it seemed as if the new-won empire was about to fall to pieces, until Darius, member of a younger branch of the royal family, succeeded in eliminating the priest Gaumata who had usurped the throne. During a reign of over thirty-five years (521-485) he organized his enormous empire in a system of satrapies, meshes of a net that he manipulated with much dexterity. Though authoritarian, he practised clemency and tolerance; subject nations were allowed to keep their religions, languages and, in several cases, their former rulers. From one or other of his many residences, at Susa, Persepolis, Ecbatana and Babylon, the 'King of Kings' administered his empire with a firm hand, but often, also, with an eye to the satisfaction of his subjects. Thus when the Jews on their return from captivity encountered difficulties in rebuilding the temple of Jerusalem, they applied for help to Darius, who promptly gave the necessary orders, with the result that the work went forward smoothly and was brought to a successful conclusion.

But all great conquerors, it seems, are destined to outreach their grasp and transgress the limits set by Fate. Darius and, after him, his son Xerxes, not content with dominating the East, crossed the Helles-pont and advanced into Europe. After the subjugation of Thrace, the Persians embarked on the campaigns against Greece, which ended in disaster for the colossus of the East. Once again David's sling laid low a seemingly invincible Goliath.

The Persian Wars had long-lasting effects not only on the political relations between East and West but also in the domain of culture. For the first time the East had come in direct contact with a non-Oriental civilization in its own climate and environment. When the Persians retreated after their misadventures in the West, their eyes had been opened to a new way of life and new ways of thought that, intermingling with their Oriental heritage, were now to lead to the production of works which, if basically composite, were in the result original. What the Achaemenians aimed at was an audacious synthesis: a blending of Western suavity with the rigid hieraticism of Mesopotamian art, second-ed by a readiness to innovate in architecture by borrowing ideas from Egypt. Thus reminiscences of Nineveh, Babylon, Thebes, and probably Athens as well, can be seen at Persepolis. But obviously it was easier to draw inspiration from the Assyrians or Neo-Babylonians, or to copy the Egyptians, than to annex the genius of Hellas.

Since the Achaemenians will form the subject of a separate volume of this series, there can be no question here of dealing with them at any length. Our purpose is simply to show the extent to which they inherited and continued the art and civilization of Mesopotamia, particularly in their Assyrian and Neo-Babylonian form.

Persian monumental art is known to us by way of three cities, still imposing though in ruins: Pasargadae, built by Cyrus the Great between 559 and 550; Persepolis, where work continued through the reigns of Darius, Xerxes I and Artaxerxes I (518-460), but which was never completed; and, lastly, Susa, where building was in progress under Darius and Xerxes I and also later, under Artaxerxes II Mnemon (405-358). The building inscription composed by Darius I and found at Susa is of exceptional interest since it lists the teams of workers of

239 - SUSA. VIEW OF THE PALACE (6th-4th CENTURIES B.C.).

many nationalities, some freemen, some conscripted, who were employed in building the palace. And no doubt the same method of team-work obtained in the other large-scale works commissioned by the king.

The importance of the inscription lies in its detailed information about the foreign sources of supply, not only of raw material, but of labour—that is to say the importation of more or less expert craftsmen from abroad. Though doubtless they had to comply with precise instructions furnished by the king, they cannot have completely discarded the techniques and skills, widely differing from those of their employers, which they had learnt in their homelands. Here we have, presumably, an explanation of the peculiar nature of Achaemenian art; it was a composite product, an amalgam of widely different ingredients deriving from a great variety of races and drawing inspiration from diverse, often conflicting sources.   And so far as can be known this was something wholly unprecedented in the Ancient East.

240 - PASARGADAE. VIEW OF THE PALACE (6th CENTURY B.C.).

What is believed to be the earliest residence of the Achaemenid sovereigns was located at Meshed-i-Sulaiman, where a great terrace was built, backed against a mountain, to which ten stairways gave access. A similar terrace, on a yet larger scale, was subsequently constructed at Persepolis. At Pasargadae, chosen by Cyrus as the site of his capital, the architecture was of a very different type and consisted of separate buildings situated in a walled park. Here we find already what were to be the three essential units of royal abodes—a triumphal gateway, an Audience Hall, a residential palace—and also one of the distinctive features of Achaemenian architecture, a lavish use of columns. Placed outside, the columns form part of porticoes; inside, they support the roofs of hypostyle halls. Totally foreign to Mesopotamia, these architectural features seem to have been borrowed from Egypt, but the use of cedar-wood beams permitted greater spans in the roofing than was possible in the Nile valley, where only stone was employed.

The decorative elements consisted largely of borrowings from countries less remote than Egypt. Thus the gate-house was guarded by stone bulls, winged in the outer entrance, human-headed within. A pillar, still *in situ*, in one of the passages was decorated with the figure of a genius with two pairs of wings and an elaborate crown of an Egyptianizing type, clearly copied from Phoenician bronzes. The lower part of the walls of the Audience Hall was embellished with carved slabs, according to Assyrian and Hittite custom. The columns had capitals executed in a style prefiguring that of Persepolis and Susa, but with more variety in the animals represented: bulls, lions (sometimes horned) and horses. Here, while the bases and shafts of columns are Ionian, the capitals are typically Achaemenian.

241 - PASARGADAE. WINGED GENIUS DECORATING A GATE OF THE PALACE (6th CENTURY B.C.).

Notable is the predilection for polychromy evidenced not only by the alternate use of white and greyish-black stone, but also by the addition of coats of vivid colours.

Pasargadae was only a beginning, if an auspicious one. Once Darius had put down the rebellions that followed his accession, and had established his authority throughout the empire, he decided to have a capital worthy of a 'King of Kings.' His choice fell on a site some twenty-four miles south of Pasargadae, in the province of Fars. Work on Persepolis continued for sixty years, from 520 to 460 B.C. After Darius, his son Xerxes and then his grandson Artaxerxes I made it a point of honour to enlarge and embellish a city that was a memorial not so much to individual rulers as to a dynasty. Thus, for a just appreciation of this period and culture, there is more to be learnt from Persepolis than from either Susa or Pasargadae.

The architectural lay-out was planned, then executed, on a spectacular scale. The terrace was a gigantic stage measuring about 1650 by 980 feet, and 42 feet in height, with for a backdrop the rugged Kuh-i-Rahmet mountains. Several palaces were erected on this site; Darius had his own, the Tatchara, and Xerxes had another built for himself, the Hadish palace. Magnificent though these were, they were dwarfed by two immense edifices, the Audience Hall (or Apadana) begun by Darius and completed by Xerxes and Artaxerxes, and the Hundred-Column Hall, started by Xerxes and finished by his son. Here architects and builders excelled themselves. Both display the characteristic features of Achaemenian architecture: a square ground-plan, stately porticoes (three in the Apadana, one in the Hundred-Column Hall), and a lavish use of columns supporting the terraced roof and topped by capitals of

242 - PERSEPOLIS. AERIAL VIEW OF THE RUINS (6th-5th CENTURIES B.C.).

a wholly novel kind. Above a fluted shaft, a corolla-shaped capital supports a block adorned with four double volutes, vertically disposed, upon which rest two animals back to back: bulls, griffins or human-headed bulls. The crossed cedar-wood beams supporting the roof rested on the animals' backs and between their horns. This structural arrangement was at once highly decorative and eminently functional. The wooden architraves permitted a wider spacing between the columns than was possible in Egyptian temples (where stone was employed throughout), and the number of columns could be reduced—there were only thirty-six in the Apadana, which was nearly 200 feet square and capable, we are told, of accommodating ten thousand people—or else increased at will (the sides of the Hall of the Hundred Columns measured 230 feet).

Not all the columns were in stone. Many were made of wood plastered and painted in bright colours (blue, red, white), as in the buildings at the foot of the cliffs, styled by Erich Schmidt the Treasury.

The same architectural methods obtained in those other portions of the palace complex which have been tentatively, somewhat unconvincingly, called the Harem, the Council Hall (Tripylon), Palace H, etc. As at Pasargadae, there was a majestic gate-house standing well to the north of the palace. It was built by Xerxes who gave it the name 'All Countries.' Four columns supported the roof of a square inner room, and two pairs of bulls guarded the outer and inner entrances. The bulls were taken over from Assyria, but the entablature was a servile copy of an Egyptian cornice.

Though blocks of stone were sometimes used for the artificial terraces, others were built in the Mesopotamian manner, that is to say with unbaked bricks. The frames of doors, windows and wall recesses, however, were always carved in stone, many of these frames being all in one piece, not assembled from three or four elements. It is hard to see why designers and craftsmen thus increased the difficulties of their respective tasks. In any case this procedure has led to somewhat curious results: while the raw brick walls of Darius' palace have crumbled into dust, the stone doorways and window-frames have remained intact, and seen from the east, stand out against the vastness of the plain: silent, yet eloquent witnesses to a splendour that has passed away.

Yet something of the splendour of Persepolis has survived in the magnificent decorative elements, buried under hundreds of tons of rubble, that have been brought to light by recent excavations. Never had decorative ensembles so complete and still located at the exact places for which they were intended, been unearthed in any of the dead cities of the Ancient East.

243 - PERSEPOLIS. MONUMENTAL STAIRWAY ON THE EAST SIDE OF THE APADANA (6th-5th CENTURIES B.C.).

With some very rare exceptions the Achaemenians employed sculpture in the round only for their capitals, whereas they had a marked predilection for the ornamental bas-relief. It was of two types: sometimes a free-standing block of stone, but oftener an element that, repeated again and again, built up a vast panoramic composition consisting of a series of prefabricated slabs aligned side by side. This obviously follows the Assyrian system of ornamentation, but the Persians carried it to such a pitch that the over-all effect is monotonous, not to say tedious. It is, however, possible that the reactions of the subjects of the Great King were different from ours; perhaps it seemed only natural to them that the power and the glory of the monarch should be extolled on these time-honoured lines. The object of the reliefs was first to catch the eye, then to fix the scene in the beholder's memory, and visitors to the palace of Persepolis were intensively subjected to this visual propaganda.

All conspired to hymn the glory of the monarch and his victories on the battlefield. Yet actual fighting is never represented; not only were scenes of warfare banned by a strict censorship but not the least allusion to them was permitted. Only the recompense of victory—long streams of tribute-bearers from twenty-eight countries—was depicted in these sculptured chronicles. Looking at them, one might well believe that this homage paid the great king by foreigners was spontaneous and that they had a real devotion to the beneficent 'King of the Earth.'

195

But even at his most courteous, the king remains distant and aloof. The Mede who, staff in hand, is shown bowing to Darius (accompanied by his son Xerxes) is under close supervision; dignitaries and soldiers in attendance are on the alert, ready to spring to action the moment any danger threatens.

Like the Assyrian palaces, the palace of Persepolis was well guarded. But whereas the safe-keeping of the former was usually ensured by tutelary celestial genii, these were omitted by the Achaemenians, who contented themselves with a few human-headed sphinxes posted outside the palace and, here and there, the emblem of Ahuramazda. Wise in their generation, the Persian kings put more confidence in their bodyguard of picked troops, the ten thousand 'Immortals.'

That the themes of this decorative sculpture are borrowed from Assyrian and Mesopotamian art is undeniable. For example, the figures upholding the throne derive from Assyria, while the motif of the hero-king clutching a lion with his right arm is an evident recall of the 'Gilgamesh with a Lion Cub' at Khorsabad. Similarly the procession of tributaries directly stems from processions in Sargon's palace. True, the Assyrian palaces were in ruins when Darius started building his, but there is no doubt that the reliefs at Nineveh, Nimrud and Khorsabad could still be seen and that the sculptors employed

244 - PERSEPOLIS. KING MASTERING A LION CUB 6th-5th CENTURIES B.C.)

I

at Persepolis drew inspiration from them.

But their technique is very different. Figures are more fully modelled, more graceful. Above all in the rendering of garments we find a notable advance; they have a rippling movement and folds are treated with a fluency far to seek in Assyrian sculpture. (The Medes, with their smooth garments, without folds, are an exception and, by contrast, cut stiff, lifeless figures.) Western influence is evident in these elegantly undulating draperies; indeed Darius in his building inscription explicitly states that the sculptors were Ionians and Sardians. To them, steeped as they were in Aegean culture, it came natural to impart to stone the fluttering movement of light tissues and the buoyancy of the Persian garments. For these foreign sculptors invented nothing; all they did was to render with a stylishness

245 - PERSEPOLIS. SERVANT OF THE PALACE OF DARIUS (6th-5th CENT. B.C.).

of which the local artists were incapable the free-flowing costumes then in fashion in the sophisticated circles of the royal capital.

From their sojourn in Hellas the Achaemenians had brought back *inter alia* this taste for loosely fitting garments that billowed in the wind. After rows and rows of stereotyped figures—one soldier is always exactly like another, an 'usher' has exactly the same features as another 'usher' —suddenly we come on figures that stand out sharply against this background of standardized imagery. Almost they seem like envoys, or intruders, from another world, in this case the Western world, for it is of the West we are inevitably reminded by the slim, beardless servants holding in one hand a perfume jar and a folded napkin in the other who figure in the palaces of Darius and Xerxes. They are poles apart from the young Assyrian eunuchs whom the prophet Daniel described as 'fair and fat in flesh' (i. 15). But for their coiffure and garments they would remind us far more of Greek ephebi than of the sturdy youngsters of the Iranian highlands.

At Susa, another royal city, Darius applied himself to making good the havoc wrought by the Assyrian Assurbanipal a century before. Unfortunately the site was ravaged by fire and it was left to Artaxerxes Mnemon (405-358) to repair the damage. Susa was much more a Mesopotamian than an Achaemenian city (this was due to its proximity to Babylon) and the contrast with Persepolis is striking. Yet the two cities have a basic affinity; the same civilization and art prevailed in both, though Babylonian influences are more pronounced in Susa.

This is evident both in the architecture and in the ornamentation. The plan of the palace at Susa, with its three open courts on an east-west axis, each surrounded by a series of rooms, is obviously reminiscent of the Neo-Babylonian palaces of Babylon. The only truly original features were the hypostyle hall with its thirty-six columns (the same number as in the Apadana of Persepolis), its pillared porticoes (two, if not three) and of course that specifically Achaemenian feature, the forked, two-headed capital.

But the decorative panels of polychrome glazed bricks were typically Babylonian. This technique was rarely practised at Persepolis where, as we have seen, there was an abundance of stone reliefs. These were very unusual at Susa, judging by the paucity of fragments of such reliefs discovered there, whereas the walls were covered with glazed brick decorations in the purest Neo-Babylonian style. The Susian lions passant could easily have replaced the ones adorning, two centuries before, the Processional Way and the throne room of Nebuchadnezzar's palace at Babylon. Similarly, except for the wings, the bulls of Susa were replicas of those on the Ishtar Gate at Babylon. But there were also animals peculiar to Susa: winged griffins, horned lions and the winged, human-headed lions which are shown, confronted, under a winged disk, but with their heads slewed round, as if to avoid looking at each other.

246 - (A) BABYLON. PLAN OF THE NEO-BABYLONIAN PALACES (B) SUSA. PLAN OF THE PALACE (C) PERSEPOLIS. PLAN OF THE PALACES

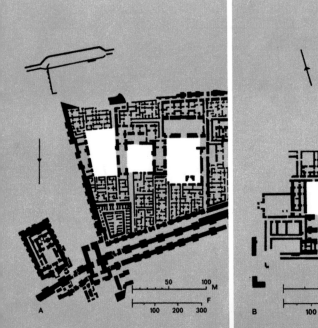

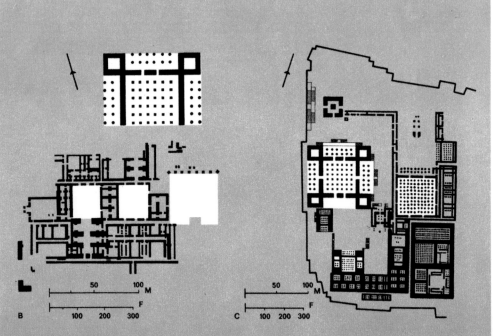

Lastly, we have complete panels reproducing in glazed bricks the processions carved in stone at Persepolis: long lines of archers with olive-green hair and costumes of several colours: white tunics with yellow sleeves, yellow tunics with brown sleeves, yellow shoes.

The gorgeously decorated uniform of the Persian soldier was so voluminous as seriously to handicap him in the field of battle. Herodotus commented on 'the disadvantage of these cumbrous, over-long garments and the lightness of the Persians' weapons': the lances with gold or silver knobs, and bows whose arrows, though they laid low the Spartans at Thermopylae, proved so ineffective at Plataea.

The lavish use of colours in the reliefs—mostly yellow, green and azure blue, diversified with passages of gold and orange-red—was paralleled in the textiles. In the first chapter of the Book of Esther we read of a feast 'in the court of the garden of the king's palace, where were white, green and blue hangings fastened with cords of fine linen and purple to silver rings and pillars of marble... upon a pavement of red, and blue, and white, and black marble.' One of the purposes of the great variety of colours employed in the palaces of the Achaemenids was doubtless to relieve the monotony that would otherwise have resulted from the persistent repetition of stereotyped motifs.

247 - SUSA. ARCHER OF THE ROYAL GUARD (5th CENTURY B.C.). — LOUVRE

248 - NAKSH-I-RUSTAM. TOMB OF DARIUS I (5th CENTURY B.C.).

What were the ideas behind these motifs? How explain, for example, the symbolic wild beasts, always in an aggressive mood? That they were animal attributes of deities seems improbable, given the tenor of Iranian culture. Were they, then, guardians? That could apply to the lions, possibly to the bulls as well; though hardly to the griffins. We can but recognize that the language of this imagery is enigmatic and all too often defies interpretation. For here, for the first time, religion seems no longer to be art's sole, invariable source of inspiration. The Assyrians, as we have seen, had qualms about representing their supreme gods in their palaces, though they made countless effigies of celestial genii. The Neo-Babylonians dispensed with both, and confined themselves to representing symbolic animals and attributes of their major gods.

Under the Achaemenians religious iconography, limited to its simplest expression, had recourse to some Assyrian formulas, such as the winged disk, sometimes topped by a bust of Ahuramazda. This imagery was used in the palaces and also on the façades of royal tombs cut into the rock-face, for example those at Naksh-i-Rustam. By the same token, the absence of temples and the celebration of religious rites in the open air, in front of fire altars, ruled out representations of the gods. And these changes reflect the remarkable simplification—not to say purification—of religious dogma under the Achaemenians.

Having no temples, the Persians would have been at a loss what to do with statues of the gods, even had they thought of making any. As it is, they seem to have produced very little sculpture in the round. Plutarch speaks of a huge statue of Xerxes at Persepolis which was broken up by Alexander's troops. Not a trace of it remains. A few isolated fragments which may or may not have belonged to statues have been unearthed at Susa. The only intact pieces are equally few and of

very small dimensions, an inch or
two in height: a head in the Stoclet
Collection and another in lapis
lazuli paste, discovered at Persepolis, which, in view of its crenellated crown, may represent Xerxes
when as a young prince he was in
charge of his father's building
operations. The absence of free-
standing statues seems all the more
puzzling in view of the sculptors'
vigorous handling of hundreds of
yards of bas-reliefs and their skill
in hewing from enormous blocks
of stone the bulls of the column-
capitals in the hypostyle halls.

The Achaemenians were not
only enterprising in their architecture and lavish in their mural
decorations, but also patronized
those 'luxury arts' which call for
delicate workmanship as well as
refined taste. Their seal cutters
kept to the Babylonian tradition
and Achaemenian seal designs were
little varied and usually symbolic.
It is curious, though not surprising, to find some of the main
themes of their large-scale decorative sculpture recurring in glyptic
art; for example the hero-king in
combat with a griffin or subduing
two horned lions, while standing
on two bearded, winged sphinxes;
the winged disk of Ahuramazda,
and winged human-headed lions.
There are obvious reminiscences
of Assyrian art in Darius' cylinder
seal, which shows the king in his
chariot hunting lions, and in another which reproduces the motif
of two acolytes upholding a winged

249 - PERSEPOLIS. PORTRAIT OF A PRINCE (5th CENT. B.C.). — TEHERAN MUSEUM

250 - SEAL IMPRESSION. THE KING, STANDING
ON TWO SPHINXES, GRAPPLING WITH
TWO LIONS (1ST MILLENNIUM B.C.).

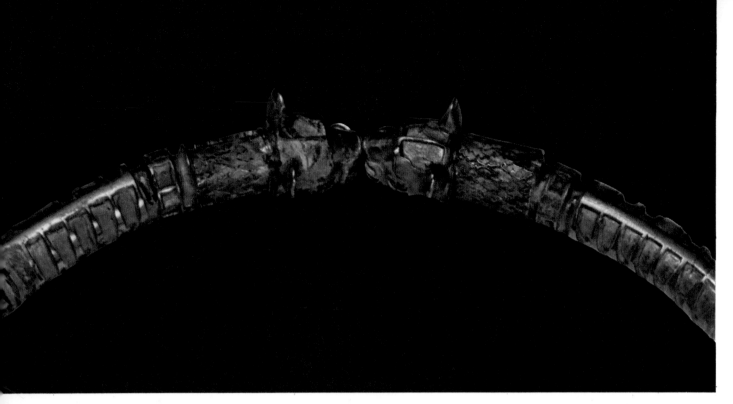

disk. Here the two bull-men have become two archers who support
the emblem with their spears, and the kneeling genius in the centre
has assumed the form of Ahuramazda himself.

It was in their metal-work that the Achaemenians excelled and
many of these objects testify not only to their skill but to their high
standard of taste. The king's table-service was worthy of the 'King of
the Earth,' judging by the magnificent silver dishes and goblets in
nielloed silver that have been discovered, and the superb rhytons in
bronze or silver with the stand representing an ibex or a goat.

Unlike the Assyrian monarchs, the Achaemenians, if the reliefs are
to be trusted, never wore jewellery, though it is clear that they were
well supplied with it. In an unplundered grave at Susa a hoard of
such articles as pendants, beads and necklaces was found, all of a similar
type and reliably dated. Most remarkable, however, was a gold torque
of exceptionally fine quality, composed of two torsades that could be
clipped together, whose finials were formed by exquisitely carved lions'
heads set with turquoises for the cheeks and mane, lapis lazuli for the
muzzle and mother-of-pearl for the eyes. Here we have another instance
of that fondness for polychromy which is also evidenced by the gold
bracelets and earrings studded with turquoises or lapis lazuli.

This fine craftsmanship was not limited to articles made for royal
use; it is also found in certain details of weapons, for example in the
dagger sheath hung on the belt of a high official, in one of the Treasury
reliefs. It has all the delicate perfection of the objects found in the

hoard of Ziwiyeh, in which animal forms were the basic motifs. These were carried over into ornamental sculpture, as can be seen at Persepolis in the decoration of the royal baldachin in the Hall of a Hundred Columns, which represents bulls and lions moving in antithetical files along two registers towards the winged globe.

There must have been many other instances in which the craftsmen's feeling for, and keen observation of, animal life found expression. If so few of their works have survived, it is because objects in metal were so highly prized and for this reason systematically looted. The Assyrians and Neo-Babylonians had set the example; the former by selling the statues found in conquered towns, the latter by carrying off to Babylon, as war booty, the pillars of brass and the 'brazen sea' in the temple of Jerusalem (II Kings xxv. 13). The Achaemenian palaces, in turn, were pillaged and razed to the ground and only scattered fragments have come down to us, but some of them give an idea of the notable achievements of this art.

One is the bronze bowl in the Louvre on which an ostrich hunt is represented. Nothing could be more animated than this hunting scene, unique of its kind since a cameleer is shown taking part in it. Then there is a small lion (also in the Louvre) very different from the plump, gorged lions of the glazed reliefs, whose leanness shows that it has gone short of food for many days. Different, again, is another lion from Susa, in which the bronze-worker has merely copied slavishly, mechanically, the Assyrian lion of Khorsabad.

252 - BOWL. OSTRICH HUNT (6th-4th CENTURIES B.C.). — LOUVRE

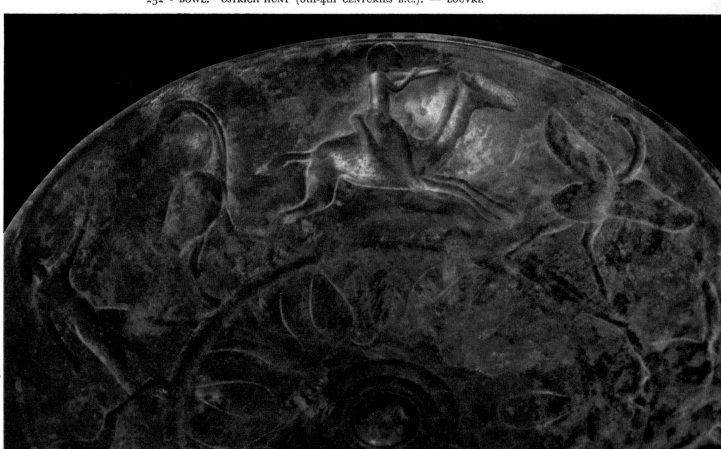

253 - SUSA. CAPITAL WITH FOREPARTS OF BULLS (5th-4th CENTURIES B.C.). — LOUVRE

Incomparable of its kind is this silver ibex inlaid with gold standing on a palmette above a satyr's head. The dainty, outspread wings add a touch of aerial lightness to the lithe elegance of the young body. All the charm of Achaemenian art finds eloquent expression in this evocation of a wild animal in strenuous movement, of which there had been intimations three millennia before in the ibexes of the Susian goblets, with preternaturally elongated horns, galloping across the desert.

In marked contrast with the aerial grace of the ibex are the ponderous double-headed capitals of Achaemenian columns. The Achaemenians never brought themselves to choose between these alternatives, which

254 - SAMSUN(?). VASE-HANDLE IN THE FORM OF A WINGED IBEX (5th-4th CENTURIES B.C.). — LOUVRE →

indeed reflected the ambivalence of their world-view. Like their politics, their architecture was so to speak a challenge to the 'nature of things,' as when they placed two bulls back to back, weighing tons, on top of a slender column sixty feet high. The least earth tremor could bring down the pillars like a row of ninepins, and the whole building with them.

But it was not an earthquake that caused the downfall of the Persian empire. It was the military genius of Alexander of Macedon who in 334 B.C., with an army of thirty-five thousand men, struck east into Asia. In the battles of Granicus, Issus and Gaugamela (near Arbela) he laid low the Persian colossus. From the Mediterranean to the Indus the Greeks had swept aside all opposition; nothing, it seemed, could halt their progress. Alexander was in his early thirties. What would have happened if his life had not been cut short in its prime and he had held the reins of power for, say, twenty-five years? Franz Cumont rightly stresses the fact that he contemplated associating Persians with Macedonians, 'the two races worthy of dominating the other Asiatic peoples,' in the government of his empire.

But this is one of the 'might have beens' of history; on the 18th of May (or June) 323 B.C., on his return to Babylon, he fell seriously ill, and ten days' illness effaced the work of ten victorious years. Alexander died, but he had succeeded in doing what none had done before him; the West had established a foothold on Oriental soil. The consequences were not merely of a political order; religion, civilization, art, all were permanently affected by Alexander's great adventure. The curtain had risen on a new era.

Even today, after five millennia, the light that rose in this primal 'Eden,' scene of the dawn of all our Western culture, still bathes the world around us with its immemorial radiance. When a traveller in France gazes at one or other of our Romanesque churches, that 'white garment' which the men of the Middle Ages spread upon our country-side in the Age of Faith, how can he fail to be struck by the frequent presence of the East in its imagery, its parables, its esoteric symbolism? In it we see, as Emile Mâle has aptly pointed out, 'all Asia bringing her gifts to Christendom, as once the Magi to the Child.' Heaven and Hell, we are often told, confront the believer the moment he enters the church, and this is true up to a point. Yet how many of the idioms of this esoteric language defy interpretation: two confronted lions having a single head, a lion-headed eagle hovering above two domestic animals, an ass playing a lyre—motifs deriving from Sumer, but no less enigmatic in the context of Sumerian art.

When, looking up at the tympanum of a Romanesque church, we see Christ in Glory, surrounded by the tetramorph, we are transported unequivocally into the East. For the four Evangelist symbols—man, lion, bull and eagle—were taken over, unchanged, by Christians from Mesopotamian symbolism. They had been already employed at Ur, long before Ezekiel, in the third millennium B.C., but separately, and it was the Assyrians who first had the bold idea of combining the four

255 - CHARTRES. TYMPANUM OF THE ROYAL PORTAL (12th CENTURY A.D.).

elements of the tetramorph in a single creature: the human-headed bull guarding their palaces. That themes like these outlast races, cultures, religions and the passing ages, proves that man's creative instinct harks back persistently to the same figurations for expressing the inexpressible. This is undoubtedly the most striking element of the legacy bequeathed by the Sumerian 'Eden': that 'quality of humanity' which, transmitted through the ages, still forms part of our Western heritage.

207

A

D

B

C

E

F

G

H

I

526-264 - ACHAEMENIAN SEAL IMPRESSIONS

CHAPTER V

FROM THE ACHAEMENIANS
TO THE DEATH OF ALEXANDER
(558-323 B.C.)

After capturing Babylon and making themselves masters of the entire Near East, the Achaemenians make a bid to extend their empire further west. They succeed in conquering Egypt, but their invasion of Greece ends in disaster. Culturally, however, they gain much by their contacts with other civilizations, from which they are wise enough to borrow freely but without ever copying slavishly. The result is that a synthetic art, stemming from many sources, now makes its appearance on Iranian soil.

Achaemenian art is best known to us through its architecture, as exemplified in the imposing ruins of the royal cities: Pasargadae, Persepolis and Susa, where generations of sculptors were employed by Cyrus, Darius, Xerxes I and Artaxerxes I and II to celebrate the blessings of the 'Achaemenian peace.' Innumerable reliefs on walls and stairways hymn the glory of the monarch and his achievements. Unlike Assyrian works, these reliefs never represent actual fighting; only the aftermath of successful warfare is shown, never its horrors and bloodshed.

Like the Neo-Babylonians, the Achaemenians decorate walls with large panels of polychrome glazed bricks, representing processions of lions, griffins and archers, as at Susa.

It is in fine metal work and jewellery that the Achaemenians perhaps most strikingly display their skill and taste. Few such works survive, unfortunately, for the royal residences were looted and destroyed by Alexander's soldiery. Enough remains, however, in the way of necklaces, bracelets, earrings, silver dishes and goblets, to show that there was no lack of luxury articles to grace the homes of the living and the graves of the dead.

KINGS	SITES
Cyrus II (558-530)	MESHED-I-SULAIMAN PASARGADAE
Cambyses (530-522)	
Darius I (521-485)	PERSEPOLIS SUSA
Xerxes I (485-465)	PERSEPOLIS SUSA
Artaxerxes I (465-424)	PERSEPOLIS
Xerxes II (424)	
Darius II (424-404)	
Artaxerxes II Mnemon (404-358)	SUSA
Artaxerxes III Ochus (358-337)	
Arses (337-335)	
Darius III Codomannus (335-330)	
Death of Alexander the Great (323)	

ARCHITECTURE	SCULPTURE	TERRACOTTA	METAL	EGYPT	AEGEAN
Palace	Capitals	Enamelled and glazed pottery			
				Psammetichus III (526-525) Conquest of Egypt by Cambyses	Beginning of Persian Wars (490)
Palace (Tatchara)	Capitals Reliefs			Persian Domination (525-404)	Thermopylae (480)
Palace	Capitals	Building Inscription of Darius	Silver and bronze vessels		
Palace (Hadish)	Capitals Reliefs Statue (?) Small head of Xerxes (?)		Gold rhyton Jewellery and ornaments		
Palace					End of Persian Wars (479) Pericles Pheidias The Parthenon (447-438)
Palace Hundred-Column Hall	Capitals Reliefs				Peloponnesian War (431-404)
Palace	Capitals	Frieze of the Archers Animals (glazed bricks)		Nectanebes (378-360) Second Persian Domination (341-333)	Plato Praxiteles Philip of Macedon (359-336) Alexander the Great (336-323)

PART TWO

MESOPOTAMIAN TECHNIQUES

268 - CATTLE ABOUT TO QUIT A STABLE (EARLY 3rd MILLENNIUM). — LOUVRE

Architecture. The natural resources of the country, rich in alluvial mud, poor in timber and stone, made Mesopotamian architecture what it was. From alluvial mud bricks were made ('And they had brick for stone. . . ,' Genesis xi. 3), while timber and stone had to be imported and were therefore used sparingly. Even in the rocky districts of the north (Middle Euphrates and Upper Tigris), where stone could be quarried in abundance, brick was used for architectural purposes; it remained, everywhere and always, the standard building material of Mesopotamia.

The earliest shelters and huts in the marshlands of Lower Mesopotamia were, however, reed constructions—tightly bound fascines of tall reeds staked in the ground in two parallel rows, with their tops tied together to form an arch and then covered with matting. Even now the natives build their *zarifehs* in just this way. That the earliest dwellings were of this type, and that they continued to be built long after other construction techniques had come into use, is evident, for we find them represented in the reliefs on stone vases.

269 - LAGASH (TELLOH), IRAQ. BUILDING A ZARIFEH (1930).

The tall reeds of the marshes used as building material by the early settlers were followed by mud plaster (clay and straw), then by *pisé* (sun-dried clods of beaten earth), and finally by mud bricks, usually unbaked. These were small blocks of clay mixed with finely chopped straw, kneaded, moulded and sun-dried. Baked bricks were made in the same way, but fired in kilns to give them added strength. They were jointed either with clay mortar or with bitumen ('. . . and slime [i.e. bitumen] had they for mortar,' Genesis xi. 3). Sometimes, in the very largest constructions (e.g. the ziggurats of Aqar Quf, Uruk and Mari), every eighth or ninth course of bricks rested on a layer of reed matting. Later, in Neo-Babylonian times, we find lime mortar mixed with bitumen; but the Achaemenians reverted to the use of clay mortar.

The size of bricks varied with the place and period. The following figures apply to unbaked (i.e. sun-dried) bricks. Those used at Uruk in protohistoric times (fourth millennium B.C.) were designated by the German excavators as *patzen* ($31^{1}/_{2}$ by $13^{3}/_{4}$ inches)—such were the bricks in the Limestone Temple—and *riemchn* ($6^{1}/_{4}$ by $2^{3}/_{8}$; 7 by $3^{1}/_{8}$; $8^{5}/_{8}$ by $3^{1}/_{2}$; $9^{1}/_{2}$ by 4 inches). Pre-Sargonid work is characterized in Lower Mesopotamia by the use of plano-convex bricks, flat on one side, curved on the other. This peculiar shape, which seems to answer to no functional purpose, has never been satisfactorily explained. Possibly it indicates the arrival of new settlers from the north who, previously accustomed to building with stone, gave their bricks what was roughly the shape of unhewn blocks of stone.

Woolley found plano-convex bricks of the following sizes at Ur: $10^{1}/_{2}$ by $6^{3}/_{4}$ by 4; 7 by $5^{7}/_{8}$ by 2; $7^{1}/_{2}$ by $6^{3}/_{4}$ by 4; 7 by $3^{1}/_{2}$ by 3 inches. The masonry often consists of alternating courses, one of

270 - KISH. PLANO-CONVEX BRICKS (3rd MILLENNIUM).

271 - LAGASH (TELLOH). WELL OF EANNATUM. HERRING-BONE WORK (SECOND HALF, 3rd MILL).

bricks bedded flat, the next of bricks laid slantwise; this herring-bone work is characteristic of Mesopotamian architecture in the pre-Sargonid period and even later, for it was still used in the time of Ur-Nammu.

Oddly enough, no unbaked plano-convex bricks have ever been found in the Middle Euphrates region. All the unbaked bricks of the buildings so far cleared at Mari are quite flat. Some of the standard sizes are as follows: 13 by 13 by $2^3/_8$; $15^3/_8$ by $15^3/_8$ by $3^1/_2$; $16^1/_2$ by $16^1/_2$ by $4^1/_2$; $17^3/_4$ by $17^3/_4$ by $4^3/_4$; $15^3/_4$ by $8^5/_8$ by $2^3/_4$ inches. Up to 1960 no bricks of the *patzen* or *riemchen* types had been found.

Baked bricks occur in Mesopotamian architecture as early as the pre-Sargonid period (early third millennium). Their upper surface is curved both at Mari and at Lagash; only slightly on the Middle Euphrates, much more markedly in Sumer. But from Sargon's time to the end of the Neo-Sumerian period baked bricks are found to be uniformly flat. The finger marks sometimes visible on the curved side of plano-convex bricks were made, before firing, by squeezing the soft clay either with the thumb (Ur-Nanshe at Lagash), with the thumb and forefinger (Eannatum), or with one or two fingers (Entemena). The grooves thus produced may have facilitated the adhesive action of the mortar, which usually consisted of a compound based on bitumen or, in rougher constructions, of a strongly diluted clay. Lagash bricks show the following measurements: $11^3/_4$ by $7^1/_2$ (Eannatum), $12^1/_4$ by $8^5/_8$ and $13^3/_8$ by $9^1/_2$ inches (Entemena).

272 - TELLOH. BRICK INSCRIBED WITH GUDEA'S NAME (22nd CENTURY B.C.).

In addition to finger marks, many baked bricks carry inscriptions, either stamped on them or engraved by hand. The length of the inscription may vary a good deal. Some of Gudea's bricks have a brief text, filling from seven to twelve compartments with some such stock formula as: 'To Ningirsu, mighty warrior of Enlil, his king, Gudea, Patesi of Lagash, his Eninnu (called) "radiant Imgig," has built.' As against this, the inscription on the foundation bricks of King Iahdun-Lim found at Mari in 1953 runs to one hundred and fifty-seven lines. And the longer the text, the better the archaeologist's chances of getting the precious information (the names of the building and its founder) that will help him to date and identify his finds. How carefully these bricks were hidden in the substructure is shown by the fact that the inscribed side is always found face down or turned inward and thus invisible from outside. Among the designs figuring on bricks are a crescent (Eridu), an eagle and a lion (Lagash). A brick occasionally turns up with an animal's footprint on it; but this, as far as we know, occurs only on flat bricks. Such footprints, in any case, must have been accidental, left perhaps by a dog that strayed into the workshop where the bricks were being moulded.

Baked bricks of the following sizes were found at Mari. Those of the earliest periods were invariably oblong: $7^7/_8$ by 5 by 2; 11 by $7^1/_2$ by $2^1/_2$; $11^3/_4$ by $7^7/_8$ by 2; $12^1/_4$ by 9 by 2; $12^1/_2$ by $8^3/_4$ by 2; $12^1/_2$ by $9^3/_4$ by 2; 13 by $4^3/_4$ by $2^3/_8$; $13^3/_8$ by $8^5/_8$ by $1^3/_4$ inches. Later, in Neo-Sumerian times, several standard sizes were adopted, based as a rule on the small or the large cubit and giving a square brick: $12^3/_8$ by $12^3/_8$ by $2^1/_8$; $12^5/_8$ by $12^5/_8$ by $2^3/_8$; $18^1/_2$ by $18^1/_2$ by $2^3/_4$ inches.

To facilitate their work masons also had at their disposal a half-brick ($11^3/_4$ by $5^7/_8$ by $2^3/_4$ inches).

Baked bricks were very sparingly used in early times, for an obvious reason: the shortage of fuel kept production down to a strict minimum. We accordingly find them only where strength and impermeability were indispensable: in plinths, in the flooring (normally of beaten earth) of certain rooms, in hygienic or hydraulic installations (well of Eannatum

273 - LARSA (SENKEREH). PALACE OF NUR-ADAD (EARLY 2nd MILL.).

at Lagash). In time, as the supply increased, they entered into the foundations, then into the walls of the ground floor (either alone or in combination with sun-dried bricks) and even into the dwelling houses of ordinary townsfolk (at Ur). Kings and high-ranking officials did not scruple to use them on a large scale in their palaces (Mari), hypogea (of Dungi and Bur-Sin at Ur, of Ur-Ningirsu and Ugme at Lagash), triumphal arches (Ishtar Gate at Babylon) and ziggurats, whose core of mud bricks was encased in a thick layer of baked bricks (Ur, Kish, Babylon). It takes a considerable effort of the imagination to realize the planning and labour required to build one of these staged towers, hundreds of feet high, with its truly prodigious number of small bricks —not to mention such elaborate architectural complexes as that of the ziggurat of Choga Zambil, with its maze of inner chambers.

Builders entirely dependent on clay were obviously labouring under a handicap. The amazing thing is that they resorted so seldom to vaulting and domes as a means of overcoming the lack of suitable roofing timber. Terraced roofs are almost exclusively the rule. Ridged roofs occur in the Upper Tigris region, but they seem to have been rare. Cross-beams had certainly to be imported from Persia, Anatolia, Lebanon and the Amanus mountains, for the trunks of palm-trees, the only wood readily available, were unsuitable for roofing. Of the timber trade of that day we can form some idea from the 'seascape' in Sargon's palace at Khorsabad (eighth century B.C.) and also from the Bible (II Kings xix. 23; Isaiah xiv. 8 and xxxvii. 24). The roof span was

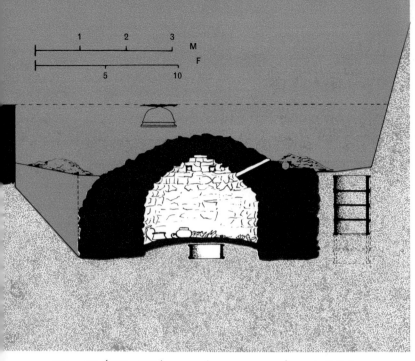

274 - UR (MUQAYYAR). TOMB (FIRST HALF, 3rd MILLENNIUM).

strictly limited by the terrace it supported (made of beaten earth over a bed of brushwood, the latter resting on a layer of matting). Consequently the oblong rooms of such buildings seldom exceeded a carefully calculated width. The throne room in the palace of Mari, for example, measuring 82 feet in length, is 32 feet wide—virtually a maximum, though wider rooms have been found at Uruk in the Limestone Temple (37 feet) and Temple D (38 feet); but these unusually wide spans were probably supported by a system of trusses. For though the arch, the corbelled vault and even the dome (tombs at Ur and Mari) were known as early as the pre-Sargonid period, they never came into general use.

The same is true of the column, of which only isolated examples are recorded, at Uruk (Hall of Columns), Kish (palace), Mari (portico in the court of the Ishtar temple) and Ur (under the Third Dynasty). It occurs at each of these sites in the form of massive pillars of unbaked bricks. Later they were made of baked bricks (at Lagash in Gudea's time) and sometimes, apparently, even of wood standing on stone bases (temple of Ninhursag, Mari). That they were used again in the Assyrian period, in the palace attributed to Sennacherib at Khorsabad, is proved by the presence of two basalt column bases found in a kind of loggia (Residence K, Room 15); the columns themselves, made of mud brick, had entirely crumbled away. They no doubt formed part of a *bit hilani* (portico), a type of structure which the Assyrians borrowed from their neighbours in Anatolia

275 - DUR SHARRUKIN (KHORSABAD). BASE OF A COLUMN (8th CENTURY B.C.).

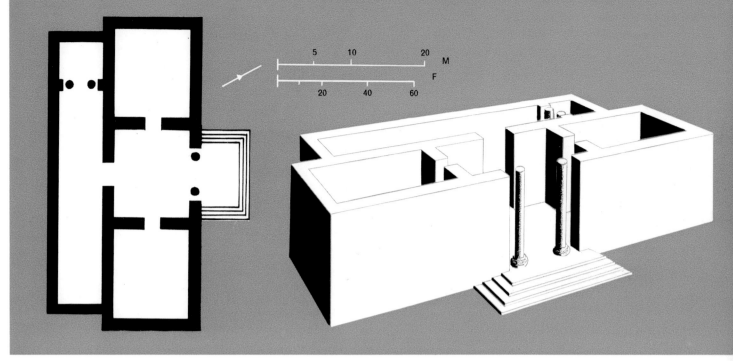

276 - DUR SHARRUKIN (KHORSABAD). PLAN AND RECONSTRUCTION OF THE 'BIT-HILANI' (8th CENTURY B.C.).

and North Syria. Though rare, then, in Mesopotamian architecture, the column came to be used extensively by the Achaemenians in their palaces.

Stone, as we have said, being almost non-existent in Lower Mesopotamia (though Woolley and Hall located a quarry in the Eridu region), had to be imported and so never came into general use. We find it, nevertheless, in buildings at Eridu, Ur, al 'Ubaid and Uruk. It is much more common in the Middle Euphrates region (tombs and foundations of large buildings) and along the Upper Tigris (terraces, basements, foundations, thresholds). Something has already been said of the part it plays in Achaemenian architecture (stairways, terraces, window frames, doorways).

Not a single Mesopotamian monument has survived in its full elevation, but reliable reconstructions can be made on the basis of the buildings occasionally represented in seal designs. The monotonous expanse of bare grey walls was relieved by pilasters and recesses, which set up a varied play of light and shade. In protohistoric times wall panels and mud-brick columns (Uruk) were decorated with cone mosaics—i.e. thousands of small pointed cones driven into the mud brick so that only their heads were visible, coloured red, black and white and forming a variety of geometric patterns. The finest surviving examples are the cone mosaics of Uruk, but others existed at Ur and Lagash where many cones have been found loose in the soil.

Other types of mural decoration consisted of stone fragments or terracotta (Uruk). Wall paintings were executed at every period:

277 - AL 'UBAID.   DAIRY SCENE (FIRST HALF, 3rd MILLENNIUM). — IRAQ MUSEUM, BAGHDAD.

temple of Tell 'Uqair (late fourth millennium); palace of Mari, royal apartments and Court 106 (early second millennium); Assyrian palaces at Nimrud, Khorsabad and Til Barsip (first millennium). Elsewhere, in the White Temple at Uruk (late fourth millennium), mud-brick walls were first coated with mud plaster (indispensable as weather-proofing) and then simply whitewashed.

More refined techniques of decoration were revealed by the discovery of the temple of al 'Ubaid (early third millennium). On the façade of the temple were friezes of animals in bronze (standing bulls, recumbent cows), shell, and stone (bulls, birds) set in bitumen; below them ran a row of large artificial flowers made of terracotta, coloured stones (white and pink) and bitumen (black). The same temple is also famous for the dairy scene showing men seated on low stools milking cows; the figures are carved in white stone and set in bitumen. An equally fine decorative effect was produced by two pillars, whose core (two palm trunks?) was covered with a mosaic of triangular or diamond-shaped flakes of shell, stone and bitumen, and which stood beside the temple entrance; the tympanum above the doorway was decorated with a bronze relief representing a lionheaded eagle hovering above two stags.

278 - AL 'UBAID. NAIL-HEADS WITH A FLOWER PATTERN (FIRST HALF, 3rd MILL.).

The same scrupulous care went to the decoration of a pre-dynastic temple discovered by Mallowan at Tell Brak, in the Upper Jezireh. Round three sides of the podium ran a frieze composed of three parallel bands of coloured stones, bordered by gold leaf studded with golden nails. Three varieties of stone were used: on the top register, blocks of blue limestone, let into the wall and grooved on their outer face with concentric circles producing the effect of a hollow cone; below this, a narrow strip of white marble; on the lower register, pieces of blue-green schist with vertical grooves. Here, too, on the outside of the temple, in imitation of the artificial flowers at al 'Ubaid, was a magnificent series of eight-petalled marguerites made of coloured stone (black schist, white marble, red limestone).

Clay now came to play an increasingly important part in the decoration of buildings. From the mid-second millennium on, baked bricks were moulded in more or less salient relief to form figure compositions: gods and goddesses with the flowing vase in the temple of Karaindash at Uruk (fifteenth century B.C.); the bull-god with a date palm and the goddess Ninhursag in the temple of Shushinak at Susa (twelfth century B.C.); Processional Way and Ishtar Gate in the palace of Babylon (sixth

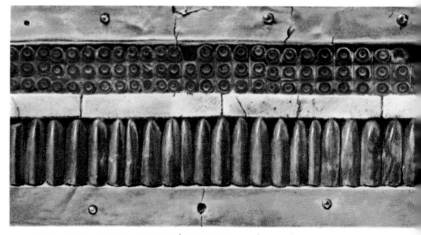

279 - TELL BRAK. FRIEZE (FIRST HALF, 3rd MILL.).

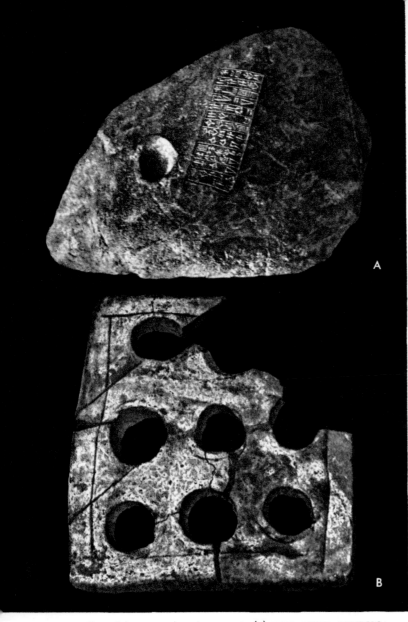

280 - (A) TELLOH. TOADSTONE   (B) TELL ASMAR. WINDOW

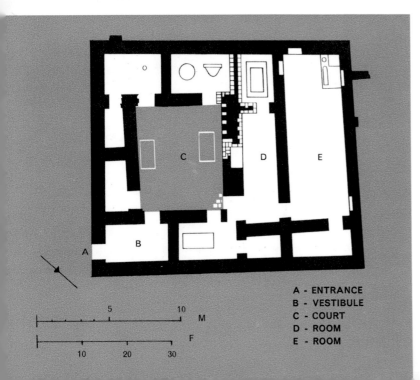

A - ENTRANCE
B - VESTIBULE
C - COURT
D - ROOM
E - ROOM

281 - TELLOH. PLAN OF A HOUSE (LATE 3rd MILL.).

century B.C.); frieze of archers, bulls, lions and griffins in the palace of Susa (sixth-fourth centuries B.C.). With the development of the technique of glazing in the Assyrian period, these moulded reliefs were enlivened with polychromy, which had also been used to distinguish the different stages of a ziggurat: Khorsabad (Assyrian period); Borsippa and Ur (Neo-Babylonian period); Babylon (Neo-Babylonian period), the only city where the upper temple had been faced with blue glazed bricks. In addition to moulded bricks in relief (glazed or unglazed), another type of decoration consisted simply of polychrome glazed bricks without relief. Very fine examples of this technique have been found at several sites: Nimrud (royal procession and palmettes); Assur (the god Assur in the *aura* drawing his bow; chariot and team; ibexes on either side of the sacred tree; a priest before a fire altar; a worshipper before Shamash); Khorsabad (winged genii with the holy-water pail, on the gates; processions in the temples). These polychrome glazes were also applied to terracotta decorations, not only in Assyria but in Babylonia and Elam.

The lighting of Mesopotamian buildings was provided for very largely, if not exclusively, by doors giving on to open courtyards. Windows certainly existed (these is archaeological evidence in proof of this), but for reasons of security from attack and protection against

282 - THE GOD ASSUR IN THE 'AURA' (9th CENTURY B.C.). — BRITISH MUSEUM.

sandstorms and extremes of heat and cold (for there are only two seasons in Mesopotamia, as we are reminded in Genesis viii. 22), they must have been very rare. In Assyrian reliefs dormer windows are sometimes visible high up in walls or towers. Oblong bays divided by colonnettes are represented on a basalt boulder from Tell Halaf. These openings must have been screened or shuttered by perforated terracotta plaques, like the one found at Ashnunnak. Buried at the angle of doorways was a block of hard stone hollowed out on the upper side, thus providing a socket for the door-hinge; very often, particularly in important buildings (temples and palaces), this stone bore an inscription recording the founder's name and other relevant information.

Mesopotamian architecture as a whole is characterized by construction techniques of the horizontal type. The very simplest houses were composed of an inner court open to the sky, from which different rooms led off, with the entrance on the street. Between the entrance and the inner court there was usually an antechamber, serving both as a passageway and as a guarantee of privacy. Larger and finer houses consisted of an interlocking series of two or more of these basic building units (court

227

283 - BABYLON. THE ZIGGURAT E-TEMEN-AN-KI (7th-6th CENTURIES B.C.).

surrounded by rooms). Terraced roofs were the rule, though they were not all on the same level, this for two reasons: to provide for the draining off of rain-water (hence a slight incline in the terraces) and for the skylights needed to admit daylight to any rooms that did not open on the courtyard. Undoubtedly the palaces and major temples had an additional storey or storeys, but the average dwelling house did not rise above the ground floor. In many houses the foot of a stairway has been found, but this in most cases led not to an upper storey but to the terraced roof (cf. Isaiah xxii. 1), where the inmates spent a large part of their time; in hot weather the entire population slept on these terraces. This horizontal architecture, however, was dominated in the larger cities by the vertical mass of the ziggurat. Thirty-four of these ziggurats, or staged towers, have now been located in twenty-seven cities of the Ancient East. The greatest of them all was that of Babylon (called *E-temen-an-ki*, house of the foundation of heaven and earth), some three hundred feet high, with seven stages crowned by a small temple. The story of the Tower of Babel in the Book of Genesis (xi. 1-9) evidently relates to the ziggurat of Babylon, while early descriptions of it have come down to us in Herodotus (*Histories*, I, 181) and the inscribed Esagil Tablet in the Louvre (AO 6555).

The degree of comfort in private houses naturally depended on the owner's station in life. As regards royal residences, the palace of Mari is particularly impressive, for many of its amenities were found either intact or remarkably well preserved. It included kitchen stoves, with covered hearths, complete with holes on either side where fuel could be fed in and openings on top for the cooking utensils; bathrooms with tiled bath-tubs, water closets *à la turque* and a hooded fireplace in the corner; schoolrooms with mud-brick benches; workshops equipped to forge and repair metal tools and implements; pottery works with kilns; storerooms and warehouses. The water supply was provided by wells built of terracotta or brickwork (baked bricks of a peculiar shape). A drainage system of terracotta conduits carried off sewage and overflow to cesspools sunk several yards below the foundations.

228

284 - JERWAN (IRAQ). AQUEDUCT OF SENNACHERIB (7th CENTURY B.C.).

One of the most impressive engineering feats of Oriental antiquity is the Assyrian water conduit from Bavian to Nineveh, a distance of over fifty miles. The work of Sennacherib (705-681 B.C.), it involved the quarrying, dressing and assemblage of over two million blocks of stone, measuring on an average about 20 by 20 by 26 inches. At some points the conduit exceeds sixty-five feet in width. At Jerwan it is carried across a broad valley by an aqueduct nearly one thousand feet long and forty feet wide, supported at one point by five arches.

Road-building was handicapped by lack of stone, indispensable for the construction of a permanent road-bed. Failing stone-paved highways, Mesopotamia had nevertheless an extensive network of cross-country tracks; these of course were unfit for traffic in the rainy season. City streets were unpaved except for the very busiest thoroughfares (e.g. at Mari, from the early second millennium) and the Processional Ways at Assur (700 B.C.), Babylon (700-600 B.C.) and Uruk (300 B.C.). At Assur the Sacred Way leading to the Ishtar temple was paved with slabs of gypsum resting on several layers of baked bricks jointed with bitumen. At Babylon a stone-paved Processional Way over half a mile long passed through the Ishtar Gate, continued in a straight line alongside the palaces and the *temenos* of the ziggurat, and then, turning at a sharp right angle, ended at the bridge over the Euphrates. In its final form the work of Nebuchadnezzar (sixth century B.C.), it was called *Ai-ibur-shabu*. The entire roadway, beneath the stone paving-slabs, was bedded with three courses of baked bricks; the mortar jointing them was a mixture of bitumen, sand and fibrous materials.

Stone. Stone was scarce in Lower Mesopotamia and therefore sparingly used for building purposes. Such stone as was required for making vases, bowls, cups, maces, statues and bas-reliefs had to be imported. It was often indispensable too in the applied arts: for stamps and cylinder seals, amulets, ornaments of various kinds. Its scarcity by no means precluded the use of many kinds of stone—which implies extensive trade relations, and this as early as the fourth millennium B.C.

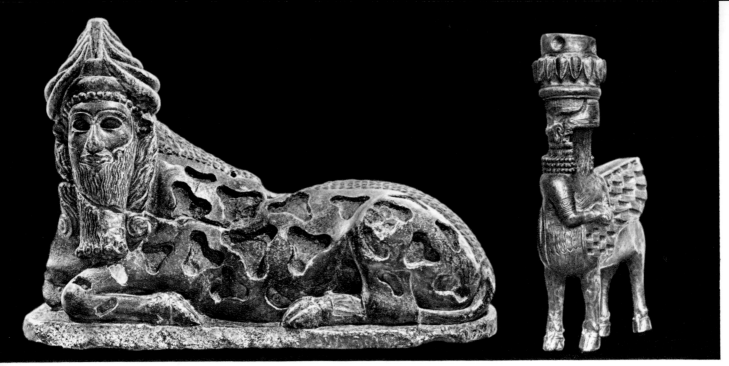

285 - TELLOH. HUMAN-HEADED BULL (SECOND HALF, 3rd MILL.). 286 - KOPRAKKALE. CENTAUR (1st MILL.).

Alongside such common rock as gypsum *(xa-u-na)* and limestone *(pilu pisu)*, easily obtainable from quarries fairly near the urban centres and thus in frequent use, we find more precious varieties, like alabaster and marble *(parutu)*, and others more difficult to manipulate, such as basalt *(na-lu-a)*, which was quarried in the Middle and Upper Euphrates regions (Birejik). Among the nobler varieties of stone, prized for their hardness and colouring (dark blue), were diorite and dolerite, imported from the 'land of Magan' (Arabia) and used for most of the Gudea statues. Smaller objects were often carved in steatite, a stone much easier to work: Gudea's libation goblet, the small head of Hammurabi, many cylinder seals and statuettes of human-headed bulls dating to the time of Gudea, and (a slightly later work) the ram's head from Ur. Haematite had much the same qualities, but only came into use somewhat later (early second millennium); though much appreciated for its dark colouring with metallic gleams, its scarcity restricted its use to cylinder seals and, on occasion, small pieces of sculpture. The fondness of the Sumerians for polychromy accounts for the abundant use of lapis lazuli *(uknu)*, extracted from a 'lapis mountain' in Media; of carnelian *(samtu)* from the land of Meluhha (Arabia); of jasper *(ashpu)* from Mount Zimur, east of Lake Urmya; of onyx, with its delicate sea-green veining; of agate, amethyst, amber, chalcedony and serpentine, in which beads, cylinder seals, amulets and ornaments were carved.

Inlays of ivory, shell or coloured stones against a darker ground occur frequently in Mesopotamian art. The love of polychromy, attested as early as the Jemdet Nasr period, was an enduring feature of this art, illustrated by a host of examples. Only a few need be mentioned here:

vases, animals with inlay holes hollowed in their flanks, the human-headed bull in the Louvre whose body was adorned with incrustations, and the human-headed bulls in bronze from the Urartu region, with their wings inlaid with coloured scales.

Little is known of the actual techniques employed in carving and polishing stone. These naturally depended on the hardness of the material used. Limestone and gypsum could easily be shaped with metal chisels (of copper or bronze), but diorite and basalt are unworkable with such tools, and for them the sculptors must have resorted to some still harder tools, probably of flint or quartz. Seal-cutters, as early as the fourth millennium, were using a bow-drill with a pointed tip or borer, to which the bow-string imparted a rotary movement in both directions. How certain particularly hard materials were polished—diorite, for example—remains unexplained. The stone is so smooth to the touch that it gives the impression of having been polished by some natural agent, like water. This explanation seems wholly inappropriate in the case of the Gudea statues, which bear no resemblance to the water-smoothed boulders of a river. Yet the work betrays no scoring, no visible trace of a cutting tool. This being so, one can only suppose the polish was obtained by rubbing with wet sand.

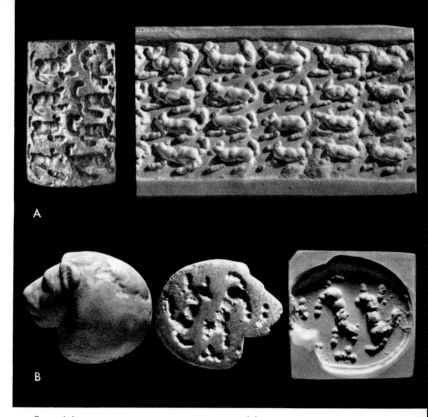

A

B

287 - (A) CYLINDER SEAL AND IMPRESSION (B) STAMP SEALS

288 - LAGASH (TELLOH). SEAL IMPRESSION — LOUVRE

289 - TEPE GAWRA. MOULD (MID-3rd MILLENNIUM).

Metal. The discovery of metal-working led to a radical change in living conditions. Stone, clay, wood and bone had hitherto supplied the raw materials needed for the manufacture of implements and weapons. By the early fourth millennium, however, copper had been introduced; this marks the beginning of the Chalcolithic or Aeneolithic period. It came from Asia Minor, Armenia, Elam and Oman, in other words from the peripheral regions around Mesopotamia; possibly, a little later (second half of the third millennium), it was also imported from Cyprus. It seems unlikely that the Mesopotamians depended for any of their copper on the Arabah mines, south of the Dead Sea, or on the Sinai mines (at Serabit el-Khadim, where there were also turquoise deposits) which supplied the Egyptians. The earliest metal implements are made of almost pure copper (*urudu* in Sumerian, *siparru* in Akkadian), but whether through deliberate experiment or the accidental use of mineral compounds, an alloy very soon became the rule. Copper was mixed—or found mixed—with small quantities of lead *(anaku)*, antimony *(guxlu)*, arsenic, zinc and above all tin. The result was bronze *(zabar* in Sumerian, *siparru* in Akkadian), a metal harder, stronger and easier to work than pure copper.

The oldest metal object found at Ur was a spear-head of almost pure copper. Analysis reveals the following composition: copper, 99.69%; arsenic, 0.16%; zinc, 0.12%; iron, 0.01%. Tin, lead, antimony, nickel, silver and manganese were totally absent.

The introduction of metal-work by no means put an end to the manufacture of stone implements, but the advantages of metal in the way of durability and malleability were so obvious that it soon came into general use. It is interesting to note that, to begin with, the new implements exactly copied the old: the flat axe of pure copper reproduces the axe of polished stone. The molten metal had simply been cast in an open mould of stone or terracotta. Graving tools, chisels and even daggers were manufactured in the same way.

The increasingly generalized use of bronze (copper with a 5 to 15% admixture of tin) led to improved and simplified techniques of producing it. The metal could either be hammered into shape or cast in one of three ways: in an open mould, in a closed mould (impracticable with pure copper), or by the *cire perdue* process. The closed mould

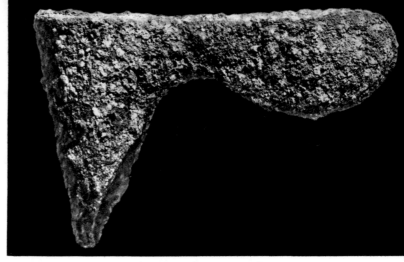

consisted of two closely fitting halves. A hollow object could be cast by inserting a terracotta core in the stone mould and pouring the molten metal around it. The technique of casting with wasted wax *(à cire perdue)* has changed little since antiquity. First the wax is modelled to the desired shape over a hard core of clay. Then the wax model is covered with several layers of the very finest clay mixed with different substances whose action does away with any porosity. When the coating is thick enough, the model is placed in a hot oven, which bakes the clay, both of the core and of the outer mould, and melts the wax, which flows off through small outlets provided for the purpose. The hollow space thus obtained, between the core and the mould, is then filled with molten metal. When the cast has hardened, the terracotta mould is broken away and the finished object emerges.

Alloys vary considerably according to the site and the nature of the object. Analysis of the metal bulls of the temple frieze at al 'Ubaid revealed the following composition: copper, 98.81%; iron, 0.98%; nickel, 0.12%; sulphur, 0.09%, with traces of tin. A Mesopotamian nail in the Baghdad Museum contains copper, 88.6%; tin, 9.77%; iron, 0.28%; sulphur, 0.17%; lead, 0.68%. Another nail from the Ishtar temple at Mari contains copper, 74.2%; lead, 24.83%; arsenic, 0.46%; tin, 0.07%, with traces of zinc.

Metallurgy developed decisively in the Bronze Age. All the excavation sites of the Ancient East have yielded axes fitted with a metal socket for the handle, together with metal chisels, gravers, gouges, drills and sickles. (In protohistoric times sickles had been made of flint mounted on a wooden handle, sometimes on an animal's jawbone; such, it may be surmised, was the 'jawbone of an ass,' in Judges xv. 15, with which Samson slew a thousand Philistines.) Metal weapons, too, increased in number and variety: triangular daggers, swords, spear-heads, arrow-heads and battle-axes. Daggers have a tang fitted with rivets to secure the blade to the handle; axe-heads have a round or oval socket for the same purpose. Vases and various containers were made of bronze, together with countless figurines and statuettes of men and animals which show how highly skilled these early bronze-founders were. One of their finest works is the head from Nineveh, usually identified with Sargon of Akkad, cast in a single piece and tooled with the chisel.

The Bronze Age was followed by the Iron Age, which in Mesopotamia began about 1200 B.C. Iron *(parzillu)* first appears in two forms: meteoric (with a high nickel content, up to 5% and even more) and mineral (magnetite, haematite and siderite). The richest iron deposits lay in the peripheral regions (Asia Minor, the Taurus range, Armenia, the Caucasus, northern Persia), but these were not exploited till later. The oldest iron objects, found at Ashnunnak and Chagar Bazar, date to about the mid-third millennium B.C. They consist exclusively of ornaments and beads, first because smelting and casting techniques had not yet been fully mastered; secondly because the Mesopotamians attributed prophylactic and even magical properties to iron, which they called (according to some Assyriologists) the 'metal of heaven.' In the course of the first half of the second millennium it was found that iron, when heated red-hot, hammered into shape and tempered in cold water, becomes harder than bronze. Thereafter utensils and weapons came increasingly to be made of iron. But just as the introduction of copper had not displaced stone, so bronze continued to be employed in the manufacture of luxury articles.

The iron pickaxes, ploughshares and above all swords, spear-heads and arrow-heads which now came into use exactly reproduce the forms these objects had been given in the Bronze Age. That the men in the workshops were competent to deal with both metals may be inferred from the passage in Genesis (iv. 22) referring to Tubal-Cain, 'an instructer of every artificer in brass (i.e. bronze) and iron.' While the technique of iron-work brought about sweeping changes in the structure of society, it gave its practitioners so decisive a superiority that they sought to establish a monopoly and in certain cases to prohibit its manufacture by subject peoples. Under Philistine domination, at the height of the Iron Age, the Israelites were forbidden to forge their own farming implements; they had to buy them from their overlords, who thereby hoped to prevent their vassals from making weapons (I Samuel xiii. 19-21).

Besides copper, bronze and iron, ancient metal-workers also made frequent use of gold and silver. The most extensive gold mines were in Nubia, but others were opened up in Arabia, Asia Minor, the Caucasus and Iran. Gold was refined by cupellation, but both in Mesopotamia and Egypt it was combined with alloys which gave it a peculiar colour. It was very often mixed with silver, in greatly varying proportions, the result being electrum, still known as 'yellow gold.' The composition of several objects found at Ur is as follows:

Dagger: gold, 91.11%; silver, 7.69%; copper, 1.2%. Onager: gold, 65.6%; silver, 31.45%; copper, 2.65% (16 carats). Helmet of Meskalamdug (15 carats).

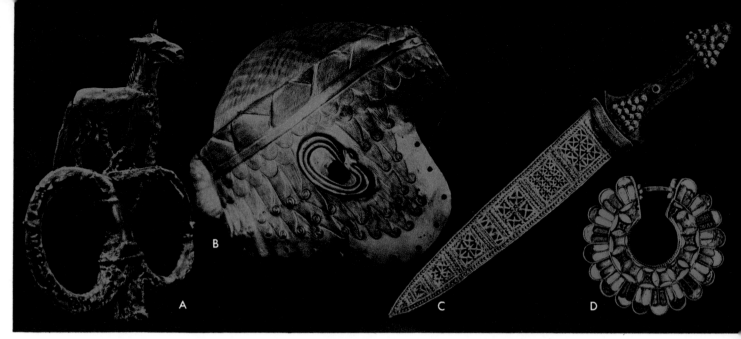

291 - UR. (A) REIN-RING (B) HELMET OF MESKALAMDUG (C) DAGGER. (D) SUSA. EARRING

Silver, like lead, was extracted from galena, which was found in abundance in Armenia and Asia Minor. The 'silver mountains' frequently mentioned in cuneiform texts in connection with an expedition of Sargon of Akkad, presumably lay in this region.

Analysis o a rein-ring from Ur (on which the small onager in electrum mentioned above was mounted) shows the following composition: silver, 93.5%; copper, 6.1%; gold, 0.08%; zinc, 0.15%.

In addition to works cast in moulds or by the *cire perdue* process, many others were made by hammering gold and silver leaf or thin sheets of bronze over a wooden or bitumen core (lions of al 'Ubaid, guardian animals of the temple of Dagan at Mari). The joints were sealed either by soldering or by studs made of the same metal. After being hammered into shape, the metal could be embellished with repoussé work, then finished with the chisel (helmet of Meskalamdug from Ur, in electrum; bronze doors of Balawat).

Several different metals sometimes entered into the manufacture of a single object: silver bowls from Ur, with decorative bands in electrum; the onager in electrum from Ur, mounted on a silver rein-ring; the silver vase of Entemena from Lagash, on a bronze stand. Even before 2500 B.C. Sumerian goldsmiths were familiar with the techniques of filigree work (gold sheath of the dagger from Ur) and jewel-setting (jewellery from Ur and Lagash) in which stones of different colours (red carnelian, blue lapis lazuli) are inset in a gold mount. We find an even more elaborate combination in the famous rams from the 'royal tombs' of Ur, whose head and belly are of gold and electrum, while the fleece is made of laths of shell and lapis. The body and wings of the Achaemenian ibex in the Louvre are made of silver inlaid with gold thread.

235

Clay. We have already emphasized the importance of **clay** in the civilization of Mesopotamia, where, owing to the scarcity of timber and stone, it was often called upon to serve as building material. We shall now deal with the clay artifacts of prime necessity in daily life: such as cooking-pots, bowls and cups.

Owing to its fragility, the conditions of nomadic life were unfavourable to its development, but with the founding of permanent settlements pottery appears in abundance. Before producing earthenware vessels, primitive man may well have made baskets and receptacles out of hide, but of this we have no proof. Potter's clay was prepared by kneading it with water and adding a tempering material or *dégraissant* (sand, powdered lime, chopped straw or finely ground potsherds), which reduced the plasticity of the clay and made it easier to handle. After the lumps of kneaded clay had been left to dry for a time in the open air, they were taken over by the potter. At first the clay was shaped entirely by hand. A slight improvement was made when 'hand-made' ware came to be 'hand-turned,' i.e. built up on a more or less circular support which could be rotated at will. A decisive step was taken with the invention of a still better support for the clay: the 'tournette,' a slowly turning wheel kept moving either by the potter himself with one hand or by an assistant. The true potter's wheel, provided with a flywheel near the base which the potter could rotate with his foot and so have both hands free to shape the clay, was a much later invention.

To make the clay less porous the potter rubbed both the inner and outer surfaces of the vessel either with his wet hand or with a piece of bone or a kind of wooden scraper, smoothing and tamping the wet clay. As a further precaution it was often coated with slip, a clay diluted to the consistency of cream and sometimes tinted. Then came the firing, whose efficacity depends on two factors: the intensity of the heat and the amount of oxygen in the surrounding atmosphere. The temperature varied from 450° to 800° C. Carried out either over an open hearth or in brick kilns constructed vertically or horizontally, firing was a matter of hours or days, depending on the temperature and the type of oven. The very fine Susa ware known as Style I was baked over a slow fire, which in part accounts for its extreme porosity.

Clay containing ferrous elements gave the ware a peculiar hue: red, if fired at a high temperature with an abundance of oxygen; grey or even black, if deprived of oxygen. The latter colour could also be induced by mixing the clay with carbonaceous matter. The pottery thus obtained is sometimes described as 'carboniferous.' A French specialist, Louis Franchet, has proposed the following classification for wares of this kind: *poteries charbonneuses* ('coal ware'), when coal has been introduced into the clay, acting at the same time as a *dégraissant; poteries fumigées dans la masse* ('smoked ware'), when the kiln has been closed and smoke has thoroughly penetrated the clay; *poteries fumigées superficiellement* ('semi-smoked ware'), when the clay has been smoked for only a short time towards the end of the firing. Broken fragments of semi-smoked ware distinctly show the two interpenetrating colours: red on the inside, black on the outside. Franchet has drawn attention to still another type of black pottery, obtained by mixing the clay with vegetable earth (humus), which also acts as a *dégraissant*.

A certain number of technical terms, relating to characteristic types of ancient pottery found in Mesopotamia, were standardized in English, French and German by a group of archaeologists, all leading specialists in the field of ceramics, at a meeting held in Baghdad on January 16, 1930 (cf. *Syria*, XI, 1930, pp. 307-308):

1. Slip (Fr. *engobe*, Ger. *Engobe*), finely levigated clay added after the vessel has been shaped.

2. Wheel-finished (Fr. *mouillé*, Ger. *geglättete Oberfläche*), applied to a vessel whose surface has been smoothed with the wet hand, on the wheel, without the use of any other tool.

3. Wash (Fr. *enduit coloré non argileux*, Ger. *Farb-Überzug*), paint or colouring matter unmixed with clay.

4. Glazed (Fr. *émaillé*, Ger. *emalliert*), coated with a siliceous composition fused to the surface of the clay by firing.

5. Burnished (Fr. *lissé*, Ger. *poliert*), smoothed with a polishing tool or a bone.

6. Matt paint (Fr. *peinture mate*, Ger. *Mattmalerei*).

7. Lustre paint (Fr. *peinture lustrée*, Ger. *Lustremalerei*).

8. Frit (Fr. *Fritte*, Ger. *Fritte*), a vitrifiable compound only partially fused.

9. Reserve slip (Fr. *réserve d'engobe*, Ger. *unterbrochene Engobe*), interruption of the slip.

On the whole, Mesopotamian pottery fails to achieve any great elegance of design. The Sumerians, moreover, produced nothing but undecorated ware. This is all the more surprising in view of the richly decorated pottery of the protohistoric period (from Samarra, Tell Halaf, Sialk and Susa, for example).

From the very start two techniques of ceramic ornamentation were employed, either separately or combined: painting and engraving. Pottery was nearly always decorated before firing. To engrave designs on the raw clay was a simple matter; painting, however, presented certain problems, for fire was fatal to organic colours. Ochre and sienna pigments had to be used, and even these changed

292 - SUSA. (A, B) DECORATED BOWLS (4th MILL.). — LOUVRE

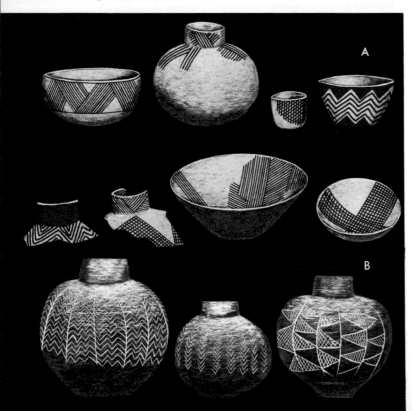

colour to some extent under the action of heat. These limitations of course ceased to operate when, occasionally, pottery was decorated after firing; then either organic or inorganic colours could be freely used. Unfired pigments, however, have the disadvantage of being less adhesive and flaking off easily; failing to blend with the body, they tend moreover to look like an arbitrary adjunct. Another decorative technique consists in incising the design through the slip to the body beneath.

The earliest decorated pottery of Mesopotamia is that of the Hassuna period. Either engraved, painted, or engraved *and* painted, the usual designs include hatchings, chevrons, chequer-work, wavy lines, lozenges and triangles. These early decorators, though we can scarcely call them artists, were none the less able craftsmen and their intricate compositions must often have entailed careful thinking out before work began. Sometimes, on the other hand, we find an untrammelled freedom of expression and utter disregard of symmetry and balance.

The art of the Samarra period, whose distinctive feature was the co-existence of an abstract and a figurative style, was followed by the more elaborate calligraphy of the Halaf period. Straight lines gave place to curves, ellipses and wave patterns. The ornamentation of dishes, in particular, is often composed of elements which,

293 - HASSUNA. (A, B) DECORATED POTTERY
(4th MILL.). — IRAQ MUSEUM, BAGHDAD

though simple and repetitive, are so ingeniously combined and multiplied that preliminary designs were certainly required.

Two dishes from Arpatchiya call for special mention as outstanding examples of this pottery of the Chalcolithic Age.

The first was, to begin with, dipped in orange-red slip, on to which the decoration in red and black was then applied. In the centre is a design which had already figured on Samarra pottery: the Maltese cross (here oblong) with a chequer pattern on the central square. At each corner is a triangle with an incurved hypotenuse. Each arm of the cross is patterned with sixteen red circles surrounded by black dots, while in the small field within the curved base of the triangle the same circles are repeated in groups of three. The outer edge is decorated with concentric designs: three rings of black wavy cable patterns interspaced with black dots.

The decoration of the other dish is no less elegant. On a buff ground tinged with pink, a flower with thirty-two petals stands out in red around a black corolla; a thin, light-coloured border encloses each element of the design. A series of concentric rings separates two circular zones, each covered with a black and red chequer pattern and dotted with white crosses on a black ground. A black zigzag runs round the outer edge.

294 - SIALK AND TEPE GIYAN. POTTERY DESIGNS (LATE 4th MILL.). — LOUVRE AND TEHERAN MUSEUMS

239

295 - (A, B) ARPATCHIYA. DECORATED PLATES (LATE 4th MILL.). — IRAQ MUSEUM, BAGHDAD

296 - ERIDU. PAINTED POTTERY (LATE 4th MILL.). — BAGHDAD

These elaborate designs give place in the following periods, well represented at Eridu and al 'Ubaid, to decoration of an almost austere simplicity. Writing had not yet been invented and our knowledge of this early culture largely depends on what can be inferred from these precious fragments of painted pottery. Comparing their ornamentation with that of the earlier pottery discussed above, we note one or two distinctive features which give this ware a place apart: both the human figure and animal forms are rare in Iran. Decoration is usually confined to geometric patterns composed of the simplest elements (straight and wavy lines, trellis-work and chequer patterns) often grouped in circular zones. Zigzags and triangles abound. In the middle of the centre design (a large Greek cross) of a dish from Eridu figures a Maltese cross; and this is the only symbolic motif found on this pottery which has any association with those on the earlier pottery discussed above.

The Uruk and Jemdet Nasr periods brought further changes in ceramic decoration. After a series of vessels simply coated with a red or grey slip, there was a return to decorated ware, but now engraved instead of painted, and always with great sobriety (Uruk period). Not till later, in the Jemdet Nasr period, does painted pottery reappear, and then only in limited quantities on a few sites.

297 - JEMDET NASR. PAINTED POTTERY
(LATE 4th-EARLY 3rd MILLENNIUM)

240

While many fine examples of painted pottery from the protohistoric periods have been found on many sites (Nineveh, Arpatchiya, Tepe Gawra, Tell Billa and Tell Halaf in Upper Mesopotamia; Eridu, al 'Ubaid and Ur in Lower Mesopotamia; Susa, Persepolis and Sialk in Iran), it disappeared almost completely at the beginning of the third millennium. Undecorated ware now becomes the rule.

Shortly before the Akkadian period, and again in the early second millennium, ceramic decoration of another kind occurs, combining incised figures with applied ornaments: e.g. flat-handled vases of the Mother Goddess type and the Larsa vase on which the goddess Ishtar appears—once incised in outline, once in the form of small plaques inlaid with slip—surrounded by animals (birds, tortoise, bull) which are also incised and even touched up with paint.

In the Larsa period (early second millennium), at Larsa, Lagash and Susa, we find cylindrical, flat-bottomed vases of an ash-grey colour whose entire decoration consists of engraved designs, each line of which is inlaid with pink or white slip. This technique of engraving enhanced with inlays reappears somewhat later (mid-second millennium) in the regions settled by the Hurrians and also in Assyria. Pottery inlaid with shell, red slip and lapis lazuli had already been produced in the pre-dynastic period.

298 - (A) MARI. FLAT-HANDLED JAR WITH ENGRAVED DESIGNS (EARLY 3rd MILLENNIUM). — LOUVRE
(B) SUSA. VASE WITH ENGRAVED DESIGNS INLAID WITH WHITE SLIP (EARLY 2nd MILL.). — LOUVRE

299 - TELL BILLA. GOBLETS (MID-2nd MILLENNIUM).

It was in the Hurrian region, in fact, in the middle of the second millennium, that an attempt was made, with remarkable success, to produce ceramics both elegantly shaped and finely decorated. These are goblets with slightly curving sides, standing on a small round stem. Divided into registers, the ornamentation combines figurative, naturalistic motifs (quadrupeds, long-necked birds, tiny suns) with abstract geometric patterns (spirals, chevrons, concentric semicircles); these stand out in white against a black or salmon-coloured ground. The Assyrians seem to have imitated this technique, judging by very similar ware excavated by the British expedition at Nineveh (British Museum) and earlier by Victor Place at Jighan near Khorsabad (Louvre). Specimens of this painted pottery are, however, fairly rare and the bulk of the production evidently consisted of undecorated household wares.

Besides these utensils for everyday use, several series of a finer ware have come to light whose lustrous glazing stamps them as *articles de luxe*. These flasks, sweetmeat boxes and blue-tinted or silver-grey phials, while never abundant in Assyria, are by no means rare from the twelfth century on. With the Assyrians, then, the ceramic art of Mesopotamia again achieved a high standard of excellence and, thanks to the technique of glazing, maintained it for many centuries to

300 - ASSUR. DECORATED VASE (1st MILL.). — BERLIN MUSEUM

242

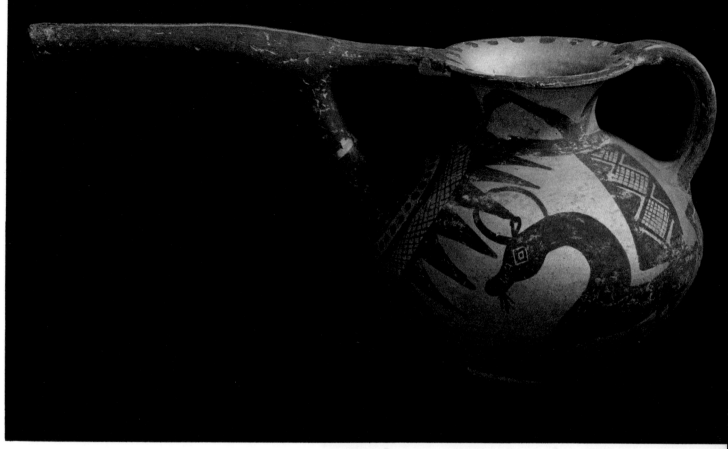

301 - SIALK. VASE WITH LONG SPOUT, DECORATED WITH GEOMETRIC AND ANIMAL DESIGNS (EARLY 1st MILL.). — LOUVRE

come, under the Achaemenians, the Seleucids, the Parthians, the Sassanians, and after them the Arabs. Ornamentation, though simple and never profuse, is not lacking in elegance: plaitwork, chevrons, marguerites, ibexes, etc. The colours always harmonize with each other: white, golden yellow, sky blue, occasionally black and dark blue. The Neo-Babylonians kept to this technique, which they undoubtedly took over from the Assyrians.

While ornamentation of this kind was also employed by the Achaemenians and, before them, by the Elamites, it must not be forgotten that some particularly fine painted pottery had been produced in Iran long before, in the protohistoric period, and that it never quite died out in the course of the second millennium. Judging by the decorated ware found by Ghirshman in Cemetery B at Sialk and dating to the early first millennium, its powers of inspiration were far from being exhausted. Jars with long spouts—a vessel undoubtedly based on a metal prototype—are gaily decorated with animal forms (horses, ibexes, bulls, birds), geometric patterns (lozenges, chequer-work) and symbolic motifs (suns).

302 - LARSA (SENKEREH). TUB-SHAPED BURIAL VESSEL

303 - LAGASH (TELLOH). CLOCHE-SHAPED BURIAL JAR

304 - LAGASH (TELLOH). TWIN-VESSEL BURIAL JAR
(LATE 3rd - EARLY 2nd MILLENNIUM).

Both the Mesopotamians and the Iranians depended on clay not only for the bulk of their utensils and nearly all their household ware (only a favoured few could afford metal dishes, cups and bowls), but also for their tombs. These were by no means always the same; burial rites evolved and the type of grave naturally varied with the dead man's station in life. In graves of the simplest kind there was not even a coffin; the body was merely wrapped in matting or hide. Others, however, with their vaults of baked or unbaked bricks, formed part of an elaborate architectural complex. Such were the 'royal tombs' of Ur and the hypogea of Shulgi (Dungi) and Bur-Sin at Ur, of Ur-Ningirsu and Ugme at Lagash. These latter were gigantic constructions requiring many tons of building material. Ordinary folk were content with less and could thus be reasonably sure of resting undisturbed. Their graves had a better chance of escaping the depredations of plunderers, for tomb robbing was one of the most inveterate and lucrative professions of the whole Ancient East, where the dead were buried with their 'grave furniture,' which in the tombs of the wealthy might add up to a considerable treasure.

The commonest type of coffin was made of clay and had several different shapes: a large earthenware vessel inverted over the body; two ribbed vessels laid sidewise

244

305 - UR.   VIEW OF THE 'ROYAL' CEMETERY (FIRST HALF, 3rd MILLENNIUM).

mouth to mouth, the join being masked by bricks; a large oval-rimmed 'tub,' with or without a cover; or a capacious lid shaped like a cloche enclosing the whole body.   The shapes of these vessels varied so markedly from one period to another that they alone suffice to distinguish a Sumerian from an Assyrian tomb, or a tomb contemporary with Hammurabi from one of the Seleucid period.   This funerary ware was produced in very large quantities, and while it has no particular aesthetic value, it nevertheless rises above the level of ordinary earthenware vessels.   It presents certain peculiarities, however, which remain unexplained, since they appear to be neither functional nor ornamental in purpose; for example, the 'sausage-roll' aspect of most of these burial jars, and the ribbing disposed in parallel rows on the large 'tubs.'   Not till after the fourth century B.C. can we speak of ornamentation properly so called, such as that on the jars in the Seleucid cemetery recently cleared at Mari; these were decorated entirely with engraved designs, both figurative and geometric. No discussion of them is called for here, since the Seleucid period lies beyond the scope of this volume.

A

B

Clay was also the medium of another prolific type of art which flourished throughout the course of Mesopotamian civilization. We have in mind the terracotta figurines, innumerable examples of which have come down to us; some of the most characteristic were illustrated in the previous volume. Here we shall deal with them from the technical angle. They are of prime importance, first, because they reflect many aspects of daily life and embody the religious beliefs of the various peoples of Mesopotamia; secondly, because they testify to an artistic evolution, particularly striking perhaps in the 'nobler' medium of stone and metal statuary, but no less evident in the figurines.

To begin with, these works were modelled in the round entirely by hand. Increased demand, however, from the Neo-Sumerian period on (late third millennium), led to the use of moulds, and accordingly to mass production. This naturally simplified and accelerated the work, but at the expense of originality. Craftsmen—much less artists—were no longer needed, mere jobbers would do, since a lump of clay had only to be pressed in the intaglio design of the mould for the desired figure to be produced, and reproduced in countless indistinguishable copies.

Figurines in the round occur at Jarmo at the height of the Neolithic period; they are made

306 - LAGASH (TELLOH). MODELLED FIGURINE
    (FIRST HALF, 3rd MILLENNIUM). — LOUVRE
307 - LARSA (SENKEREH). FIGURINE OF A NUDE
    WOMAN (EARLY 2ND MILLENNIUM). — BAGHDAD

of roughly modelled, sun-dried clay and conform already to the Mother Goddess type. The figure is either seated or crouching. Sometimes a wash has been spread over the object. A very similar type of figurine recurs later in the Halaf period; many examples have been found on sites in northern Mesopotamia, at Tepe Gawra, Arpatchiya, Chagar Bazar and Tell Halaf; also (in 1960) at Tepe Sarab in Iran. The woman represented is always seated or crouching, with heavy, sagging breasts. These terracotta figurines sometimes show traces of painting, perhaps intended to represent tattooing or jewellery.

The figurines of the al 'Ubaid period discovered in Lower Mesopotamia, also in the round, are of a totally different type. Best known are the ones from Ur: tall slender female figures erect and completely nude, with snake-like faces surmounted by a bitumen toque or wig. Some have their hands on their hips, others hold a suckling child with their left arm. The bodies are ornamented: incised lines indicate their sex, tiny pellets of clay are dotted over their shoulders and upper arms, and the breast or back is picked out with irregular touches of paint. The only known example of a male figurine of this type comes from Eridu: nude, with a headdress in the form of an elongated *polos*, the body studded with clay pellets, like the goddesses from Ur.

308 - TELL HALAF. 'MOTHER GODDESS' (4th MILL.).
309 - (A) UR. NUDE SNAKE-HEADED FEMALE FIGU-
      RINE (4th MILL.). — BRITISH MUSEUM
      (B) ERIDU. MALE FIGURINE (4th MILL.).
      IRAQ MUSEUM, BAGHDAD

247

310 - LAGASH (TELLOH). (A) NUDE FEMALE FIGURINE   (B) MALE FIGURINE   (C) NUDE FEMALE FIGURINE — LOUVRE

Besides this well-documented type there are others, like the female figurines from Lagash, all of them headless unfortunately. Touches of black paint on the slim bodies may be interpreted as indicating tattooing or ornaments. None of these women carries a child. Another series of figurines almost certainly represents men, but with many ambiguities. The head is generally an undefined blob of clay drawn out and pinched off at the top; the shoulders are summarily rounded off without any indication of arms. No doubt there is room here for differing interpretations; the present writer, however, finds it difficult to accept the view put forward by A.J. Tobler, who regards similar figurines excavated by him at Tepe Gawra as anthropomorphic game pieces, analogous to the kings and queens of chess.

Figurines continued to be modelled in the round in the pre-Sargonid and Sargonid periods, but were of a noticeably different type. The men and Mother Goddesses of the al 'Ubaid period gave place to crudely modelled male and female figures intended to stand erect, judging by their broad base. As before, incised lines indicate hair and sex, and tiny pellets of clay represent eyes (greatly elongated), breasts and necklaces,

248

but the figures themselves in no way resemble those of earlier times. There is now no trace of painting.

The Neo-Sumerians, as we have said, revolutionized the whole technique of figure-making by inventing the mould. The use of terracotta moulds made it a simple matter to reproduce the small effigies (men and women, gods and goddesses, mythical heroes) described in the previous volume as figure-plaques—i.e. small, flat, rectangular plaques on which the figure stands out in more or less salient relief. (It is curious that, while these terracotta reliefs have been found by thousands, so few moulds have come to light.) The figure as a rule is represented in full front view; only in the Larsa period does it appear in profile with any frequency. It was then, too, that West Semitic civilization introduced a fresh stock of themes. Sites like Larsa and Ashnunnak have yielded figure-plaques much more lively and varied than those from the great Sumerian cities like Lagash and Ur, where stock subjects were found by the dozen, indeed by hundreds—'woman with a drum,' 'man carrying a goat' (prototype of the Good Shepherd of Early Christian art), couples (husband and wife) face to face or side by side.

312 - LAGASH . FIGURINE: DEMON. —LOUVRE. 313 - FIGURINE: WARRIOR. —BAGHDAD

Mass production by means of moulds did not, however, put an end to figurines hand-modelled in the round. These became rarer, it is true, and surviving examples of this type are often all the more precious for the fact that they are unique of their kind. Such is the case with two statuettes from Lagash: a lion-headed demon clutching a bird with its two paws and a turbaned, bearded warrior with an adze, which may very well have been the model for a large-scale statue. Indeed, there are good grounds for believing that the clay figurines often served as models for monumental statuary. We have conclusive evidence of this practice in a figure-plaque in the Louvre from Ashnunnak, representing bull-gods, erect and gripping the trunk of a palm-tree with their hands, for this very theme occurs on an Elamite mural decoration of moulded bricks (*Sumer*, fig. 405). The size of these terra-cotta figure-plaques varies considerably. Most of them measure from 4 to 8 inches in height. The Burney Plaque, however, is $19^5/_8$ inches high, and Woolley found two plaques at Ur measuring 24 and $28^3/_4$ inches respectively: a bull-god and a goddess with the flowing vase.

While the manufacture of figurines slackened off after the period of the First Dynasty of Babylon, it did not altogether cease. The Assyrians still resorted to them to represent genii or spirits *(apkallu)*: hybrid beings with two pairs of wings, shown full face; winged, hawk-headed genii in profile; bearded men whose bodies are sheathed in the skin of a fish (these 'fish-men' also appear on stone and bronze reliefs); bearded warriors, full face. Produced from moulds, all these figurines conform to stereotyped models; a few are painted, all show traces of whitewash. They were probably thus adorned as part of a magic rite, for these figurines—as we now know, thanks to excavations at Assur, confirmed by those at Nimrud—were buried in chests placed in the basements of houses, which they protected against demons and evil spirits.

The clay figurines Botta brought back from Khorsabad have a slightly different aspect. Some, $8^5/_8$ inches high, represent gods of high rank (since they are wearing crowns with three rows of horns), with their bodies painted blue; others, $9^1/_2$ inches high, show Gilgamesh dressed in a short tunic and holding a thick staff with both hands. These works, though modelled individually, not in moulds, are obvious imitations of figures in the large palace reliefs.

Keeping to the practice of the Assyrians, the Neo-Babylonians, too, buried either figurines of *Papsukal* (crowned divinities) in the foundations of their temples, such as were found by Koldewey at Babylon and Langdon at Kish; or demons in unbaked clay, modelled in the round, such as Woolley found at Ur. Assignable to the same period is a very different series of figurines, of which we discovered several examples at Larsa representing a chubby-faced woman suckling a child. Here again we have the age-old theme of the Mother Goddess: emerging at the very dawn of Mesopotamian civilization (Jarmo, late fifth millennium) and taking a modified form as the Woman with a Child (al 'Ubaid, fourth millennium), it was reinterpreted by the Neo-Sumerians in their own distinctive style (late third millennium) and by the Neo-Babylonians (sixth century B.C.). And even then its course was not yet run.

314 - WINGED EAGLE-HEADED GENIUS HOLDING A STAFF
      (FIRST HALF, 1st MILL.). — LOUVRE

315 - KHORSABAD. GILGAMESH HOLDING A STAFF (8th
      CENT. B.C.). — LOUVRE

316 - LARSA. MOTHER NURSING HER CHILD (7th-6th
      CENT. B.C.). — LOUVRE

317 - UR. DECORATION OF A BOX, DETAIL (EARLY 3rd MILL.).

318 - UR. GILGAMESH GRAPPLING WITH TWO BULLS (EARLY 3rd MILL.).

Shell and Ivory. The Mesopotamians made extensive use of both materials in their decorative art and handled them with much skill and taste.

Conch-shells they found in abundance on the shores of the Persian Gulf, of a size and texture enabling them to peel off flat thin plaques which could be cut out to form either purely geometric elements (triangles, rectangles, squares, lozenges) or figures (men, women, warriors, animals); these separate pieces were then arranged on panels so as to form large decorative inlays. Woolley discovered some wonderful examples of such work in the 'royal tombs' of Ur.

He noted three different working methods. (1) Cut out and polished, the shell plaque was engraved with a chisel; the grooved lines were then incrusted with a red or black paste, thus bringing out the design (usually animals surrounded by stylized plant forms). (2) First the subject was engraved with the chisel; then the ground was cut back to the depth of a millimetre or so and filled in with bitumen, thus leaving the subject silhouetted against a dark background. (3) The third procedure derived from the second. First the background was cut away altogether, leaving the silhouetted figure in slight relief; anatomical or other inner details were incised with the chisel, and these lines were filled in with a black or red paste. The surrounding field was

319 - THE 'STANDARD' OF UR, DETAIL (EARLY 3rd MILL.). — BRITISH MUSEUM

usually built up with a mosaic composed of small irregular pieces of lapis lazuli set with bitumen. Sometimes, too, the shell plaque, hollowed out by the technique known as intaglio relief, was mounted on a bitumen ground. It comes as something of a surprise to note that the lapis lazuli elements used in these inlays are of all shapes and sizes; obviously they were not fashioned with an eye to any particular work, the pieces being made to fit in anywhere. The inevitable result was a certain number of flaws and even gaps in the finished inlay, though these could to some extent be concealed by the dark bitumen ground. Shell, moreover, is so brittle that parts of certain figures generally had to be left uncut; the areas between the legs, between the arms and the body, or between the paws of animals. These areas were accordingly hollowed out and filled with black paste.

Among the finest shell inlays discovered at Ur are the famous Standard (British Museum), the gaming boards, the toilet box of Shubad, and the soundboxes of several lyres and harps.

Many vestiges of this art have also been found at Lagash and Kish, but so shattered and incomplete that it is impossible to piece them together or even to tell whether they formed part of decorative panels, figure compositions or the ornamentation of goblets.

320 - THE 'STANDARD' OF UR. (A) 'PEACE.' (B) 'WAR.' (EARLY 3rd MILLENNIUM B.C.). — BRITISH MUSEUM

321 - UR. GAMING BOARD (3rd MILL.). — BRITISH MUSEUM

322 - UR. SOUNDBOX PANEL (3rd MILL.). — PHILADELPHIA

323 - UR. DECORATION OF A BOX (3rd MILL.). — BAGHDAD

234 - MARI. 'STANDARD' (EARLY 3rd MILL.). — ALEPPO AND LOUVRE   325 - WARRIOR WITH AN ADZE (EARLY 3rd MILL.). — LOUVRE

Mari has yielded similar fragments which, in the light of the complete ensembles from Ur, can be restored to their original lay-out. They form a scene representing the aftermath of war: the Numbering of the Captives, who are being led in single file, naked, their arms bound at the elbows, towards the victorious commanders wearing their battle dress. The Mari panel, found in pieces in the ruins of the Ishtar temple, consisted of several registers, three if not more, with dividing lines made of particles of shell and red stone. The figures were cut in plaques of mother of pearl with a delicate precision that is all the more remarkable, considering the extreme fragility of the material, and then mounted on a bitumen ground enclosed in a wooden frame. The empty spaces between the figures were filled in with small, irregularly shaped pieces of stone, not lapis lazuli as at Ur, but grey-black schist. The scene as a whole was bordered with a double row of rectangular flakes of stone and shell, alternately red and white.

Another figure carved in a thick plaque of shell, also from Mari, represents a warrior armed with an adze. Its convex shape suggests that it was originally mounted on a sword-hilt or the grip of a dagger. As there are no traces of studding, it was presumably made fast with bitumen.

Some cylinder seals were also carved in shell, but only very rarely, owing to the brittleness of the material.

Curiously enough, while shell inlays were in high favour during the third millennium, and particularly in the pre-Sargonid period (2750-2450 B.C.), they ceased being made at all in the following centuries.

An even more precious substance than shell, ivory seems to have been in demand more or less continuously from the very earliest times. It appears in the Palaeolithic period, but came into general use only in the Chalcolithic age. It was obtainable in abundance, for there were great herds of elephants at that time not only in Upper Egypt, Abyssinia and Eritrea, but also in Syria, in the marshes of the Upper Euphrates, and in the Indus valley with which Mesopotamia had established trade relations by the early third millennium. From Ophir (? India, Arabia, Madagascar or the Somali Coast) Solomon's navy brought 'gold, and silver, ivory, and apes, and peacocks' (I Kings x. 22). In Ezekiel's time (sixth century B.C.) Tyre was one of the great seaports of the East and ivory is mentioned among the many commodities in which it plied a thriving and remunerative trade (Ezekiel xxvii. 15).

The technique of ivory carving is clearly derived from that of the shell carvers. Plaques of ivory are handled in the same way, the figure being either engraved with the chisel, worked in low relief, or silhouetted with or without open-work.

Though assertions to the contrary have been made, the Mesopotamians not only were familiar with ivory but employed it frequently. Excavations at Mari prove it to have been in general use as early as the first half of the third millennium, at the height of the pre-Sargonid period. The many fragments found there by us since 1934, and particularly in 1953, leave no doubt that ivory inlays were produced on quite as large a scale as those composed of shell and mother of pearl; and that they contained the usual figures (men, women, dignitaries) and representations of animals then to be seen in Mesopotamia (onagers, lions, etc.). The scenes of which these fragments formed part related either to the official life of the city or to cult ceremonies (several of the Mari ivories depict the ritual sacrifice of a ram). From the start the yellowish hue of the ivory was deliberately played off against darker elements (fragments of lapis lazuli, for example) used as fillings or inset in open spaces. Sometimes the bodies of animals are pitted with holes which once contained small coloured inlays—yet another instance of that love of polychromy so characteristic of the Sumerians.

It is a curious fact that, at the end of the pre-Sargonid period (c. 2450 B.C.), ivory, like shell, went out of fashion. It does not reappear till early Assyrian times, at some indeterminate date between the sixteenth and thirteenth centuries B.C. (and thus roughly contemporaneous with the great caches of ivories found along the Mediterranean

coast, at Lachish, Megiddo and Ras Shamra). The most characteristic come from Assur and, as regards technique, fall into separate groups: engraved designs (a pyx and combs from Burial Vault 45); carvings in the round or in high relief (pins and a case fitted with tenons carved in the form of heads, from Burial Vault 45); elements cut out in the flat, engraved with inner details, and forming part of a larger composition (mountain-god with flowing vase, winged lion passant and trees with volutes, from the outside of the palace).

These ivories are specifically Assyrian; they were made, that is to say, in Assyria itself by local craftsmen. This was not always the case with the various groups of ivories found in the palaces of Khorsabad and Nimrud; a large number of these were products of Syro-Phœnician or North Syrian workshops and were either imported by Assyrian traders ox carried off as war booty by Assyrian armies.

As for the ivories of a later date however (ninth-eighth centuries B.C.), many are the work of native Assyrian craftsmen. The most characteristic were executed in the following techniques (already current in the third millennium): outline engraving, champlevé work, and open-work silhouettes, often enhanced with overlays of thin gold leaf or with cloisonné insets of lapis lazuli or coloured glass-paste. In studying a batch of such works discovered in the course of his excavations at Arslan Tash, in a provincial palace of Upper Syria, Thureau-Dangin succeeded in identifying the cuneiform names of these techniques: *tamlu* (inlay) and *ihzu* (overlay). Some of the ivories recently discovered by Mallowan at Nimrud illustrate this distinction perfectly.

These ancient ivory workers are seen at their boldest in some of the pieces from Nimrud, notably several female heads. One large fragment shows the combined use of ivory, gold overlays (on the hair) and coloured paste for the eyes, the eyebrows and the kiss-curls hanging over the forehead from beneath a triple headband studded with rosettes.

This chryselephantine technique is also illustrated by many female heads found in 1955 in the throne room of Esarhaddon's palace *(Illustrated London News*, January 28, 1956) and in Fort Shalmaneser (*ibid.*, January 17, 1959).

As regards the technique of the two small ivories from Nimrud representing a lioness mauling an Ethiopian, some comment is called for here. The two pieces are identical and might well pass for cloisonné work; actually, however, a different, more elaborate technique was employed. Carved in the ivory plaque, the flowers of the lotus brake were first overlaid with gold foil, then incrusted with carnelian and lapis lazuli set with a mortar of carbonate of calcium and powdered blue frit. The gold was stuck to the ivory with some organic adhesive.

Small ivory plaques served to decorate furniture, beds of state, couches, toilet boxes, and thrones (Solomon's was made of ivory overlaid with gold, cf. I Kings x. 18-20 and II Chronicles ix. 17-19, where it is described in detail).

327 - NIMRUD. HEAD OF A WOMAN WITH A DIADEM, FRAGMENT

328 - LAGASH (A, B) DECORATIVE MOTIFS (FIRST HALF 3RD MILLENNIUM). — LOUVRE

329 - ASSUR. PALACE OF TUKULTI-NINURTA I. MOUNTAIN GOD WITH FLOWING VASE (13th CENTURY B.C.). — BERLIN

330 - KALAKH (NIMRUD). LILITH (EARLY 1st MILL.).

When the Bible speaks of the 'ivory house' which Ahab made at Samaria (I Kings xxii. 39), we may take this to mean that ivory was used on a really lavish scale; it fails to specify, however, whether this was confined to architectural ornamentation. Figure compositions, in any case, may be assumed to have been employed in the revetment of doors, where the scenes represented did not require to be treated on a large scale (cf. the bronze doors of certain Christian churches and, in Assyria, the bronze doors of Balawat).

It should be added that ivory was often carved in the round; excavations at Nimrud have brought many such works to light.

The tools employed by Mesopotamian ivory carvers—chisel, saw and drill—are identifiable from the traces they have left behind. A polish was obtained not with files, but by means of abrasives, chiefly sand.

The Louvre recently acquired a silver plaque that forms the support of an ivory carving representing a lion and a lioness about to attack a frightened antelope. The animals were mounted on the metal plaque, but the recesses provided for them are somewhat smaller than the animal silhouettes. These, then, must have been fastened originally to intermediate mounts (now lost) which fitted into the recesses beneath; this inference is borne out by the small holes drilled in the back of the ivory animal figures. This work appears to be unique of its kind.

331 - LIONS AND ANTELOPE ON A WOODED HILLSIDE (EARLY 1st MILL.). — LOUVRE

Painting. We here confine ourselves to the wall paintings mentioned in this and our previous volume, to the exclusion of the painted pottery of early times and such figurines, reliefs and sculptures in the round as still bear traces of paint. Wall paintings were in high favour with the ancient Mesopotamians and the surviving works are obviously but a tithe of what formerly existed. Here time has taken a greater toll than in the other art forms dealt with above. For one thing, the colours have often failed to resist erosion and moisture of the ground; for another, the excavators of last century overlooked many fragments that might still have been salvaged from the ruins.

The earliest wall paintings (fourth millennium B.C.) of which traces still remain were found in houses at Tepe Gawra, Eridu and Uruk; their three colours—red, white and black—are the same as those used in cone mosaics. The

332 - TELL 'UQAIR. ALTAR DECORATION (LATE 4th-EARLY 3rd MILL.).

earliest coherent body of paintings, however, comes from the much more modest site of Tell 'Uqair, where they decorated the altar and inner walls of a temple on a high platform. They were executed on the fresh, whitewashed plaster of the mud-brick walls. The initial design had been laid in first in red or orange, then rectified or emphasized with black. Two guardian animals were still recognizable, their bodies picked out with touches of black, their ears, eyes, manes and the tips of their tails emphasized with a 'fast colour.' Of the remaining tones employed we are told that there was 'a great variety' of them, with the 'notable omission' of blue and green. At a slightly later period (early third millennium) a chapel of the temple of Ninhursag at Mari was decorated with a procession of figures standing on a bull, all of them treated in a schematic, filiform style: each consisting of only a few streaks of black hastily slashed on to the plaster coating of the wall.

The palace of Mari contained a great number of wall paintings, dating from the opening centuries of the second millennium; their variety of themes, diversified techniques and boldness of inspiration were unparalleled by any previous finds.

First came alternating parallel bands of black and red ochre (Rooms 43 and 46), then a double frieze in cobalt blue, composed of two S-shaped torsades with a white border and central point (Court 31). Four primary colours were used: black, white, red and blue. Made up entirely of geometric patterns, these paintings were often executed on the mud plaster which, as usual, overlaid the rough masonry of unbaked bricks. Mud plaster being a highly unsatisfactory support, it was sometimes covered with a more or less thick coat of white plaster or gesso, to which the paints were applied while it was still wet. Such was the case with the upper face of a podium (Room 64), whose panels, painted in imitation of marble, stand in a frame that combines running spirals with a flame pattern. The only colours used in this decoration are red and yellow ochre and white. The same technique recurs in a large sacrificial scene found in pieces under a mass of rubble. This was a large-scale figure composition, with animals. The design was first blocked out in black on the plaster ground, then the paints were laid in. The colours used were black, white, red ochre, dark red ochre, and red ochre of a lighter shade, applied directly to the plaster in flat tones.

The large panel, which we have called 'The Investiture of the King of Mari,' illustrates a different technique. First, the outlines of figures were incised with a sharp point. The ground is not white plaster as before, but a mere mud wash spread over the

333 - MARI. SACRIFICIAL SCENE, DETAIL. — LOUVRE

334 - MARI. 'THE INVESTITURE,' DETAIL
(18th CENTURY B.C.). — LOUVRE

mud plaster of the wall. The actual support, then, amounted to a very thin film, and to this not only the usual colours were applied (red and orange ochre and white) but also carmine, yellow, green and blue. We noticed that in several parts of the painting the colours, instead of being brushed in, seemed to have been applied with a palette knife, thus standing slightly in relief and like an inlay filling the spaces between the incised lines.

One cannot help wondering why painters had recourse to so fragile a support as mud plaster when gesso was available and would have ensured better results. Yet we find mud again on the walls of the Audience Chamber (132), where the figures are more like tinted drawings than paintings, most of them clearly outlined with thick black lines, then filled in with a limited range of flat colours (red ochre, black and white). In another part of the palace were similar figures with bronzed flesh tints, clad in light-coloured costumes (blue and white); contours were drawn with a sharp point, but

335 - AQAR QUF (DUR KURIGALZU). DIGNITARY (14th CENTURY B. C.)

always on the same mud-plaster support. The palace of Mari thus vouches for the existence of a long-standing tradition of painting still obtaining round about 1750 B.C., and shows that there now flourished a new category of trained artists—the painters.

It would have been surprising indeed had so vigorous a tradition speedily died out. That it did not is proved by a series of later paintings discovered at Nuzi, Kar-Tukulti-Ninurta (thirteenth century B.C.) and above all at Dur Kurigalzu (fourteenth century B.C.) where a Kassite palace was decorated with processions of men painted in distemper on a yellowish ground. The following colours were used: red, scarlet, yellow, black, cobalt blue and Prussian blue.

336 - TIL BARSIP (TELL AHMAR). WALL PAINTING. IBEX (8th-7th CENTURIES B.C.). — ALEPPO

We come now to the Assyrian period, for which our documentation would be even more abundant than it is, had the excavators of last century (Place and Layard in particular) kept a more careful record of their finds. But concerned as they were with reliefs and statuary, they took little notice of the fragments of paintings that undoubtedly lay scattered amid the debris of the palaces they cleared.

In the provincial residence at Til Barsip (Tell Ahmar) the Thureau-Dangin expedition brought to light some wall paintings (ninth-seventh centuries B.C.) but it proved impracticable to detach them; the copies executed by Lucien Cavro, however, supply us with documentation of the

262

337 - TIL BARSIP (TELL AHMAR). WALL PAINTING. IBEX (7th CENTURY B.C.). — LOUVRE

highest value. Again we find the extraordinary gift for animal representation which the Assyrians always displayed in depicting the animals
of the open steppes or the royal preserves: ibexes rising to their feet,
a horse moving at a gallop, a lion pouncing on its prey. The pigments
—size paints or distemper—were applied in flat tints. Two styles are
observable: one characterized by outline drawing in black before the
application of the colours, the other by red contours emphasized here
and there at key points by black underscorings. Black, red and blue
are the only colours employed; green and yellow are altogether absent.
The red is an ochre pigment, a natural compound of clay and oxide

263

338 - TIL BARSIP (TELL AHMAR). WALL PAINTING IN THE PALACE, ARCHER (8th CENTURY B.C.). — ALEPPO

TIL BARSIP. WALL PAINTINGS. 339 - GALLOPING HORSEMAN (7th CENT. B.C.) 340 - ROARING LION (8th OR 7th CENT. B.C.).

341 - KHORSABAD. WALL DECORATION (8th CENTURY B.C.).

of iron. Analysis of the blue, which was very close to cobalt, showed the following composition: silica, 74.27%; oxide of copper, 10.37%; lime, 9.19%, together with minute quantities of alumina, oxide of iron, oxide of manganese, magnesia, potassium and soda; these, however, were mere impurities. The fatty substance that served as a binding medium had disappeared; this accounts for the powdery aspect of the blue-painted surfaces and for the fact that the paint crumbled into dust almost immediately after being uncovered. The originals of some of these paintings are preserved in the Louvre and the Aleppo Museum.

At Khorsabad the American expedition of the Oriental Institute of Chicago confirmed the earlier discoveries of Place when it found large fragments of wall paintings datable (with unusual precision) to the reign of Sargon II (721-705 B.C.). Technical analysis of these works tallied with the findings of the Thureau-Dangin expedition and may be summed up as follows. The plastered surface of

342 - TIL BARSIP (TELL AHMAR). WALL DECORATION (8th CENTURY B.C.).

the wall had first been coated with a lime wash, and on this the flat colours were laid in. They included not only the familiar dominants (blue, red and black) but also green and brown. Yellow never occurs. The blue pigment was made from lapis lazuli; the red is a mercuric sulphide, with the clay of the wall surface apparently acting as a binding medium. As a finishing touch, forms and figures were given thick black outlines. A comparison of paintings and sculptures shows no difference of style or inspiration, though it is clear that each of the two art forms had its own well-defined stock of themes; the two antithetical bulls on either side of a geometric motif, for example, or the two winged human-headed genii with the

266

343 - TIL BARSIP (TELL AHMAR). WALL PAINTING IN THE PALACE. PANELS WITH GEOMETRIC DESIGNS (8th CENT. B.C.).

situla or the sacred plant, kneeling on either side of a large disk, were never represented by sculptors. It comes as no surprise, however, to find that the themes of mural decorations are closely connected with those treated on glazed plaques and bricks without relief, for both were designed by painters.

Our knowledge of Assyrian painting is necessarily based on a relatively small number of surviving works, all of them damaged and fragmentary. It seems safe to say, nevertheless, that our present appraisal of it is in the main correct and unlikely to be invalidated by any subsequent discoveries.

267

344 - TIL BARSIP. WALL PAINTING. ANATOLIAN(?) CAPTIVES (8th CENT. B.C.).

345 - TIL BARSIP (TELL AHMAR). WALL PAINTING IN THE PALACE. LARGE HUNTING SCENE WITH CHARIOTS (7th CENTURY B.C.). →

268

MESOPOTAMIAN LITERATURE

LITERATURE

For all the abundance and variety of the painting, statuary and reliefs dealt with in this and the preceding volume, our survey of the art of the Ancient East would be incomplete if we failed to discuss, however briefly, two other forms of artistic expression in which the Mesopotamians seem to have been pioneers: literature and music.

There can be no question here of drawing up a complete catalogue of the literary works (several volumes would be needed), or of advancing any speculative theories as regards the music, for which our documentation is far scantier. We shall merely draw attention to the remarkable scope of this literature which seems to have included all types and genres; and, as regards the music, to the high stage of evolution vouched for by a range of instruments comparable with that of the modern orchestra.

Probably no other ancient civilization has bequeathed to the world so vast a corpus of written documents as that of Mesopotamia. This seems all the more extraordinary when we remember that it arose in an age when oral tradition still bulked large and the epic narratives were normally transmitted by word of mouth. Yet, despite the prevalence of this oral tradition, the written record successfully competed with it, even in very early times. No other race (except perhaps the Egyptians) had such a propensity for building up archives covering

← 348 - TIL BARSIP. WALL PAINTING. TWO SCRIBES (8th CENTURY B.C.).

279

350 - FRANÇOIS THUREAU-DANGIN (1872-1944)

every aspect of human existence: historical events, social conditions and religious beliefs. Had they been inscribed on a perishable substance such as papyrus or vellum, little or nothing of these records would have stood up to the ravages of time and the moisture of the soil during the Mesopotamian winter. Fortunately clay tablets were used and, whether baked or sun-dried, they have survived intact and whole collections of them have been unearthed by archaeologists. Hundreds of thousands of cuneiform tablets are now available. At Nineveh, Nippur, Lagash and Mari entire libraries have been found, not to mention the thousands of texts found at other sites, notably Shuruppak, Uruk, Ur, Larsa, Ashnunnak, Kish, Nimrud and Assur.

Thus, thanks to the labours of several generations of Assyriologists from all parts of the world, a whole literature has emerged from the buried cities of ancient Mesopotamia.

This is not the place to describe the gradual stages (1849, 1854, 1857) of the decipherment of the cuneiform script. Suffice it to say that the key was found in the trilingual inscriptions at Behistun and Persepolis, and it soon became apparent that the so-called 'Assyro-Babylonian' system of writing derived from a much earlier age and was undoubtedly of Sumerian origin. The Sumerians were not only the inventors of writing, they were also the creators of literature in the modern sense. When in the seventh century B.C. Assurbanipal founded his great library at Nineveh, his scribes were set to copying the ancient texts. For recent excavations have made it clear that the so-called Akkadian versions were in many cases transcriptions or adaptations of much older Sumerian originals.

It was in 1905 that the French savant François Thureau-Dangin (1872-1944) published his *Inscriptions de Sumer et d'Akkad*. The texts reproduced were mainly historical and relating to reigning monarchs, quite a number being dedications. In 1943, the eminent American

Sumeriologist Professor Samuel Kramer discovered in the collections of the University Museum in Philadelphia a tablet from Nippur which proved to be a library catalogue. It listed sixty-two items, dating back to the end of the third millennium B.C. Some years later Professor Kramer identified Tablet AO 5393 in the Louvre as being another book list, cataloguing sixty-eight titles. The two lists are not identical, only forty-three items being common to both. There could be no better evidence of the widespread contemporary interest in literature of all descriptions.

Among these works are numerous mythological or epic narratives: *Enki and Ninhursag* (a 'paradise' tale); *Dumuzi and Enkimdu* (the rivalry between a shepherd-god and a farmer-god, curiously resembling that of Cain and Abel); *Gilgamesh and Agga* (the conflict between two cities, throwing light on the political conditions of the age); *Gilgamesh and the Land of the Living* (man's horror of the thought of death); *The Death of Gilgamesh* (death and the after-life); *Inanna's Descent to the Netherworld* (Inanna, visiting the infernal regions, is helped by Enki to return to the land of the living); *Enmerkar and the Lord of Aratta* (conflict between the King of Uruk and the ruler of a city-state in southern Iran); *The Deluge* (prototype of the Biblical and Babylonian flood-stories, in which Noah is named Ziusudra).

351 - SAMUEL N. KRAMER (b. 1897)

352 - TABLET WITH LIBRARY CATALOGUE (2nd MILLENNIUM). — LOUVRE

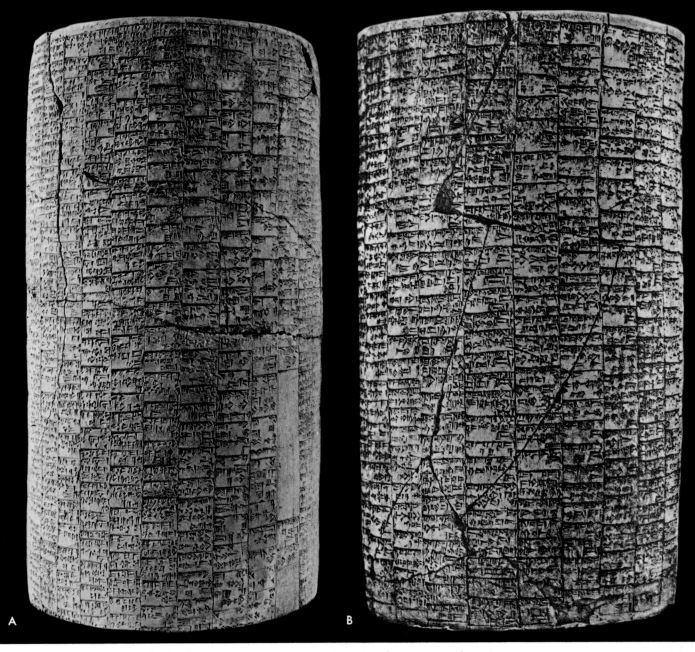

354 - TELLOH (LAGASH). CYLINDERS A AND B OF GUDEA (22nd CENTURY B.C.). — LOUVRE

Besides these specifically Sumerian works, mention must also be made of what we owe to Gudea, Patesi of Lagash: not only the inscriptions engraved on his statues but also the texts on his clay cylinders, A and B, which throw so much light on the cultic and ritual conceptions prevailing at the close of the third millennium B.C. Religion and history marched side by side, since the gods controlled all the activities of the rulers, their viceregents on earth. The inscription on the Stele of the Vultures bears out its iconography, which shows the two worlds, human and divine, closely intermingled. For Eannatum owed his victory to the active collaboration of the gods.

← 353 - TELLOH (LAGASH). GUDEA, 'THE ARCHITECT WITH A PLAN' (22nd CENTURY B.C.). — LOUVRE

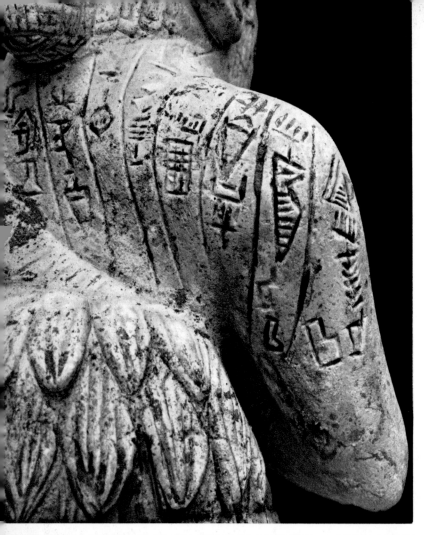

355 - MARI. INSCRIPTION ON THE STATUE OF LAMGI-MARI — ALEPPO MUSEUM

356 - MARI. INSCRIPTION ON THE STATUE OF IDI-NARUM — ALEPPO MUSEUM

The Sumerians were masters of a great variety of literary forms, including epics, myths, legends, royal or religious hymns, lamentations (for example over the fall of Ur and Nippur), Ludingirra's elegies on the deaths of his father and his wife, inscriptions commemorating historical events, dedications, law codes (Ur-Nammu's, Lipit-Ishtar's), cultic and ritual formulas, and books of proverbs. Besides these texts many thousands of written contracts have been unearthed and they tell us much about the everyday life, commerce and business methods of the Sumerians.

In business the Sumerians were scrupulous record keepers and everywhere archives give us detailed accounts of the agriculture and industries of the age. What is more, not only have the archives familiarized us with the careers of kings, and high officials such as Gin-ak, the Patesi, but they also have much to say about the life of the common people, of which, but for the labours of these nameless scribes, we should know nothing. For *inscribed* statues or statuettes are extremely rare.

At the end of the third millennium the Sumerians disappeared from the political scene, but their language persisted as a *lingua sacra*. As for their traditions, it is clear that these were a source of inspiration for all the literature, usually described as 'Akkadian' or 'Assyro-Babylonian,' of a later age.

357 - DIYALA REGION. INSCRIPTION ON THE STATUE OF GIN-AK — LOUVRE →

For at the beginning of the second millennium there was a large and varied output of literary works and for this the Semites were responsible. Outstanding amongst these are two great works, the Babylonian Poem of Creation and the Epic of Gilgamesh.

The former, inscribed on seven tablets, is named after the first two words of the first tablet, *Enuma Elish* ('When on high. . .'). This poem, which was recited on the fourth day of the New Year festival, is a sort of Mesopotamian Genesis, a Babylonian account of the Creation. Assurbanipal had it recopied in the seventh century B.C. for his library at Nineveh, from originals which probably dated back to the time of the First Dynasty of Babylon (nineteenth-eighteenth centuries B.C.).

The final recension of the Gilgamesh Epic was written on twelve tablets from an original version which contained, it seems, only ten. Of the two additional tablets the eleventh described the Deluge, and the twelfth appears to have been directly drawn from Sumerian sources. There can be no question that the Epic of Gilgamesh is one of the noblest and most poignant masterworks of ancient literature. It covers all the essential aspects of human life: love and friendship, struggle and adventure, and, last but not least, the sense of death and the craving for immortality that have always haunted the minds of men. The hero Gilgamesh, the 'shepherd of Uruk,' joins forces with the half-animal being Enkidu and, after combats with wild beasts, goes with him to the Cedar Forest, where they slay the giant Humbaba. When on their return from this perilous adventure Enkidu dies, Gilgamesh is filled with despair. Not only has he lost his dearest friend, but he is reminded of the fact that the same fate awaits him. His one thought now is to win the immortality bestowed by the gods on Ut-napishtim and his wife, sole survivors of the Deluge, and with this in mind he descends into the Land of No Return. He has a brief interview with Enkidu who gives his friend a gloomy picture of the realm of the dead. 'Have you seen that man whose dead body lies in the plain? I have seen him; his spirit has no rest in the underworld. That man whose spirit has none to care for it—have you seen him? I have seen him; all he has to eat is the scourings of the pot, the left-over scraps of food that are flung into the street!'

That the rulers of the underworld, Nergal and Ereshkigal, are of a far from amiable disposition is evidenced by the myth, *Ishtar's Descent to the Netherworld*. As the goddess passes through each of the seven gates leading to the Netherworld, she is stripped of her garments and jewels piece by piece and roughly treated. While she is absent from the upper world, all life is in abeyance; on her return, it recommences, men and beasts reawaken to the joys of love.

358 - NUDE WINGED GODDESS (EARLY 2nd MILLENNIUM). — NORMAN COLVILLE COLLECTION →

Other myths tell the stories of Adapa who broke the wings of the South Wind and was summoned to 'the heaven of Anu' to account for his misdeed; of the shepherd Etana who went up to heaven on an eagle in quest of 'the plant of life'; of Atrahasis the sage, whose exemplary life distinguished him from the common run of mortals. True, these were 'special cases'; nevertheless all men partook of godhead, for had not man been fashioned out of clay mixed with the blood of a slain god? His life was determined by the will of Enlil, keeper of the tablets of destiny (which on one occasion were carried off by the bird-god Zu).

Associated with these epic poems were hymns and prayers celebrating the greater gods or pleading for their aid. Examples are the hymns in praise of Ishtar who bestowed her blessings on King Ammiditana; of Sin, 'hero of the gods,' and Shamash who dispensed justice and equity. Thus, too, we have a psalm glorifying Marduk on his return to his temple; a prayer to the gods of Night who, like men, have periods of repose; a prayer to an unnamed god, soliciting his pardon since mankind had, involuntarily, lapsed into evil ways.

362 - TABLET OF 'THE RIGHTEOUS SUFFERER' (2nd MILLENNIUM). — LOUVRE

This constant desire to keep in contact with the celestial powers is evident also in the rites. The description of one of these, relating to the Ishtar cult, was unearthed by us at Mari and others, of much interest, have been found at Uruk. Copies made at comparatively late dates (from the Assyrian to the Seleucid epoch) and mostly transcriptions of older Babylonian originals, they have much to relate about the highly elaborate ceremonies performed in the city dear to Anu and help us to picture the magnificence of the ritual prescribed for offerings and sacrifices.

Another branch of Mesopotamian literature was of a didactic nature. There certainly existed a Sumerian Book of Wisdom. In 1960 an American scholar, Dr Edmund Gordon, revealed the existence of two large collections of proverbs (some 366 in all). The Babylonians, too, practised this genre and many of their proverbs seem to foreshadow those of Ecclesiastes. Some of them, moreover, have a penetration and poignancy equalling those of the Book of Job. Thus Professor Kramer has been able to prove the existence of a 'Sumerian Job,' followed up in Babylonia by 'The Righteous Sufferer,' a dramatic tale recorded on a number of tablets.

First to be discovered were the *monologue* of the righteous man (*ludlul bel nemeqi*, 'I shall pray to the Lord of Wisdom') and the acrostic *dialogue* between the righteous man and his friend. A definitive rendering of the latter was supplied by Edouard Dhorme in 1923. Since 1952 an older (Babylonian) version has been available (Tablet AO 4462, Louvre), published by Jean Nougayrol. A man is visited with affliction though he is not merely innocent but a paragon of virtue. The prologue —which was lacking in the first discovered tablet—is evidently intended to lead up to the intervention of the friend who pleads the victim's cause with his god. Despite the ills that have unjustly befallen him he has not lost his faith. To this the god replies: 'Your path is made smooth, my blessing is upon you, you have found favour in my eyes and, lo, you are healed for ever.' This 'happy ending' absolves all concerned; no one need reproach himself for anything, the god has not turned a deaf ear, the advocate has won his suit and the sufferer regained health and prosperity—as was the case with the Biblical Job.

After these excursions into theology and moral philosophy, we may turn to a group of works relating to other aspects of human existence: legislation, historiography and correspondence, for all of which there is a copious documentation.

It was long thought that the most ancient Mesopotamian law code was that drawn up at the behest of Hammurabi, King of Babylon (eighteenth century B.C.).

363 - CODE OF HAMMURABI, DETAIL (18th CENTURY B.C.). — LOUVRE

It comprises 282 laws covering, it would seem, all the acts that were then regarded as infringements of the rights of individuals or the community. But it is now known that similar codes had been enacted at even earlier dates: by Lipit-Ishtar, fifth king of the Isin Dynasty (c. 1860 B.C.); by a king of Ashnunnak (c. 1925 B.C.); and by Ur-Nammu of the Third Dynasty of Ur (c. 2050 B.C.). Couched in a precise, juristic style, these law codes are models of brevity and clarity. Here are a few extracts from the Code of Hammurabi:

§ 14. A thief stealing from a child is to be put to death.

§ 25. A thief stealing from a burning house is to be burnt.

§ 215. A physician who operates on a but slightly wounded man with the bronze scalpel shall have his hands cut off.

§ 229. A builder who builds a house which falls and causes the death of the owner is to be put to death.

§ 230. In the case of its killing the son of the owner, the builder's son is to be put to death.

The effects of this praiseworthy attempt to regulate social and economic life made themselves felt over a long period, and in this context mention may be made of the codification of the Assyrian laws between the fifteenth and twelfth centuries B.C., recorded on clay tablets found at Assur.

Great as was their concern for law and justice, the Sumerians, Babylonians, Assyrians and Neo-Babylonians were even more interested in history—in the annals of their own past, needless to say. Hundreds, indeed thousands of texts have been discovered in which are chronicled with scrupulous exactitude the salient events of each reign with, in the case of the Assyrians, an emphasis on the military exploits of their kings. Some of these documents are contemporaneous with the events described, while others are the works of scribes who, writing at a later date, drew their information from reliable sources. The care taken to ensure factual accuracy is evident in such works as the so-called 'Chronicles of Sargon,' which have much to tell of such outstanding figures as Sargon of Akkad, his son Naram-Sin, Shulgi of Ur and Hammurabi of Babylon. Here the conscientiousness and abilities of the chronicler are evident; his descriptions in sober prose of the chief incidents in the careers of these royal empire-builders could hardly be bettered.

More tendentious doubtless are the official narratives of successful campaigns, which, from Tiglathpileser I to Assurbanipal, record with much precision the routes followed, defeats of hostile coalitions, the towns taken by storm and the booty amassed. The general effect is apt to be tedious, but there are occasionally lighter touches, as when Sennacherib describing his Palestine campaign speaks of shutting up King Hezekiah in his city of Jerusalem 'like a bird in a cage.' Unfortunately such passages are rare, whereas long accounts of massacres and deportations are all too frequent. None the less this zeal for getting every detail 'on the record' has greatly helped us to an understanding of the history of some fifteen hundred years and enabled us to build up a solid chronological framework.

As a sidelight on this historical documentation there is a wealth of letters unparalleled in any other ancient civilization. The First Dynasty of Babylon (early second millennium B.C.) witnessed an exceptional development of letter-writing. Thus the royal archives of Mari alone have yielded several thousand letters, all of which can be positively dated to the eighteenth century B.C. Besides carefully drawn up reports, they contain private messages which have much to say about the daily life of the correspondents. Queen Shibtu dictates a letter to her husband Zimri-Lim, then at the 'front': 'Tell this to my lord. Thus says his servant Shibtu. All goes well in the Palace. May my lord keep in good health. I am sending him a garment of the best quality, a cloak of the best quality, two *gish-shub* and three jars.'

Then we have a treaty of defensive alliance, copied and sent by a spy to the King of Mari. 'Rim-Sin has written to Hammurabi as follows: "My men are mustered in my country. Let the men of your country do likewise. If the enemy plans to attack you, my men and my boats will join forces with you. But if he attacks me, let your troops and boats come to join me."'

A letter from King Shamshi-Adad to Iasmah-Adad, his son, viceroy at Mari, runs as follows: 'How long shall we have to guide your steps perpetually? You are still a little boy, you are not a man, your chin is beardless! While your brother, here, kills the *davidum*, you over there lie supine amongst women. Be a man!'

The letters offer us glimpses of the everyday life lived by flesh-and-blood beings whose behaviour never surprises us, so much does it resemble what ours might well have been in similar circumstances. Moreover these letters are drawn up in business-like fashion, the names of sender and addressee are always stated, the subject-matter concisely set forth, often with a striking psychological acumen and an engaging spontaneity —in a word, they vividly reflect the many-sided life of the age when they were written.

One of the best descriptions of a military campaign (the eighth of Sargon of Assyria) is couched in the form of a letter from the

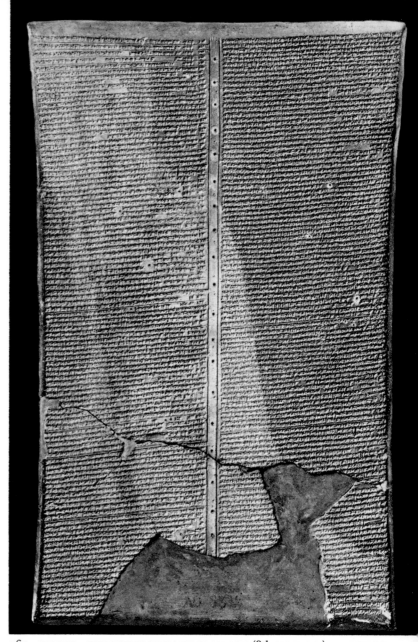

364 - TABLET. THE EIGHTH CAMPAIGN OF SARGON (8th CENT. B.C.). — LOUVRE

365 - MARI. A SCHOOLROOM IN THE PALACE (18th CENTURY B.C.).

king to his god, Assur. It opens with a grandiose salutation: 'Hail, all hail to Assur, to the father of the gods and mighty lord who dwells in his great temple, the *E-har-sag-gal-kur-kur-ra*.' After citing the gods and goddesses of the city, of the people and the palace (to whom, also, the letter is addressed), the king continues: 'With Sargon, holy priest, thy servant, who fears thy mighty godhead, all is well.' There follows a report of over four hundred closely written lines inscribed on a large tablet 'engraved by Nabu-shallimshunu, chief scribe of the king, learned doctor, master-of-arts of Sargon.'

The huge literary output of the age was, in fact, the work of a whole army of scribes. They were trained in special schools, where they spent laborious days writing on small clay tablets, many of which have come down to us intact. We spoke above of the great 'libraries' of ancient Mesopotamia. That of Nineveh was one of the most extensive. Assurbanipal was not only a great general but also a great humanist, proud of his ability to read and write. Under his orders recensions were made of the legends and traditions of the remote past, and so it was that on December 3, 1872, the Assyriologist George Smith was able proudly to announce that, after sorting the thousands of broken tablets brought from Nineveh to the British Museum, and fitting the fragments together, he had discovered the Babylonian account of the Flood described in the Bible.

MESOPOTAMIAN MUSIC

367 - TELLOH (LAGASH). MUSICIANS WITH A DRUM (22nd CENTURY B.C.). — LOUVRE

MUSIC

Most Biblical scholars hold that the fourth chapter of the Book of Genesis embodies several traditions, originally independent, relating to the early history of mankind. From Cain, according to one tradition, descend the three main orders of men which went to form the nomadic society of those early times: shepherds, smiths and—surprisingly enough—musicians. The Bible even specifies that Jubal was 'the father of all such as handle the harp and organ' (Genesis iv. 21). Particular emphasis, then, is laid on the importance of music, which was evidently regarded not only as a means of expression and a delight to the senses, but also as a communal activity prescribed by religion.

The Gudea texts from Lagash (twenty-second century B.C.) are no doubt the most explicit in this respect. Again and again they remind the worshipper how pleasing to the gods, to Ningirsu especially, are the sacred hymns, the psalms and lamentations chanted by trained singers in accordance with a well-defined liturgy, to the accompaniment of divers instruments: lyres, flutes, cymbals and drums. These were made by expert craftsmen, with loving care, for each had, so to speak, a personality of its own and each was given a name appropriate to its qualities. The lyre deposited in the sanctuary of Ningirsu bore the name of *usum-gal-kala(m)-ma;* it was said to be 'beloved' of the god and to produce 'perfect music.' With his flute, En-lulim the goatherd 'filled with joy the forecourt of the *eninnu.*'

It would be pleasant to be able to record the discovery of a written score, complete with instrumentation, of this ancient music. Several specialists have conjecturally identified musical notation on an Assyrian

← 366 - THE 'STANDARD' OF UR, DETAIL: A MUSICIAN (FIRST HALF, 3rd MILL.). — BRITISH MUSEUM

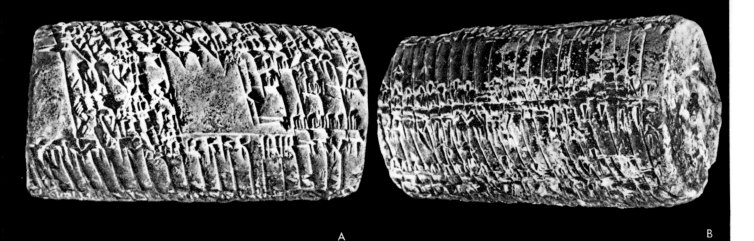

tablet of the ninth century B.C., found at Assur and now in the Berlin Museum.   The cuneiform inscription is engraved in three columns. It has been ascertained that two of them contain a Sumerian hymn with its Assyrian translation; the third column is assumed to provide the music. The same interpretation has been proposed for the inscription on a clay cylinder seal discovered in 1945 at Tell Harmal, near Baghdad. But in both cases these are mere hypotheses, with little to commend them. In actual fact our knowledge of Mesopotamian music is largely derived from the instruments themselves, a few of which have by an extraordinary chance survived virtually intact, and even more from the many representations of musicians in reliefs, inlays and other works of art.

The surviving instruments were found by Sir Leonard Woolley in the 'royal' cemetery of Ur.   They include two harps, four well-preserved lyres and the elements of several others. The most interesting harp (U. 10412) comes from the tomb of 'Queen' Shubad. Its rectangular soundbox was embellished with an edging of mosaic (lapis lazuli, shell and red stone). The front of the soundbox was decorated with four superimposed panels representing mythological scenes, and above these, like a figure-head, projected a calf's head of gold leaf over a wooden core, its hair and beard made of lapis lazuli. There were eleven strings fastened to the upright by gold-headed nails. The second harp (from Tomb 1130) was of a simpler make and had no figure-head. Since fifteen copper nails were found on it, it presumably had fifteen strings.

There is a great variety of lyres. Most famous is the large gold lyre from the 'death-pit' (Tomb 1237). Its soundbox, with a curved hollow in the upper surface, was bordered with a mosaic inlay. The front of the soundbox was decorated with superimposed mosaic panels; above these projected a magnificent bull's head wrought in heavy gold. The number of strings is estimated at eight.

An equally fine instrument is the silver lyre from the same tomb. Its wooden soundbox, entirely covered with thin sheet silver, seems to have been intended to represent an animal's body, in highly stylized form. On the front is a superimposed sequence of small mosaic panels, surmounted by a silver cow's head. There seem to have been eleven strings attached, not directly to the cross-bar, but to loops of some woven fabric (perhaps canvas). Against the cross-bar were found eleven silver-plated rods; by inserting these in the loops and twisting them the pitch of the strings could be adjusted and the instrument tuned.

Very different is the lyre in the form of a high-prowed boat, also from the 'death-pit' (Tomb 1237). It is made of wood overlaid with silver. On the prow is an antlered stag standing on its hind legs. Again there were eleven strings.

The fourth lyre ('Royal' Tomb 1151), made of wood, was almost entirely decayed. But by pouring plaster of Paris into the holes left in the earth by the soundbox and uprights, Woolley succeeded in making a cast of the instrument, reproducing the original with absolute precision. Projecting from the front was a copper cow's head, found intact. Faint imprints of ten strings (possibly eleven) were discernible in the soil.

Other instruments are pictured on various works excavated in the same sector of Ur, and there is

UR (FIRST HALF OF THE THIRD MILLENNIUM).
369 - ELEVEN-STRINGED HARP — BRITISH MUSEUM
370 - LYRE FROM THE DEATH-PIT — PHILADELPHIA
371 - LYRE FROM THE ROYAL TOMB — BAGHDAD

372 - UR. (A) SOUNDBOX PANEL, DETAIL — PHILADELPHIA. (B, C, D) SEAL IMPRESSIONS. BANQUETS AND MUSICIANS — PHILADELPHIA AND BAGHDAD

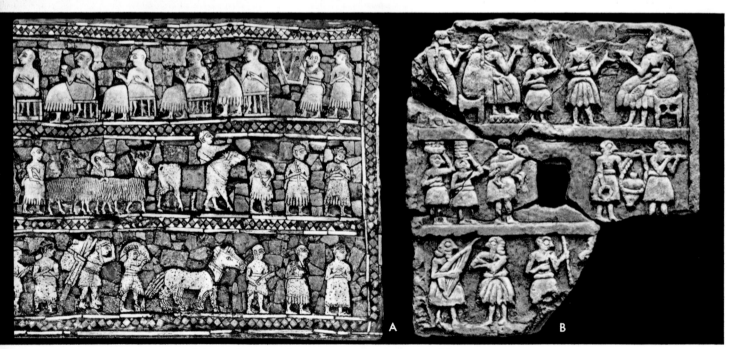

373 - (A) THE 'STANDARD' OF UR — BRITISH MUSEUM   (B) KHAFAJE.   VOTIVE PLAQUE — CHICAGO

374 - ADAB (BISMAYA). PROCESSION WITH TWO HARPISTS (FIRST HALF, 3rd MILL.). — CHICAGO

much to be learned from a study of these representations. On one of the panels decorating the front of the soundbox of a lyre from Tomb 789, we see a donkey playing an eight-stringed lyre whose soundbox represents the body of a recumbent bull with its legs tucked under it. A musician with an eleven-stringed lyre figures on the upper register of the 'Standard' of Ur, on the side representing 'peace.' There are only five strings to the lyre on the cylinder of Dumu-kisal and on the gold cylinder, and only four to the harp on another cylinder seal.

The works from Ur invite comparison with representations of stringed instruments from other sites. First, chronologically speaking, we have a fragment of a vase unearthed at Bismaya and dating to the early third millennium, on which we see a procession of figures with curious headdresses. Two are musicians, each playing a harp with a 'horizontal arc'; the first has seven, the second five strings. This instrument was also known in the Diyala region of Middle Mesopotamia, for we find it pictured on a votive plaque from Khafaje.

301

Another lyre figures on a Gudea stele. The musician is seated behind it and with his right hand plucks the strings (there are eleven of them). Several centuries, then, after the period represented by the 'royal' cemetery of Ur, there still existed an identical type of instrument, with its soundbox adorned in front with a projecting bull's head. Identical except in one particular: here a miniature bull is represented standing on the soundbox. We may hazard the opinion that these animal forms were not merely decorative and that the figure-head—bull, cow, calf or stag —designated the tone of the instrument. Thus, if this interpretation is correct, there are grounds for thinking that, as early as the third millennium B.C., the Sumerians already had a well-developed system of harmony.

A potsherd of the early second millennium which we discovered at Larsa shows a musician seated on a folding stool, behind a large eight-stringed lyre with a rectangular soundbox standing on legs. The sherd, remnant of a large vase, was unfortunately so much disfigured that it is quite impossible to tell whether the musician was a man or a woman (probably a man) or to see how the strings were fastened to the upper cross-bar.

Figurines of the same period, happily quite intact, show us two types of harp. One, with a 'vertical arc,' the seated musician holds in his lap, the strings (seven

302

379 - ASHNUNNAK. HARPIST — LOUVRE   380 - LUTE PLAYER (2nd MILL.). — LOUVRE

in all) well to the fore, the longest being the furthest away. The second, with a 'horizontal arc,' is held between the left arm and the body; the strings (seven in all) lie on a horizontal plane and seem to have been plucked with a plectrum. The instrument could be played either seated or standing, and even by a marching man.

In addition to harps and lyres, we find illustrations of a peculiar type of lute, with a tiny, pear-shaped body and a very long neck. It is always played by a man, who is uniformly represented in the nude, except now and then for a tiny belt. In every case but one he is shown in front view. The single exception is a youth seen in profile, his long hair falling on either side of his right ear, and wearing a narrow belt wrapped four times about his waist. Nudity being the rule in certain rites, we may assume these musicians to be taking part in some religious ceremony and chanting the liturgy to their own accompaniment.

303

The function of music was primarily a religious one—that is the inference to be drawn from these works. But it had its secular uses too, as in the banquet scene on the Standard of Ur marking the victorious conclusion of a military campaign.   Here, holding a lyre with both hands, a man is accompanying a woman singing behind him with her hands crossed on her breast.   That women musicians, who also sang and danced, existed as early as the first half of the third millennium is shown by the small statue of Ur-Nina, 'The Great Singer,' discovered at Mari. Besides the complete statue, we found in the same sanctuary, dedicated by the same woman, another piece of sculpture sadly damaged, unfortunately; there only remain the torso and parts of a hand holding a musical instrument. Ur-Nina, then, played, sang and danced, no doubt with equal proficiency and to the entire satisfaction of her sovereign, Iblul-il, to whom she dedicated these statues. Did she perform in a temple or in the palace? Probably in both, for she was doubtless equally adept in sacred and in profane music.

Presumably we have a scene with religious music on the votive plaque from Khafaje, generally believed (though this is far from certain) to illustrate the New Year celebrations.   Beside a harpist stands a bearded, long-haired singer with his arms crossed on his chest.

After these performances of 'chamber music' involving one or two musicians, we may turn to the instrumental ensembles that sometimes amounted to small orchestras. These often figure in Assyrian times (in the first millennium B.C.), but what comes as a genuine surprise is to find them represented some twenty centuries earlier. Here, to lyres and harps are added percussion instruments, beginning with the most natural form of percussion: the clapping of hands to mark the tempo of the music. This elementary method of beating time was elaborated by the introduction of cymbals. All this is illustrated on several cylinder seals from Ur. Various combinations are shown: here a harpist and two singers clapping their hands; there a lyre player, two cymbalists and a singer; elsewhere a small orchestra complete with a conductor, with his baton on his shoulder, and six performers, all women: a lyre player, two cymbalists and three singers. In all three instances the musicians are entertaining at a banquet. Whether a sacred symposium or a convivial gathering is hard to say; it could be either.

Again we have an orchestra, but a very unusual one, represented on the front of a lyre from Ur. Here we are plunged into a frankly grotesque world of myth and legend. Disposed on four registers, these scenes are easier to describe than to interpret: scanning from top to bottom, we first have Gilgamesh gripping two human-headed bulls; a dog and a lion acting as butler and cup-bearer; then the orchestra with which we are now concerned; then a scorpion man followed by a gazelle walking on its hind legs, holding a goblet with each paw. In these surroundings the orchestra is quite in keeping, since it consists of a donkey sitting on its haunches, gravely strumming an eight-stringed lyre; a seated jackal shaking a sistrum with its right paw and beating a tabor with its left; and a bear who seems to be setting the tempo and dancing as well.

An equally intriguing scene from Ur is the serenade given by a procession of music-making equidae, brandishing harps and clappers with their forepaws. Later, at the end of the second or the beginning of the first millennium, even larger 'animal orchestras' are represented on two stone slabs from the palace of Kapara at Tell Halaf. A wild saraband is in full swing; it is as if the animals (bear, donkey, jackal and lion) had purloined the instruments of a real orchestra and were parodying the movements of human beings.

382 - UR. SEAL IMPRESSIONS. BANQUETS AND MUSICAL PERFORMANCES (FIRST HALF, THIRD MILLENNIUM).

Although both animals and instruments are badly defaced, lyres and tabors are still clearly recognizable.

Cymbals were not the only percussion instruments in use. Drums of different kinds are often represented. They vary greatly in size, ranging from the large 'bass drum' to a small tabor or timbrel held by a woman with both hands. Countless numbers of small figure-plaques of the time of Gudea or the Third Dynasty of Ur popularized the latter theme, featuring a female musician, no doubt a temple slave or hierodule, with no attempt at all to veil her physical charms. The 'bass drums' pictured on a vase from Telloh (?), on a stele from Telloh and on the stele of Ur-Nammu from Ur must have measured over three feet in diameter. The parchment stretched over the circular frame was fastened to the rim with huge nails, which also served to strengthen the frame, for the drum could only be moved by rolling it. Two drummers were required for the instrument to produce its full effect. On the Telloh vase is an enigmatic detail: the big drum is surmounted by a human form with the head of an animal. Why this musician should be a hybrid being has never been satisfactorily explained.

Last of the percussion group we have a sort of rattle. Made of hard-baked clay, it contained clay pellets, which clattered when the container was shaken. But this may have been only a child's toy.

306

387 - LARSA. MONKEY PLAYING THE FLUTE — LOUVRE   388 - LARSA. WOMAN WITH PAN-PIPE — LOUVRE

By the early third millennium wind instruments were also in use among the Mesopotamians. On a cylinder seal found by Woolley in the 'royal' cemetery of Ur, we see a monkey playing a long flute in the shade of a tree, surrounded by other animals. The tradition of a flute-playing monkey, whether with a single- or a double-piped instrument, persisted for a long time, for at Larsa we discovered a figurine representing exactly the same theme. Actual flutes have been found at Ur with four equidistant finger-holes in the silver tubing. It was certainly not until much later, doubtless in the Seleucid period, that the pan-pipe made its appearance; such, anyhow, was the case at Larsa. This instrument is like a mouth-organ, whose pipes, though externally of the same length, are actually stopped inside at different lengths so as to change the pitch of the notes. On the small Larsa plaque we see a woman playing this instrument, thus giving the earliest known demonstration of a method of music-making destined to have remarkable developments in succeeding ages.

389 - MARI. WALL PAINTING IN THE PALACE. HORN PLAYER (18th CENTURY B.C.).

There may be mention of the trumpet in Sumerian texts, but the exact meaning of the term used remains conjectural. In a wall painting in the palace of Mari, we see a horn held in a curious position between the thumb and fingers of the right hand by a bearded man with long hair. Here, also, it must be admitted, there is an element of doubt: is this really the musical instrument subsequently known to the Israelites as a *shofar*, or only a receptacle for some holy oil?

From the Ishtar temple at Mari comes a more positive piece of evidence. A statuette found in the outhouses of the sanctuary represents a pair of musicians, their heads covered with a low, frizzled wig or toque. Their faces are so thoroughly comic that one might easily take them for clowns. But they are definitely playing the horn, and we are probably justified in regarding them as musicians attached to the temple staff. As a work of art, this statuette has nothing to commend it; its value lies in the fact that it proves the horn to have been in existence as early as the first half of the third millennium B.C.

The foregoing remarks sum up our knowledge of the instruments in use and the place occupied by music in Mesopotamia from the earliest times to the beginning of the second millennium B.C. It played a large part in daily life, in the home and above all in the temples. No religious ceremony was complete without musical accompaniment and, as we have seen, a great variety of instruments was employed.

390 - MARI. TWO HORN-PLAYERS — LOUVRE →

391 - NINEVEH. RELIEF. FOUR MUSICIANS (7th CENT. B.C.). — LOUVRE

Coming down to later times, we find that music has lost none of its popularity. If anything, its scope has been extended. The Assyrian kings, as was to be expected, were quick to see the purpose it might serve in warfare and employed it to stimulate the ardour of their soldiers. Here, at a far remove, we have the origin of our military bands.

A relief from Nineveh, dating to the time of Assurbanipal (seventh century B.C.), leaves no room for doubt. Between a register of foot-soldiers evidently singing (since they are clapping their hands in time) as they file past and a scene of horsemen and archers engaged in battle, the intermediate register shows a groom leading four restive, unharnessed horses and behind him four musicians, facing each other two by two. Their postures make it clear that they are on the move, pacing back and forth alternately. Two men on one side are playing a tabor and a lyre (or perhaps a psaltery); those on the other have cymbals and an eight-stringed lyre.

392 - NINEVEH. RELIEF. MILITARY BAND (7th CENTURY B.C.). — BRITISH MUSEUM

From the same period dates a large sculptured slab commemorating Assurbanipal's victory over the Elamite king Teuman. Musicians followed by women and children clapping their hands are celebrating the accession to the throne of Ummanigash, a refugee Elamite prince. Well in view are seven harpists, two double-pipe players and a man with a tabor.

393 - NINEVEH. CAPTURED MUSICIANS (7th CENT. B.C.). — BRITISH MUSEUM

A temple in conquered territory—perhaps in Judea, judging by figures and dress similar to those of the inhabitants of Lachish as pictured on the famous stele of Sennacherib —also had musicians attached to it. We see three lyre players being led into captivity by an Assyrian soldier. Whatever their real feelings may be, they are compelled to strike up a tune as they go. Later, the exiled Jews were asked to play and sing for their captors, but they refused. 'By the rivers of Babylon, there we sat down, yea, we wept, when we remembered Zion. We hanged our harps upon the willows in the midst thereof. For there they that carried us away captive required of us a song; and they that wasted us required of us mirth, saying, Sing us one of the songs of Zion. How shall we sing the Lord's song in a strange land?' (Psalm cxxxvii. 1-4). The three musicians on the Nineveh slab evidently thought it safest to comply with the conqueror's whim.

But even with the Assyrians music was by no means confined to the battlefield. Harpists, flutists and lyre players figure on the walls both of Assurnasirpal's palace at Nimrud and of Sennacherib's palace at

394 - KALAKH (NIMRUD). PYX, RECONSTRUCTION. BANQUET SCENE (9th CENTURY B.C.). — BRITISH MUSEUM

395 - KALAKH (NIMRUD). PYX, DETAIL. MUSICIANS (9th CENTURY B.C.). — BRITISH MUSEUM

Nineveh. Then, too, there is the famous scene of the 'Feast in a Garden,' where we see Assurbanipal giving the queen an account of his Elamite campaign, while a harpist makes music in the shade of a tree from which hangs the head of Teuman, the defeated king of Elam. Elsewhere, returning from a successful hunting expedition, the Assyrian monarch pours a libation over the dead animals, to a musical accompaniment.

Several ivory pyxes discovered at Nimrud by W.K. Loftus throw further light on the music of ancient Mesopotamia. One of them is decorated with a banquet scene. Seated on a throne is a woman —perhaps a goddess but more probably, in our opinion, a princess. With a cup in her hand, she is about to do honour to the dishes set before her on a high pedestal table. Behind her are five young musicians, two playing the double pipes, two the psaltery and one the tabor. Here, then, once again we have a small orchestra composed of all three families of instruments (winds, percussion and strings) described above.

Thus, alongside sculptors, painters and builders, men of letters and musicians contributed much to the multiform achievements of ancient Mesopotamian civilization. And we of today, in retrieving and appraising the cultural legacy of these men of three, four and even five millennia ago, have found that in all its manifestations it still retains that power of suggestion which is the hallmark of imperishable works—of works that are, above all, a 'dialogue with the invisible.'

PART THREE

GLOSSARIAL INDEX

Each work reproduced is listed under the place where it was discovered. Items marked with an asterisk are commented on in separate entries under the corresponding letter of the alphabet.

ABDIMILKUTTI — King of Sidon, represented on the stelae of Esarhaddon* found at Zinjirli and Tell Ahmar . . . . *p.* 35
— Held in leash by Esarhaddon . . . *fig.* 39*c*, 86

ABEL — Son of Adam . . . . *p.* 281

ABU HABBA (SIPPAR) — Akkadian city, with temple of Shamash. Excavated by Rassam (1879-82), Scheil (1894), and Jordan and Andrae (1927). Famous monument: tablet of Nabu-apal-iddin (British Museum). The stele with the Code of Hammurabi may have been erected here . . . . *p.* 168, 182
Sculpture:
— Tablet of Nabu-apal-iddin* . . . *fig.* 213, 215

ABU SHAHREIN (ERIDU) — City in southern Mesopotamia, centre of the cult of Enki-Ea, god of subterranean waters. Excavations have revealed here a phase of Mesopotamian protohistory preceding the al 'Ubaid period. *p.* 220, 223, 240, 241, 259
Male figurine . . . . *fig.* 309*b*
Painted pottery . . . . *fig.* 296

ABYSSINIA — Present-day Ethiopia . . . *p.* 255

ACHAEMENIDS — Persian dynasty, of which Cyrus (546 B.C.) was the first king to reign over the whole country. Ends in 330 B.C. with the death of Darius III Codomannus. . . *p.* 128, 142, 182, 189, 190, 194, 196, 197, 200, 201, 202, 204, 218, 223, 243

ADAD — Akkadian storm god, known as Hadad in Syria, Phœnicia and Canaan . . *p.* 4, 9, 35, 71, 76, 78, 170
— With thunderbolt, standing on a bull . . *fig.* 84

ADAD-NIRARI III — Assyrian king (809-782 B.C.). *p.* 20, 22, 35
— Statue of Nabu* dedicated by Bel-tarsi-iluma* for the life of Adad-Ninari and Sammuramat*. *fig.* 24

ADAPA — In Sumerian mythology . . . . *p.* 288

ADZE — Iron axe with arched blade . . . *fig.* 290
— Warrior with an adze . . . . . *fig.* 313, 325

AENEOLITHIC AGE — Early cultural phase characterized by the simultaneous use of metal (copper) and stone. Also known as the Chalcolithic Age. *p.* 232

AGATE — A form of variegated chalcedony, the colours veined in stripes or cloudy streaks.

AHURA MAZDA — In the Achaemenian religion the supreme god, creator of heaven and earth, by whose grace kings reign on earth. Represented half-length, emerging from a rayed disk. *p.* 196, 200, 201, *fig.* 264

AI-IBUR-SHABU — Name of the Processional Way at Babylon, leading from the Ishtar Gate to the temple of Marduk . *p.* 172, 174, 226, 229, *fig.* 220

AKKAD — An ancient city (perhaps Deir) and State. Its first king was Sargon (25th century B.C.), whose dynasty ended in the 23rd century B.C. The name 'Agade' is also used to designate the city, the kingdom or the dynasty . . . . *p.* 1, 182, 241

AKKADIANS — Name applied to the kings of the Semite dynasty founded by Sargon or to the inhabitants of their kingdom . . . . *p.* 1

ALABASTER — Calcareous or gypseous stone, sometimes translucent, taking a high polish, in which the Mesopotamians carved their most precious statuettes . . . . *e.g. fig.* 60
— Black alabaster . . . . *e.g. fig.* 40 *b*
— Gypseous alabaster . . . . *e.g. fig.* 15

ALAJA HÜYÜK — Ancient city in Anatolia, northeast of Boghazkeuy, where tombs filled with very fine grave furniture have been discovered (mid-3rd millennium B.C.) . . . . *p.* 138

ALEXANDER THE GREAT (356-323 B.C.) — King of Macedon and conqueror of Western Asia. Died at Babylon . . . . *p.* 189, 200, 206, 210

AL'OHEIMIR (KISH) — Sumerian city, seat of several dynasties (I-IV), north-east of Babylon. Excavated from 1912 on (Genouillac), then from 1923 to 1933 (Joint Expedition). *p.* 221, 222, 251, 253, 280
— Plano-convex bricks . . . . *fig.* 270

ALTAR — Architectural element made of baked or unbaked bricks, occasionally of stone. Its position varies; in Neo-Babylonian temples it was located in the court, opposite the door to the cella. . . *p.* 4

ALTMAN (C) — Gordon Loud's associate in the Khorsabad excavations from 1933 on.
— Reconstruction by Altman . . . . . *fig.* 11, 12

AL'UBAID — Small site near Ur, excavated in 1919, which gave its name to a phase of Mesopotamian protohistory between the Halaf and Uruk periods (4th millennium B.C.) . *p.* 83, 223-225, 233, 235, 240, 241, 247, 248, 251
— Dairy scene. . . . . *fig.* 277
— Nail-head with flower pattern . . . . *fig.* 278

AMANUS — Mountain range north of Antioch dominating the Cilician plain. Its forests provided the Mesopotamians with timber. An episode of the Gilgamesh* Epic is located there . . . . *p.* 221

AMMIDITANA — Early Sumerian king. . *p.* 288

AMYITIS — Daughter of Astyages, king of the Medes, and wife of Nebuchadnezzar, king of Babylon, who built the Hanging Gardens of Babylon for her. *p.* 176

ANATOLIA — Central province of Asia Minor. *p.* 1, 221, 223

ANDRAE (Walter) (1875-1956) — Famous German architect and archaeologist, disciple of R. Koldewey and excavator of Assur (1903-14) . . . . . *p.* 74

ANIMAL MUSICIANS . . . . *fig.* 322

ANIMAL ORCHESTRA — Theme of Mesopotamian iconography, on the soundbox of a lyre from Ur (Tomb 789) and on a relief from Tell Halaf. *p.* 91, 305, *fig.* 100

ANNALS OF THE ASSYRIAN KINGS — Official accounts of the exploits, chiefly military campaigns, of the Assyrian kings . . . . *p.* 6

ANTELOPES — Frequently represented, notably in hunting scenes with Gilgamesh* and Enkidu*.
p. 117, 133, 154, 156, *fig.* 258

ANTIMONY — Bluish white metal, hard and brittle.
p. 232

ANTITHETICAL ANIMALS — Frequent theme in Mesopotamian iconography: two animals facing each other on either side of a central motif.
p. 130, 139, 149, 203

ANU — Supreme god of the Mesopotamian pantheon. Temple at Uruk . . . . *p.* 288, 290

ANUBIS — Egyptian god of the dead, with the head of a jackal . . . . *p.* 154

ANZAN — Iranian city north-west of Susa. It figures in royal titles . . . . *p.* 182

APKALLU — Genii or spirits of various kinds, by which the Assyrians believed men to be continually surrounded . . . . *p.* 250

APSU — Underground body of fresh water, domain of Enki-Ea . . . . *p.* 169

AQAR QUF (DUR KURIGALZU) — Site of the ancient Kassite capital, west of Baghdad. Excavated by the Iraqi Department of Antiquities (1942-45).
p. 218, 261
Painting:
— Procession of dignitaries . . . . . . *fig.* 335

AQUEDUCT OF JERWAN* — Built by Sennacherib* (704-681 B.C.) to supply Nineveh with water.
p. 229, *fig.* 284

ARABAH — Jordanian region extending south from the Dead Sea to the Gulf of Aqaba . . . *p.* 232

ARABIA — The region, largely desert, lying south of Syria and Mesopotamia, between the Red Sea (on the west), the Persian Gulf and the Gulf of Oman (on the east) . . . . *p.* 3, 230, 234

ARBELA (ERBIL) — Assyrian city . . . . *p.* 206

ARCHER — Represented on painted pottery from Susa.
fig. 99a, 338
— Archer shooting a bull . . . . *fig.* 193
— Archer shooting at a Sphinx . . . . . *fig.* 196
— Archer shooting a winged quadruped . *fig.* 232

ARCHERS (ACHAEMENIAN) — Represented on stone reliefs (Persepolis) and on glazed brick panels in relief (Susa). Louvre. *p.* 199, 201, 210, 226, *fig.* 247

ARMENIA — Mountainous region to the north of Mesopotamia, known to the ancients as Urartu.
p. 3, 112, 232, 234, 245

ARPATCHIYA — Small site near Nineveh excavated by Mallowan in 1933. Revealed evidence of several protohistoric cultures (Samarra, Halaf, 'Ubaid). Ancient name unidentified . . . *p.* 239, 241, 247
Pottery:
— Dish with Maltese Cross . . . . . . *fig.* 295a
— Dish with rosette, dotted with small crosses.
fig. 295b

ARSLAN TASH (HADATU) — Site in Upper Syria excavated by the Thureau-Dangin expedition in 1928. Reliefs, statues and a magnificent collection of ivories discovered there (Louvre and Aleppo Museum).
p. 22, 76, 124, 144, 148, 154, 256
Sculpture:
— Adad* with lightning-fork, standing on a bull.
fig. 84
— Bull passant . . . . *fig.* 88
— Cow suckling its calf . . . . *fig.* 181
— Genius* with a box . . . . . . *fig.* 27a-b-c, 28
— Guardian lion . . . . *fig.* 33
— Winged ram-headed sphinxes . . . . *fig.* 326

ARTAXERXES I — Achaemenian king (465-424 B.C.), son of Xerxes I . . . . *p.* 190, 193, 210

ARTAXERXES II MNEMON — Achaemenian king (405-358 B.C.), successor of Darius II.
p. 190, 198, 210

ASHNUNNAK, see TELL ASMAR.

ASHTAMAKU — King of Syria
— Captured by Shalmaneser III . . *fig.* 123, 124

ASSUR (City), see QALAAT SHERGAT.

ASSUR (God) — Supplanted Enlil as 'lord' of the city of Assur. Supreme god of the Assyrian pantheon.
p. 4, 8, 11, 35, 71, 74, 99, 226, 294
— In the 'aura' . . . . *fig.* 282
— Standing on animal attribute (with Sennacherib* adoring him) . . . . *fig.* 81
— Surrounded by scorpion-men . . . *fig.* 214
Well of the temple of the god Assur:
— Ritual basin adorned with gods with the flowing vase and genii with the situla (found in the well).
fig. 82, 83

ASSURBANIPAL — King of Assyria (668-631 B.C.), famous for his palace and library discovered at Nineveh by Layard, Rassam and Loftus. Immortalized by the Lion Hunt and Feast in a Garden reliefs (British Museum) *p.* 3, 24, 35, 42, 43, 52, 60, 80, 100, 116, 146, 150, 179, 198, 267, 280, 286, 292, 294, 310-312
— As a basket bearer . . . . *fig.* 40a
— 'Feast in a Garden' . . . . *fig.* 60
— Lion-hunt . . . . *fig.* 63, 65, 68
— Making a libation on dead lions . . . *fig.* 76

ASSURBANIPAL (CAMPAIGNS OF) — Townsfolk led into captivity . . . . *fig.* 53, 54, 56

ASSURBELKALA — King of Assyria
— Female statue inscribed in his name . . . *fig.* 26

ASSURDAN — Name of three Assyrian kings. The headless statuette inscribed with this name probably represents King Assurdan II (993-912 B.C.).
p. 119, *fig.* 134a-b

ASSURNASIRPAL I — Assyrian king (1049-1031 B.C.).
p. 35

ASS

ASSURNASIRPAL II — Assyrian king (883-859 B.C.) who embellished Kalakh (Nimrud). Palace containing reliefs (British Museum, Louvre, Baghdad Museum) and precious objects (ivories, British Museum and Baghdad Museum). Stone statue (British Museum) . *p.* 3, 9, 13-15, 34-36, 42, 54, 71, 112, 142, 146, 149, 150, 179, *fig.* 22, 23, 41, 42, 183, 312
— Bull-hunting . . . . *fig.* 62
— Lion-hunting . . . . *fig.* 64
— Stele of Assurnasirpal II . . . . . *fig.* 14, 39a
— Waging war . . . . *fig.* 18

ASSURSHARRAT — Wife of Assurbanipal. Represented in the 'Feast in a Garden' (British Museum) and on the fragment of a stele from Assur (Berlin Museum) . . . . *p.* 52, 150

ASSYRIA — Region of the Upper Tigris, several cities of which were great cultural centres: Assur (Qalaat Shergat), Kalakh (Nimrud), Nineveh (Kuyunjik), Dur Sharrukin (Khorsabad).
p. 1, 2, 6, 138, 142, 144, 242

ASSYRIANS. . *p.* 1-4, 12, 30, 100, 112, 127, 144, 148, 150, 160, 164, 167, 190, 200, 203, 207, 242, 243, 250, 262

ASTYAGES — King of the Medes. His daughter Amyitis was Nebuchadnezzar's wife . . . *p.* 176

ATHENS — Taken and devastated by the army of Xerxes (480 B.C.). . . . . *p.* 180

ATRAHASIS — Sage in Sumerian mythology . *p.* 288

AURA — Subtle emanation given off by divine beings
— Assur shooting an arrow in the aura . . . *fig.* 282

AXE — Teshub brandishing thunderbolt and axe.
fig. 87, 89

BAAL — Collective name of the Canaanite gods in the Old Testament. May, however, have been applied to a specific god. . . . . *p.* 78

BABEL (TOWER OF) — In Genesis xi. 1-9. Identifiable with one of the ziggurats of Babylonia, perhaps with that of Babylon itself . . *p.* 11, 176, 228

BABYLON — Great capital city in the heart of Mesopotamia, on the Euphrates, some 50 miles south of Baghdad. Mentioned as early as the 24th century B.C. Particularly prosperous under Hammurabi (1792-1750) and later under the Neo-Babylonians (626-538). Its last king, Nabonidus, was defeated by Cyrus the Persian. According to the judicious chronology of S. Smith and Ungnad, which we have adopted here, the 'dynasty of Babylon' lasted from 1894 to 1595 B.C. *p.* 1, 3, 4, 9, 11, 103, 127, 167, 168, 170, 172, 174, 178, 179, 181, 182, 186, 189, 190, 197, 198, 203, 206, 210, 221, 226, 250, 251, 286
Architecture:
— City and ziggurat (plan). . . . . *fig.* 218, 219
— Palace (plan) . . . . *fig.* 223, 246a
— Temple of Ishtar* (plan). . . . . . *fig.* 225
Sculpture:
— Assurbanipal* as a basket-bearer . . . *fig.* 40a
Cylinder seal:
— Figure (priest?) approaching a ziggurat . *fig.* 6

BAL

BABYLON (BASALT LION) — Discovered in the *Hauptburg.* Dating and interpretation remain controversial. . . . . *fig.* 226

BABYLON (BULLS) — Represented in glazed brick on the Ishtar Gate. Animal attribute of Adad.
fig. 221c

BABYLON (DRAGONS) — Represented in glazed brick on the Ishtar Gate. Animal attribute of Marduk, the city-god. . . . . *fig.* 221b

BABYLON (HANGING GARDENS) — Built by Nebuchadnezzar for his wife Amyitis. Located at the north-east corner of the *Südburg.*
p. 176, 186, *fig.* 220

BABYLON (ISHTAR GATE) — Defensive works, of the Neo-Babylonian period, on the north side of the city. Decorated with 575 dragons and bulls.
p. 172, 176, 186, 198, 221, 226, 229, *fig.* 220, *p.* 172, 176, 186, 198, 221, 226, 229, *fig.* 220, 222

BABYLON (PROCESSIONNAL WAY) — See AI-IBUR-SHABU.

BABYLON (THRONE ROOM, so-called) — In the *Südburg,* opening on the third inner court.
p. 176, *fig.* 224

BABYLON (ZIGGURAT) — Seven-staged tower with *Esagila,* temple of Marduk, called *E-temen-an-ki* (house of the foundation of heaven and earth). Over 300 feet high. Prototype of the Tower of Babel (Genesis xi) . *p.* 172, 186, 221, 228, 229, *fig.* 218, 220, 283

BABYLONIA — Strictly speaking, the region in the immediate neighbourhood of Babylon, but often used to designate a large part of central and southern Mesopotamia . . . . *p.* 112, 198, 210

BABYLONIANS — Inhabitants of the Babylon region. Sometimes used, by extension, to designate the inhabitants of a much wider area, embracing central and southern Mesopotamia. Some archaeologists therefore speak, for example, of an 'Assyro-Babylonian' civilization. . . . . . *p.* 167, 168, 176, 178, 186

BAKING OF BREAD . . . . *fig.* 144

BALAWAT (IMGUR BEL) — Site east of Mosul, excavated by Rassam (1882) and Mallowan (1956) who discovered remains of a palace and a temple to the god Mahir built by Shalmaneser III and Assurnasirpal II. The most sensational find was the 'bronze doors' decorated with reliefs illustrating the campaigns of Shalmaneser III and Assurnasirpal II.
p. 13, 112, 116, 235
Reliefs ('bronze doors'):
— Baking bread . . . . *fig.* 144
— Boats with tribute from Tyre. . . . *fig.* 122
— Carrying off war booty . . . . . *fig.* 139, 145
— Capture of Ashtamaku* . . . . . *fig.* 123, 124
— Cities on fire and trees felled. . . . *fig.* 140
— City of Khazunu on fire. . . . . . *fig.* 141
— Dedication of a stele. . . . . . *fig.* 138, 143
— Invalid king of Hama surrendering.
fig. 121, 126, 129
— Massacre of prisoners . . . . *fig.* 142
— Prisoners impaled . . . . *fig.* 125
— Prisoners led out of Sugunia* . . . . *fig.* 146
— Siege of Dabigu* . . . . . . *fig.* 127, 128, 145

BAND (MILITARY) — Its origins in Assyria.
p. 310, fig. 392

BARNETT (R.D.) — English Assyriologist, curator of Department of Western Asiatic Antiquities at the British Museum. . . . . p. 119

BARREKUB — Aramaean king residing at Zinjirli (8th century B.C.) . . . . p. 146

BASALT — Dark grey stone of volcanic origin, sometimes imported and used by Mesopotamian sculptors.
e.g. fig. 87

BASIN (RITUAL) — Found at Assur. . fig. 82, 83

BASKET-BEARER — Assurbanipal* as a basket-bearer . . . . fig. 40a

BASRA — City of modern Iraq, on the Shatt el-Arab (mouth of the Tigris and Euphrates). . . p. 172

BASS DRUM — Ancient Mesopotamian musical instrument. . . . . p. 306, fig. 385

BATTLE-AXE — Among the Luristan bronzes.
p. 134
— Axe with a lion rampant. . . . . . . fig. 155
— Ceremonial axe . . . . fig. 163
— Decorated socket . . . . fig. 164-166

BAVIAN — Site some 30 miles north-east of Nineveh, famous for its rock reliefs . . . . . p. 71, 229
Sculpture:
— Relief of Sennacherib* (adoring the god Assur*).
fig. 81

BEHISTUN — Village in the Zagros range (Persia) where Darius I* had a great cuneiform inscription engraved in three languages; it was copied and deciphered by Sir Henry Rawlinson (1835-45). p. 280

BEL — In Isaiah xlvi. 1, where it designates Marduk*.
p. 76

BEL-TARSI-ILUMA — Governor of Kalakh (Nimrud) who dedicated four statues 'for the life of' Adad-Nirari III (809-782 B.C.) . . . . p. 20
— Statue of Nabu* dedicated by Bel-tarsi-iluma 'for the life of' Adad-Nirari and Sammuramat* . fig. 24

BELT PLAQUES — From Luristan, often decorated with hunting scenes. Fine specimen in the Louvre.
p. 128, 133, fig. 159

BIBLE . . . . p. 6, 221, 258, 294

BIRD. . . . . p. 96, 119
— Bird of prey on a capital . . . . . . fig. 105
— Hero fighting three birds . . . . . fig. 228

BIRD (RED) — Of the Han dynasty (China), compared with Luristan ibexes. . . . . p. 134, fig. 160

BIREJIK — Turkish city on the Upper Euphrates (left bank) . . . . p. 230

BIRS NIMRUD (BORSIPPA) — Ancient site near Babylon, excavated by Koldewey in 1902. The god Nabu was worshipped there in the temple called *Ezida* . . . . p. 178, 226

BISMAYA (ADAB) — Site south-east of Nippur.
— Vase with musicians in a procession.
p. 301, fig. 374

BIT HILANI — Type of building of Anatolian or North Syrian origin, used by the Assyrian kings in their palaces, in imitation of the buildings they saw in the course of their campaigns abroad . . . fig. 276

BITS — A great many of the Luristan bronzes are horses' bits, patterned with real or imaginary animals.
p. 128, 129, 164, fig. 148-150

BITUMEN — Black hydrocarbon, found on the Middle Euphrates and Upper Tigris, much employed by the Mesopotamians in architecture, sculpture, implements, sumptuary arts, etc.

BOAR — Represented on a bronze belt plaque from Luristan (Louvre) . . . . p. 133

BOOKS OF WISDOM—In Sumerian literature. p. 290

BOOK OF PROVERBS — In Sumerian literature.
p. 284, 290

BOOMERANG . . . . p. 88, 92
— Teshub* brandishing mace and boomerang.
fig. 98b

BORSIPPA, see BIRS NIMRUD.

BOTTA (Paul-Emile) (1802-70) — French consul at Mosul, who discovered and excavated Khorsabad in 1843-44 . . . . p. 251

BOUNDARY STONES, see KUDURRUS.

BOW — Symbol of victory or fighting.
— Assurnasirpal* holding a bow . . . . fig. 42
— Hunting with bow and arrows . . . . fig. 66

BOXES decorated with ivories . . . . . . fig. 27

BRAIDS — Oriental motif possibly symbolizing water.
p. 95, 148, 149

BRANCH (FLOWERING) . . . . p. 6

BRAZEN SEA — Large tank of bronze in the temple of Solomon at Jerusalem (I Kings vii. 23-26). Perhaps a symbolic reminiscence of the *apsu* . . . . p. 203

BREAD-MAKING . . . . fig. 144

BRICK (BAKED) — Clay moulded into blocks, fired in kilns and used as building material. . . . p. 218
— With a thumb-print (Ur-Nanshe). . . p. 219
— With a thumb- and a finger-print (Eannatum).
p. 219
— With one or more fingerprints (Entemena).
p. 219

BRICK (GLAZED) — Used for decorative work, either flat or moulded in relief. First appears in the Assyrian period. Very popular with the Neo-Babylonians and Achaemenians p. 8, 98, 198, e.g. fig. 247

BRICK (PLANO-CONVEX) — A type of baked or unbaked brick flat on one side, curved on the other. Building material characteristic of the Early Dynastic* or Pre-Sargonid* period in Sumer.
p. 218, 219, e.g. fig. 270

BRICK (UNBAKED) — Clay moulded into blocks and sun-dried, used as building material. . . p. 218

BRONZE — Alloy of copper and tin, much used from the early 3rd millennium on. . . . . *p.* 232, 233

BRONZE DOORS — Discovered by Rassam (1882) and Mallowan (1956) at Balawat (Imgur Bel); the work of Assurnasirpal II (883-859 B.C.) and Shalmaneser III (858-824 B.C.). Baghdad Museum, Louvre, British Museum. . . . . *p.* 112, 235, 258

BUCK — Animal represented on a bronze belt plaque from Luristan . . . . *p.* 133

BULL *p.* 120, 133, 141, 150, 156, 158, 225, 226, 302
— Adad* holding a thunderbolt, standing on a bull.
fig. 84
— Bull attacked by a lion . . . . *fig.* 328a
— Bull-hunt . . . . *fig.* 62, 97a, 177a, 193
— Bull passant. . . . . *fig.* 88, 184, 258
— Bull's head . . . . *fig.* 136, 137
— Lion attacking a bull . . . . *fig.* 201
— Teshub brandishing thunderbolt and axe, standing on a bull . . . . *fig.* 89
— Winged bull with female bust . . *fig.* 119, 192

BULL (FIVE-LEGGED) — Conventional characteristic of Assyrian bulls guarding the palaces. . *p.* 14

BULL (HUMAN-HEADED) — Often represented in seals, reliefs, statuettes, apparently symbolizing a beneficent power under constant attack from an evil one (lion-headed eagle). *p.* 30, 70, 141, 142, 168, 192, 198, 201, 203, 230, *fig.* 215, 285

BULL (WINGED HUMAN-HEADED) — Guardian animal at the gates of Assyrian palaces (Kalakh, Nineveh, Dur Sharrukin) *p.* 9, 27, 71, 88, 101, 119, 207, 231, *fig.* 2, 30, 32, 34a-b, 35, 37, 98c, 110

BULLS (CONFRONTED) — A frequent theme in Assyrian wall painting . . . . . *p.* 99, *fig.* 108

BURIAL RITES — From clay coffins to royal hypogea. *p.* 244, 245

BURNEY PLAQUE — Terracotta plaque representing a naked, winged goddess with lions and owls. *p.* 250, *fig.* 358

BUR-SIN — King of the First Dynasty of Isin (20th century B.C.) and of the Third Dynasty of Ur (21st century B.C.). . . . . *p.* 221, 244

BUSINK (T.A.) — Dutch architect who has made a special study of ziggurats . . . . *p.* 11
— Ziggurat of Dur Sharrukin (elevation according to Busink). . . . . *fig.* 13b

CAIN — Son of Adam. . . . . . . *p.* 281, 297

CAMBYSES — Achaemenian king (528-522 B.C.), son of Cyrus. . . . . *p.* 189

CAMPS — Representation of Assyrian military camps in the field, on several reliefs (British Museum, Berlin Museum) . . . . *p.* 48
— Camp scene (interior of a tent). . . . *fig.* 58

CAPITAL (ACHAEMENIAN) — Composed of foreparts of two animals back to back (bulls, lions, horses). Capital from Susa in the Louvre.
p. 120, 193, 198, 204, *fig.* 136

CAPTIVITY (TOWNSFOLK LED INTO).
p. 44, *fig.* 53-56, 59

CARCHEMISH — Hittite city and kingdom of the first millennium B.C. (now in Turkey) *p.* 112, 154

CARNELIAN — A reddish variety of chalcedony, imported into Mesopotamia from the land of Meluhha (Arabia).

CASTING TECHNIQUES — In an open or a closed mould and by the *cire-perdue* process. . . *p.* 232, 233

CAUCASUS — Mountain range between the Black and the Caspian Sea, rich in mineral deposits.
p. 234

CAVALRY — Formed an important part of the Assyrian military forces. . . . . *p.* 46
Painting:
— Galloping horseman . . . . *fig.* 339

CAVRO (Lucien) — French architect-draughtsman who made copies of the Til Barsip wall paintings *p.* 100, 262

CEDAR FORESTS — Famous cedar forests of Lebanon and the Amanus range, where Solomon and the Assyrian kings got the timber needed for their buildings (temple of Jerusalem, palaces on the banks of the Tigris) . . . . *p.* 146, 176, 192, 194

CELLA — The innermost sanctuary of the temple, the Holy of Holies, where the god resided and his statue stood, often surrounded by ex-votos . . . *p.* 178

CENTAUR
— Centaur against a lion. . . . . *fig.* 199
— Winged centaur against a lion . . . . *fig.* 224

CENTAUR-LION — Hybrid being figuring as a guardian animal at the gates of Assyrian palaces (Nimrud) and represented in seal designs.
fig. 199, 286

CHAGAR BAZAR (SHUBAT ENLIL?) — Tell in the Upper Khabur region, excavated by Mallowan (1935-37). Its ancient name is still uncertain.
p. 234, 247

CHALCEDONY — A translucent variety of quartz, of many different colours . . . . . . *e. g. fig.* 197

CHALCOLITHIC AGE — Cultural phase characterized by the simultaneous use of metal (copper) and stone. One of the essential traits of the Halaf period . . . . *p.* 232

CHAMPLEVÉ WORK — A technique in which a metal plate is hollowed out, leaving thin raised lines which form the outline of the design. The background not occupied by the design can then be filled with coloured, vitreous paste. . . . . . . *p.* 256

CHARIOT — War chariots, invented by the Sumerians, were developed and exploited tactically in the Assyrian period. . . . . *p.* 46

CHERT — A flint-like quartz, usually dark in colour.
e.g. fig. 235

CHINA — Contacts with Luristan . . . . *p.* 134

CHOGA ZAMBIL — Elamite site in the Susa region, dominated by a five-storied ziggurat cleared by Ghirshman. . . . . *p.* 221

'CHRONICLES OF SARGON' . . . . . . *p.* 292

CHRYSELEPHANTINE TECHNIQUE — Combined use of ivory and gold . . . . *p.* 257

CIMMERIANS — An ancient people of the Crimea who began crossing the Caucasus in the 8th century B.C. and invaded northern Assyria and north-western Iran . . . . *p.* 128

CIRE-PERDUE — Technique of metal-casting. *p.* 233

CLOISONNÉ — A technique in which copper wire was used to make a trellis-work inset with stones of various colours. . . . . *p.* 256

COCK — Seldom represented, though it occurs on a cylinder seal from Nimrud and a pyx from Assur, both of the Assyrian period . . . . . *p.* 146, 161

COFFIN — Usually made of terracotta (jars, tubs, etc.). *p.* 244, 245, *fig.* 304

COLUMN-FIGURES — Supporting figures sculptured on a large scale (portico of the 'temple palace', Tell Halaf) or on a very small one (Nimrud ivories). *p.* 86, *fig.* 25, 95, 96

'CONSISTORIAL-RAT' — Pre-Sargonid male statuette from Assur, so named by the German excavators. . . . . *fig.* 5

COMB — Made of bone or ivory, usually decorated. *p.* 146, *fig.* 179a

CONE MOSAICS . . . . *p.* 223

COPPER — Metal used for the manufacture of implements in the protohistoric period (transitional phase from prehistory to historic times). Its alloy with tin (i.e. bronze) was the first metal compound to come into general use. Hence the name of an early cultural phase: the Bronze Age (early 3rd millennium on).

CORBELLED VAULTING — Building technique known as early as the Pre-Sargonid period, executed in stone or brick. . . . . *p.* 221, 222

COW SUCKLING ITS CALF — A frequent theme on ivories from Arslan Tash and Nimrud; it appears even earlier, on Babylonian cylinder seals of the early 2nd millennium . . . . . . *p.* 148, 154, *fig.* 181

CRAFTSMAN AT WORK . . . . *fig.* 265

CRESCENT — Symbolic motif on Kassite seals and boundary stones, connected with Sin*. . *p.* 181, 220

CROSS (GREEK) — Cross with four arms of equal length, figuring frequently on Susa pottery. . *p.* 240

CROW — Seldom represented in Mesopotamian art. Figures on an Assyrian pyx from Assur . . *p.* 146

CUMONT (FRANZ) (1868-1947) — Famous Belgian Orientalist, a specialist in the history of ancient religions, particularly Oriental and Roman cults. *p.* 206

CUP-BEARER — Servant at the Assyrian court having a post of great responsibility: whatever the king drank passed through his hands . . . . *p.* 36, 37

CYMBALS — Ancient Mesopotamian musical instrument. . . . . *p.* 297, 304, 306, 310

CYPRUS — Island in the Eastern Mediterranean, often mentioned in cuneiform documents under the name of *Alashia*. A centre of copper production. *p.* 3, 176, 232

CYRUS — King of Anzan (558-528 B.C.) and conqueror of Babylon (539). He allowed the Jews deported by Nebuchadnezzar (586) to return to Palestine. *p.* 182, 189, 190, 192, 210

DABIGU — Syrian town north of Aleppo.
Sculpture:
— Capture of Dabigu by the Assyrians.
fig. 127, 128, 145

DAGAN — A god worshipped at Mari and at Terqa (upstream from Zimri-Lim's capital). . . . *p.* 235

DAGGER . . . . *p.* 140, 141, 233

DAIRY SCENE — Represented at al 'Ubaid.
fig. 277

DAMASCUS — Capital of the Aramaean kingdom of that name. Destroyed by Tiglathpileser III (745-727 B.C.). The collection of ivories found at Arslan Tash probably came originally from Damascus, whence it was carried off as war booty by Adad-Nirari III (809-782) . . . . *p.* 6, 148

DAMGALNUNNA — 'Great wife of Nun,' appellation of the goddess Ninhursag*.

DAMKINA — Contracted form of Dam-ki-anna (lady of heaven and earth), another name for Damgalnunna*.

DANIEL — Hebrew prophet of the 7th century B.C. *p.* 103, 181, 182, 197

DARIUS I — Persian nobleman (521-485 B.C.) who became king upon the death of Cambyses, despite the intrigues of Gaumata . *p.* 189, 190, 193, 194, 196-198, 201, 210

DARIUS (BUILDING INSCRIPTION OF) — Foundation document discovered at Susa, probably written between 494 and 490 B.C. (Louvre) . *p.* 190, 191

DAVID — King of Judah, father of Solomon *p.* 190

'DEATH OF GILGAMESH' — A mythological tale. *p.* 281

'DELUGE' (The) — Theme of Biblical and Babylonian Flood stories. . . . . *p.* 281

DEMON — Animal-headed demon holding a bird.
fig. 312

DHORME (Edouard) — French Assyriologist, b. January 15, 1881. Member of the French Institute. Honorary Professor at the Collège de France. . . . . *p.* 290

DIABASE — A species of rock commonly called Diorite (q. v.)

DIORITE — An extremely hard, blue-black, eruptive rock, imported into Mesopotamia from the land of Magan (Arabia?). Several Gudea statues are carved in diorite . . . . *e.g. fig.* 353

DISK UPHELD BY TWO ACOLYTES — A frequent theme in seal designs and reliefs (Tell Halaf). There is a variant on a relief from the citadel of Aleppo: acolytes upholding a rayed disk within a crescent.
p. 88, 161, 198, 200, 201, *fig.* 191a
— Gilgamesh* and Enkidu* upholding the winged disk. . . . . *fig.* 97b
— Woman on a throne surmounted by the winged disk. . . . . *fig.* 189

DISK (RAYED). . . . . *p.* 169, *fig.* 215

DISK (WINGED) — A frequent emblem in Assyrian iconography, taken over from Egypt. Symbol of Assur and Shamash *p.* 14, 35, 71, 77, 141, 155, *fig.* 2, 205, 231, 233, 264

DISTEMPER — A technique of painting in which powdered colours, bound by glue and diluted with water, are applied to a dry surface. . *p.* 261, 263

DIYALA — Tributary on the eastern side of the Tigris, which it joins about 12 miles south-east of Baghdad. *p.* 2, 301

EUPHRATES — One of the two great Mesopotamian rivers . . . . *p.* 2, 78, 170, 186, 229

EUPHRATES (MIDDLE) — The region between Meskine in the north and Ramadi in the south.
p. 83, 217, 219, 223, 230

EUPHRATES (UPPER) — The region between its source (in Turkey) and Meskine, east of Aleppo, in the United Arab Republic. . *p.* 144, 230, 255

EYESTONE. . . . . *e.g. fig.* 250

EZEKIEL — Hebrew prophet, exiled in 597, whose visions are often inspired by Mesopotamia.
p. 32, 101, 207, 255

EZIDA — Name of the temple of [Nabu at Borsippa, excavated by Koldewey (1902) . . . . . . *p.* 179

FARS — Iranian province, also called Persis. . *p.* 193

FEAST IN THE GARDEN — A famous relief from Nineveh (British Museum), showing Assurbanipal lounging on a couch, under shade trees, with the queen seated beside him . . . . *fig.* 60

FIG-TREE — Decorative element on some of the glazed brick panels in the palace of Khorsabad.
p. 99, *fig.* 107

FILIGREE WORK — Delicate open-work designs made of fine wire on jewellery and ornaments.
p. 138, *fig.* 291c

FIRE ALTAR. . . . . *p.* 68, 226

FISH. *p.*74

FISH-MAN — Figure in Assyrian iconography, whose function is still not clear . . *p.* 250, *e.g. fig.* 82M

FLOOD — Babylonian account of the Flood described in the Bible . . . . *p.* 294

FLOWERS (ARTIFICIAL) — In wall decorations (al 'Ubaid, Tell Brak), assembled from stones of different colours . . . . *p.* 224, 225

FLOWING VASE — Mesopotamian theme symbolizing fertility and plenty *p.* 6, 20, 74, 225, *e.g. fig.* 25 M 82, 83

FLUTE — Ancient Mesopotamian musical instrument.
p. 297, 307, *fig.* 387

FLY-WHISK — Often represented in the hands of a servant in Assyrian reliefs and seal designs. *fig.* 41

FOX — Represented on a bronze belt plaque from Luristan. . . . . *p.* 133

FRANCHET (Louis) — French chemist, specialist in ceramics. . . . . *p.* 237

FRIT — Clay with a high proportion of silica, used to produce fine table service, figurines, beads. *p.* 237

FRUIT TREES — Victorious armies made a point of cutting down the enemy's fruit trees . . . *p.* 112

FURNITURE — Often decorated with ivory (e.g. Assyrian chairs, thrones and beds). *p.* 134, 255, 257

GADD (Cyril John) — English Assyriologist (b. 1893), sometime curator of the Egyptian and Assyrian Department of the British Museum, eminent specialist in Assyrian antiquities (*vide* Bibliography). Professor of Semitic Languages and Cultures in the School of Oriental and African Studies. . . . . *p.* 14

GALENA — An ore of lead sulphide, bright bluish grey in colour . . . . *p.* 235

GAUGAMELA — Site near Arbela, where Alexander the Great defeated Darius III Codomannus (331 B.C.) and cleared the way for his advance into Mesopotamia and Iran . . . . *p.* 206

GAUMATA — Magian priest who usurped the Persian throne by pretending to be Bardiya (Smerdis), brother of Cambyses, then on an expedition to Egypt. After a brief reign he was put to death in 521 B.C.
p. 189

GAZELLES — Represented in hunting scenes on Assyrian reliefs (Nineveh) *p.* 59, 67, 86, 146, 149, *fig.* 73, 202

GENESIS — First book of the Old Testament. Except for Chapter X (the table of nations), the first eleven chapters are obviously based on Mesopotamian events and beliefs. . . *p.* 169, 227, 228, 234, 297

GENII — Deities of inferior rank very frequently figuring in Assyrian reliefs, sometimes as winged human beings, sometimes as winged hybrids, half-human, half-animal *p.* 70, 83, 91, 99, 101, 117, 142, 149, 156, 192, 196, 200, 226, *fig.* 2, 16, 27a-b-c, 28, 241
— Genius protecting Horus . . . . . . *fig.* 180b
— Winged eagle-headed genius holding a staff.
fig. 314
— Winged genius as an atlas . . . . . . *fig.* 99c
— Winged genius leading a bull. . . . . *fig.* 109
— Winged genius with situla (on a ritual basin).
fig. 30, 82
— Winged, human-bodied, eagle-headed genius before a sacred tree . . . . *fig.* 78

GENII (FEMALE) — On certain ivories. Often identified with Isis and Nephtys. . . . . *p.* 147, 148

GENIUS BINDING PAPYRUS — A frequent theme on ivories from Arslan Tash and Nimrud, obviously of Egyptian inspiration. . . . . *p.* 148

GENIUS (WINGED HUMAN-HEADED) — Represented in high relief behind the guardian bull at certain gates of Khorsabad . *p.* 32, 37, 101, 145, 158, *fig.* 30, 37, 42, 77, 241

GENOUILLAC (Abbé Henri de) (1881-1940) — French Assyriologist, excavated Kish (1912) and Telloh (1929-31).

GHIRSHMAN (Roman) — French archaeologist (b. 1895), excavator of Tepe Giyan, Sialk, Susa and Choga Zambil . . . . *p.* 243

GIANT . . . . *p.* 91
— Execution of a bearded giant by two acolytes.
fig. 99d
— Giant headsman. . . . . *fig.* 1

GILGAMESH — Epic hero of Mesopotamian mythology, hailing from Uruk, represented countless times, often with Enkidu, in combat with wild animals.
p. 9, 32, 91, 116, 251, 281, 286, 305, *fig.* 322
— Gilgamesh and Enkidu* upholding the winged disk. . . . . *fig.* 97b
— Gilgamesh holding a staff . . . . . . *fig.* 315
— Gilgamesh subduing two human-headed bulls.
fig. 318

'GILGAMESH AND AGGA' — A mythological tale.
p. 281

HERODOTUS — Greek historian born at Halicarnassus about 484 B.C. His account of his travels in Egypt, Mesopotamia and Iran is an invaluable source of information, more trustworthy than is often supposed. . . . . . . *p.* 172, 176, 199, 228

HERRING-BONE WORK — Ancient building technique in which bricks are laid in parallel courses, alternately flat and slantwise. . . . . . . *p.* 219

HEZEKIAH — Son of Ahaz and king of Judah (late 8th - early 7th century B.C.). . . . . . . *p.* 292

HIEROGLYPHICS — Ancient picture writing in which the forms of objects, instruments, plants and human beings (in whole or in part) are recognizable. In Mesopotamia this mode of writing was soon supplanted by the cuneiform script. . . . . *p.* 77

HILLEH — Modern city in Iraq, south of Babylon, with a great palm grove. Largely built with bricks from Babylon . . . . *p.* 172

HINES — Site in the Gomel Valley, north of Nineveh, famous for its rock sculptures executed at the behest of Sennacherib (human-headed bulls, Gilgamesh, Assur, Ninlil) . . . . *p.* 71
— Reliefs of Sennacherib* . . . . . . *fig.* 80, 81

HITTITES — An ancient people who settled in Anatolia in the early 2nd millennium. The capital of their kingdom was Boghazkeuy. . . . . . *p.* 141

HORN — Ancient Mesopotamian musical instrument. *p.* 308, *fig.* 389, 390

HORSES — Seem to have existed in Mesopotamia as early as the beginning of the 3rd millennium, but were not represented in art till later (Gawra VI figurines). The animals represented in mosaic inlays from Ur and Mari are onagers. *p.* 39, 108, 192

Sculpture:
— Plumed horses' heads . . . . *fig.* 45
Painting:
— 'Brown and black horses'. . . . . . . *fig.* 119
— Horses and lancers. . . . . *fig.* 347
— 'Pink horse' . . . . *fig.* 120
— 'White horses' . . . . *fig.* 118

HORSE (WINGED) — In Assyrian seal designs of the 13th-11th centuries B.C.. . . . . . . *fig.* 200

HORUS — Egyptian god, son of Isis and Osiris. *p.* 148, 154, 158, *fig.* 180*b*

HUMBABA (also read HUWAWA) — Guardian of the cedar forest in the Epic of Gilgamesh. Killed by the hero with the help of Enkidu. Represented on many small figure plaques . . . . *p.* 91, 286

HUNTING — One of the leading themes in Assyrian reliefs (Assurnasirpal II, Sargon II, Assurbanipal). Also occurs frequently in seal designs
— Assurbanipal* hunting . . . . . . *fig.* 63, 65
— Assurbanipal making a libation over dead lions. *fig.* 76
— Assurnasirpal II bull-hunting. . . . *fig.* 62
— Assurnasirpal II lion-hunting . . . . *fig.* 64
— Bull-hunt. . . . . *fig.* 97*a*, 177*a*, 193
— Dying lioness . . . . *fig.* 70
— Grooms bringing in a dead lion . . *fig.* 74, 75
— Hunting wild asses. . . . . *fig.* 72
— Hunting with chariots (painting) . . . *fig.* 345
— Huntsman holding a mastiff in leash . *fig.* 68

— Lion and lioness in a park. . . . . . . *fig.* 71
— Lion-hunt. . . . . *fig.* 177*b*
— Ostrich-hunt . . . . *fig.* 252
— Sennacherib* (?) hunting and hawking. *fig.* 66, 67
— Stag-hunt . . . . *fig.* 97*c*

HURRIANS — A people of Upper Mesopotamia, whose political and cultural status is uncertain. Specimen of Hurrian art of the mid-3rd millennium: bronze lion of Tissari, king of Urkish . . . *p.* 96

HUWAWA, see HUMBABA.

HYPOGEUM — Underground tomb chamber. One of the most famous is that of the kings of the Third Dynasty of Ur. . . . . *p.* 244

IAHDUN-LIM — King of Mari whose foundation bricks were discovered in 1953 in the substructure of the temple of Shamash. A disk inscribed with his name (Louvre) had previously been found in the palace of Mari. Inscriptions translated by F. Thureau-Dangin (disk) and G. Dossin (foundation bricks). *p.* 220

IASMAH-ADAD — Son of Shamshi-Adad I, king of Assur, who acceded to the throne of Mari by a *coup d'état* (18th century B.C.). Statue of Shamash inscribed with his name (Aleppo Museum). *p.* 2, 293

IBEX *p.* 139, 140, 142, 143, 161, 202, 226, 240, *fig.* 171, 337
— Ibex leaning against a shrub. . . . . *fig.* 328*b*
— Hero subduing ibexes . . . . *fig.* 198

IBEX (FILIFORM) — Represented on bronze pinheads from Luristan . . . . . . *p.* 130, 134

IBEX (SACRIFICIAL). . . . . *p.* 37
— Sargon II* carrying the sacrificial ibex. *fig.* 43

IBEX (SILVER) — Inlaid with gold, forming the handle of a vase (Louvre). An identical work is in the Berlin Museum. Both were clandestine finds, but are undoubtedly Achaemenian works. *p.* 204, 285, *fig.* 254

ID — Name of the river-god

IDOL — Figures in the art of Luristan, but the interpretation is questionable. *p.* 131, 132, *fig.* 153, 154

IMGIG — Another reading of the name Im-Dugud (bird of the storm wind) . . . . *p.* 210

IMGUR BEL, see BALAWAT.

IMMORTALS — Name given to the soldiers of the royal guard of the Achaemenian kings. Represented as archers in glazed brick panels (Louvre). *p.* 196, *fig.* 247

'INANNA'S DESCENT TO THE NETHERWORLD' — A mythological tale . . . . . . *p.* 281, 286

INDO-EUROPEAN — Designates both a family of languages and the peoples speaking them, who originated somewhere in Asia or Europe and seem quite distinct from the Semitic races . . . *p.* 189

INDUS — Region with which Mesopotamia was in contact by the early 3rd millennium. Objects from this region include cylinder seals, steatite vases, and carnelians inlaid with white paste. The name is often used to designate the river Sind in India (present-day Pakistan) . . . . *p.* 206, 255

INLAYS — Used to decorate pottery and mosaic panels and to make statues and reliefs more life-like.

INURTA — Another reading of the name Ninurta*.

IONIA — Region of Asia Minor, more particularly the Aegean littoral and the neighbouring islands (Samos, Chios). . . . . *p.* 192

IONIANS. . . . . *p.* 197

IRON AGE — Begins in Mesopotamia about the 13th century B.C. . . . . *p.* 234

ISAIAH — Hebrew prophet of the 8th century B.C. *p.* 76, 221, 228

ISHTAR — Goddess of love and war *p.* 2, 4, 22, 71, 146, 161, 222, 229, 241, 254, 288, 290, 308, *fig.* 203

ISHTAR OF ARBELA — One of the most famous goddesses of Mesopotamia, patron of warriors, particularly venerated by Assurbanipal. . . . . *p.* 76
— Standing on a lion . . . . *fig.* 85

ISRAEL — Generic term designating the Jewish people after their return Egypt, when they settled in the land of Canaan. After the schism (10th century B.C.) it applies only to the northern region, as distinct from the kingdom of Judah . . . . *p.* 144

ISSUS — Cilician town where the Achaemenian troops were defeated by Alexander the Great (333 B.C.). *p.* 206

IVORY — From the tusks of elephants and wild boars, used in the sumptuary arts of the Mesopotamians. *p.* 139, 144, 150, 255, 256, 268, *e.g. fig.* 181

JACKAL — Music-making jackal . . *p.* 305, *fig.* 322

JARMO — Prehistoric settlement dated by Carbon 14 tests to about 5000 B.C. One of the oldest sites in Iran, explored by Braidwood. . . . *p.* 247, 251

JASPER — A variety of quartz, coloured yellow, red or green depending on its composition. Imported into Mesopotamia from the region east of Lake Urmya . . . . *e.g. fig.* 194

JEHU — King of Israel (842-815 B.C.) represented on the obelisk of Shalmaneser III, making his submission. No mention is made of this event in the Old Testament . . . . *p.* 35

JEMDET NASR — Site north-east of Kish, excavated by the Langdon-Mackay-Watelin expedition (1925-28), which gave its name to a phase of Mesopotamian protohistory (late 4th-early 3rd millennium). *p.* 230, 240
— Painted vase . . . . *fig.* 297

JERUSALEM — Besieged by Sennacherib (701 B.C.), captured by Nebuchadnezzar (586 B.C.). *p.* 37, 179, 182, 186, 190, 203

JERWAN — Town in Iraq with remains of an aquedut built by Sennacherib to bring water from Bavian to Nineveh.

JEWS. . . . . *p.* 182, 190, 311

JEZIREH (UPPER) — Region in northern Syria, between the Tigris and Euphrates, watered by the Khabur. . . . . *p.* 225

JIGHAN — Site near Khorsabad, where Place found some decorated pottery (Louvre). . . . . *p.* 242

JOB — Old Testament patriarch who endured affliction with fortitude and faith. . . . . *p.* 290, 291

JUBAL — The inventor of music (Genesis iv. 21). *p.* 297

KALAKH, see NIMRUD.

KALAR DASHT — A mountainous, thickly wooded district in the Mazanderan province of Iran. *p.* 141
— Bowl adorned with lions. . . . . . . *fig.* 172

KANDALANU — Last king of Babylon of the 'J' Dynasty (747-726 B.C.), a vassal of the Assyrian kings . . . . *p.* 168

KAPARA — King of the Assyrian city of Guzana (present-day Tell Halaf), who built a palace decorated with hundreds of reliefs (9th century B.C.). (Aleppo, Berlin, Cologne Museums, Louvre, etc.). *p.* 83, 124, 305
Architecture:
— Palace of Kapara: Plan . . . . *fig.* 93
Portico (reconstruction) . . . . *fig.* 95
Scorpion Gate (reconstruction). . . . . *fig.* 92
Sculpture:
— Column-figures (gods and goddess on their animal attributes) . . . . *fig.* 95, 96

KARAINDASH — Kassite king (15th century B.C.) who built a temple at Uruk decorated with brick reliefs (gods and goddesses with the flowing vase). *p.* 225

KAR-TUKULTI-NINURTA — City founded on the left back of the Tigris, opposite Assur, by Tukulti-Ninurta I (1243-1207 B.C.) to commemorate his victory over Babylon. Ziggurat, palaces, paintings, cleared by Andrae . . . . *p.* 4, 261
Painting:
— Animals on either side of the sacred tree, palmettes, rosettes, winged genii . . . . *fig.* 7

KASSITES — Invaders from the mountains northeast of Mesopotamia who put an end to the First Dynasty of Babylon (last king: Samsuditana, 1625-1595 B.C.) and founded a new dynasty (36 kings, reigning 576 years, from 1730 to 1155 B.C.). *p.* 1, 2, 96, 131, 146, 160, 169

KELERMES
— Lioness. . . . . *fig.* 175

KHABUR — Tributary on the east bank of the Euphrates, taking its rise in the Upper Jezireh, near the present Turkish frontier . . . . *p.* 83, 95, 124

KHAFAJE (? TUTUB) — Site in the Diyala region.
— Votive plaque with musicians.
p. 301, 304, *fig.* 373*b*

KHAZANU — Phœnician city burnt down by the Assyrians (860 B.C.).
— City of Khazanu on fire. . . . . . . *fig.* 141

KHORSABAD (DUR SHARRUKIN) — Site some 10 miles north-east of Mosul, where in 1843 Botta discovered the palace of Sargon II of Assyria (721-705 B.C.). *p.* 8, 9, 11, 20, 30, 32, 37, 39, 43, 59, 71, 80, 98-101, 116, 144, 147, 148, 154, 164, 182, 196, 203, 222, 224, 226, 242, 251, 256, 266

Architecture:
— Bit-hilani (plan). . . . . *fig.* 276
— Citadel (Gate A) . . . . *fig.* 30
— Column base . . . . *fig.* 275
— 'Harem': so called by Place (1854) but the excavations of the Oriental Institute of Chicago (1930) have shown it to be a religious complex. *p.* 98, 116
— 'Harem,' Gate Z (reconstruction) . . . *fig.* 107
— Palace of Sargon, the largest royal residence in the Ancient Near East (covering some 25 acres).
                                    p. 8, 9
— Palace (plan). . . . . *fig.* 10*b*
— Palace (plan showing the temples) . . *fig.* 10*c*
— Palace (over-all view). . . . . *fig.* 12
— Plan of the city of Khorsabad . . . . *fig.* 10*a*
— View of the city from the ziggurat. . *fig.* 11
— Ziggurat, a perhaps seven-storied tower, 140 feet high. dominating the temple area of the palace of Khorsabad.   Built by Sargon II (721-705 B.C.). Excavated by Place. The latest reconstruction of it is that of Businck* (five storeys) . . *p.* 91, *fig.* 13*a-b*
Sculpture:
— Column-figure (god with flowing vase). *fig.* 45
— Crouching lion . . . . *fig.* 132
— Gilgamesh* subduing a lion . . . . *fig.* 36, 38
— Genius protecting Horus . . . . . . *fig.* 180*b*
— Human-headed bulls followed by winged genii*.
                                    fig. 30
— Plumed horses' heads . . . . *fig.* 45
— Sargon II* (side view) . . . . *fig.* 15
— Sargon II carrying the sacrificial ibex. *fig.* 43
— 'Seascape': reliefs decorating Court VIII of Sargon palace. . . . . *p.* 40, 221, *fig.* 48, 267
— Sennacherib* (?) hunting and hawking.
                                    fig. 66, 67
— Sphinx. . . . . *fig.* 180*c*
— Threshold of the palace with floral ornamentation. . . . . *fig.* 207
— Tributaries . . . . *fig.* 44
— Winged human-headed bull* . . *fig.* 34*a-b*, 35
— Winged human-headed genius* with pine-comb and situla . . . . *fig.* 37, 77
— Woman in the window. . . . . . . *fig.* 180*a*
Painting:
— Animal and geometric designs . . . . *fig.* 341
— Decoration in Residence K. . . *p.* 99, *fig.* 108

KISH, see AL 'OHEIMIR.

KOLDEWEY (Robert Johann) (1855-1925) — German architect and archaeologist, began his career as an excavator in 1882 at Assos (an ancient city in Mysia, Asia Minor, opposite Lesbos) and went on to Mesopotamia, where he distinguished himself above all in the exploration of Babylon (1899-1917).
                                    p. 251

KRAMER (Samuel Noah) — American Sumeriologist (b. 1897). Curator of the University Museum of Pennsylvania. . . . . *p.* 281, *fig.* 351

KUANG — Ritual vase in the form of a sauce-boat, whose lid represents an animal (Shang dynasty, China) . . . . *fig.* 161

KUDURRUS — Black boundary stones, decorated with reliefs, covered with inscriptions and deposited in temples, where they were supposed to ensure the permanence of the boundary. Kassite period. *p.* 96

KUH-I-RAHMAT — Mountain dominating Persepolis.
                                    p. 193

KURDISTAN — Province in north-eastern Iraq.
                                    p. 138

KURKH
Sculpture:
— Stele of Shalmaneser III* . . . . . . *fig.* 39*b*

KUTHA, see TELL IBRAHIM.

KUYUNJIK (NINEVEH) — Tell north of the Khoser, on the left bank of the Tigris, opposite Mosul. One of the capitals of the Assyrian kingdom, famous for the palaces of Sennacherib and Assurbanipal.   A whole phase of protohistory has also been revealed there. *p.* 1, 3, 6, 9, 20, 30, 35, 52, 60, 80, 101, 112, 138, 144, 162, 167, 168, 182, 189, 190, 196, 229, 233, 241, 242, 267, 280, 286, 294, 310, 311
Sculpture:
— Assurbanipal* lion-hunting . . . . . *fig.* 63, 65
— Assurbanipal making a libation* over dead lions.
                                    fig. 76
— Camp scene (interior of a tent) . . . *fig.* 58
— Captives (Siege of Lachish*) . . . . . *fig.* 55
— Captives resting and eating . . . . . *fig.* 59
— Defeat of the Elamites* . . . . *fig.* 50
— Dying Lioness . . . . *fig.* 70
— 'Feast in the Garden'*. . . . . *fig.* 60
— Gazelles in flight . . . . *fig.* 73
— Grooms bringing in a dead lion . . *fig.* 74, 75
— Horseman shouting . . . . *fig.* 57
— Hunting wild asses. . . . . *fig.* 72
— Huntsman holding a dog in leash . . *fig.* 68
— Lion and lioness . . . . *fig.* 71
— Lion released from its cage. . . . . . *fig.* 69
— Military band . . . . *fig.* 392
— Musicians. . . . . *fig.* 61, 391
— 'Obelisk' of Tiglathpileser I* . . . . *fig.* 40*c*
— Prisoners playing the lyre . . . . . . *fig.* 393
— Sack of the city of Hamaan*. . . . . *fig.* 46
— Sennacherib* at the siege of Lachish*. *fig.* 49
— Sow and its young in the marshlands . *fig.* 51
— Statue of a woman, inscribed with the name Assurbelkala . . . . *fig.* 26
— Townsfolk led into captivity . . *fig.* 53, 54, 56
— Warfare in the marshes . . . . . . *fig.* 52

LABARTU — Evil spirit responsible for fever and illness, who had to be exorcised. *p.* 117, *fig.* 130*a-b*

LACHISH — City of ancient Palestine, southwest of Jerusalem in present-day Israel (Tell el-Duweir).
                                    p. 256, 311

LACHISH (SIEGE OF) — Relief from Nineveh (British Museum) commemorating the surrender of the city to Sennacherib in 701 B.C. *p.* 40, 43, *fig.* 49, 55

LAGASH, see TELLOH.

LAMASSU — Name given to the guardian animal whose statue stood at the gates of Assyrian palaces and temples . . . . *p.* 27

LANGDON (Stephen Herbert) (1876-1937) — English Assyriologist, in charge of the Joint Expedition to Kish and Jemdet Nasr (1923-33) . . . . . *p.* 251

LAPIS LAZULI — Azure blue stone composed of silicates, imported from Media, where there was a 'lapis mountain' . . . . *e.g. fig.* 229

LARSA, see SENKEREH.

LAW CODES — Cf. HAMMURABI, LIPIT-ISHTAR and UR-NAMMU . . . . *p.* 284, 291

LAYARD (Sir Austen Henry) (1817-94) — English archaeologist and diplomatist, excavator of Nineveh, Nimrud, Assur, Babylon and Kish (1845-51).
p. 138, 164, 226

LEAD. . . . . *p.* 232

LEBANON — Region of Western Asia, on the Mediterranean coast, famous for its cedar forests. Today an independent republic (capital Beirut) . *p.* 221

LEONIDAS — King of Sparta (490-480 B.C.) killed in the defence of Thermopylae against the Persians.
p. 199

LETTER-WRITING. . . . . *p.* 292, 293

LIBATION — Religious rite often represented in reliefs and seal designs. The celebrant (king, priest or simple worshipper), naked or clad, pours water into a vase from which a plant emerges *p.* 54, 68, *fig.* 76

LIBRARIES — At Nineveh, Nippur, Lagash and Mari.
p. 280, 286, 294

LIGHTING — In Mesopotamian architecture.
p. 226, 227

LIGHTNING-FLASH — Symbol of the storm-god Adad*. . . . . *p.* 76, 77
— Adad* holding lightning, standing on a bull.
fig. 84
— Teshub* brandishing lightning and axe.
fig. 87, 89

LIMESTONE — Frequently used by Mesopotamian sculptors.

LION — Very often represented either under its natural aspect or in a composite form (winged lion, centaur-lion, human-headed lion) *p.* 64, 66, 67, 133, 140-143, 154, 158, 159, 192, 198, 203, 206, 210, *fig.* 63-65, 69, 74-76, 172, 177*b*, 199, 200, 201
Sculpture:
— Bounding lion . . . . *fig.* 173*a-b*
— Bronze lion with dorsal ring; many such were found at Nimrud, Khorsabad and Susa (Louvre, British Museum). Served an undetermined purpose.
p. 116, *fig.* 132
— Centaur-lion, guardian animal (palace of Nimrud).
p. 27, 70
— Crouching lion . . . . *fig.* 132
— Guardian lion . . . . . . *p.* 27, *fig.* 31, 33
— Horned lion, Urartian art (first millennium B.C.), carrying a god on its back (Louvre). Also figures in glazed brick panels from Susa (Louvre).
p. 119, 192, 198, *fig.* 135
— Hunter spearing a lion. . . . . . . *fig.* 192
— Ishtar* of Arbela standing on a lion . *fig.* 85
— Lion and lioness in hunting relief of Assurbanipal (British Museum). . . . . *p.* 61, *fig.* 71
— Lion and lioness attacking an antelope. *fig.* 258
— Lion erect . . . . *fig.* 99*b*
— Lion passant . . . . . . *fig.* 98*a*, 221*a*, 252
— Lion's head in gold (torque) . . . . *fig.* 251
— Lion roaring . . . . *fig.* 234
— Winged human-headed lion, high relief (Nimrud).
p. 27, *fig.* 29
— Winged human-headed lion, in glazed brick panels from Susa, Achaemenian period (Louvre).
p. 198, 201, 226, *fig.* 29
Painting:
— Lion roaring . . . . *fig.* 340

LIONESS. . . . . *p.* 152, *fig.* 174, 175

LIONESS (DYING) — Relief from Nineveh.
p. 61, 66, *fig.* 70

LIONESS MAULING AN ETHIOPIAN (?).
fig. 186, 187

LIPIT-ISHTAR — Fifth king of the Isin Dynasty (c. 1860 B.C.). Drew up a law code.. . . *p.* 284, 291

LOFTUS (Sir William Kennet) — English archaeologist, excavated Susa (1851), explored southern Babylonia (Nippur, Uruk, Ur, Eridu) and Larsa, and was sent to Nineveh and Nimrud by Rawlinson (1954). Found the relief of Assurbanipal called the 'Feast in the Garden' (British Museum) and a large collection of ivories (British Museum).
p. 148, 150, 164, 312

LOTUS — Plant and flower often figuring in ivory carving of Syro-Phœnician provenance . . *fig.* 110

LUDINGIRRA'S ELEGIES. . . . . . . *p.* 284

LURISTAN — Mountainous province in the Kermanshah region of Iran, famous for the bronzes found there . . . . . *p.* 120, 127, 130, 132, 134, 164
Bronzes:
— Axes. . . . . *fig.* 155, 163-166
— Belt plaque. . . . . *fig.* 159
— Bits . . . . *fig.* 148-150
— Head of a warrior. . . . . *fig.* 147
— Idol . . . . *fig.* 153
— Pin-heads. . . . .*fig.* 151, 152, 209-212
— Situlae. . . . . *fig.* 158*a-b*
— Standard. . . . . *fig.* 156
— Sword with open-work hilt. . . . . *fig.* 208

LUTE — Represented in Mesopotamian art.
p. 303, *fig.* 380

LYDIA — Kingdom in Asia Minor (capital Sardis). In the Achaemenian period its king was Croesus, who was defeated and captured by Cyrus (546 B.C.).
p. 189

LYRE — A musical instrument very popular with the Mesopotamians *p.* 91, 206, 253, 297-299, 301, 302-306, 310, 311, *fig.* 370, 371

MACEDON — Ancient kingdom of Europe, lying to the north of Greece. Its greatest kings, Philip (359-336) and Alexander (336-323 B.C.), were contemporary with the Achaemenians . . . . *p.* 206

MACE — Weapon often represented in the hands of the gods . . . . . *p.* 16, 35, 88, *fig.* 20-22, 39
— Teshub* brandishing mace and boomerang*.
fig. 98*b*

MADAGASCAR — Sometimes identified with the ancient Ophir. . . . . *p.* 255

MAGAN (LAND OF) — Identified with Arabia. Supplied the Mesopotamians with hard stones like diorite and dolerite. . . . . *p.* 230

MAGI — Priests of ancient Media and Persia, the 'kings' or 'wise men of the east' (Matthew ii. 1). *p.* 206

MALACHITE — A natural green carbonate of copper.
p. 199

MALE (EMILE) (1862-1954) — French scholar and art historian, a specialist in Christian iconography.
p. 206

Standard of Ur, a mosaic panel inlaid on both sides, one with scenes of war, the other with scenes of peace. Discovered in the 'Royal' Cemetery (Tomb 779), now in the British Museum
— Lyre player. . . . . *fig.* 373a
— Musician. . . . . *fig.* 366
— Servant and guest in the banquet scene *fig.* 319
— Side representing 'peace'. . . . . . *fig.* 320a
— Side representing 'war' . . . . . . *fig.* 320b
Sculpture:
— Nude snake-headed woman. . . . . *fig.* 309a
— Ram's head. . . . . *p.* 230
Metal-work:
— Dagger with sheath. . . . . *fig.* 291c
— Helmet of Meskalamdug* . . . . . *fig.* 291b
Inlays:
— Decoration on a box. . . . . *fig.* 323
— Decoration on a box: animal passant . *fig.* 317
— Gaming board . . . . *fig.* 321
— Gilgamesh and human-headed bulls. . *fig.* 318
— Soundbox of a harp: Gilgamesh, animals at a banquet, animal musicians, scorpion-man *fig.* 322
— Soundbox of a lyre: music-making donkey.
. . . . *fig.* 372a
Cylinder seals:
— Banquet scenes with musical entertainment.
. . . . *fig.* 372b-c-d, 382a-b-c
Perforated plaque:
— Relief presumably fixed as a votive offering to the wall of a temple.

MUSHRUSSHU — Horned dragon, symbol of Marduk. . . . . *p.* 181, 186

MUSICIANS . . . . *fig.* 61
— Animal musicians . . . . *fig.* 322

MUSIC-MAKING ANIMALS — A frequent theme in Mesopotamian art, e.g. on a lyre from Ur (Tomb 789) and a relief from Tell Halaf.
p. 91, 305, *fig.* 100

MUSRI (MOUNT) — Near Khorsabad . . . *p.* 8

MYCENAE — Ancient city of the Peloponnese, excavated by Schliemann (1876-77), famous for the gold jewellery and ornaments found in the tombs.
p. 138

NABONIDUS — Last king of the Neo-Babylonian* dynasty (555-538 B.C.), defeated by Cyrus*.
p. 170, 178, 179, 182

NABOPOLASSAR — Founder of the Neo-Babylonian* dynasty, reigned 625-605 B.C.
p. 168, 170, 178, 179, 182, 186

NABU — Son of Marduk. God of scribes and writing, worshipped at Borsippa in the temple called *Ezida*.
p. 8, 9, 20, 99, 116, 169, 170, *fig.* 24

NABU-APAL-IDDIN — Babylonian king of the 'H' Dynasty (885-852 B.C.). Rebuilt the temple of Shamash* at Sippar. Foundation tablet (British Museum).. . . . . *p.* 168, 169, *fig.* 215

NABU-SHALLIMSHUNU — Chief scribe of Sargon* of Assyria. . . . . *p.* 294

NAIL-HEAD — With a flower pattern. . . *fig.* 278

NAKSH-I-RUSTAM — Site in the neighbourhood of Persepolis* with Achaemenian fire temples and rock tombs . . . . *p.* 200
— Tomb of Darius I. . . . . *fig.* 248

NAQIA — Wife of Sennacherib* (704-681 B.C.) and mother of Esarhaddon* (680-669 B.C.). Represented on a bronze relief (Louvre) . . . . . *p.* 118, 150
— Esarhaddon and Naqia. . . . . . . *fig.* 133

NARAM-SIN — King of the Akkadian dynasty (c. 2300 B.C.), son of Sargon . . . . . . *p.* 292

NEBO — Mentioned in Isaiah (xlvi. 1): synonym of the god Nabu*. . . . . *p.* 76

NEBUCHADNEZZAR II — King of the Neo-Babylonian* Dynasty (604-562 B.C.), a great builder and conqueror of Jerusalem *p.* 170, 172, 176, 178, 179, 186, 198, 229

NEO-ASSYRIAN — The final period of Assyrian domination (8th-7th centuries B.C.).

NEO-BABYLONIAN PERIOD — Begins with Nabopolassar* (625-605 B.C.), founder of the Neo-Babylonian Dynasty, and ends with Nabonidus* (538 B.C.).
p. 80, 170, 178, 179, 190, 200, 203, 210, 243, 251

NEO-SUMERIAN PERIOD — The period extending from the end of the Akkadian dynasty (23rd century B.C.) to the fall of the Third Dynasty of Ur (20th century B.C.). . . . . . . *p.* 246, 249, 251

NERGAL — Ruler of the Underworld* . . *p.* 286

NILE — The great river, rising in East Africa, which waters Egypt. Sacred river of ancient Egypt.
p. 6, 80, 192

NIMROD — Mentioned in Genesis (x. 9) as 'a mighty hunter before the Lord.' His name subsists in Arab place-names of Iraq: Nimrud (Kalakh), Birs Nimrud (Borsippa). A variant of Gilgamesh . . . . *p.* 61

NIMRUD (KALAKH) — One of the Assyrian capitals, south of Nineveh, excavated by Layard (1845-51) and Mallowan (since 1949) *p.* 9, 16, 20, 22, 27, 30, 37, 80, 100, 101, 112, 116, 142, 144, 147-150, 154, 156, 164, 179, 196, 224, 226, 250, 256-258, 280
— Assurnasirpal II* . . . *fig.* 22, 23, 41, 42, 183
— Assurnasirpal II bull-hunting. . . . . *fig.* 62
— Assurnasirpal II lion-hunting . . . . . *fig.* 64
— Assurnasirpal II waging war . . . . . *fig.* 18
— Bull passant. . . . . *fig.* 184
— Capture of a town by Tiglathpileser III*. *fig.* 17
— Decoration of a bed. . . . . *fig.* 191a-b
— Fugitives swimming with water-skins. . *fig.* 47
— Guardian animal . . . . *fig.* 31
— Hero subduing a wild beast . . . . . *fig.* 190
— King and winged genius* on either side of the sacred tree* . . . . *fig.* 16
— Lilith. . . . . *fig.* 330
— Lioness mauling an Ethiopian. . *fig.* 186, 187
— 'Monna Lisa'. . . . . *fig.* 185
— Mythological scene. . . . . *fig.* 204
— Nabu. . . . . *fig.* 24
— 'Obelisk' of Shalmaneser III*. . . . . *fig.* 40b
— Pyx with musicians . . . . . . *fig.* 394, 395
— Servant with fly-whisk. . . . . . . *fig.* 41
— Stele of Assurnasirpal II* . . . *fig.* 14, 39a
— Winged bull . . . . *fig.* 32
— Winged, human-bodied, eagle-headed genius before the sacred tree* . . . . *fig.* 78
— Winged human-headed genius. . . . . *fig.* 42
— Winged human-headed lion. . . . . . *fig.* 29
— Winged sphinx . . . . *fig.* 188
— Woman with a crown and long braids *fig.* 182
— Woman seated on a throne, and winged disk.
fig. 189
— Woman's head with diadem . . . . . *fig.* 327

NINEVEH, see KUYUNJIK.

NINGAL — Goddess worshipped at Ur and Harran, consort of the moon-god Nannar. Represented on the Stele of Ur-Nammu (University Museum, Philadelphia) . . . . *p.* 9

NINGIRSU — God of fertility, worshipped at Lagash in particular. His emblem is the lion-headed eagle.
p. 220, 297

NINHURSAG — Goddess of fertility (literally, 'lady of the mountain'), worshipped throughout Mesopotamia. Temple at Mari . . *p.* 169, 222, 225, 259

NINLIL — Goddess, consort of Enlil, god of Nippur.
p. 71

NINURTA — War god . . . . . . *p.* 9, 16, 71

NIPPUR — Sumerian city, residence of the god Enlil. Excavated from 1889 to 1900, and since 1948 by an American joint expedition. . . . . . *p.* 281, 284

NOAH — Old Testament patriarch, builder of the Ark, by means of which he and his family survived the Flood. . . . . *p.* 281

NOSE — Flattening of the nose as a sign of humility.
p. 118

NOUGAYROL (Jean) — French Assyriologist, Director of Studies at the École des Hautes Études. Former Curator at the Louvre. . . . . *p.* 290

NUBIA — Region to the south of ancient Egypt, between the first cataract and Bahr el-Ghazal, traversed by the Nile. Today it lies partly in Egypt, partly in the Sudan . . . . *p.* 35, 234
— Nubian trampled by a lioness *p.* 152, *fig.* 186, 187

NUMBERING OF CAPTIVES — A frequent theme in scenes representing the aftermath of war.
e.g. fig. 324a

NUR-ADAD — King of the Larsa Dynasty. His palace was discovered in 1933
— Palace of Nur-Adad. . . . . *fig.* 273

NUSKU — Fire-god, symbolized by a lamp. Often represented on boundary stones . . . . *p.* 4, 170

NUZI, see YORGAN TEPE.

OBELISK — A pointed, four-sided pillar, tapering as it rises. The top of Assyrian obelisks is given the form of a ziggurat.

OMAN — Country south-east of Saudi Arabia.
p. 232

ONAGERS — Wild asses of the Mesopotamian desert, domesticated and harnessed to chariots (represented in works from Ur, Mari and Khafaje). *fig.* 291a

ONYX — A variety of quartz allied to agate with layers of different colours . . . . *p.* 230

OPHIR — A country mentioned in the Bible from which Solomon's navy brought back 'gold, and silver, ivory, and apes, and peacocks' (I Kings x. 22). Conjecturally identified with India, South Arabia, the Somali coast and even Madagascar . . . *p.* 255

ORIENTAL INSTITUTE OF CHICAGO — Has sponsored important expeditions to the Diyala region, Khorsabad and Nippur and throughout Mesopotamia.
p. 266

ORTHOSTATS — Stone reliefs set on along the base of a wall, which they reinforced and decorated at the same time. Most Assyrian reliefs had this dual purpose . . . . *p.* 34, 88

OSTRICH — On an Achaemenian cup (Louvre). Also figures in Neo-Babylonian seal designs
— Ostrich-hunt . . . . *fig.* 252
— Winged hero fighting an ostrich . . . *fig.* 236
— Winged hero subduing two ostriches. . *fig.* 235

PAINTING, see WALL PAINTING.

PALACE OF SARGON II (Khorsabad) — The largest royal palace of the ancient Near East. *p.* 8, 9

PALAEOLITHIC PERIOD — Phase of prehistoric culture, characterized by rough or chipped stone implements, preceding the Neolithic Period.

PALMETTE — Highly stylized plant form, often represented in Assyrian reliefs and Syro-Phœnician ivories *p.* 91, 145, 149, 154, 156, 162, 226, *fig.* 191a

PALM TREE — Widely cultivated in Mesopotamia. Famous palm groves at Basra, Hilleh (near Babylon) and Ana (on the Middle Euphrates). Ceases to grow beyond a point about 60 miles north of Abu Kemal. Very frequently represented in Mesopotamian art.
p. 70, 146, 161, 225, *fig.* 201

PAN-PIPE — Ancient Mesopotamian musical instrument . . . . *p.* 307, *fig.* 388

PAPYRUS — Egyptian plant used as writing material, very frequently represented in ivories of Syro-Phœnician provenance . . . . *p.* 148

PARTHIANS — An ancient people who, driven out of Scythia*, moved south and settled in Hyrcania (south-east of the Caspian Sea). In 250 B.C. the Parthian Arsaces founded a dynasty which lasted until A.D. 226, when it gave place to the Sassanians*.
p. 243

PASARGADAE — The first Achaemenian capital, built by Cyrus* (between 559 and 550 B.C.). Its ruins lie about 60 miles north-east of Shiraz (Iran).
p. 190, 192, 193, 210
Architecture:
— View of the palace . . . . *fig.* 240
Sculpture:
— Winged genius . . . . *fig.* 241

PATZEN — Type of large, unbaked brick found (and so designated) and the German excavators of Warka* (Uruk) . . . . *p.* 218, 219

PAZUZU — Evil spirit represented in the Neo-Sumerian (amulets, figurines) and Assyrian periods.
p. 117, *fig.* 131

PECTORAL — Ornament of precious metal often found in unrifled tombs on the dead man's breast.
p. 139, 154, *fig.* 167, 168, 174

PERCUSSION INSTRUMENTS . . . *p.* 304-306

PERSEPOLIS — Royal Achaemenian city, famous for its palaces, some 30 miles north-east of Shiraz.
p. 182, 190, 192-200, 203, 210, 241
— Aerial view of the ruins . . . . *fig.* 242
— Trilingual inscriptions . . . . *p.* 280

Architecture:
— Apadana: large audience hall prolonged on three sides by porticoes with double colonnades, built by Darius I, Xerxes I and Artaxerxes I.
p. 193, 194, 198
— East stairway of the Apadana . . . . *fig.* 243
— Hadish, palace of Xerxes. . . . . . . *p.* 193
— Hall of the Hundred Columns, built by Xerxes I and Artaxerxes I. . . . . *p.* 193, 194, 202
— Harem, in the palace quarter, west of the Treasury and south of the Hundred-Column Hall. . . *p.* 194
— Plan of the palaces . . . . *fig.* 246c
— Tatchara, palace of Darius. . . . . *p.* 193
— Treasury, architectural unit at the south-east corner of the palace . . . . *p.* 194
— Tripylon, or 'Council Chamber,' square in plan, with four columns in the centre and three doors.
p. 194

Sculpture:
— Babylonian tributaries. . . . . . . *fig.* 239
— Capital in the Apadana. . . . . . *fig.* 253
— Portrait of Xerxes (?). . . . . . . *fig.* 249
— Servants of the palace. . . . . . . *fig.* 245

PERSIAN GULF — Here the Mesopotamians procured their supplies of shell and mother-of-pearl. *p.* 3, 252

PERSIANS — A federation of agricultural and nomadic tribes, of which the Achaemenians formed one clan.
p. 189, 190, 197, 200, 206, 210

PHARAOH — Title of the kings of ancient Egypt.
p. 189

PHOENICIA — Region on the Mediterranean seaboard, extending from Latakia in the north to Mount Carmel in the south . . . . *p.* 77, 112

PHILISTIA — Narrow strip of coast-land in ancient Palestine, from Mount Carmel in the north to the Gaza region in the south. Confederation of five towns: Gath, Gaza, Ekron, Ashdod, Ascalon. Palestine takes its name from the Greek form of Philistia (Palaestina) . . . . *p.* 6

PHILISTINES — Formed part of the 'sea peoples' who invaded Egypt and were driven back by Ramesses III (1191-1190 B.C.). They settled shortly afterwards on the Mediterranean coast of Palestine. Cf. PHILISTIA. . . . . *p.* 6, 233

PILASTERS — Engaged piers projecting from the wall, used to break up the monotony of uniform wall surfaces and to set up plays of light and shade *p.* 223

PINE-CONE — Represented as a sprinkler in the hands of Assyrian kings and genii, when making the gesture of purification (or fructification) *p.* 32, 70, 117, 149, 156, *e.g. fig.* 37, 77

PIN-HEADS — A great many of the Luristan bronzes are pin-heads, variously ornamented. *p.* 128, 130
— Hero subduing two mastiffs. . . . *fig.* 151, 152
— Hero subduing two serpents . . . . . *fig.* 212
— Mask in salient relief . . . . *fig.* 209
— Torsades . . . . *fig.* 210
— Wild animals fighting . . . . *fig.* 211

PISÉ — Sun-dried clods of beaten earth, used as a primitive building material . . . . . . *p.* 218

PLACE (VICTOR) (1818-75) — French consul, excavator of Khorsabad (1852-54). The greater part of his finds were lost in an accident which sent them to the bottom of the Tigris. Two notable works, however, reached the Louvre: a human-headed bull and a large winged genius with a situla.
p. 11, 98, 242, 262, 266
— Elevation of the ziggurat of Khorsabad according to Place . . . . *fig.* 13a

PLATAEA — Greek victory over the Persians (479 B.C.).
p. 199

PLOUGH — Emblem of Ningirsu on a boundary stone from Susa. Often represented in seal designs. Decorative element on the glazed brick panels of the palace of Khorsabad . . . . *p.* 99, *fig.* 107

PLUTARCH (A.D. c. 45-c. 125) — Greek historian, born at Chaeronea (Bœotia), who travelled in Asia Minor . . . . *p.* 200

PODIUM — Low pedestal in Mesopotamian temples, where the divine statue stood. . . . *p.* 71, 225
— Frieze on the podium at Tell Brak* . . . *fig.* 279

POEM OF CREATION, see 'ENUMA ELISH.'

POLOS — A high headdress, tapering off at the top and fastened at the bottom with a broad ribbon.
p. 247, *fig.* 309b

PORTICO . . . . *p.* 193

POTTER'S WHEEL. . . . . *p.* 236

POTTERY — The fragments of decorated or undecorated pottery found on a given site are one of the archaelogist's most precious means of working out a relative chronology . . . . . . *p.* 83, 236, 243

POTTERY (CARBONIFEROUS). . . . . *p.* 236

POTTERY ('COAL WARE'). . . . . . . *p.* 237

POTTERY ('SMOKED WARE'). . . . . *p.* 237

PROTOHISTORY — Phase of civilization beginning at the end of prehistoric times (c. 5000 B.C.) and ending when epigraphically recorded history begins (early third millennium B.C.). . . . . *p.* 83

PSALTERY — Ancient musical instrument.
p. 310, 312

PYX — Small round or rectangular box, with a flat bottom and a lid, holding jewellery and ornaments.
p. 146, *fig.* 179b, 394, 395

QALAAT SHERGAT (ASSUR) — One of the capitals of the Assyrian kingdom, on the right bank of the Tigris, excavated by Andrae (1903-14).
p. 1-4, 6, 9, 15, 71, 80, 100, 116, 138, 144, 146, 152, 164, 167, 186, 229, 250, 256, 280, 292
Sculpture:
— Altar of Tukulti-Ninurta I* . . . . . *fig.* 8
— Comb* with religious scene . . . . . *fig.* 179a
— 'Der Consistorial-Rat'*. . . . . *fig.* 5
— Pyx with symbolic scene. . . . . . . *fig.* 179b
— Ritual basin with gods with the flowing vase and genii with situla. . . . . *fig.* 82, 83
— Shalmaneser III*. . . . . *fig.* 19
— Vegetation god. . . . . *fig.* 9
— Zariqum*. . . . . *fig.* 4
Pottery:
— Decorated vase . . . . *fig.* 300
Glazed brick:
— Scene of worship . . . . *fig.* 79
Tablet:
— Eighth campaign of Sargon* . . . . . *fig.* 364

RAM — Represented in later seal designs and at Ziwiyeh. . . . . *p.* 139, 142, 235

RAMESSES III (1198-1166 B.C.) — Defeated the 'sea peoples' in their attempt to invade Egypt. This victory is commemorated in the temple reliefs at Medinet Habu in Upper Egypt. . . . . *p.* 6

RASSAM (Hormuzd) (1826-1910) — A Chaldean Christian who excavated most of the cities of Assyria and Babylonia for the British Museum. For an account of his methods, see our *Archéologie mésopotamienne,* I, *p.* 22, 52

RAS SHAMRA (UGARIT) — One of the largest Phœnician cities of the second millennium B.C., on the Mediterranean coast north of Latakia. Excavations, begun by C. Schaeffer in 1929, entered their 21st season in 1960. . . . . *p.* 154, 256

RATTLE — Ancient Mesopotamian musical instrument (or toy) . . . . *p.* 306, *fig.* 384

REEDS — Used as a primitive building material. *p.* 217

REIN-RING — Adorned with an onager*. *fig.* 291*a*

REPOUSSÉ WORK — Technique of decorating metal by beating it into relief. . . . . *p.* 140

REVETMENT PLAQUES — In the Ziwiyeh treasure. . . . . *fig.* 170*b*, 173*a-b*

RHYTON — Ceramic or metal vessel in the form of an animal. . . . . *p.* 202

RIEMCHEN — Type of small unbaked brick*, so called by the German excavators of Warka* (Uruk). *p.* 218, 219

'RIGHTEOUS SUFFERER' (THE) — Babylonian tale of an innocent man visited with affliction (like Job). . . . . *p.* 290, *fig.* 263

ROADS AND ROAD-BUILDING . . . . *p.* 229

ROSETTE — Symbolic theme in Kassite seal designs. *p.* 5, 138, 162, *fig.* 191*b*

SACRIFICIAL ANIMALS — Thrown into the water (thus represented on the 'bronze doors' of Balawat). *p.* 112

'ST GEORGE AND THE DRAGON.' *p.* 156, *fig.* 190

SAMARIA — Capital of the kingdom of Israel*, founded by Omri (9th century B.C.), captured by Sargon II* (721 B.C.) . . . *p.* 6, 144, 154, 258

SAMARRA — City on the left bank of the Tigris, north of Baghdad, excavated in 1914 by Herzfeld. It revealed a phase of protohistoric culture. *p.* 83, 237, 239

SAMMURAMAT — Wife of Adad-Nirari III*, 'Lady of the Palace,' known to the Greeks as Semiramis*. *p.* 20
— Statue of Nabu* dedicated by Bel-tarsi-iluma* 'for the life of' Adad-Nirari and Sammuramat. *fig.* 24

SAMSON — Hebrew judge, prototype of the Oriental Hercules. His exploits are related in Judges (xiii-xvi). Many traits in common with the Mesopotamian Gilgamesh . . . . *p.* 233

SANGAR — King of Carchemish* who paid tribute to Shalmaneser III* . . . . *p.* 112

SARDIS — Capital of the ancient kingdom of Lydia (Asia Minor), on the Pactolus. Captured by Cyrus* in 546 B.C. . . . . *p.* 197

SARDONYX — A deep orange-red variety of chalcedony, with bands of different colours. *e.g. fig.* 233

SARGON OF AKKAD — Founder of the Akkadian dynasty. His dates are roughly 2470-1412 B.C. The famous bronze head from Nineveh (Baghdad Museum) is believed to be a portrait of him *p.* 233, 235, 292

SARGON II OF ASSYRIA (721-705 B.C.) — Conqueror of Samaria* and builder of Khorsabad* (Dur Sharrukin). The largest collection of his reliefs is in the Louvre *p.* 8, 9, 11, 13, 20, 30, 37, 59, 152, 169, 179, 196, 266, 293, 294
Architecture:
— Palace of Sargon (over-all view) . . . *fig.* 12
Sculpture:
— Sargon II (side view) . . . . *fig.* 15
— Sargon II carrying the sacrificial ibex. *fig.* 43
Tablet:
— Eighth campaign of Sargon. . . . . . *fig.* 364

SASSANIAN ART — The art of the Sassanian dynasty of Iran (A.D. 225-651) . . . . *p.* 143, 243

SATRAPIES — Provinces of the Achaemenian* empire, administered by satraps. . . . . *p.* 189

SCHIST — Dark grey rock having a foliated structure and readily split into slabs or sheets. *e.g. fig.* 279

SCHMIDT (Erich) — American archaeologist (b. 1897), excavated Fara (1931), Persepolis* and Surkh Dum* (1938). . . . . *p.* 127, 130

SCORPION GATE — Palace of Kapara* at Guzana. *fig.* 92

SCORPION-MAN — Composite figure in Assyro-Babylonian mythology. . . *p.* 96, 305, *fig.* 91, 94, 322
— Scorpion-men accompanying Assur . . *fig.* 214

SCRIBES — On a wall painting from Tell Ahmar*. *fig.* 348

SCYTHIANS — People of Iranian origin who crossed the Caucasus and invaded Urartu and Assyria in successive waves, from the 8th century B.C. on. *p.* 128, 143, 168, 186

SEA-LAND DYNASTIES — Ruled the whole of Lower Mesopotamia from the 18th to the 11th century B.C. *p.* 167

SELEUCID DYNASTY — A line of kings founded by Seleucus who ruled over a large part of Persia and Asia Minor after the death of Alexander the Great* (fourth to first century B.C.) *p.* 243, 290, 307

SEMIRAMIS — Greek name of Sammuramat* *p.* 176

SENKEREH (LARSA) — Prospected by Loftus (1853-54) and Andrae (1903), soundings made by A. Parrot (1933). The Larsa Dynasty (2023-1761 B.C.) was founded by Naplanum and ended with Rim-Sin, defeated by Hammurabi*, king of Babylon. *p.* 241, 249, 251, 280, 302, 307

Architecture:
— Palace of Nur-Adad* . . . . *fig.* 221
Figurines:
— Monkey playing a flute . . . . . . *fig.* 387
— Woman nursing a child . . . . . . *fig.* 316
Figure-plaques:
— Turbaned figure . . . . *fig.* 311*a*
— Woman with a pan-pipe. . . . . . *fig.* 388
Potsherd:
— Harpist . . . . *fig.* 376
Tomb:
— Tub-shaped burial vessel . . . . . . *fig.* 302

SENNACHERIB — King of Assyria (705-681 B.C.). Represented at the siege of Lachish (British Museum). *p.* 30, 43, 59, 71, 74, 118, 150, 167, 170, 179, 222, 229, 292, 311
— Aqueduct of Sennacherib . . . . . . *fig.* 284
— At the siege of Lachish (Room 36 of the palace of Sennacherib) . . . . *fig.* 49
— Hunting and hawking . . . . . . *fig.* 66, 67
— Relief of Sennacherib (Hines) . . . . *fig.* 80
— Relief of Sennacherib (Bavian) worshipping the god Assur . . . . *fig.* 81

SERABIT EL-KHADIM — Site of mineral deposits in the Sinai* peninsula. The rocks are covered with graffiti commemorating Egyptian expeditions made under the Middle Kingdom (2160-1580 B.C.) . . *p.* 232

SERPENTINE — Mineral or rock, basically a hydrous magnesium silicate . . . . *e.g. fig.* 192

SHALMANESER III — Assyrian king (858-824 B.C.) represented on several monuments, e.g. the 'obelisk' from Kalakh* (British Museum). Three statues of him from Assur *p.* 13, 15, 16, 35, 112, 144, 149, 152, 179, 257, *fig.* 19-21
— 'Obelisk' of Shalmaneser ('black obelisk'). *fig.* 40*b*
— Stele of Shalmaneser . . . . *fig.* 39*b*

SHAMASH — Sun-god, worshipped at Larsa and Sippar in particular *p.* 4, 9, 71, 99, 138, 168, 226, 288, *fig.* 213, 215

SHAMSHI-ADAD I (or SHAMSHI-ADDU) OF ASSUR — One of the greatest of Mesopotamian kings (1823-1791 B.C.), contemporary and adversary of Hammurabi*. Much has been learned about him from the Royal Archives of Mari *p.* 2, 293

SHAMSHI-ADAD V — Assyrian king (823-810 B.C.). Stele found at Nimrud* . . . . *p.* 35

SHANG DYNASTY — Ritual vase of the Shang dynasty of ancient China (c. 1523-1028 B.C.) compared with certain Luristan bronzes. . . . . *p.* 134

SHEDU — Name given to the guardian animal whose statue stood at the gates of Assyrian palaces and temples. . . . . *p.* 27

SHELL — Often used in Mesopotamian inlaid work. *e.g. fig.* 317

SHIBTU — Queen of Mari, wife of Zimri-Lim*. *p.* 292

SHOFAR — Ancient trumpet of the Hebrews. *p.* 308

SHUBAD — 'Queen' buried in the cemetery of Ur (Tomb 800) with a treasure of 270 pieces: vessels of gold, silver and stone, a harp, ornaments, etc. *p.* 253

SHUQAMUNA — Kassite divinity, presiding over the fecundity of the flocks. . . . . . . *p.* 170

SHURUPPAK (FARA) — Ancient Sumerian city, home of Utnapishtim*, excavated by Koldewey and Andrae (1902-3) and by Schmidt (1931). *p.* 280

SHUSHINAK — Susian divinity whose temple was found by J. de Morgan and R. de Mecquenem. *p.* 225

SIALK — Iranian site excavated by Ghirshman (1933-37). Some very important archaeological evidence was revealed by its early settlements and cemeteries. *p.* 237, 241, 243
— Pottery with human figures. . . . . . *fig.* 294
— Vase with long spout . . . . . . *fig.* 301

SIBITTI ('The Seven') — Seven gods of the heavens or of the underworld, or seven stars identified with the Pleiades. Represented by seven small spheres on cylinder seals, boundary stones and stelae. Temple of the Sibitti discovered at Khorsabad* . . . . *p.* 35

SICKLE — Made in early times of flint (set with bitumen on a handle of bone or wood), later of bronze. Sickles were also made of terracotta in the al 'Ubaid period . . . . *p.* 233

SIDON — Phœnician port, whose king Abdimilkutti* is represented on the stele of Esarhaddon*. The necropolis has yielded many sarcophagi, including the Alexander Sarcophagus (Istanbul Museum). *p.* 35

SILVER — Figurines, statuettes and receptacles of value were often made of silver (usually in combination with copper). Divine figurines were often overlaid with silver.

SILVER MOUNTAINS — Located in the Taurus* range . . . . *p.* 235

SIN — Semitic name of the moon-god, worshipped at Ur and Harran in particular. Cf. NANNAR. *p.* 4, 9, 35, 71, 78, 288

SINAI — Mountain on the Sinai peninsula where Moses received the Tables of the Law (Exodus XIX. 20).
— Copper and turquoise mines . . . . . *p.* 232

SIPPAR. see ABU HABBA.

SISTRUM — Ancient musical instrument . . *p.* 305

SITULA — Holy-water pail often held by winged Assyrian genii with the head of a bird of prey or a man *p.* 34, 70, 74, 117, 142, 149, 156, *fig.* 37, 77, 82, 158*a-b*, 191*a*
— Decorated bronze situlae from Luristan (?) in the Louvre (9th century B.C.). . . . . . . *p.* 133

SIZE PAINT, see DISTEMPER.

SKYLIGHTS . . . . *p.* 228

SLIP — Potter's clay in a liquid state, added after the vessel has been shaped . . . . . . *p.* 236, 237

SMITH (George) (1840-76) — English Assyriologist. *p.* 294

SNAKE-HEADED FIGURINES — Of the al 'Ubaid period, from Ur. . . . . *p.* 247, *fig.* 309*a*

SOCKET — Round or oval, for the handles of weapons or implements . . . . *fig.* 164, 166

SOLOMON — Son of David and king of Israel, who built the temple of Jerusalem (10th century B.C.). *p.* 255, 257

SOMALI COAST — In East Africa, flanking the Gulf of Aden. . . . . *p.* 255

SOW — Sow and its young in the marshlands of Lower Mesopotamia. . . . . *fig.* 51

SPADE — Triangular spade, symbol of Marduk, often figures on reliefs and in glyptic art. Cf. *Marru.*

SPARTANS — Soldiers or inhabitants of the city of Sparta. . . . . *p.* 199

SPHINX — Symbolic animal, often winged.
p. 139, 142, 154

SPHINX (WINGED) — Frequent in Assyrian seal designs (13th-11th centuries B.C.), Oriental ivories, in the Tell Halaf reliefs and Luristan bronzes *p.* 86, 129, 148, 154, 158, 159, 169, *fig.* 158*a*, 180*c*, 188, 196, 197, 326

SPREE — German river, flows through Berlin and at Spandau joins the Havel, a tributary of the Elbe.

SPRINKLING — Genii with pine-cone sprinkler making the ritual gesture of purification (or fructification) . . . . *p.* 32, 70, 117, 149, 156

STAFF — Topped by a disk and held by acolytes.
p. 130, *fig.* 314, 315

STAG — A frequent theme of Mesopotamian art.
p. 86, 88, 154, 156, 302
— Stag-hunt . . . . *fig.* 97*c*

STANDARD OF LURISTAN . . . . . . *fig.* 156

STANDARD OF MARI . . . . *fig.* 324

STANDARD OF UR . . . . *fig.* 320

STEATITE — A species of medium-hard, greenish-blue stone in which the Mesopotamians carved many statuettes, figurines and cylinder seals.
p. 32, *e.g. fig.* 193, 195

STELE — A commemorative slab or pillar of stone generally rounded off at the top, decorated with reliefs and often inscribed. . . . . *e.g. fig.* 143

STEPPES (ART OF THE) — Characterized by impetuous life and movement, expressed in a racy, schematic style. Much of this art is usually ascribed to the Scythians** . . . . *p.* 139, 164
— Lioness . . . . *fig.* 175

STONE — Used as a building material *p.* 223, 225, 229, 231

STRINGED INSTRUMENTS . . . . . *p.* 298-304

STYLUS — Emblem of Nabu*, god of scribes and writing . . . . *p.* 181

SUGUNIA — Armenian town, taken by the Assyrians in 860 B.C. . . . . *fig.* 146

SUMER — Region of Lower Mesopotamia, south of Kish, largely confined to the area between Nippur and Eridu. The great majority of its inhabitants were Sumerians . . . . . *p.* 132, 182, 206, 219

SUMERIANS — A non-Semitic people who settled in Lower Mesopotamia in the middle of the fourth millennium B.C., probably during the Uruk period.
p. 1, 150, 230, 235, 255

SURKH DUM — Iranian site excavated in 1938 by E. Schmidt*, who cleared a temple there. *p.* 127

SUSA — A great metropolis in south-western Iran, systematically excavated since 1897, where some of the finest works of Mesopotamian art have been found (Stele of Naram-Sin, Code of Hammurabi, Kassite boundary stones). A great centre of pottery manufacture in ancient times *p.* 116, 182, 190, 192, 193, 198, 199, 200, 202, 210, 225, 226, 237, 241
— Archer of the royal guard. . . . . . *fig.* 247
— Code of Hammurabi, detail . . . . . *fig.* 363
— Ear-ring . . . . *fig.* 291*d*
— Engraved and inlaid vase . . . . . *fig.* 298*b*
— Ornamented bowls. . . . . *fig.* 292*a-b*
— Plan of the palace. . . . . *fig.* 246*b*

SWORD — With open-work hilt (Luristan) *fig.* 208

SYRIA — In ancient times, the Land of Aram. Today bounded by Lebanon to the west, Turkey to the north, Iraq to the east, Jordan and Israel to the south. Capital: Damascus. Forms with Egypt the United Arab Republic . . . *p.* 6, 76, 112, 255

SYRIA (UPPER) — Region around Aleppo, bordering on present-day Turkey . . . *p.* 76, 223, 256

TABOR — Small drum represented in Mesopotamian art. . . . . *p.* 305, 306, 310-312, *fig.* 383

TAHARQA — King of Egypt and Nubia (689-663 B.C.), XXVth Dynasty . . . . *p.* 35, 154

TAMLU — Akkadian name for a terrace . *p.* 256

T'AO-T'IEH — Animal heads decorating certain Chinese bronzes, somewhat similar to the Luristan bronzes. . . . . *p.* 135, *fig.* 162

TARTAR — High-ranking official at the Assyrian court. . . . . *p.* 104, 105

TAURUS — Mountain range between Cilicia and Cappadocia, crossed by way of the Cilician Gates. Its timber and mineral deposits made it a constant objective of expeditions sent out by Mesopotamian rulers . . . . *p.* 234

TEHERAN — Capital of present-day Iran . *p.* 142

TEIMA — Oasis of Saudi Arabia, 60 miles north-east of Moda'in, on the route from Petra to the Persian Gulf. Nabonidus* lived there from 552 to 544 B.C. The place is forbidden to Europeans, a few of whom have visited it at the risk of their life (Doughty, Euting, Huber, Janssen, Savignac) . . . . *p.* 179

TELL — Arab name for an artificial mound formed by the accumulation of ancient ruins.

TELL AHMAR (TIL BARSIP) — Capital of the Aramaean state of Bit Adini in Upper Syria, on the left bank of the Euphrates, conquered by Shalmaneser III (859-824 B.C.). Excavated by the Thureau-Dangin expedition(1927-31). Wall paintings, statues and stelae *p.* 35, 76-78, 100, 101, 108, 124, 224, 262, 267

Sculpture:
— Ishtar* of Arbela standing on a lion . . . *fig.* 85
— Stele of Esarhaddon*: Esarhaddon holding in leash the kings Abdimilkutti* and Ushanahuru*.
fig. 86
— Teshub* brandishing lightning and axe.
fig. 87, 89

Painting:
— Archer. . . . . *fig.* 338
— 'Brown and black horses'. . . . . . *fig.* 119
— Execution of a prisoner . . . . . *fig.* 115, 116
— Galloping horseman . . . . *fig.* 339
— Geometric and animal designs . . *fig.* 342, 343
— Giant headsman . . . . *fig.* 1
— Head of a dignitary. . . . . . . *fig.* 346
— Horses and lancer. . . . . *fig.* 347
— Ibex. . . . . *fig.* 337
— Large hunting scene with chariots. . . *fig.* 345
— Lion roaring . . . . *fig.* 340
— 'Pink horse' . . . . *fig.* 120
— Prisoners harnessed to a chariot. . . . *fig.* 117
— Scribes at work. . . . . *fig.* 348

TEMENOS — Sacred precinct within which the temples are located . . . . *p.* 229

TEMPLE OF JERUSALEM — Built by King Solomon (10th century B.C.) with the help of Phœnician craftsmen . . . . *p.* 37
— Reconstruction . . . . *p.* 190

TENT SCENE — Figures on Assyrian reliefs and on the 'bronze doors' of Balawat. . . . . *fig.* 58

TEPE GAWRA — Site north-east of Nineveh, excavated from 1927 to 1938, where a well-preserved sequence of strata yielded evidence of each successive cultural phase from the Neolithic Age to the mid-second millennium B.C. . . . . . . *p.* 241, 247, 248, 259
— Mould . . . . *fig.* 289

TEPE GIYAN — Iranian tell excavated by Contenau and Ghirshman in 1931-32. It yielded a large quantity of pottery of the early Iranian period.
— Pottery with human figures. . . . . . *fig.* 294

TEPE SARAB — Iranian town in the province of Azerbaijan, some 60 miles east of Tabriz. *p.* 247

TERRACED ROOFS — The usual type of roofing in Mesopotamian houses. . *p.* 9, 221, 222, 227, 228

TESHUB — Great Hittite god of the elements, a variant of Adad*. The bull was his animal attribute. *p.* 77, 78, 88
— Teshub brandishing lightning and axe. *fig.* 87, 89
— Teshub brandishing mace and boomerang. *fig.* 98*b*

TETRAMORPH — The four elements (man, lion, bull, eagle) symbolizing the four Evangelists, a frequent theme on the tympanums of Romanesque churches . . . . *p.* 207

TEUMAN — King of Elam*, whose severed head is hanging from the branch of a tree in the 'Feast in the Garden'* from Nineveh . *p.* 52, 311, 312, *fig.* 60

THEBES — Capital of Upper Egypt, taken by Assurbanipal* in 663 B.C. . . . . . *p.* 3, 6, 80, 190

THERMOPYLAE — The pass in Thessaly where Leonidas, king of Sparta, made an heroic attempt to hold back the Persians (480 B.C.) . . . *p.* 199

THOMAS (Félix) (1815-75) — French architect, awarded the Grand Prix de Rome, who accompanied the Fresnel (1852) and Place (1853-55) expeditions to Khorsabad, where he made plans and drawings of many of the monuments (for *Ninive et l'Assyrie*). *p.* 11

THRACE — Region of northern Greece, along the Aegean, the Black Sea and the Sea of Marmora *p.* 190

THRONES — Decorated with ivory or with gold overlays. . . . . *p.* 144, 156
— Woman seated on a throne. . . . . . *fig.* 189

THUNDERBOLT — Symbol of the god Adad*. Cf. LIGHTNING-FLASH.

THUREAU-DANGIN (François) (1872-1944) — Famous French Assyriologist, excavated Arslan Tash (1928) and Tell Ahmar (1929-31). His *Inscriptions de Sumer et d'Akkad* (1905) first established Sumerology on a sound basis and is still a standard work.
p. 100, 256, 262, 266, 280, *fig.* 350

TIAMAT — Personification of salt water, enemy of Marduk* and dominated by him. . . . . . *p.* 159

TIARA — A crown with one or more rows of horns forming the headdress of gods and goddesses.
p. 155, 168, 251

TIGLATHPILESER I — Assyrian king (1112-1074 B.C.), the first whose armies reached the Mediterranean coast. Obelisk bearing his name found at Nineveh. . . . . *p.* 3, 35, 292
— 'Obelisk' of Tiglathpileser I. . . . . *fig.* 40*c*

TIGLATHPILESER III — Assyrian king (745-727 B.C.) who devastated Damascus and invaded Israel. Reliefs from Nimrud* (British Museum, Louvre). . . . . *p.* 14, 22, 179
— Capture of a town by Tiglathpileser. . *fig.* 17
— Tiglathpileser giving audience (paintings).
fig. 111-114, 266

TIGRIS — One of the two great Mesopotamian rivers.
p. 2, 6, 71, 78, 80, 83, 103, 119, 168
— Map. . . . . *fig.* 3

TIGRIS (UPPER) — From Jezireh ibn-Omar to Assur. Also used to designate the surrounding region.
p. 1, 12, 160, 217, 221, 223

TIL BARSIP, see TELL AHMAR.

TIMBER — Represented floating off the Phœnician coast . . . . *p.* 40, *fig.* 48, 267

TOBLER (A.J.) — American archaeologist, editor of the second volume devoted to the excavations at Tepe Gawra* by a joint American expedition. *p.* 248

TORQUE — A stiff necklet usually made of bronze, but sometimes of gold . . *p.* 140, 202, *fig.* 170*a*, 251

TOURNETTE — Hand-wheel used by primitive potters . . . . *p.* 236

TREE (SACRED) . . . . *p.* 14, 70
— Adoration of the sacred tree *fig.* 205, 231, 233
— King and winged genius on either side of the sacred tree . . . . *fig.* 16
— Winged, human-bodied, eagle-headed genius before the sacred tree . . . . *fig.* 78

TRUSSES — Assemblage of beams supporting a roof. *p.* 222

TUBAL-CAIN — The first smith (Genesis iv. 22). *p.* 234

TUKULTI-NINURTA I — Assyrian king (1243-1207 B.C.), conqueror of Babylon*. Built a new city on the left bank of the Tigris opposite Assur: Kar-Tukulti-Ninurta . . . . *p.* 3, 4, 51
— Altar of Tukulti-Ninurta I . . . . . . *fig.* 8

TURQUOISE — A blue stone (variety of phosphate of aluminium) found in Persia . . . . . *p.* 232

TYMPANUM — The space over a church doorway between the lintel and the arch . . *p.* 207, *fig.* 255

TYRE — Phœnician seaport, seat of the cult of the god Melkart. Its king, Hiram, helped Solomon to build the temple of Jerusalem (10th century B.C.). Tribute from the king of Tyre to Shalmaneser III ('bronze doors' of Balawat*) . . *p.* 112, 255, *fig.* 122

UGME — Son of Ur-Ningirsu, and Patesi of Lagash. His hypogeum was discovered in 1932. *p.* 221, 244

UMMANIGASH — Elamite prince . . . . *p.* 311

UNDERWORLD — Domain of the god Nergal.
p. 117

URAEUS — Representation of a goddess in the form of an angry cobra . . . . *p.* 154

URARTU — Ancient name of present-day Armenia. Urartian art was influenced by that of Assyria, but retained a highly original character of its own.
p. 119, 120
— Bulls of Urartu: bronzes, some in a very powerful style recalling that of Sumer. . . . . . . *fig.* 137
— Centaur . . . . *fig.* 286
— God standing on a horned lion. . . . *fig.* 135
— King Assurdan*. . . . . *fig.* 134*a-b*

URMYA (LAKE) — In the Azerbaijan province of north-western Iran, between Turkey and the Caspian Sea. . . . . *p.* 138, 230

UR-NAMMU — Founder of the Third Dynasty of Ur, author of a code of laws identified by Kramer*. A great builder (2124-2107 B.C.) *p.* 2, 9, 284, 291

UR-NINA — Also read Ur-Nanshe or Ur-Nazi (Stephens); the correct form is uncertain. One of the first Patesis of Lagash (c. 2800 B.C.) *p.* 35, 219

UR-NINGIRSU — Patesi of Lagash, son of Gudea (22nd century B.C.) . . . . *p.* 221, 244

URUK, see WARKA.

USHANAHURU — Son of Taharqa*, king of Egypt and Nubia (689-663 B.C.), shown held in leash on the stelae of Esarhaddon* discovered at Zinjirli* and Tell Ahmar*. . . . . *p.* 35
— Held in leash by Esarhaddon*. . . *fig.* 39*c*, 86

UT-NAPISHTIM—Mentioned in the Epic of Gilgamesh
p. 286

VAN (LAKE) — In Armenia (present-day Turkey). Sacrifice offered there by the troops of Shalmaneser III, represented on the 'bronze doors' of Balawat*.
p. 112, 119

VINES . . . . *p.* 52, *fig.* 60

VULTURES (STELE OF THE) — Famous Sumerian monument erected by Eannatum, king of Lagash.
p. 283

WARFARE — The leading theme of Assyrian reliefs, though it had already figured in Sumerian (Stele of the Vultures) and Akkadian works (Stele of Naram-Sin). *fig.* 17, 18, 46, 49, 50, 52-59, 115-117, 123-125, 127, 128, 139-142, 145, 146, 257

WARKA (URUK) — Sumerian capital, seat of several dynasties (I-V) and home of Gilgamesh*. One of the great centres of Mesopotamian art and civilization. The name (Uruk) is also used to designate a phase of protohistoric culture corresponding to Levels XIV-VI of the excavated site (second half of the fourth millennium B.C.) *p.* 9, 218, 222-225, 229, 240, 259, 280, 290

WASH — Painting or colouring matter on pottery, unmixed with clay . . . . *p.* 237, 247

WATER-SKINS — Fugitives swimming across a river with water-skins . . . . *fig.* 47

WELLS — Built of bricks or terracotta . . *p.* 228

WHEEL-FINISHED — Vessel whose surface has been smoothed with the wet hand, on the potter's wheel. . . . . *p.* 237

WIND INSTRUMENTS . . . . . . *p.* 307, 308

WINDOWS — Their existence in ancient Mesopotamian architecture is confirmed by archaeological evidence (Ashnunnak, Tell Halaf, Assyrian reliefs) and they are represented on Syro-Phœnician ivories.
p. 226, 227

WOMAN AT THE WINDOW — A frequent theme of Syro-Phœnician ivories found in Mesopotamia. Its interpretation is still a matter of controversy. Regarded by some as a woman of easy virtue accosting passers-by . . . . . . *p.* 147, 148, 154, *fig.* 180*a*

WOMAN (NUDE) — *p.* 20, 100, *fig.* 26, 307, 309*a*, 310*a*, 310*c*

WOMAN WITH A CHILD — Many figurines represent a woman suckling a child or holding it in her arms . . . . *p.* 247, 251

WOMAN WITH A CROWN . . . . *fig.* 182

WOOLLEY (Sir Leonard) (1880-1960) — English archaeologist, made world-famous by his discovery of the 'royal tombs' at Ur (1927-29). From 1936 to 1949 he excavated Atchana (Alalakh) in northern Syria (now Turkey). *p.* 218, 223, 250-252, 298, 307

WRITING — Pictographic writing first appears in Mesopotamia shortly before 3000 B.C. *p.* 240, *fig.* 349

XERXES I — Achaemenian* king (485-465 B.C.), son of Darius*. Invaded Greece, defeated at Salamis (480) and Plataea (479). *p.* 190, 193, 196, 197, 200, 201, 210

YORGAN TEPE (NUZI) — Ancient city about 8 miles south-west of Kirkuk, excavated by the American School of Baghdad and Harvard University (1925-31) . . . . *p.* 261

ZAB (GREAT) — Tributary of the Tigris (left bank), which it joins a few miles south of Kalakh (Nimrud).
p. 2
— Map. . . . . *fig.* 3

ZAGROS MOUNTAINS — In north-eastern Mesopotamia, from which invading tribes often swept down into the plains . . . . *p.* 140, 141
— Zagros art: bracelet . . . . *fig.* 170*e*

ZARIFEH — Reed-built hut, common in the villages of southern Iraq . . . . *fig.* 269

ZARIQUM — Assyrian king, contemporary with the Third Dynasty of Ur. Headless statue from Assur.
p. 2, *fig.* 4

ZIGGURAT — A staged tower, the characteristic type of sacred architecture in ancient Mesopotamia. The Tower of Babel (Genesis xi) was a ziggurat. *p.* 4, 11, 35, 36, 218, 226, 228, *fig.* 6, 13a-b

ZIMRI-LIM — Last king of Mari (1790-1759 B.C.), defeated by Hammurabi* . . . . *p.* 292

ZIMUR (MOUNT) . . . . *p.* 230

ZINJIRLI — Site in Turkey, capital of a kingdom of the Neo-Hittite period (1200-709 B.C.), excavated by the Von Luschan expedition (1888-1902). Fortress, temples, palace, many reliefs. Stele of Esarhaddon*.
p. 35, 146, 154

Sculpture:
— Stele of Esarhaddon: Esarhaddon holding in leash the kings Abdimilkutti* and Ushanahuru*.
fig. 39c

ZIUSUDRA — The Babylonian Noah* . . . *p.* 281

ZIWIYEH — Iranian site south-east of Lake Urmya*, where peasants discovered a magnificent treasure hoard (1947) now scattered throughout the world
p. 138-141, 145, 146, 164, 203
— Banquet scene. . . . . *fig.* 178
— Bracelets . . . . *fig.* 170c-d
— Bronze bowl . . . . *fig.* 176
— Bull-fight. . . . . *fig.* 177a
— Head of a griffin* . . . . *fig.* 169
— Ibex. . . . . *fig.* 171
— Lion-hunt. . . . . *fig.* 177b
— Pectoral* . . . . *fig.* 167, 168, 174
— Revetment plaques . . . . . *fig.* 170b, 173a-b
— Torque* . . . . *fig.* 170a

ZU — Bird-god. . . . . *p.* 288, *fig.* 360, 361

BIBLIOGRAPHY

I. HISTORIES OF ART

ANDRAE (Walter) and SCHAEFER (H.). — DIE KUNST DES ALTEN ORIENTS. DIE KUNST VORDERASIENS, in PROPYLÄEN KUNSTGESCHICHTE, 11, pp. 133-168, Berlin, Propyläen Verlag, 1925.

Short presentation of the masterpieces of Mesopotamian art; excellent plates (pp. 467-580), brief descriptive notices, and basic bibliography.

CONTENAU (Georges). — L'ART DE L'ASIE OCCIDENTALE ANCIENNE, Paris and Brussels, G. van Oest, 1928.

Concise general survey (55 pages, 64 figures) of Oriental art, including Hittite art, from the origins to the third century A.D.

CONTENAU (Georges) and CHAPOT (V.). — L'ART ANTIQUE: ORIENT, GRÈCE, ROME, in L'HISTOIRE UNIVERSELLE DES ARTS, edited by Louis Réau, Paris, Armand Colin, 1930.

Studies the monuments by millennia and continually intermingles Egypt and Asia.

CONTENAU (Georges). — L'ANTIQUITÉ ORIENTALE, in L'HISTOIRE GÉNÉRALE DE L'ART, I, pp. 35-65, Paris, Flammarion, 1950.

Concise but substantial account; well-chosen, well-reproduced illustrations.

DELAPORTE (Louis). — L'ART DE L'ASIE ANTÉRIEURE in NOUVELLE HISTOIRE UNIVERSELLE DE L'ART, edited by Marcel Aubert, I, pp. 27-51, Paris, Firmin-Didot, 1932.

Brief account of a field greatly broadened and enriched since the date of publication.

DELAPORTE (Louis). — L'ART DE L'ASIE OCCIDENTALE AVANT LA CONQUÊTE D'ALEXANDRE, in L'ART DES ORIGINES A NOS JOURS, edited by Léon Deshais, I, pp. 27-42, Paris, Larousse, 1932.

Sixteen pages (including illustrations) can obviously not give a complete picture of Mesopotamian art; yet well-chosen illustrations include some of the latest finds then available (notably from the excavations at Ur).

FRANKFORT (Henri). — THE ART AND ARCHITECTURE OF THE ANCIENT ORIENT, in THE PELICAN HISTORY OF ART, Harmondsworth and Baltimore, Penguin Books, 1954.

One of the best and most recent histories of the art of the ancient Near East (279 pages, 192 plates), by an outstanding specialist on the region, who died prematurely in 1954.

GODARD (André). — L'ART DE LA PERSE ANCIENNE, in NOUVELLE HISTOIRE UNIVERSELLE DE L'ART, edited by Marcel Aubert, I, pp. 167-178, Paris, Firmin-Didot, 1932.

Brief account of Iranian art in the Median (650-560 B.C.) and Achaemenian (560-331 B.C.) periods. A limited number of well-chosen illustrations.

HUYGHE (René) (editor). — L'ART ET L'HOMME, vol. I, Paris, Larousse, 1958.

General survey laid out along new lines, showing the interpenetration of different civilizations; early periods of Mesopotamia treated by Dr Contenau (pp. 65-70, 129-140). Contains a 'précis d'histoire de l'art,' written by Philippe Jean (pp. 164-168).

PERROT (Georges) and CHIPIEZ (Charles). — HISTOIRE DE L'ART DANS L'ANTIQUITÉ, vol. II: CHALDÉE ET ASSYRIE, Paris, Hachette, 1884.

The first comprehensive study of Oriental art, under the two general headings: Assyria (excavations of the Assyrian triangle) and 'Chaldea' (Sarzec's excavations at Telloh). Well-documented and abundantly illustrated with line engravings.

PERROT (Georges) and CHIPIEZ (Charles). — HISTOIRE DE L'ART DANS L'ANTIQUITÉ, vol. V: PERSE, PHRYGIE, LYDIE ET CARIE, Paris, Hachette, 1890.

The study of Persia (pp. 403-897) is based essentially on the excavations of the Dieulafoys, before those of de Morgan had begun. The very existence of the period preceding the Achaemenians was then unsuspected.

POPE (A. Upham). — A SURVEY OF PERSIAN ART FROM PREHISTORIC TIMES TO THE PRESENT, vol. IV, London and New York, Oxford University Press, 1938.

Magnificent survey of the most famous and most characteristic monuments of Iranian civilization: pottery, bronze vessels and glazed-brick panels from Susa, Luristan bronzes, reliefs from Persepolis, etc. Plates are commented on in a volume of text (vol. I).

REINACH (Salomon). — APOLLO: HISTOIRE GÉNÉRALE DES ARTS PLASTIQUES (6th ed.), Paris, Hachette, 1910. APOLLO, tr. from the French by Florence Symmonds, new ed., Heinemann, London, 1907.

Very few pages (pp. 23-30) are devoted to the art of 'Chaldea and Persia.'

SARRE (F.). — L'ART DE LA PERSE ANCIENNE, French translation by P. Budry, Paris, Crès, n.d. (after 1920).

Covers pre-Islamic Persian art from 550 B.C. to the end of the Sassanian period (A.D. 636), with one chapter devoted to Achaemenian art (pp. 3-19). A few 'comments on the illustrations' are followed by an album of 150 plates, 52 of them showing Achaemenian works.

TERRASSE (Charles). — HISTOIRE DE L'ART DEPUIS LES ORIGINES JUSQU'A NOS JOURS, vol. I: L'ART DE L'ASIE OCCIDENTALE, pp. 49-75, Paris, Henri Laurens, 1938.

Very succinct account (14 pages devoted to Mesopotamia, including illustrations); dates, however, need to be moved forward in time to bring them into line with the new chronology.

II. REPRODUCTIONS AND ILLUSTRATED SURVEYS

BARNETT (R.D.). — ASSYRISCHE PALASTRELIEFS, Prague, Artia, 1961.

An album of Assyrian reliefs (9th-7th centuries B.C.) from the British Museum (173 plates in black and white, 24 colour plates), with an introduction. Includes the 'bronze doors' of Balawat (plates 137-173). The colour plates illustrate the later works, from Babylon and Susa.

CONTENAU (Georges). — MUSÉE DU LOUVRE, DÉPARTEMENT DES ANTIQUITÉS ORIENTALES. LES ANTIQUITÉS ORIENTALES. I. Sumer, Babylonie, Elam. II. Monuments hittites, assyriens, phéniciens, perses, judaïques, cypriotes, araméens. Paris, Morancé, 1927-30.

Presentation of the outstanding works in the Department of Oriental Antiquities, with descriptive notices; excellent reproductions (108 collotype plates).

Encyclopédie Photographique de l'Art (parts 6-13), Paris, Editions Tel, 1935-36.

Excellent reproductions, from unpublished photographs by André Vigneau, of the most important and aesthetically interesting works in the Oriental collections of the Louvre; short descriptive captions.

GRESSMANN (Hugo). — ALTORIENTALISCHE BILDER ZUM ALTEN TESTAMENT (2nd ed.), Berlin and Leipzig, Walter de Gruyter, 1927.

Valuable selection of works from the Ancient Near East (678 figures) chosen for their possible bearing on the Old Testament; excellent descriptive and bibliographical notices.

HALL (Harry Reginald). — BABYLONIAN AND ASSYRIAN SCULPTURE IN THE BRITISH MUSEUM, Paris and Brussels, G. van Oest, 1928.

Presentation of the finest examples of Mesopotamian sculpture in the British Museum, from the Jemdet Nasr period to Assyrian times.

MALRAUX (André). — LE MUSÉE IMAGINAIRE DE LA SCULPTURE MONDIALE, Paris, La Galerie de la Pléiade, Gallimard, 1952.

Mesopotamia is abundantly represented in this magnificent panorama, in which the works of each period and place are seen in due perspective as part of an organic whole. Mesopotamian sculpture: figs. 6-30, 45-53, 94-102.

MALRAUX (André). — Vol. II. LE MUSÉE IMAGINAIRE DE LA SCULPTURE MONDIALE, DES BAS-RELIEFS AUX GROTTES SACRÉES, Paris, La Galerie de la Pléiade, Gallimard, 1954.

Many works from Mesopotamia (figs. 58-106 bis) take their place in this long sequence of bas-reliefs from many different periods and places.

PARROT (André). — MARI, Neuchâtel and Paris, Ides et Calendes, 1953.

Photographs of the most attractive works (sculpture, painting, architecture, glyptics) discovered at Mari from 1933 to 1953 (132 collotype figures, 3 plans, 132 descriptive notices).

PRITCHARD (J.B.). — THE ANCIENT NEAR EAST IN PICTURES RELATING TO THE OLD TESTAMENT, Princeton, University Press, 1954.

Excellent reproductions of 769 works, with accurate descriptive notices and bibliography. Covers the entire Near East, including Egypt.

SPEISER (Werner). — VORDERASIATISCHE KUNST, Berlin, Safari, 1952.

Good general outline of Oriental art, from the earliest times to the Parthians.

ZERVOS (Christian). — L'ART DE LA MÉSOPOTAMIE DE LA FIN DU QUATRIÈME MILLÉNAIRE AU XVᵉ SIÈCLE AVANT NOTRE ÈRE. ELAM, SUMER, AKKAD. Paris, Editions "Cahiers d'Art," 1935.

Photographic survey of the most important monuments of ancient Mesopotamia. Works from Susa are also included.

III. HISTORICAL WORKS

AYMARD (André) and AUBOYER (Jeannine). — L'ORIENT ET LA GRÈCE ANTIQUE, in HISTOIRE GÉNÉRALE DES CIVILISATIONS, edited by Maurice Crouzet, Vol. I, Paris, Presses Universitaires de France, 1953.

Part II (p. 111-178), devoted to 'Mesopotamian Civilization,' contains an up-to-date chapter on 'les créations artis-

tiques.' *A few pages (191-206) on the Achaemenians. Well-chosen, well-reproduced illustrations.*

Cambridge Ancient History. — I. EGYPT AND BABYLONIA, 1924. III. THE ASSYRIAN AND PERSIAN EMPIRES, 1925. IV. THE PERSIAN EMPIRE AND THE WEST, 1926. Cambridge, University Press.

DELAPORTE (Louis). — LES PEUPLES DE L'ORIENT MÉDITERRANÉEN. I. LE PROCHE-ORIENT ASIATIQUE, Paris, Collection "Clio," Presses Universitaires de France, 1938.

Excellent account of the history of the Near East from the earliest times to Alexander, with an extensive bibliography. Needs to be supplemented, however, with the knowledge acquired since the date of publication.

DELORME (Jean). — CHRONOLOGIE DES CIVILISATIONS, Paris, Collection "Clio," Presses Universitaires de France, 1949.

Chronology of the world's great civilizations, based on the latest researches.

DHORME (Edouard) and CONTENAU (Georges). — LES PREMIÈRES CIVILISATIONS, first volume of the series "Peuples et Civilisations," Paris, Presses Universitaires de France, 1950.

Several chapters on our subject contributed by the authors.

EDZARD (Dietz Otto). — DIE "ZWEITE ZWISCHENZEIT" BABYLONIENS, Wiesbaden, Otto Harrassowitz, 1957.

Scrupulously accurate account of the Babylonian period from the accession of Ishbi-Irra of Isin to that of Rim-Sin of Larsa.

GHIRSHMAN (Roman). — L'IRAN, DES ORIGINES A L'ISLAM, Paris, Payot, 1951. IRAN: FROM THE EARLIEST TIMES TO THE ISLAMIC CONQUEST, Harmondsworth, Penguin Books, 1954.

The civilization, history and archaeology of Iran up to the Islamic conquest. A few reproductions of objects from the Sakkiz treasure (Ziwiyeh).

GOOSSENS (Godefroy). — ASIE OCCIDENTALE ANCIENNE, in HISTOIRE UNIVERSELLE I "Encyclopédie de la Pléiade," pp. 289-495, Paris, Gallimard, 1957.

One of the most recent syntheses of the history of Western Asia in ancient times, making full use of the latest archaeological discoveries.

KING (L.W.). — A HISTORY OF BABYLON FROM THE FOUNDATION OF THE MONARCHY TO THE PERSIAN CONQUEST, London, Chatto and Windus, 1915.

Historical study of the great capital with an account of archaeological explorations. Needs to be brought up to date.

LLOYD (Seton). — TWIN RIVERS, Oxford University Press, 2nd edition, 1947.

Short history of Iraq from the antediluvian age to the 20th century.

MASPERO (Gaston). — HISTOIRE ANCIENNE DES PEUPLES DE L'ORIENT CLASSIQUE, 3 volumes, Paris, Hachette, 1895-99.

Despite the vast increase in our knowledge, this remains a masterly study remarkable for its broad, synthetic grasp of the subject and the depth and penetration of the author's views. Will long remain a standard work.

MASPERO (Gaston). — THE DAWN OF CIVILISATION, EGYPT AND CHALDAEA, ed. by A.H. Sayce, tr. by M. L. McClure, 5th ed., London, Society for Promoting Christian Knowledge, 1910. New York and Toronto, The Macmillan Co., 1922.

MASPERO (Gaston). — THE STRUGGLE OF THE NATIONS, EGYPT, SYRIA AND ASSYRIA, ed. by A.H. Sayce, tr. by M. L. McClure, 2nd ed., London, Society for Promoting Christian Knowledge, 1910.

MASPERO (Gaston). — THE PASSING OF THE EMPIRES, 850 B.C.-330 B.C., ed. by A.H. Sayce, tr. by M. L. McClure, ist ed. (no later editions), London, Society for Promoting Christian Knowledge, 1900.

The three preceding works published as:

MASPERO (Gaston). — HISTORY OF EGYPT, SYRIA, BABYLONIA AND ASSYRIA, ed. by A.H. Sayce, tr. by M. L. McClure, London, The Grolier Society, Limited Edition, 1903.

MOORTGAT (Anton) and SCHARFF (Alexander). — AEGYPTEN UND VORDERASIEN IM ALTERTUM (pp. 193-535), Munich, E. Bruckmann, 1950.

One of the most recent histories of the Ancient Near East, from the earliest times to Alexander, by specialists fully conversant with the latest archaeological discoveries.

OLMSTEAD (A.T.). — A HISTORY OF ASSYRIA, New York and London, Charles Scribner, 1923.

Begins with the archaic temples of Assur and ends with the fall of Nineveh.

SCHMÖKEL (Hartmut). — GESCHICHTE DES ALTEN VORDERASIEN. HANDBUCH DER ORIENTALISTIK, ed. by B. Spuler, Vol. 2, Leiden, Brill, 1957.

Excellent reappraisal of the history of the Ancient Near East, taking the latest discoveries into account.

SCHMÖKEL (Hartmut). — HAMMURABI VON BABYLON: DIE ERRICHTUNG EINES REICHS, Munich, R. Oldenburg, 1958.

The reign of King Hammurabi of Babylon, studied in the light of the latest discoveries, drawing in particular on the royal archives of Mari.

SMITH (Sidney). — EARLY HISTORY OF ASSYRIA TO 1000 B.C., London, Chatto and Windus, 1928.

Despite the title, this is more particularly a history of Babylon, written by one of the foremost authorities on the chronology of ancient history.

IV. ARCHAEOLOGY

AMANDRY (Pierre). — CHAUDRONS A PROTOMES DE TAUREAU EN ORIENT ET EN GRÈCE, in THE AEGEAN AND THE NEAR EAST, STUDIES PRESENTED TO HETTY GOLDMAN, pp. 239-261.

Study of four bulls' heads of 'Urartian' origin (British Museum; Walters Art Gallery, Baltimore; N.K. Collection, Paris). All four may well come from Rassam's excavations at Toprak Kale in 1880. Parallels drawn with finds from Greece, Italy, Cyprus, and Altin Tepe.

AMANDRY (Pierre). — FRENCH BIBLIOGRAPHICAL DIGEST. ARCHAEOLOGY (1945-1955). II. THE NEAR EAST, New York, The Cultural Center of the French Embassy, 1957.

An accurate, detailed, fully documented bibliography of French archaeological publications.

AMANDRY (Pierre). — ORFÈVRERIE ACHÉMÉNIDE, in ANTIKE KUNST, I (1958), pp. 9-23, pl. 7-15.

An important study of gold and silver jewellery of the Achaemenian period dispersed throughout the world, with special emphasis on necklets and bracelets. The author dates the precious grave furniture from the famous tomb at Susa (Louvre) to between 350 and the opening years of the third century B.C.

AMANDRY (Pierre). — TOREUTIQUE ACHÉMÉNIDE, in ANTIKE KUNST (1959), pp. 38-56, pl. 20-30.

Study of fine household ware, in particular of amphoras with handles. The Louvre and Berlin ibexes belong to the same vase, which probably comes from Samsun and dates to the first half of the fourth century B.C.

AMIET (Pierre). — LA ZIGGURAT D'APRÈS LES CYLINDRES DE L'ÉPOQUE DYNASTIQUE ARCHAIQUE, in REVUE D'ASSYRIOLOGIE, XLV (1951), pp. 80-88.

A study of cylinder seals engraved with scenes relating to the construction of a ziggurat.

AMIET (Pierre). — ZIGGURATS ET 'CULTE EN HAUTEUR' DES ORIGINES A L'ÉPOQUE D'AKKAD, in REVUE D'ASSYRIOLOGIE, XLVII (1953), pp. 23-33.

A study based on works from Uruk, Ur and Susa. Disk of Enganduanna. The temple on a high platform served both as an altar and a shelter for the divine couple during the ceremony of hierogamy.

AMIET (Pierre). — LES COMBATS MYTHOLOGIQUES DANS L'ART MÉSOPOTAMIEN DU TROISIÈME ET DU DÉBUT DU SECOND MILLÉNAIRE, in REVUE D'ASSYRIOLOGIE, XLII (1953), pp. 129-164.

The scenes of the Akkadian period are in the tradition of Pre-Sargonid times. The theme of victory interpreted as a transposition of national triumphs on to the religious plane. The local god exerted himself to destroy the enemies of his city.

AMIET (Pierre). — LE SYMBOLISME COSMIQUE DU RÉPERTOIRE ANIMALIER EN MÉSOPOTAMIE, in REVUE D'ASSYRIOLOGIE, L (1956), pp. 113-126.

The repertory of animal themes so popular in the period of the early dynasties remained in use to the end of Assyro-Babylonian civilization. An important study, seeking to explain the significance of certain animals, such as the scorpion, the bull (human-headed or bull-man) and the eagle.

AMIET (Pierre). — NOTES DE GLYPTIQUE ORIENTALE, in CAHIERS DE BYRSA, VII (1957), pp. 23-27.

Deals with a very fine Kassite cylinder seal bearing a long inscription relating to Gilgamesh.

AMIN (Mahmud el-). — DIE RELIEFS MIT BEISCHRIFTEN VON SARGON II IN DUR SHARRUKIN, in SUMER IX (1953), pp. 35-59; X (1950), pp. 23-42.

Reliefs from Rooms V (campaign of 720), II (campaign of 716), XIV (campaign of 715), XIII (campaign of 714) and VIII. Identification, by means of inscriptions, of the cities captured.

ANDRAE (Walter). — DAS GOTTESHAUS UND DIE URFORMEN DES BAUENS IM ALTEN ORIENT, Berlin, Hans Schœtz, 1930.

An important study of sacred architecture and its distant antecedents in the form of reed constructions. A book that will be consulted for a long time to come.

ANDRAE (Walter). — DIE IONISCHE SÄULE. BAUFORM ODER SYMBOL? Berlin, Koldewey Gesellschaft, 1933.

The author's theory is that the Ionic column and capital may have originated in the cluster of reeds bound into a solid bundle.

ANDRAE (Walter). — DIE JÜNGEREN ISCHTAR- TEMPEL IN ASSUR. WISSENSCHAFTLICHE VERÖFFENTLICHUNGEN DER DEUTSCHEN ORIENT-GESELLSCHAFT, 58, Leipzig, J.C. Hinrichs, 1935.

Temples of Tukulti-Ninurta I (altar), Assur-resh-ishi I and Shalmaneser III. Sanctuary of Nabu. Group of lead figurines.

ANDRAE (Walter). — DAS WIEDERERSTANDENE ASSUR, Leipzig, J.C. Hinrichs, 1938.

Remarkable synthesis of the results obtained by the archaeological exploration of the Assyrian capital. All the essential monuments are reproduced (86 plates).

ANDRAE (Walter). — FARBIGE KERAMIK AUS ASSUR, Berlin, Scarabaeus Verlag, 1923.

Publication lavishly illustrated with colour plates (after water colours), reproducing not only ceramics but panels of painted tiles: Assur with Bow and Arrow (8), Worshipper with Locust (10) etc. Indispensable for the study of Assyrian pictorial art.

ANDRAE (Walter). — KULTRELIEF AUS DEM BRUNNEN DES ASSUR TEMPELS ZU ASSUR. WISSENSCHAFTLICHE VERÖFFENTLICHUNGEN DER DEUTSCHEN ORIENT-GESELLSCHAFT, 53, Leipzig, J.C. Hinrichs, 1931.

Above, 'mountain-god' with capridae nibbling at the plants he holds; below, small figures with the flowing vase.

ANDRAE (Walter). — VORDERASIEN, see *OTTO* (W.).

BACHMANN (W.). — FELSRELIEFS IN ASSYRIEN: BAWIAN, MALTAI UND GUNDÜK. WISSENSCHAFTLICHE VERÖFFENTLICHUNGEN DER DEUTSCHEN ORIENT-GESELLSCHAFT, 52, Leipzig, J.C. Hinrichs, 1927.

Rock reliefs showing the Assyrian king paying homage to a procession of gods. Excellent photographs both of the entire compositions and of details.

BAQIR (Taha). — IRAQ GOVERNMENT EXCAVATIONS AT AQAR QUF, in IRAQ, 1944, 1945, 1946.

Exploration of the Kassite capital Dur Kurigalzu (ziggurat, wall paintings, etc.).

BARNETT (R.D.). — THE NIMRUD IVORIES AND THE ART OF THE PHOENICIANS, in IRAQ, II (1935), pp. 179-210.

Though published over twenty-five years ago, this remains a fundamental study for a knowledge of the ivories found on Mesopotamian soil.

BARNETT (R.D.). — EARLY GREEK AND ORIENTAL IVORIES, in JOURNAL OF HELLENIC STUDIES, LXVIII (1948), pp. 1-25.

Comparative study of Oriental ivories (from Nimrud in particular) and those of archaic Greece (Samos, Delphi). The most important piece from Delphi is a God and Lion (cf. Pierre AMANDRY, in Syria, XXIV, 1944-45, pp. 149-174).

BARNETT (R.D.). — FINE IVORY-WORK, in A HISTORY OF TECHNOLOGY (pp. 663-683).

Excellent survey of ivory-work, based on finds made in the Near East.

BARNETT (R.D.). — THE TREASURE OF ZIWIYE, in IRAQ, XVIII (1956), pp. 111-117.

Challenging Godard's dating, the author holds the treasure to have been buried about 600 B.C.

BARNETT (R.D.). — THE EXCAVATIONS OF THE BRITISH MUSEUM AT TOPRAK KALE NEAR VAN, in IRAQ, XII (1950), pp. 1-43.

BARNETT (R.D.). — PHOENICIA AND THE IVORY TRADE, in ARCHAEOLOGY, 9 (1956), pp. 87-97.

Reproduces well-known ivories; also a drawing by Layard (relief from Sennacherib's palace at Nineveh) in which the author identifies the city of Tyre and the temple of Melkart.

BARNETT (R.D.). — PERSEPOLIS, in IRAQ, XIX (1957), pp. 55-57, pl. XV-XXIII.

A critical recension of E. Schmidt's work, Persepolis, I, Structures, Reliefs, Inscriptions, and a summing-up of the chronological data arrived at (Persepolis founded by 504 B.C. by Darius). Contains a catalogue of sculptures from Persepolis now dispersed throughout the world. Identification of subject nations (23 delegations are represented on the Apadana stairway). Discusses the origins of Achaemenian art.

BARNETT (R.D.). — A CATALOGUE OF THE NIMRUD IVORIES WITH OTHER EXAMPLES OF ANCIENT NEAR EASTERN IVORIES IN THE BRITISH MUSEUM, London, The Trustees of the British Museum, 1957.

Exhaustive repertory of the British Museum collection of ivories. Historical survey of their discovery; characteristics of Syrian and Phoenician art; Nimrud ivories studied in the light of the two great series of ivories found by Layard and Loftus; descriptive catalogue (pp. 169-230), 132 plates.

BARNETT (R.D.). — THE SIEGE OF LACHISH, in ISRAEL EXPLORATION JOURNAL, VIII, 3 (1958), pp. 161-164.

A fresh interpretation of the reliefs from Sennacherib's palace at Nineveh. It may have been the foreign exiles who mutilated the reliefs, as an act of vengeance, upon the death of the Assyrian monarch.

BARNETT (R.D.). — THE ASSYRIAN SCULPTURES IN THE COLLECTION OF THE ROYAL GEOGRAPHICAL SOCIETY, in THE GEOGRAPHICAL JOURNAL, CXXV (1959), pp. 197-198, 4 plates.

These sculptures (from the Rawlinson Estate) come from the palaces of Sennacherib and Assurbanipal at Nineveh. Highly interesting works, illustrating the Assyrian campaigns against the insurgent peoples of Chaldea.

BARNETT (R.D.). — CANFORD AND CUNEIFORM. A CENTURY OF ASSYRIOLOGY, in THE MUSEUM JOURNAL, 60, November 1960, pp. 192-200.

A fresh appraisal of the work of nineteenth-century Assyriologists, mentioning the disputes that sometimes arose between them, like that between Budge and Rassam, the latter backed by Layard. To his father-in-law Sir John Guest, of Canford Manor, Layard gave seven reliefs from Nineveh, which recently came to light and were sold in 1959. Cf. SMITH, William Stevenson.

BARNETT (R.D.) and WISEMAN (D.J.). — FIFTY MASTERPIECES OF ANCIENT NEAR EASTERN ART IN THE DEPARTMENT OF WESTERN ASIATIC ANTIQUITIES AT THE BRITISH MUSEUM, London, The Trustees of the British Museum, 1960.

BARRELET (Marie-Thérèse). — UNE PEINTURE DE LA COUR 106 DU PALAIS DE MARI, in STUDIA MARIANA, pp. 9-35, Leiden, E.J. Brill, 1950.

New interpretation of the 'Investiture' painting, described by A. Parrot in Syria, XVIII (1937), pp. 335-346.

BEER (M.A.). — ATLAS VAN HET TWEESTROMEN-LAND, Amsterdam and Brussels, 1960.

Deals with the geography, history, art and religion of Mesopotamia. Abundantly illustrated (296 figures), with 22 maps of the region from the earliest times to the present-day Republic of Iraq.

BERAN (Thomas). — ASSYRISCHE GLYPTIK DES 14. JAHRHUNDERTS, in ZEITSCHRIFT FUR ASSYRIOLOGIE, 18 (1957), pp. 141-215.

A survey of Assyrian glyptics, based on works found at Assur. The author distinguishes two groups: Assyrian (14th century) and the Kerkuk style. 104 works described and interpreted.

BIROT (Pierre) and DRESCH (Jean). — LA MÉDITERRANÉE ET LE MOYEN-ORIENT, Vol. II: LA MÉDITERRANÉE ORIENTALE ET LE MOYEN-ORIENT, Paris, Presses Universitaires de France, 1956.

Sound, up-to-date treatment of the subject under both its physical and human aspects.

BOSSERT (H.T.). — JANUS UND DER MANN MIT DER ADLER- ODER GREIFENMASKE, Istanbul, Nederlands Historisch-archaeologisch Instituut in het Nabije Oosten, 1959.

Iconographic study of several mythological or religious figures that occur frequently in Mesopotamian art: the man with two faces and the man with the head of an eagle or griffin.

BOTTA (Paul-Émile) and FLANDIN (Eugène). — MONUMENT DE NINIVE DÉCOUVERT ET DÉCRIT PAR M. P.-E. BOTTA, MESURÉ ET DESSINÉ PAR M. E. FLANDIN, Paris, 5 vols., 1849-50.

Monumental publication of Botta's discoveries at Khorsabad, which he took to be ancient Nineveh; hence the title of the work.

BRITISH MUSEUM. — A SUMMARY GUIDE TO THE ANTIQUITIES OF WESTERN ASIA, London, British Museum, 1952.
Contains a few reproductions: Gudea with shaven head, Lion Hunt of Assurbanipal, ivories from Nimrud, bracelet from the Oxus treasure.

BUCHANAN (Briggs W.). — THE CYLINDER SEALS OF THE YALE BABYLONIAN COLLECTION, in YALE UNIVERSITY LIBRARY GAZETTE, 35, July 1960, pp. 23-24.
The Yale Babylonian Collection contains 655 seals, 512 of them cylinder seals. The author, one of the leading specialists in the field of Oriental glyptics, has arranged them chronologically, from the Uruk period to Achaemenian times. The dating seems accurate and reliable.

BUDGE (E.A. Wallis). — ASSYRIAN SCULPTURE IN THE BRITISH MUSEUM. REIGN OF ASHUR-NASIR-PAL, 885-860 B.C. London, British Museum, 1914.
Statuary and reliefs of the time of Assurnasirpal (53 plates) with short descriptive notices. Excellent reproductions.

BUDGE (E.A. Wallis). — A GUIDE TO THE BABYLONIAN AND ASSYRIAN ANTIQUITIES, London, British Museum, 3rd edition, 1922.

BUSINK (T.A.). — LA ZIGGURAT DE DUR-SARRUKIN, in COMPTE RENDU DE LA TROISIÈME RENCONTRE ASSYRIOLOGIQUE INTERNATIONALE, pp. 105-122. Leiden, Nederlandsch Instituut voor het Nabije Oosten, 1954.
Criticizes the theories of Place and Thomas and proposes a new reconstruction of the Khorsabad ziggurat.

BUSINK (T.A.). — DARSTELLUNGEN ALTMESOPOTA-MISCHER BAUWERKE, in JEOL, 15 (1957-58), pp. 219-231, Leiden, E.J. Brill.
With ancient Mesopotamian architecture now largely in ruins, many features of it can only be studied in representations of ancient buildings. Of these the author, a Dutch architect, makes the best possible use.

BUSINK (T.A.). — DE BABYLONISCHE TEMPELTOREN, Leiden, E.J. Brill, 1949.
Well-informed, up-to-date monograph by one of the best qualified specialists on the subject.

CONTENAU (Georges). — MANUEL D'ARCHÉOLOGIE ORIENTALE, DEPUIS LES ORIGINES JUSQU'A L'ÉPOQUE D'ALEXANDRE, 4 volumes of text (2378 pages), abundantly illustrated (1311 figures in the text), Paris, Picard, 1927, 1931, 1947.
Exhaustive recapitulation of the results obtained from many excavation sites in the Near East, up to a fairly recent date.

CONTENAU (Georges). — L'ÉPOPÉE DE GILGAMESH, POÈME BABYLONIEN, Paris, L'Artisan du Livre, 1939.
A French translation of the epic poem whose hero figures so prominently in the Mesopotamian iconography.

CONTENAU (Georges) and GHIRSHMAN (Roman). — FOUILLES DU TÉPÉ-GIYAN PRÈS DE NÉHA-VEND, 1931 et 1932, Paris, Geuthner, 1935.
Publication of the excavations at Tepe Giyan, which revealed the early periods of Iranian civilization. The examples of pottery are among the most important found so far.

CONTENAU (Georges). — MONUMENTS MÉSOPOTA-MIENS NOUVELLEMENT ACQUIS OU PEU CONNUS. MUSÉE DU LOUVRE. Paris, Editions d'Art et d'Histoire, 1934.
Works ranging from the Jemdet Nasr period to Achaemenian times (stone, bronze, shell).

CONTENAU (Georges). — L'INCRUSTATION SUR MÉTAL ET L'ORFÈVRERIE CLOISONNÉE EN MÉSOPOTA-MIE, in SYRIA, XXXIII (1956), pp. 58-62.
Study of metal inlays and cloisonné work, with examples from Sumerian art, where these techniques appear for the first time.

Corpus of Ancient Near Eastern Seals in North American Collections, edited by Edith Porada, 2 volumes, Washington, Bollingen Foundation, 1948.
Excellent publication on the Oriental glyptics in the Pierpont Morgan Collection, with 176 plates of the highest order illustrating 1157 items. Cf. PORADA.

DELAPORTE (Louis). — CATALOGUE DES CYLINDRES ORIENTAUX ET DES CACHETS ASSYRO-BABYLO-NIENS, PERSES ET SYRO-CAPPADOCIENS DE LA BIBLIOTHÈQUE NATIONALE. INSTITUT DE FRANCE, FONDATION EUGÈNE PIOT. 1 vol. of text, 1 vol. of plates, Paris, Ernest Leroux, 1910.
Descriptive catalogue of 650 seals preserved in the Bibliothèque Nationale.

DELAPORTE (Louis). — CATALOGUE DES CYLINDRES ORIENTAUX. MUSÉE DU LOUVRE. I. Fouilles et Missions, 1920. II. Acquisitions, 1923, Paris, Hachette.
Exhaustive catalogue of the cylinder seals preserved in the Louvre.

DELOUGAZ (P.). — PLANO-CONVEX BRICKS AND THE METHOD OF THEIR EMPLOYMENT. STUDIES IN ANCIENT ORIENTAL CIVILIZATION, 7. Chicago, University of Chicago Press, 1934.
Excellent monograph by a qualified specialist in mud-brickwork (Khafaje).

DELOUGAZ (P.). — POTTERY FROM THE DIYALA REGION. ORIENTAL INSTITUTE PUBLICATIONS, LXIII. Chicago, University of Chicago Press, 1952.
A valuable, fully documented work with 204 plates, 16 in colour.

DESHAYES (Jean). — LES OUTILS DE L'AGE DU BRONZE, Paris, Geuthner, 1960.
An important technical and stylistic study of the tools and implements of the Ancient Near East.

DHORME (P.). — CHOIX DE TEXTES RELIGIEUX ASSYRO-BABYLONIENS, Paris, Gabalda, 1907.
Publication of the standard religious texts, inviting comparison with representations on many Mesopotamian works.

DHORME (Edouard). — LES RELIGIONS DE BABY-LONIE ET D'ASSYRIE. Paris, Collection Mana, Presses Universitaires de France, 1949.
A work of the highest order, dealing with every aspect of Mesopotamian religion. The best study of its kind in French.

DIEULAFOY (Marcel). — L'ART ANTIQUE DE LA PERSE, Paris, Morel, Des Fosses et Cie, 2 vols., 1884-85.

Large-scale study of ancient Persian art, from the Achaemenians to the Sassanians. The text is now out of date, but the illustrations and documentary material are first-rate. Photographs by Madame Dieulafoy, photogravures by P. Dujardin.

DIEULAFOY (Marcel). — LES ANTIQUITÉS DE SUSE DÉCOUVERTES ET RAPPORTÉES PAR LA MISSION DIEULAFOY (1884-1896), Paris, Leroux, 1913.

Concise catalogue of the Susian antiquities discovered by the Dieulafoy Expedition and now in the Louvre.

DOSSIN (Georges). — L'INSCRIPTION DE FONDATION DE IAHDUN-LIM ROI DE MARI, in SYRIA, XXXII (1955), pp. 1-28.

An historical inscription of the highest interest, of the 18th century B.C., discovered in 1954 in the temple of Shamash, copied, translated and commented on by the epigrapher of the Mari expedition.

DUCHESNE-GUILLEMIN (Marcelle). — LA MUSIQUE EN ÉGYPTE ET EN MÉSOPOTAMIE ANCIENNE, in HISTOIRE DE LA MUSIQUE, I, Encyclopédie de la Pléiade, Paris, Gallimard, 1960, pp. 353-361.

An excellent account of the musical instruments of the Ancient East, dealing in particular with the various types of harps. On harps, see also the article by the same author in Revue d'Assyriologie, *1937, pp. 29-41.*

DYSON (Robert H.). — A GIFT OF NIMRUD SCULPTURES, in BULLETIN OF THE BROOKLYN MUSEUM, XVIII (1957), 3, pp. 1-12.

Publication of 12 reliefs from Nimrud, presented to the Brooklyn Museum in 1955.

FALKENSTEIN (A.). — ZUR CHRONOLOGIE DER SUMERISCHEN LITERATUR, in COMPTE RENDU DE LA SECONDE RENCONTRE ASSYRIOLOGIQUE INTERNATIONALE, Paris, Imprimerie Nationale, 1951, pp. 12-27.

A study of outstanding importance. The author divides Sumerian literary texts into two groups, one dating to the 'Old Babylonian' period, the other to between 1100 and the Seleucid period; but he carefully distinguishes between copies and the initial composition of texts.

FALKENSTEIN (A.). and SODEN (W. von). — SUMERISCHE UND AKKADISCHE HYMNEN UND GEBETE, Zurich and Stuttgart, Artemis Verlag, 1953.

A remarkable compilation by the two leading German specialists in Sumero-Akkadian literature. The texts (hymns and prayers) are divided into various types: Götterlieder, Königshymnen, Lieder auf Tempel, Klagelieder, Beschwörungen, etc. With detailed notes and index of names.

FARMER (Henry George). — THE MUSIC OF ANCIENT MESOPOTAMIA: ANCIENT AND ORIENTAL MUSIC (pp. 228-254), London, Egon Wellesz, 1957.

FORBES (R.J.). — METALLURGY IN ANTIQUITY. A NOTE-BOOK FOR ARCHAEOLOGISTS AND TECHNOLOGISTS, Leiden, E.J. Brill, 1950.

An account of our present knowledge of ancient metallurgy.

FORBES (R.J.). — STUDIES IN ANCIENT TECHNOLOGY, I (1955), II (1955), III (1955), IV (1956), V (1957), VI (1958), Leiden, E.J. Brill.

Well-documented works dealing with all the creative activities of early times.

FORBES (R.J.). — EXTRACTING, SMELTING AND ALLOYING, in HISTORY OF TECHNOLOGY, pp. 572-599.

Concise account of the technique of ancient metallurgy.

FORBES (R.J.). — BIBLIOGRAPHIA ANTIQUA, PHILOSOPHIA NATURALIS. II. METALLURGY. Leiden, Nederlandsch Instituut voor het Nabije Oosten, 1940-50.

Exhaustive bibliography, listing 10,751 references to ancient science and technology.

FRANCHET (Louis). — LA CÉRAMIQUE PRIMITIVE. INTRODUCTION A L'ÉTUDE DE LA TECHNOLOGIE. Nouvelles Archives des Missions Scientifiques, Ministère de l'Instruction publique, XVI, Paris, 1911.

A detailed technical study which remains a standard work.

FRANKFORT (Henri). — CYLINDER SEALS, A DOCUMENTARY ESSAY ON THE ART AND RELIGION OF THE ANCIENT NEAR EAST, London, Macmillan, 1939.

One of the most valuable compilations of Oriental glyptics, not only grouping the seals chronologically and geographically but also interpreting them. The best general study so far made.

FRANKFORT (Henri). — STUDIES IN EARLY POTTERY OF THE NEAR EAST. I. MESOPOTAMIA, SYRIA AND EGYPT AND THEIR EARLIEST INTERRELATIONS. London, The Royal Anthropological Institute of Great Britain and Ireland, 1924.

Shows the importance of pottery as a source of knowledge of early history and civilization. Remains a standard work.

FRANKFORT (Henri). — TOWN PLANNING IN ANCIENT MESOPOTAMIA, in THE TOWN PLANNING REVIEW, XXI (1950), pp. 99-115.

With illustrations of aerial views, ground plans and reconstructions of Mesopotamian architecture.

FRANKFORT (Henri). — THE ORIGIN OF THE BIT HILANI, in IRAQ, XIV (1952), pp. 120-131.

Study of an architectural form found in Mesopotamia (Tell Halaf, Khorsabad), whose origin is still a matter of controversy. Frankfort regards it as a product of Syrian (not Anatolian) civilization.

FRANKFORT (Henri), GROENEWEGEN-FRANKFORT (H.A.), WILSON (John) and JACOBSEN (Thorkild). — THE INTELLECTUAL ADVENTURE OF ANCIENT MAN, Chicago, University of Chicago Press, 1946. Published in England as BEFORE PHILOSOPHY, Harmondsworth, Penguin Books, 1949.

A most interesting study of the primitive myths, beliefs and speculations of the Egyptians and Mesopotamians.

GADD (C.J.). — HISTORY AND MONUMENTS OF UR, London, Chatto and Windus, 1929.

General survey of the history of the great Sumerian capital, illustrated with works excavated there, including the 'royal' tombs.

GADD (C.J.). — THE ASSYRIAN SCULPTURES, London, British Museum, 1934.
Excellent monograph with valuable notes on the Assyrian sculptures in the British Museum.

GADD (C.J.). — THE STONES OF ASSYRIA. THE SURVIVING REMAINS OF ASSYRIAN SCULPTURE. THEIR RECOVERY AND THEIR ORIGINAL POSITIONS. London, Chatto and Windus, 1936.
An account of Assyrian excavations and discoveries (Botta and Flandin; Layard; Rassam; Place; Loftus and Boucher). Listing of Assyrian reliefs in the principal museums of the world.

GADD (C.J.). — THE HARRAN INSCRIPTIONS OF NABONIDUS, in ANATOLIAN STUDIES, VIII (1958), pp. 35-92.
Publication of three Neo-Babylonian stelae discovered in 1956 by D.S. Rice at Harran. They throw light on Nabonidus' religious activity and his stay at Teima.

GALPIN (Francis W.). — THE MUSIC OF THE SUMERIANS AND THEIR IMMEDIATE SUCCESSORS, THE BABYLONIANS AND ASSYRIANS, Strasbourg, Heitz, 1955.
A study of musical instruments, from representations of them. The instruments are divided into three groups: percussion, wind, strings. Extensive bibliography (pp. 87-98).

GARELLI (Paul). — GILGAMESH ET SA LÉGENDE, Cahiers du Groupe français Thureau-Dangin, I, Paris, Imprimerie Nationale, 1960.
Studies brought together on the occasion of the VIIe Rencontre Assyriologique Internationale, Paris, 1958. A highly important compilation, with an exhaustive bibliography.

GHIRSHMAN (Roman). — MASJID-I-SOLAIMAN, RESIDENCE DES PREMIERS ACHÉMÉNIDES, in SYRIA, XXVII (1950), pp. 205-220.
This architecture stems from Urartian traditions and inspired that of Pasargadae and Persepolis.

GHIRSHMAN (Roman). — LE TRÉSOR DE SAKKEZ, LES ORIGINES DE L'ART MÈDE ET LES BRONZES DU LURISTAN, in ARTIBUS ASIAE, XIII (1950), pp. 181-206.
Publication of various pieces from the Ziwiyeh (or Sakkez) treasure acquired by private collectors. The provenance indicated by the dealers concerned may well be questioned (cf. DUSSAUD, in Syria, XXVIII, p. 290).

GHIRSHMAN (Roman) and others. — VILLAGE PERSE-ACHÉMÉNIDE (MEMOIRES DE LA MISSION ARCHÉOLOGIQUE EN IRAN XXXVI), Paris, Presses Universitaires de France, 1954.
A settlement about half a mile east of the royal Elamite acropolis of Susa. Publication of the archaeological material found there, compared with works from Sialk, Luristan, Sakkez (Ziwiyeh), Tepe Giyan, Persepolis, etc.

GODARD (André). — LES BRONZES DU LURISTAN. ARS ASIATICA, XVII, Paris, G. Van Oest, 1931.

GODARD (André). — LE TRÉSOR DE ZIWIYEH (KURDISTAN). Publication du Service Archéologique de l'Iran. Haarlem, J. Enschedé, 1950.
Publication of one of the most important finds made in Iran, south-east of Lake Urmya, in 1947.

GOOSSENS (G.). — RELIEFS D'ASSURNAZIRPAL II, in BULLETIN DES MUSÉES ROYAUX D'ART ET D'HISTOIRE, 28 (1956), pp. 31-39, Brussels.
Publication of several Assyrian reliefs (sacred tree, winged genius, stele) in the Brussels Museum.

GOVERNMENT OF IRAQ. — Directorate General of Antiquities. A GUIDE TO THE IRAQ MUSEUM COLLECTIONS, Baghdad, Government Press, 1942.
Excellent guide with good reproductions of famous works (Warka vase, statuettes from Khafaje and Ashnunnak, woman's head from Warka, helmet of Meskalamdug from Ur, statue of Alla from Lagash, Assyrian reliefs from Khorsabad).

GRESSMANN (Hugo). — ALTORIENTALISCHE TEXTE ZUM ALTEN TESTAMENT, Berlin and Leipzig, Walter de Gruyter, 2nd edition, 1926.
Though published a good many years ago, this book has lost none of its value. Cf. PRITCHARD for an excellent complement to it.

GROENEWEGEN-FRANKFORT (H.A.). — ARREST AND MOVEMENT: AN ESSAY ON SPACE AND TIME IN THE REPRESENTATIONAL ART OF THE ANCIENT NEAR EAST, London, Faber and Faber, 1951.
Analysis of styles, themes and composition in Mesopotamian art, pp. 145-181.

GÜTERBOCK (HANS G.). — A NOTE ON THE STELA OF TUKULTI-NINURTA II FOUND NEAR TELL ASHARA, in JOURNAL OF NEAR EASTERN STUDIES, XVI (1957), p. 123.
The author rectifies the translation given in Annales Archéologiques de Syrie, II (1952), pp. 169-190. Representation of Adad-Nirari II on one side of the stele erected by his son Tukulti-Ninurta II. Cf. TOURNAY and SAOUAF.

GÜTERBOCK (HANS G.). — NARRATION IN ANATOLIAN, SYRIAN, AND ASSYRIAN ART, in AMERICAN JOURNAL OF ARCHEOLOGY, LXI (1957), pp. 62-71.
The palace of Assurnasirpal II at Nimrud is the earliest known example of a building decorated with orthostats adorned with reliefs. Study of the Balawat bronze plaques, reliefs from Khorsabad, and the hunting scenes with Assurbanipal ('continuous style').

HALLER (Arndt) and ANDRAE (W.). — DIE HEILIGTÜMER DES GOTTES ASSUR UND DER SIN-SHAMASH-TEMPEL IN ASSUR. WISSENSCHAFTLICHE VERÖFFENTLICHUNGEN DER DEUTSCHEN ORIENT-GESELLSCHAFT, 67. Berlin, Mann, 1956.
From the temple of Assur come (among other works) the relief of the mountain-god and the large basin with the god Ea. The temple of Sin-Shamash is a double temple, each with its own cella and ante-cella.

HALLER (Arndt). — DIE GRÄBER UND GRÜFTE VON ASSUR. WISSENSCHAFTLICHE VERÖFFENTLICHUNGEN DER DEUTSCHEN ORIENT-GESELLSCHAFT, 65. Berlin, Mann, 1954.
Publication of 1140 graves cleared at Assur. The 'Assyrian' tombs correspond to three different periods and the following types: clay, covered or uncovered; brick; jars; sarcophagi; vaults (No. 45 is the largest); royal tombs (Shamshi-Adad V, Assurbelkala, Sennacherib ?).

HANFMANN (G.M.A.). — FOUR URARTIAN BULLS' HEADS, in ANATOLIAN STUDIES, VI (1956), pp. 205-213.
Study of four bulls' heads (Emery Collection, Cincinnati; Fogg Art Museum, Harvard; Cleveland Museum; Louvre), which undoubtedly adorned large receptacles. The author proposes to date them to between the late 8th and the late 7th century B.C. These works may be compared with the heads from Toprak Kale, capital of Urartu.

HEINRICH (Ernst). — DIE STELLUNG DER URUKTEMPEL IN DER BAUGESCHICHTE, in ZEITSCHRIFT FÜR ASSYRIOLOGIE (1949), pp. 21-44.
Study of outstanding importance in which the Uruk sanctuaries are assigned their due place in the architectural tradition of Mesopotamia. Needs to be supplemented now with the discoveries made at Eridu.

HEINRICH (Ernst). — BAUWERKE IN DER ALTSUMERISCHEN BILDKUNST, Wiesbaden, Otto Harrassowitz, 1957.
A study of Sumerian architecture as represented in works of art.

HEUZEY (Léon). — LES ORIGINES ORIENTALES DE L'ART, Paris, Leroux, 1891-1915.
This 'recueil de mémoires archéologiques et de monuments figurés' contains a number of studies devoted to Mesopotamian works (Stele of the Vultures, the flowing vase, maceheads, statuette of Assurdan, etc.). Also contains a curious article on 'Oriental Antiquity' at the Paris World's Fair of 1889.

HINKE (W.J.). — A NEW BOUNDARY STONE OF NEBUCHADREZZAR I FROM NIPPUR, Philadelphia, University of Pennsylvania, 1907.
Deals with the discovery of a kudurru. Useful contribution to the study of Kassite boundary stones.

HOOKE (S.H.). — BABYLONIAN AND ASSYRIAN RELIGION, London, Hutchinson's University Library, 1953.
On gods, temples, festivals, religious life and Babylonian myths.

HROUDA (Barthel). — DIE BEMALTE KERAMIK DES ZWEITEN JAHRTAUSENDS IN NORDMESOPOTAMIEN UND NORDSYRIEN, Berlin, Mann, 1957.
Publication of painted vases discovered at Assur and a general survey of the painted pottery of the ancient Near East of the third and second millennia B.C. (Khabur, Nuzi, Cappadocia, Palestine).

JACOBSEN (Thorkild) and LLOYD (Seton). — SENNACHERIB'S AQUEDUCT AT JERWAN. ORIENTAL INSTITUTE PUBLICATIONS, XXIV, Chicago, The University of Chicago Press, 1935.
On one of the most important engineering feats of the Assyrian period, bringing water from Jerwan to Nineveh.

JACOBSEN (Thorkild). — MESOPOTAMIA, in THE INTELLECTUAL ADVENTURE OF ANCIENT MAN, pp. 125-219. (Cf. FRANKFORT.)
An excellent appraisal of Mesopotamian religious beliefs. Indispensable for the identification of religious scenes represented on monuments.

JASTROW (Morris). — BILDERMAPPE ZUR RELIGION BABYLONIENS UND ASSYRIENS (1 vol. of text, 1 vol. of plates). Giessen, Alfred Töpelmann, 1912.
Well-chosen illustrations of 226 monuments. Now somewhat out of date.

JEREMIAS (Alfred). — HANDBUCH DER ALTORIENTALISCHEN GEISTESKULTUR, Berlin and Leipzig, Walter de Gruyter, 2nd edition, 1929.
A remarkable study of Mesopotamian civilization and the iconography of the gods (pp. 324-391), based on the works known at the date of publication.

KANTOR (H.J.). — ORIENTAL INSTITUTE MUSEUM NOTES, 8: ACHAEMENID JEWELRY IN THE ORIENTAL INSTITUTE, in JOURNAL OF NEAR EASTERN STUDIES, XVII (1958), pp. 1-23.
Excellent reproductions giving a good idea of an outstanding collection rich in animal imagery, with lions predominating.

KING (L.W.). — BABYLONIAN BOUNDARY-STONES AND MEMORIAL TABLETS, London, British Museum, 1912.
Exhaustive publication of the kudurrus in the British Museum.

KING (L.W.). — BRONZE RELIEFS FROM THE GATES OF SHALMANESER, KING OF ASSYRIA, 860-825 B.C., London, British Museum, 1915.
Exhaustive publication of the bronze plaques from Balawat.

KINSKY (George). — ALBUM MUSICAL, Paris, Delagrave, 1930.
An album with 1560 illustrations, three pages of which are devoted to the Near East. Nothing on Ur, as Woolley's discoveries had not yet been published.

KOLDEWEY (Robert). — DAS WIEDERERSTEHENDE BABYLON, Leipzig, J.C. Hinrichs, 1913, later edition, 1925. English edition: THE EXCAVATIONS AT BABYLON, London, Macmillan, 1914.
Synthesis of the results obtained in the excavations at Babylon. All the essential works are reproduced (255 figures in the text, several inset plates).

KOLDEWEY (Robert). — DIE TEMPEL VON BABYLON UND BORSIPPA. WISSENSCHAFTLICHE VERÖFFENTLICHUNGEN DER DEUTSCHEN ORIENT-GESELLSCHAFT, 15. Leipzig, J.C. Hinrichs, 1911.
Temples of Ninmah and Ninurta, Temple Z (Babylon), Esagila (Babylon) and, even more important, the Temple of Nabu and the ziggurat at Borsippa (Birs Nimrud).

KOLDEWEY (Robert). — DAS ISCHTAR-TOR IN BABYLON (WVDOG, 32), Leipzig, J.C. Hinrichs, 1918.
The Ishtar Gate was a highly complex structure decorated with symbolic themes. Several colour plates give some idea of the tones of the polychrome reliefs.

KOLDEWEY (Robert) and WETZEL (F.). — DIE KÖNIGSBURGEN VON BABYLON (WVDOG, 54), Part One, Leipzig, J.C. Hinrichs, 1931.
Publication of the Südburg, which forms the nucleus of this architectural complex.

KOLDEWEY (Robert) and WETZEL (F.). — DIE KÖNIGSBURGEN VON BABYLON (WISSENSCHAFTLICHE VERÖFFENTLICHEN DER DEUTSCHEN ORIENT-GESELLSCHAFT 55), Part Two, Leipzig, J.C. Hinrichs, 1932.
Publication of the Hauptburg and the 'summer palace' of Nebuchadnezzar on the hill of Babil.

KRAMER (S.N.). — SUMERIAN MYTHOLOGY, Philadelphia, The American Philosophical Society, 1944.
A work of fundamental importance on Sumerian mythology.

KRAMER (S.N.). — FROM THE TABLETS OF SUMER, Indian Hills, Colorado, The Falcon's Wing Press, 1956. Subsequent editions: HISTORY BEGINS AT SUMER, London, Thames and Hudson, and New York, Doubleday and Company, 1957.

A new study, with additions, of the literary documentation dealt with in the same author's Sumerian Mythology. *Many iconographic parallels are proposed.*

KRAMER (S.N.). — SUMERIAN LITERATURE. A GENERAL SURVEY in THE BIBLE AND THE ANCIENT NEAR EAST, dedicated to W.F. Albright. New York, Doubleday and Company, 1961.

Some well documented pages (pp. 249-266) summing up the data available (in October, 1959) on the subject.

KRAMER (S.N.). — MYTHOLOGY OF SUMER AND AKKAD in MYTHOLOGIES OF THE ANCIENT WORLD, pp. 95-137. New York, Doubleday and Company, 1961.

A survey of the leading themes of Sumero-Akkadian mythology, illustrated by some typical excerpts dealing with, inter alios, Enlil, Enki, Ninurta, Inanna, Dumuzi (as for the Sumerians); Marduk, Nergal, Adapa, Etana and Ishum (as for the Akkadians).

LABAT (René). — LE POÈME BABYLONIEN DE LA CRÉATION, Paris, Adrien Maisonneuve, 1935.

A critical edition of the Babylonian Poem of Creation, Enuma-elish, with introduction, transcription and annotated translation.

LAESSOE (Jorgen). — A STATUE OF SHALMANESER III FROM NIMRUD, in IRAQ, XXI (1959), pp. 147-157.

Fragments of a statue (now reconstituted in Baghdad Museum) discovered by a peasant in 1956 at the foot of the acropolis. Datable to 827 or 826 B.C.

LAESSOE (Jorgen). — BUILDING INSCRIPTIONS FROM FORT SHALMANESER, NIMRUD, in IRAQ, XXI (1959), pp. 38-41.

Inscriptions on the base of a throne, in a courtyard and on a doorstep. They relate to campaigns to the sources of the Tigris and Euphrates and to the erection of statues.

LANGENEGGER (F.), MÜLLER (K.) and NAUMANN (R.). — TELL HALAF, II: DIE BAUWERKE, Berlin, Walter de Gruyter, 1950.

Publication (edited by Naumann after the death of Langenegger and Müller) of the architectural remains excavated at Tell Halaf by von Oppenheim. For the reliefs, see MOORTGAT.

LAYARD (Austen Henry). — DISCOVERIES IN THE RUINS OF NINEVEH AND BABYLON, London, John Murray, 1853, and New York, Harper and Brothers, 1856.

An account written in the style of the period but full of valuable information. Lavishly illustrated with outline drawings.

LAYARD (Austen Henry). — THE MONUMENTS OF NINEVEH FROM DRAWINGS MADE ON THE SPOT, London, John Murray, 2 vols., 1849-53.

The reconstructions (in colour) of a 'Hall in an Assyrian Palace' (pl. 2) and 'The Palaces of Nimrud' on the banks of the Tigris now have no more than a documentary value.

LEGRAIN (L.). — UR EXCAVATIONS X, SEAL CYLINDERS, London and Philadelphia, Trustees of the British Museum and of the University Museum, University of Pennsylvania, 1951.

Descriptive catalogue of the seals found at Ur, dating from the Jemdet Nasr period to Seleucid and even Parthian times.

LENZEN (Heinrich). — DIE ENTWICKLUNG DER ZIKURRAT, VON IHREN ANFÄNGEN BIS ZUR ZEIT DER III. DYNASTIE VON UR, Leipzig, Otto Harrassowitz, 1941.

General study of Mesopotamian ziggurats, from the archaic periods to the Third Dynasty of Ur.

LENZEN (Heinrich). — DIE TEMPEL DER SCHICHT ARCHAISCH IV IN URUK, in ZEITSCHRIFT FÜR ASSYRIOLOGIE, N.F. XV (1949), pp. 1-20.

A study of capital importance, with plans, dealing in detail with the architecture of the great temples of the Jemdet Nasr period at Uruk.

LEVEY (Martin). — CHEMISTRY AND CHEMICAL TECHNOLOGY IN ANCIENT MESOPOTAMIA, Amsterdam, 1959.

LIMET (Henri). — LE TRAVAIL DU MÉTAL AU PAYS DE SUMER AU TEMPS DE LA IIIᵉ DYNASTIE D'UR, Paris, 'Les Belles-Lettres,' 1960.

An important study, both philologically and historically, on ancient metal-work, dwelling particularly on metallurgy and goldsmith's work: metals and alloys, provenance, organization of the workshops, enumeration of objects and metals mentioned in records, identification and characteristics.

LLOYD (Seton). — BUILDING IN BRICK AND STONE, in A HISTORY OF TECHNOLOGY, pp. 456-473.

A brief chronological account of Mesopotamian building techniques.

LLOYD (Seton). — FOUNDATIONS IN THE DUST, Oxford University Press, 1947, and Penguin Books, 1954.

A survey of archaeological research in Mesopotamia and the development of Assyriology. A highly readable account of the activities of the early explorers and excavators: Rich, Layard, Rassam and George Smith, giving due credit to the preponderant part played by Rawlinson.

LLOYD (Seton) and SAFAR (Fuad). — TELL UQAIR. EXCAVATIONS BY THE IRAQ GOVERNMENT DIRECTORATE OF ANTIQUITIES IN 1940 AND 1941, in JOURNAL OF NEAR EASTERN STUDIES, II,2 (1943), pp. 131-158, pls. III-XXXI.

Report on the excavations at Tell Uqair.

LOUD (G.). — KHORSABAD, I. EXCAVATIONS IN THE PALACE AND AT A CITY GATE. ORIENTAL INSTITUTE PUBLICATIONS, XXXVIII. Chicago, University of Chicago Press, 1936.

LOUD (G.) and ALTMAN (C.B.). — KHORSABAD, II. THE CITADEL AND THE TOWN. ORIENTAL INSTITUTE PUBLICATIONS, XL. University of Chicago Press, 1938.

Systematic excavation of the Citadel, alongside the Palace, revealed the remains of several large buildings: residences of court officials and the temple of Nabu.

MACHABEY (A.). — LA MUSIQUE SUMÉRO-CHALDÉENNE ET ÉGYPTIENNE, in LA MUSIQUE DES ORIGINES A NOS JOURS, edited by Norbert Dufourcq, Paris, Larousse, 1946, pp. 59-62.

A brief article incorporating the discoveries made at Ur and Lagash.

MALLOWAN (M.E.L.) and ROSE (Cruikshank). —
EXCAVATIONS AT TELL ARPACHIYAH, 1933,
London, separate reprint from IRAQ, II, Part I,
1935.

Publication of exceptional interest for the wealth of its docu-
mentation. The Halaf period, in particular, here takes on a
new lustre.

MALLOWAN (M.E.L.). — THE EXCAVATIONS AT
NIMRUD (KALHU), in IRAQ, XII (1950),
pp. 147-183; XIII (1951), pp. 1-20 (ivories);
XIV (1952), pp. 1-23 (stele, ivory of Assurnasirpal) and 45-53 (ivories); XV (1953),
pp. 1-42 ('Monna Lisa' ivory); XVI (1954),
pp. 59-114 and 115-163 (figurines, ivories);
XVIII (1956) (palace, temple of Nabu);
XIX (1957) (temples of Nabu and Ninurta);
XIX (1957) (excavations on and around the
acropolis; 'Fort Shalmaneser'; ivories); XXI
(1959), pp. 93-97 ('Fort Shalmaneser' and
ivories).

MALLOWAN (M.E.L.). — Articles in THE ILLUSTRAT-
ED LONDON NEWS, July 22, 1950 (ivories);
July 29, 1950 (exorcism plaque, cylinder
seal); August 16, 1952 ('Monna Lisa' and
chryselephantine ivories); August 23, 1952
(reliefs); August 8, 1953 ('Monna Lisa' ivory
restored); August 15, 1953 (foundation
figurines); August 22, 1953 (ivories, cylinder
seals, alabaster statuettes); January 21,
1956 (god with a box); January 28, 1956
(ivories); November 23, 1957 (ivory from
Fort Shalmaneser, Aramaean *ostracon*);
November 30, 1957 (magnificent batch of
ivories from the same sector); December 7,
1957 (third series of ivories); January 17,
1959 (Fort Shalmaneser and three pages of
ivories reproduced in colour); January 30,
1960 (two pages in colour); June 25, 1960
(unpublished ivories, just repaired, including
'St George and the Dragon').

MALLOWAN (M.E.L.). — TWENTY-FIVE YEARS OF
MESOPOTAMIAN DISCOVERY (1932-1956), Lon-
don, The British School of Archaeology in
Iraq, 1958.

A remarkable summing up of the results obtained on sites
excavated by the British School of Archaeology, in Iraq (Arpat-
chiyah, Nimrud) and Syria (Khabur and Balik region).

MARCEL-DUBOIS (Claudie). — A PROPOS DE
'SCÈNES DE MUSIQUE ET DE DANSE', in REVUE
DES ARTS ASIATIQUES, X (1936), pp. 110-112.

The author dwells on the symbolic, magical and cultic aspects
of ancient music, and elucidates the names of several instruments.

MARYON (Herbert) and PLENDERLEITH (H.J.).
— FINE METAL-WORK, in A HISTORY OF TECH-
NOLOGY, pp. 623-662.

A factual account of the techniques employed in working various
metals.

MEISSNER (Bruno). — GRUNDZÜGE DER ALTBABY-
LONISCHEN PLASTIK, Leipzig, J.C. Hinrichs,
1914 (Part I of GRUNDZÜGE DER BABYLONISCH-
ASSYRISCHEN PLASTIK, 1915).

Still a valuable work, though allowance must be made for the
state of archaeological knowledge at the time.

MEISSNER (Bruno). — GRUNDZÜGE DER BABYLONISCH-
ASSYRISCHEN PLASTIK. DER ALTE ORIENT,
XV. Leipzig, J.C. Hinrichs, 1914-15.

Lavishly illustrated monograph (260 figures in the text).
Remains indispensable for an understanding of Assyro-Baby-
lonian art.

MEISSNER (Bruno). — BABYLONIEN UND ASSYRIEN,
I-II, Heidelberg, Carl Winter, 1920-25.

After a quarter of a century this remains a fundamental contri-
bution to our knowledge of the Mesopotamian world under
all its aspects. The picture it gives naturally needs to be filled
out on the basis of discoveries made since 1925.

MENANT (Joachim). — COLLECTION DE CLERCQ.
CATALOGUE METHODIQUE ET RAISONNÉ. ANTI-
QUITÉS ASSYRIENNES. I (1888), II (1903).

MERTZENFELD (C. Decamps de). — INVENTAIRE
COMMENTÉ DES IVOIRES PHÉNICIENS ET APPA-
RENTÉS DÉCOUVERTS DANS LE PROCHE-ORIENT,
Paris, de Boccard, 1954.

Deals with the 'Phoenician' ivories of the Assyrian period
discovered in Mesopotamia.

MEYER (G.R.). — STAATLICHE MUSEEN ZU BERLIN.
DURCH VIER JAHRTAUSENDE ALTVORDERASIATI-
SCHER KULTUR. Berlin, Vorderasiatisches
Museum, 1956.

This guide-book throws light at last on the fate of the vast
Oriental collections in the Berlin Museum, which suffered severe-
ly from air raids during the Second World War, and which,
since the war, has been located in the Russian Zone. The
Museum has been rebuilt and completely reorganized, and
the great architectural complexes (e.g. the Processional Way,
the Ishtar Gate and the Throne Room of the Neo-Babylonian
palace, all from Babylon) are again on display.

MEYER (G.R.). — WAS URALTE DENKMÄLER ERZÄHLEN.
KURZE WEGLEITUNG DURCH DAS VORDERASIA-
TISCHES MUSEUM. Berlin, Vorderasiatisches
Museum, 1960.

An excellent guide, concise and carefully illustrated. By no
means a repetition of the previous work.

MINKOWSKI (Helmut). — DER TURM ZU BABEL, in
HERAKLITH RUNDSCHAU, n.d. (1960?).

The most recent and comprehensive survey of the iconography
of the Tower of Babel, from the sixth century A.D. to the
different reconstructions proposed by contemporary archaeologists.
Over 500 items cited.

MOORTGAT (Anton). — DIE BILDENDE KUNST DES
ALTEN ORIENTS UND DIE BERGVÖLKER, Berlin,
Hans Schoetz, 1932.

A systematic study of the documentary material from Northern
Mesopotamia.

MOORTGAT (Anton). — VORDERASIATISCHE ROLL-
SIEGEL, Berlin, Mann, 1940.

Publication of the collection of cylinder seals in the Berlin
Museum. Catalogue of 783 works, fully described and extreme-
ly well reproduced (92 plates).

MOORTGAT (Anton). — TELL HALAF, III. DIE BILD-
WERKE. Berlin, Walter de Gruyter, 1955.

Publication of the innumerable reliefs found by von Oppenheim,
from the descriptive notes of D. Opitz. The dates now proposed
for Kapara fall in the ninth century B.C., but several sculptures
might be earlier than that (e.g. the female statues).

MOORTGAT (Anton). — ALTVORDERASIATISCHE MALEREI, Berlin, Safari Verlag, 1959.

Brief survey of painting in the Ancient Near East, in the light of the most recent discoveries, with 12 colour reproductions.

MOORTGAT-CORRENS (Ursula). — ALTORIENTALISCHE ROLLSIEGEL IN DER STAATLICHEN MÜNZSAMMLUNG MÜNCHEN, in MÜNCHNER JAHRBUCH DER BILDENDEN KUNST, VI (1955), pp. 7-27.

A small collection of 44 items, some of them of great value for the iconography of the gods: e.g. No. 16 (Ishtar of Love and Ishtar of War, juxtaposed), No. 24 (Adad standing on a winged lion), No. 27 (nude, winged potnia theron).

MORGAN (Jacques de). — MÉMOIRES DE LA DÉLÉGATION DE PERSE, Paris, Vols. I-XIII, Leroux, 1900-12.

The series thereafter changed its name several times:
MÉMOIRES DE LA MISSION ARCHÉOLOGIQUE DE SUSIANE, Vol. XIV, 1913.
MISSION ARCHÉOLOGIQUE DE PERSE, Vol. XV, 1914.
MÉMOIRES DE LA MISSION ARCHÉOLOGIQUE DE PERSE. MISSION EN SUSIANE, Vols. XVI-XXVIII, 1921-39.
MÉMOIRES DE LA MISSION ARCHÉOLOGIQUE EN IRAN. MISSION EN SUSIANE, Vol. XXIX on.

MOSCATI (Sabatino). — LE ORIGINI DELLA NARRATIVA STORICA NELL'ARTE DEL VICINO ORIENTE ANTICO, Rome, Accademia Nazionale dei Lincei, 1961.

An important study based on the work of Mrs. Groenewegen-Frankfort and supplementing it in many ways. Draws on the latest discoveries.

MOSTRA D'ARTE IRANICA. — Milan, Silvana Editoriale d'Arte, 1956.

Catalogue of an exhibition of Iranian art held in Rome (June-October 1956), grouping characteristic works from the earliest times (prehistoric and protohistoric pottery) to the 17th century of our era. Excellent summing-up of the problems they raise. The Luristan bronzes are dated to between the 14th and 11th centuries B.C. Two fine colour plates reproducing the small crowned head in lapis lazuli from Persepolis and the gold goblet from Kalar Dasht.

NAGEL (Wolfram). — MEISTER AND GESELLENARBEIT IN NEUASSYRISCHEN RELIEFS, in JAHRBUCH DES DEUTSCHEN ARCHÄOLOGISCHEN INSTITUTS, 73 (1958), pp. 1-8.

An attempt to distinguish between the work of master-sculptors and that of mere journeymen in Assyrian reliefs.

NAGEL (Wolfram). — GLYPTISCHE PROBLEME DER LARSA-ZEIT, in ARCHIV FÜR ORIENT-FORSCHUNG, XVIII (1958), pp. 319-327.

Dating and stylistic study of cylinder seals of the time of the Isin-Larsa dynasties. The Abisare cylinder of Larsa is dated to 2044-2034 B.C.

NAGEL (Wolfram). — FRUHE TIERWELT IN SUDWESTASIEN, I, in BERLINER BEITRAGE ZUR VOR- UND FRUHGESCHICHTE, Vol. 2 (1959), pp. 106-118, pl. 9-14, 23-27.
Identification of the animals represented on Mesopotamian monuments: onager, zebra (?), horse, camel, ox.

NORTH (R.). — STATUS OF THE WARKA EXPEDITION, in ORIENTALIA, XXVI (1957), pp. 185-256.

A summing up of sixteen seasons of excavation at Warka (Uruk).

NOUGAYROL (Jean). — UNE VERSION ANCIENNE DU 'JUSTE SOUFFRANT', in REVUE BIBLIQUE, 1952, pp. 239-250.

Publication of the Babylonian text in the Louvre (Tablet AO 4462).

OATES (David). — FORT SHALMANESER. AN INTERIM REPORT, in IRAQ, XXI (1959), pp. 98-127.

On the results of the 1957-58 excavations. Only a third of the fortress buildings (55 rooms) had then been cleared.

OATES (David). — EZIDA: THE TEMPLE OF NABU, in IRAQ, XXIX (1957), pp. 26-39.

Four statues stood in the temple of Nabu. Two are in the British Museum (dedication of Bel-tarsi-iluma, governor of Nimrud, for the life of Adad-Nirari and his mother Sammuramat); they date to 798 B.C. Of the two others, only a drawing by Boucher and a foot remain. The temple was destroyed about 612 B.C.

OATES (Joan). — LATE ASSYRIAN POTTERY FROM FORT SHALMANESER, in IRAQ, XXI (1959), pp. 130-146.

Study and classification of the various types of pottery found.

OPITZ (Dietrich). — DIE VOGELFÜSSIGE GÖTTIN AUF DEN LÖWEN, in ARCHIV FÜR ORIENT-FORSCHUNG XI (1937), pp. 350-353.

A study of the famous Burney plaque, throwing doubt on its authenticity.

OSTEN (H.H. von der). — ANCIENT ORIENTAL SEALS IN THE COLLECTION OF MRS. E. T. NEWELL. ORIENTAL INSTITUTE PUBLICATIONS, XXII. Chicago, University of Chicago Press, 1934.

One of the finest collections of Oriental glyptics, published with painstaking care (695 items on 41 plates). Includes several very clever fakes.

OSTEN (H.H. von der). — ANCIENT ORIENTAL SEALS IN THE COLLECTION OF MRS. AGNES BALDWIN BRETT. ORIENTAL INSTITUTE PUBLICATIONS, XXXVII. Chicago, University of Chicago Press, 1936.

Descriptive catalogue of 166 seals, with a study of the themes and motifs represented.

OSTEN (H.H. von der). — DIE WELT DER PERSER, Stuttgart, Gustav Kilpper, 1956.

A survey of the Iranian region from the earliest times to the Sassanians. Fine selection of illustrations, chronology, bibliography.

OTTO (W.). — HANDBUCH DER ARCHAEOLOGIE. VORDERASIEN by W. Andrae, Munich, C.H. Beck, 1939.

Handbook with an excellent survey of Mesopotamian archaeology (pp. 643-796), abundantly illustrated (pls. 113-182) and giving architecture the place it deserves.

PALLIS (S.A.). — THE ANTIQUITY OF IRAQ, Copenhagen, Einar Munksgaard, 1956.
Contains a wealth of documentary material on the excavations, history and civilization of Mesopotamia.

PARROT (André). — LES PEINTURES DU PALAIS DE MARI, in SYRIA, XVIII (1937), pp. 325-354.
General presentation of the wall paintings from various rooms and courts of the palace of Mari.

PARROT (André). — ARCHÉOLOGIE MÉSOPOTAMIENNE. I. LES ÉTAPES, Paris, Albin Michel, 1946.
General study of the progress of archaeological research in Mesopotamia.

PARROT (André). — ARCHÉOLOGIE MÉSOPOTAMIENNE. II. TECHNIQUE ET PROBLÈMES, Paris, Albin Michel, 1953.
On excavation technique and problems of Mesopotamian archaeology (protohistory, chronology).

PARROT (André). — ZIGGURATS ET TOUR DE BABEL, Paris, Albin Michel, 1949.
Comprehensive study of the Mesopotamian ziggurats and the problems (literary, epigraphical, archaeological, architectural and religious) which they raise.

PARROT (André) and LAMBERT (Maurice). — GLYPTIQUE MÉSOPOTAMIENNE. Fouilles de Lagash (Tello) et de Larsa (Senkereh) (1931-1933), Paris, Imprimerie Nationale, 1954.
Descriptive catalogue of 325 cylinder seals and stamps found in excavations at Lagash and Larsa. They range from the Jemdet Nasr period to Neo-Babylonian times.

PARROT (André). — MISSION ARCHÉOLOGIQUE DE MARI. I. LE TEMPLE D'ISHTAR, Paris, Geuthner, 1956.
Definitive publication of the Temple of Ishtar. Many reproductions.

PARROT (André). — MISSION ARCHÉOLOGIQUE DE MARI. II. LE PALAIS, Vol. I, ARCHITECTURE; Vol. II, PEINTURES MURALES; Vol. III, DOCUMENTS ET MONUMENTS (with the collaboration of Mme Barrelet and MM. Dossin, Ducos and Bouchud), Paris, Geuthner, 1958-59.
Definitive publication of the palace of the Zimri-Lim dynasty, with methodical studies of its architecture, wall paintings, statuary, furniture, implements, glyptics, etc.

PARROT (André) and NOUGAYROL (Jean). — ASARHADDON ET NAQIA SUR UN BRONZE DU LOUVRE (AO 20185), in SYRIA, XXXIII (1956), pp. 147-160.
Publication of a relief on which, thanks to the inscription, Jean Nougayrol identified King Esarhaddon and his mother Naqia, wife of Sennacherib.

PARROT (André). — PLAQUES ASSYRIENNES, in SYRIA, XXXV (1958), pp. 171-175; ORFÈVRERIE ET BIJOUTERIE IRANIENNES, ibid., pp. 175-185.
Publication of works recently acquired by the Louvre: Assyrian plaques in bronze (lions and ox; archer and goat) and silver and ivory (lions and goats); figured goblet in electrum (AO 20281), plaques and jewels from Ziwiyeh (AO 20177, 20178, 20180).

PATERSON (A.). — ASSYRIAN SCULPTURE. PALACE OF SINACHERIB, The Hague, Martinus Nijhoff, 1915.
Reproductions of all the reliefs from Sennacherib's palace, showing their exact position in the various rooms of the great residence. 114 plates.

PERKINS (Ann). — NARRATION IN BABYLONIAN ART, in AMERICAN JOURNAL OF ARCHEOLOGY, LXI (1957), pp. 54-62.
The examples, both secular and religious, are taken from famous Mesopotamian works: the Warka vase, the Lion Hunt stele, the plaque of Ur-Nanshe, the 'Standard' of Ur, the stelae of the Vultures, of Naram-Sin, of Ur-Nammu, the Mari paintings, the Code of Hammurabi. Two methods of narration: 'culmination' and 'episodic.'

PEZARD (M.) and POTTIER (E.). — MUSÉE NATIONAL DU LOUVRE. CATALOGUE DES ANTIQUITÉS DE LA SUSIANE, Paris, Musées Nationaux, 2nd edition, 1926.
Scrupulously accurate catalogue of works from Susiana, classified in chronological order under several main headings.

PILLET (Maurice). — LE PALAIS DE DARIUS Ier A SUSE, Paris, Geuthner, 1914.
Short monograph in which the author, a professional architect, attempts to reconstruct the palace excavated by de Morgan (see fig. 22).

PINCHES (T.G.). — THE BRONZE ORNAMENTS OF THE PALACE GATES OF BALAWAT, London, 1880-1902.
Publication of Rassam's discoveries, now in the British Museum (Cf. KING, Bronze Reliefs.).

PIOTROVSKY (B.B.) and others. — OURARTOU, Paris, A. Maisonneuve, 1954.
A useful study of the art of Urartu. See for example pp. 13-65.

PIRENNE (Jacques). — CIVILISATIONS ANTIQUES, Paris, Albin Michel, 1951.
A panoramic survey of the ancient civilizations, with a fairly well-balanced treatment of Mesopotamia and the West (Aegean and Greek civilization).

PLACE (Victor). — NINIVE ET L'ASSYRIE AVEC DES ESSAIS DE RESTAURATION PAR FÉLIX THOMAS, Paris, 3 vols., 1867-70.
Monumental publication of Place's discoveries at Khorsabad, with plans and reconstructions by the artist Félix Thomas, 'Grand Prix de Rome.'

PLENDERLEITH (H.J.). — METALS AND METAL TECHNIQUE, in WOOLLEY, UR EXCAVATIONS, II, pp. 284-298.
Invaluable information about ancient techniques of metalworking, with analyses of objects from the 'royal cemetery' of Ur.

PLENDERLEITH (H.J.) and MARYON (Herbert). — FINE METAL-WORK, in A HISTORY OF TECHNOLOGY, pp. 623-662.
A factual account of the techniques employed in working various metals.

PLESTERS (Joyce). — REPORT ON EXAMINATIONS OF PIGMENTS FROM THE THRONE-ROOM OF FORT SHALMANESER, in IRAQ, XXI (1959), pp. 127-129.

Analysis of the remains of wall paintings in the throne-room, revealing blue, red, black and white pigments and the absence of a binding medium.

POLIN (Claire C.T.). — MUSIC OF THE ANCIENT NEAR EAST, New York, Vantage Press, 1954.

PORADA (Edith). — THE GREAT KING, KING OF ASSYRIA: ASSYRIAN RELIEFS IN THE METROPOLITAN MUSEUM, New York, 1945.

Fine illustrations, with a short commentary, of the reliefs of Assurnasirpal II in the Metropolitan Museum. Some useful enlargements showing details of the royal costume.

PORADA (Edith). — THE COLLECTION OF THE PIERPONT MORGAN LIBRARY, in CORPUS OF ANCIENT NEAR EASTERN SEALS IN NORTH AMERICAN COLLECTIONS, 1 vol. of text, 1 vol. of plates, Washington, Bollingen Foundation, 1948.

Remarkable publication of a very important collection of glyptics (1157 items, including some fakes), by one of the best specialists in the field.

POTRATZ (J.A.H.). — DIE MENSCHLICHE RUNDSKULTUR IN DER SUMERO-AKKADISCHEN KUNST, Istanbul, Nederlands Historisch-archaeologisch Instituut in het Nabije Oosten, 1960.

Stylistic study of 'Sumero-Akkadian' sculpture in the round, from the Tell Asmar statues to those of Nimrud (Shalmaneser III and Assurnasirpal II). Brief account of the technique of the bas-relief.

POTTIER (Edmond). — MUSÉE NATIONAL DU LOUVRE. CATALOGUE DES ANTIQUITÉS ASSYRIENNES. Paris, Musées Nationaux, 2nd edition, 1924.

Description of Assyrian works in the Louvre (sculpture and objects in stone, metal and clay) grouped according to site (Nimrud, Khorsabad, Nineveh).

PREUSSER (Conrad). — DIE WOHNHÄUSER IN ASSUR. A. DIE BAUDENKMÄLER AUS ASSYRISCHER ZEIT. WISSENSCHAFTLICHE VERÖFFENTLICHUNGEN DER DEUTSCHEN ORIENT-GESELLSCHAFT, 64. Berlin, Mann, 1954.

A comprehensive study of Assyrian dwelling-houses, in chronological order (1960-1600 B.C.; 1500-1200 B.C.; 1100-600 B.C.). Certain examples (the 'red house,' the 'great house') are described in great detail; the inhabitant of one of them is presumed to have been a 'wizard priest.'

PREUSSER (Conrad). — DIE PALASTE IN ASSUR. WISSENSCHAFTLICHE VERÖFFENTLICHUNGEN DER DEUTSCHEN ORIENT-GESELLSCHAFT, 66. Berlin, Mann, 1955.

Publication of the royal residences: the 'old palace,' the palaces of Tukulti-Ninurta I, Adad-Nirari I and Tiglathpileser I, and Assurnasirpal II. Vestiges of a residence begun by Sennacherib, intended for one of his sons.

PRITCHARD (J. B.). — ANCIENT NEAR EASTERN TEXTS RELATING TO THE OLD TESTAMENT, Princeton University Press, 2nd edition, 1955.

Though the texts were chosen for their bearing on the Old Testament, this book forms a magnificent anthology of Mesopotamian literature, with the most recent translations by the best qualified specialists.

RAVN (O.E.). — A CATALOGUE OF ORIENTAL CYLINDER SEALS AND IMPRESSIONS IN THE DANISH NATIONAL MUSEUM, Copenhague, Nationalmuseet, 1960.

164 seals described in chronological order, by periods (Jemdet Nasr to the Achaemenian period), and forming a complete sequence of the usual Mesopotamian themes. The work ends with eight or ten pieces of doubtful authenticity.

RICE (D.S.). — FROM SIN TO SALADIN: EXCAVATIONS IN HARRAN'S GREAT MOSQUE, WITH NEW LIGHT ON THE BABYLONIAN KING NABONIDUS AND HIS 104-YEAR-OLD MOTHER, in ILLUSTRATED LONDON NEWS, September 21, 1957.

A brief report on the discovery in the Great Mosque of Harran of three Neo-Babylonian stelae with reliefs and inscriptions. Cf. GADD.

RUTTEN (M.). — SCÈNES DE MUSIQUE ET DE DANSE. MUSÉE DU LOUVRE, ANTIQUITÉS ORIENTALES, in REVUE DES ARTS ASIATIQUES, IX (1935), pp. 218-224.

Musical instruments as represented in Mesopotamian and Susian works. The usual classification in three groups: percussion, wind, strings.

RUTTEN (M.). — ARTS ET STYLES DU MOYEN-ORIENT ANCIEN (BABYLONIE, ASSYRIE, PERSE, etc.), Paris, Larousse, 1950.

In the series edited by Norbert Dufourcq, a brief essay on Oriental art, with geographical and historical introduction. Good choice of illustrations.

SAFARI (Fuad). — THE TEMPLE OF SIBITTI AT KHORSABAD, in SUMER, XIII (1957), pp. 219-221.

Discovery of a hitherto unknown temple outside the citadell between the city gate (No. 7) and Gate A. Several altars with inscriptions. The identification of the temple as that of the 'Sibitti' is borne out by inscriptions.

SANDARS (N.K.). — THE EPIC OF GILGAMESH, Harmondsworth, Penguin Books, 1960.

Excellent English translation with a long and informative introduction.

SCHMIDT (E.F.). — PERSEPOLIS, I. STRUCTURES, RELIEFS, INSCRIPTIONS. ORIENTAL INSTITUTE PUBLICATIONS, LXVIII. Chicago, University of Chicago Press, 1953.

Sumptuous publication of the results obtained at Persepolis by the Oriental Institute Expedition from 1931 to 1934 (under E. Herzfeld) and from 1934 to 1936 (under Schmidt). 205 plates of the very highest quality.

SCHMÖKEL (Hartmut). — DAS LAND SUMER, Stuttgart, Kohlhammer, 1955.

Historical study with illustrations of excavated works. Traces Sumerian influence as far as Romanesque art.

356

SCHMÖKEL (Hartmut). — UR, ASSUR UND BABYLON. DREI JAHRTAUSENDE IM ZWEISTROMLAND, Stuttgart, Gustav Kilpper, 1955. French edition: LE MONDE D'UR, ASSUR ET BABYLONE, Paris, Buchet-Chastel, 1957.
Mesopotamian art from the earliest times to the Neo-Babylonians. Excellent reproductions (118 plates) of the most important works.

SCHNITZLER (Ludwig). — FRÜHE PLASTIK IM ZWEI-STROMLAND, Stuttgart, H.E. Günther, 1959.
Selection of 48 plates illustrating Mesopotamian sculpture from the Warka head (early third millennium) to a Susa stele (18th century B.C.). Short introduction, chronological table, map.

SEGALL (Berta). — THE ARTS AND KING NABONIDUS, in AMERICAN JOURNAL OF ARCHEOLOGY, LIX (1955), pp. 315-318.
Resumes the discussion of a statuette which turned up at Aden in 1939 and deals with the bronze discovered at Marib by the W. Philips Expedition. It is to be hoped that excavations will be undertaken at Teima and Dedan.

SMITH (Sidney). — ASSYRIAN SCULPTURE IN THE BRITISH MUSEUM, FROM SHALMANESER III TO SENNACHERIB, London, British Museum, 1938.
Short descriptive notices and excellent reproductions.

SMITH (William Stevenson). — TWO ASSYRIAN RELIEFS FROM CANFORD MANOR, in BULLETIN OF FINE ARTS, Boston, Vol. LVIII, No. 312, 1960, pp. 45-56.
Publication of two reliefs from Sennacherib's palace at Nineveh, formerly at Canford Manor, acquired in 1959. They represent the deportation of Bablonians and fighting in the mountains. Cf. BARNETT.

SPEISER (E.). — EXCAVATIONS AT TEPE GAWRA, I, Philadelphia, University of Pennsylvania Press, 1935.
Official publication of the discoveries made on the first eight levels.

STARR (Richard F.S.). — NUZI. REPORT ON THE EXCAVATIONS AT YORGAN TEPE NEAR KIRKUK, IRAQ, 1927-1931, 1 vol. of text, 1 vol. of plates, Cambridge, Mass., 1937-39.
Unusually well-illustrated report (142 plates and 44 plans) of the discoveries made at Nuzi.

STAUDER (W.). — DIE HARFEN UND LEIERN DER SUMERER, Frankfurt am Main, J.W. Goethe-Universität, 1957.
Good iconographic study of Sumerian harps and lyres.

TECHNOLOGY (A HISTORY OF), edited by SINGER (Charles), HOLMYARD (E.J.) and HALL (A.R.). — I. FROM EARLY TIMES TO THE FALL OF THE ANCIENT EMPIRES, Oxford, Clarendon Press, 1954.
For the relevant contributions by various authors, see BARNETT, FORBES, LLOYD, MARYON and PLENDERLEITH.

THUREAU-DANGIN (F.), BARROIS (A.), DOSSIN (G.) and DUNAND (M.). — ARSLAN-TASH, Paris, Geuthner, 1931.
Important publication dealing with (among other things) the magnificent collection of ivories discovered near the palace, now in the Louvre and the Aleppo Museum.

THUREAU-DANGIN (F.). — LA COMPOSITION DES BRIQUES D'ARSLAN-TASH, in REVUE D'ASSYRIOLOGIE, XXXII (1935), pp. 87-88.
Chemical analysis of bricks from Arslan Tash.

THUREAU-DANGIN (F.) and DUNAND (M.) with contributions by CAVRO (L.) and DOSSIN (G.). — TIL-BARSIB, Paris, Geuthner, 1936.
In addition to Assyrian stelae and others in the Hittite style, the site yielded over 500 feet of wall paintings. Excellent copies by the architect Lucien Cavro.

TOURNAY (R.J.) and SAOUAF (Soubhi). — STÈLE DE TUKULTI-NINURTA II, in LES ANNALES ARCHÉOLOGIQUES DE SYRIE, II (1952), pp. 169-190.
Publication of a very important monument, with curious iconographic features (Ada). Cf. Güterbock.

UNGER (Eckhard). — DIE RELIEFS TIGLATPILESARS III AUS NIMRUD, Constantinople, Ottoman Museums, 1917.
Résumé of the excavations, catalogue, position of the reliefs, reproductions (6 plates). Unger draws a very suggestive parallel between Reliefs No. 11 (often cited) and No. 8 (a lesser known work).

UNGER (Eckhard). — ASSYRISCHE UND BABYLONISCHE KUNST, Breslau, Ferdinand Hirt, 1927.
Brief monograph still of considerable value, reproducing little known works: stelae of Sabaa and Adad-Nirari III; stele of Sennacherib from Nineveh with the divine symbols sculptured in the style of those on boundary stones.

UNGER (Eckhard). — BABYLON. DIE HEILIGE STADT NACH DER BESCHREIBUNG DER BABYLONIER. Berlin and Leipzig, Walter de Gruyter, 1931.
A remarkable synthesis, grouping important monuments discovered at Babylon and studying them in the light of inscriptions and literary works.

UNGER (Eckhard). — DER OBELISK DES KÖNIGS ASSURNASIRPAL I AUS NINIVE, in MITTEILUNGEN DER ALTORIENTALISCHEN GESELLSCHAFT VI (1932), pp. 1-2.
The attribution to Assurnasirpal I is by no means certain; Landsberger proposes Assurnasirpal II.

UNGER (Eckhard). — DIE WIEDERHERSTELLUNG DER STATUE DES KÖNIGS SALMANASAR III VON ASSYRIEN, in TÜRK ARKEOLOJI DERGISI, 7 (1957), pp. 42-48.
The scarcity of Assyrian sculpture in the round makes this reconstruction of a royal statue all the more valuable (pp. 16-17).

VAN BUREN (Elizabeth Douglas). — CLAY FIGURINES OF BABYLONIA AND ASSYRIA, YALE ORIENTAL SERIES, Researches Vol. 16, New Haven, Yale University Press, 1930.
Catalogue of the most characteristic Mesopotamian figurines, grouped according to types and themes. Includes 1334 items.

VAN BUREN (E.D.). — FOUNDATION FIGURINES AND OFFERINGS, Berlin, Hans Schoetz, 1931.
Monograph on the various types of foundation figurines found in the substructure of Mesopotamian edifices.

VAN BUREN (E.D.). — THE FLOWING VASE AND THE GOD WITH STREAMS, Berlin, Hans Schoetz, 1933.
Iconographical study of the frequently recurring theme of the god or man holding a flowing vase.

VAN BUREN (E.D.). — A FURTHER NOTE ON THE TERRACOTTA RELIEF, in ARCHIV FÜR ORIENTFORSCHUNG, XI (1937), pp. 354-357.
Deals with the Burney relief, accepting its authenticity.

VAN BUREN (E.D.). — THE FAUNA OF ANCIENT MESOPOTAMIA AS REPRESENTED IN ART. ANALECTA ORIENTALIA, 18. Rome, Pontificium Institutum Biblicum, 1939,
Excellent repertory, very well illustrated (107 figures on 32 plates).

VAN BUREN (E.D.). — SYMBOLS OF THE GODS IN MESOPOTAMIAN ART. ANALECTA ORIENTALIA, 23. Rome, Pontificium Institutum Biblicum, 1945.
An invaluable repertory of symbols, with countless bibliographical references. Unfortunately very few illustrations.

VAN BUREN (E.D.). — THE DRAGON IN ANCIENT MESOPOTAMIA, in ORIENTALIA, 15 (1946), pp. 1-45.
Iconography of the dragon, a frequent theme in Mesopotamian art, from the Jemdet Nasr period to Neo-Babylonian times.

VAN BUREN (E.D.). — THE ROD AND RING, in ARCHIV ORIENTALNI, XVII (1949), pp. 434-450.
Study of a controversial theme. In no case are they measuring instruments, but always symbolize divine power.

VAN BUREN (E.D.). — REPRESENTATION OF FERTILITY DIVINITIES IN GLYPTIC ART, in ORIENTALIA, 24 (1955), pp. 345-376.
Deals with cylinder seals from the Jemdet Nasr period to Akkadian times ('boat god').

VAN BUREN (E.D.). — HOW REPRESENTATIONS OF BATTLES OF THE GODS DEVELOPED, in ORIENTALIA, 24 (1955), pp. 24-41.
Chiefly in cylinder seals of the Akkadian period, in one of which the author has succeeded in identifying the death of Kingu.

VAN BUREN (E.D.). — CATALOGUE OF THE USSA COLLECTION OF STAMPS AND CYLINDER SEALS OF MESOPOTAMIA, with LIST OF RECENT ACQUISITIONS, by Dr Ugo Lissa, Rome 1959.
All periods are represented, from al 'Ubaid to the Sassanids.

VANDEN BERGHE (L.) and MUSSCHE (H.F.). — BIBLIOGRAPHIE ANALYTIQUE DE L'ASSYRIOLOGIE ET DE L'ARCHÉOLOGIE DU PROCHE-ORIENT, Leiden, Brill, 1956.
Excellent bibliography classified by regions, with each region subdivided into several main headings.

VANDEN BERGHE (L.). — ARCHÉOLOGIE DE L'IRAN ANCIEN, Leiden, E.J. Brill, 1959.
An excellent survey, from prehistoric times to the Sassanians. Geographical classification, 173 plates, plans of Pasargadae and Persepolis, synchronological table. Extensive bibliography. For the Luristan bronzes, see pp. 177-183.

VANDEN BERGHE (L.). — DE BESCHILDERDE CERAMIEK IN VOOR-AZIE VAN DE DUDSTE TIJDEN TOT ± 2000 VOOR ONZE JAARTELLING, Antwerp, de Sikkel, 1953-54.
This is an excerpt from a larger work covering 878 manuscript pages together with 7 albums containing over 8,000 drawings and photographs. Deals with painted pottery of the archaic periods in Mesopotamia and Iran. For the Tell Halaf ware, the author proposes a new classification in four groups.

VAN DIJK (A. M.). — LA DÉCOUVERTE DE LA CULTURE LITTÉRAIRE SUMÉRIENNE ET SA SIGNIFICATION POUR L'HISTOIRE DE L'ANTIQUITÉ ORIENTALE, in L'ANCIEN TESTAMENT ET L'ORIENT, Louvain, 1957.
Enumeration of the various literary forms in which the Sumerians excelled. This legacy fell to the Semites at the beginning of the second millennium, and a 'canonization' of the texts took place about 1300-1400 B.C.

VIEYRA (M.). — ISHTAR DE NINIVE, in REVUE D'ASSYRIOLOGIE, LI (1957), pp. 83-102, 130-138.
The author has collated a number of Hittite and Akkadian texts relating to the ritual of Ishtar of Nineveh.

VIEYRA (M.). — NOTES D'HISTOIRE. I. LA PLAQUE DES TRIBUTAIRES DE KALAKH, in REVUE D'ASSYRIOLOGIE, LIII (1959), pp. 205-208.
The ivories representing tributaries, found by Mallowan at Nimrud (Illustrated London News, January 28, 1956), date not from the time of Esarhaddon, but probably from that of either Assurnasirpal or Shalmaneser III.

VIROLLEAUD (Charles). — LITTÉRATURE ASSYRO-BABYLONIENNE, in HISTOIRE DES LITTÉRATURES, I, Paris, Encyclopédie de la Pléiade, Gallimard, 1956, pp. 253-276.
A survey of the major works of Babylonian literature: Poem of Creation, Epic of Gilgamesh, The Deluge, Adapa, Ishtar in the Netherworld, Code of Hammurabi, etc.

WEBER (Otto). — ALTORIENTALISCHE SIEGELBILDER, in DER ALTE ORIENT, XVII-XVIII, Leipzig, J.C. Hinrichs, 1920.
A study of ancient Oriental glyptics, classified by themes and scenes.

WEBER (Otto). — ASSYRISCHE KUNST, Berlin, Ernst Wasmuth, 1924.
Short presentation of Assyrian art from the earliest sculptures of the Ishtar temple at Assur to the Lion Hunt of Assurbanipal. 48 well-chosen plates.

WEGNER (M.). — DIE MUSIKINSTRUMENTE DES ALTEN ORIENTS, Münster (Westphalia), Aschendorffsche Verlagsbuchhandlung, 1950.

A general survey, both archaeological and literary, of the musical instruments known in Egypt, Israel, Mesopotamia, Anatolia and Greece, with bibliography, plates and chronological table of ancient instruments.

WEIDNER (E.F.). — DIE RELIEFS DER ASSYRISCHEN KÖNIGE, in ARCHIV FÜR ORIENT-FORSCHUNG, from X (1935) to the latest issues (with the collaboration of M. Falkner and O.E. Ravn).

Corpus of Assyrian reliefs scattered among various public and private collections throughout the world.

WEIDNER (E.F.). — SÄULE AUS NAHUR, in ARCHIV FÜR ORIENT-FORSCHUNG, XVII (1954-55), pp. 145-146.

Columns carried off to Assyria as war booty by Adad-Nirari I (1304-1273 B.C.), proving that the Assyrians were acquainted fairly early with this architectural form.

WETZEL (Friedrich). — ASSUR UND BABYLON, Berlin, Mann, 1949.

A small volume (70 pages) containing excellent reproductions of Assyrian, Kassite and Babylonian works in the Berlin Museum.

WETZEL (Friedrich) and WEISSBACH (F.). — DAS HAUPTHEILIGTUM DES MARDUK IN BABYLON. ESAGILA UND ETEMENANKI. WISSENSCHAFTLICHE VERÖFFENTLICHUNGEN DER DEUTSCHEN ORIENT-GESELLSCHAFT, 59. Leipzig, J.C. Hinrichs, 1938.

Indispensable for a knowledge of the architecture of the temple of Marduk and its staged tower.

WETZEL (Friedrich), SCHMIDT (E.) and MALLWITZ (Alfred). — DAS BABYLON DER SPÄTZEIT. WISSENSCHAFTLICHE VERÖFFENTLICHUNGEN DER DEUTSCHEN ORIENT-GESELLSCHAFT, 62. Berlin, Mann, 1956.

Publication of the later monuments: group of 'Homera' hills, theatre, palaestra. Earlier buildings were remodelled under the Achaemenians (the Qasr), Alexander the Great (Babil) and the Seleucids (Esagila and Etemenanki). Description of several important works: boundary stones of Adad and Marduk; remains of a divine god's stamp and cylinder seals, etc.

WILKINSON (Charles K.). — THE ART OF THE ANCIENT NEAR EAST, in THE METROPOLITAN MUSEUM OF ART BULLETIN, March 1949, pp. 186-198.

Reproductions of important Sumerian sculptures: heads of Gudea (?) and Ur-Ningirsu, and a worshipper statue from Ashnunnak; of three metal objects: the head of a bearded bull (Ur type), a foundation figurine (Shulgi type), and the head of an Elamite; and of Achaemenian reliefs.

WISEMAN (D.J.). — THE VASSAL TREATIES OF ESARHADDON, in IRAQ, XX (1958), London, The British School of Archaeology in Iraq, 1958.

Publication of a treaty written in 672 B.C. in which Esarhaddon, just before his death, divided the kingdom between his two sons: to Assurbanipal went Assyria, to Shamash-shum-ukin, Babylonia. The treaty was sealed with three cylinders: one of Sennacherib, one of the god Assur, and another of a king whose name is no longer legible (Tiglathpileser I or Tukulti-Ninurta II).

WISEMAN (D.J.). — ILLUSTRATIONS FROM BIBLICAL ARCHAEOLOGY, London, The Tyndale Press, 1958.

Biblical history in the light of archaeology. Carefully chosen illustrations, well reproduced. Several works in the British Museum are here reproduced for the first time.

WISEMAN (D.J.). — CYLINDER SEALS OF WESTERN ASIA, London, Batchworth Press, 1959.

A selection of 118 seals from the British Museum, many of them hitherto unpublished.

WOOLLEY (Sir C.L.). — EXCAVATIONS AT UR, A RECORD OF TWELVE YEARS' WORK, London, Ernest Benn, and New York, Crowell, 1954.

Woolley's Ur of the Chaldees (1929; latest edition 1950) summed up the results of seven years' excavations. This later book is a well-illustrated résumé along the same lines, but for a full account of the Ur excavations the reader is referred to the official publications of the Joint Expedition of the British Museum and the Pennsylvania University Museum.

WOOLLEY (C.L.). — UR EXCAVATIONS, II: THE ROYAL CEMETERY, A REPORT ON THE PREDYNASTIC AND SARGONID GRAVES EXCAVATED BETWEEN 1927-1931, London and Philadephia, British Museum and Pennsylvania University Museum, 1934.

Official publication, lavishly illustrated (1 volume of 274 plates accompanying the volume of text), of one of the most sensational archaeological discoveries made in Mesopotamia.

WOOLLEY (C.L.). — UR EXCAVATIONS, V: THE ZIGGURAT AND ITS SURROUNDINGS, London and Philadelphia, British Museum and Pennsylvania University Museum, 1939.

Official publication of the ziggurat of Ur, from the first archaic construction to the Neo-Babylonian tower of Nabonidus. Numerous reconstructions.

WOOLLEY (Sir C.L.). — UR EXCAVATIONS, IV: THE EARLY PERIODS, London and Philadelphia, British Museum and Pennsylvania University Museum, 1956.

Publication of works extending from the al 'Ubaid period to the Third Dynasty of Ur.

LIST OF ILLUSTRATIONS

Frontispiece - *Assyrian Art. Til Barsip.* Lion Hunting. *7th century* B.C. *Copy by Lucien Cavro, Paris. Painting, height 34¼ inches.*
This scene formed part of a large composition, some 22 feet in length, which adorned—surprisingly enough—a bathroom *(Room 27 in Plan of the Palace).*

PREFACE

XV - *Assyrian Art.   Til Barsip.* Winged Genius kneeling. *Ca. 8th century* B.C. *Louvre, Paris. Painting, height* 21¼ *inches, width* 19½ *inches. (Draeger).*
There must have been another identical figure facing this; between them was a rayed disk. *(*Vide *Thureau-Dangin, Til Barsip, Pl.* XLVI*).*

XVI - *Assyrian Art. Til Barsip.* Soldier with lance and buckler. *8th century* B.C. *Aleppo Museum. Painting, height* 17½ *inches. Detail of plate on page* XVII. *(Schneider-Lengyel).*

XVII - *Assyrian Art.   Til Barsip.* Armed Soldier escorting the Royal Chariot. *8th century* B.C. *Painting, height* 4 *feet,* 8¾ *inches. Copy by Lucien Cavro, Paris.*

NOTICE

TIL BARSIP

A word of explanation is necessary concerning the difference of tone and texture in the reproduction of paintings from Til Barsip. The plates on page XV of the preface and plates 111 and 337 in the text reproduce fragments preserved in the Louvre in the condition in which they were discovered by Thureau-Dangin in 1930. The plates on page XVI of the preface and plates 114, 336, 338 and 346 in the text reproduce fragments belonging to the Aleppo Museum and protected with a heavy coat of varnish.

The remaining plates are reconstitutions from drawings made by Lucien Cavro at Til Barsip at the time of the discovery of the frescoes. They are utilized because the originals left at the site no longer exist. Exposure to the air has caused their disintegration.

ASSYRIA

1. *Assyrian Art. Til Barsip (Tell Ahmar).* The Giant Headsman. *8th-7th centuries B.C. Copy by L. Cavro, Paris. Height 49 1/2 inches.*
Published in black and white on a smaller scale by Thureau-Dangin, *Til Barsip*, pl. LII (XLVIId).

2. *Assyrian Art.* Cylinder Seal. Mythological Scene with Worshipper, Winged Human-headed Bulls, Winged Genii and Winged Disk. *First half of the 1st millennium B.C. Louvre, Paris (AO 9046). Carnelian. (Louvre).*

3. *The 'Assyrian Triangle.'* Map of the area bounded by the Tigris and Great Zab.

4. *Mesopotamian Art. Assur (Qalaat Shergat).* Statue of Zariqum(?), King of Assur. *Late 3rd millennium B.C. Istanbul Museum. Gypsum, height 32 5/8 inches. (Istanbul Museum).*

5. *Mesopotamian Art. Assur (Qalaat Shergat).* Pre-Sargonid Statue of a Man, named 'Der Consistorial-Rat.' *First half of the 3rd millennium B.C. Berlin Museum. Gypsum, height 18 inches. (Berlin Museum).*

6. *Assyrian Art. Babylon, Merkes Quarter.* Cylinder Seal. Figure (?Priest) walking towards a Ziggurat. *Late 2nd millennium B.C. Berlin Museum. Agate, height 1 7/8 inches. (Berlin Museum).*

7. *Assyrian Art. Kar-Tukulti-Ninurta.* Wall Painting, *13th century B.C. Height 21 5/8 inches. (Claude Abeille. after W. Andrae, I, pl. 2).*

8. *Assyrian Art. Assur (Qalaat Shergat).* Altar of Tukulti-Ninurta I. *13th century B.C. Berlin Museum. Gypsum, height 20 7/8 inches. (Marburg).*
The king is represented twice as a worshipper before the altar of Nusku. This altar was discovered at the gate of the Temple of Ishtar.

9. *Kassite Art (?). Assur (Qalaat Shergat).* Vegetation God. *Second half of the 2nd millennium B.C. Berlin Museum. Gypsum, height 4 3/8 inches. (Marburg).*
May have been taken to Assur as war booty. Discovered in the well of the temple of the god Assur.

10a. *Assyrian Art. Dur Sharrukin (Khorsabad).* Plan of the City of Dur Sharrukin. *8th century B.C. Plan by C. Abeille, after André Parrot,* Archéologie Mésopotamienne, I.

10b. *Assyrian Art. Dur Sharrukin (Khorsabad).* Plan of the Palace. *8th century B.C. Plan by C. Abeille, after André Parrot,* Archéologie Mésopotamienne, I.

10c. *Assyrian Art. Dur Sharrukin (Khorsabad).* Plan of the Palace. Detail of the temples. *8th century B.C. Plan by C. Abeille, after André Parrot,* Archéologie Mésopotamienne, I.

11. *Assyrian Art. Dur Sharrukin (Khorsabad).* View of the City of Dur Sharrukin from the Ziggurat. *8th century B.C. Reconstruction by Charles Altman.*

12. *Assyrian Art. Dur Sharrukin (Khorsabad).* Bird's-eye View of Sargon's Palace. *8th century B.C. Reconstruction by Charles Altman.*

13a. *Assyrian Art. Dur Sharrukin (Khorsabad).* The Ziggurat. *8th century B.C. Elevation according to Victor Place.*

13b. *Assyrian Art. Dur Sharrukin (Khorsabad).* The Ziggurat. *8th century B.C. Elevation according to T.A. Busink.*

14. *Assyrian Art. Kalakh (Nimrud).* Stele of Assurnasirpal. *9th century B.C. British Museum. Limestone, height 9 feet 7 inches. (British Museum).*

15. *Assyrian Art. Dur Sharrukin (Khorsabad).* King Sargon II. *8th century B.C. Turin Museum. Gypseous alabaster, height 35 inches. (Turin Museum).*

16. *Assyrian Art. Kalakh (Nimrud).* King and Winged Genius beside the Sacred Tree. *9th century B.C. British Museum. Gypseous alabaster, height 6 1/2 feet. (British Museum).*

17. *Assyrian Art. Kalakh (Nimrud).* Capture of a Town by Tiglathpileser. Exodus of the populace; counting up the spoils. *8th century B.C. British Museum. Gypseous alabaster, height 39 3/4 inches. (British Museum).*

18. *Assyrian Art. Kalakh (Nimrud).* Assurnasirpal at War. *9th century B.C. British Museum. Gypseous alabaster, height 39 inches. (British Museum).*

19. *Assyrian Art. Assur (Qalaat Shergat).* King Shalmaneser III. *9th century B.C. British Museum. Basalt, height 51 inches. (British Museum).*

20. *Assyrian Art. Kalakh (Nimrud).* King Shalmaneser III, side view. *Istanbul Museum. Basalt. (Istanbul Museum).*

21. *Assyrian Art. Kalakh (Nimrud).* King Shalmaneser III, full face. *Istanbul Museum. Basalt. (Istanbul Museum).*

22. *Assyrian Art. Kalakh (Nimrud).* Statue of Assurnasirpal II. *9th century B.C. British Museum. Limestone, height of statue 41 3/4 inches; height of pedestal 21 inches. (British Museum).*

23. *Assyrian Art. Kalakh (Nimrud).* Statue of Assurnasirpal II, detail. *9th century B.C. British Museum. Limestone. (British Museum).*

24. *Assyrian Art. Kalakh (Nimrud).* Statue thought to represent the God Nabu. *9th-8th centuries B.C. British Museum. Limestone, height 5 feet 3 inches. (British Museum).*
Dedicated by the Governor Bel-tarsi-iluma 'for the life of' Adad-Nirari and his wife Sammuramat.

25. *Assyrian Art. Dur Sharrukin (Khorsabad).* 'Caryatid' column Figure. Deity with Flowing Vase. *8th century B.C. Oriental Institute, Chicago. Stone, height 4 feet 11 inches. (Oriental Institute).*

26. *Assyrian Art. Nineveh (Kuyunjik).* Statue of a Woman. *11th century B.C. British Museum. Limestone, height 37 inches. (British Museum).*
Inscribed on the back with the name of Assurbelkala, King of Assyria.

27a, b, c. *Assyrian Art. Hadatu (Arslan Tash).* Genius holding a Box. *8th century B.C. Aleppo Museum. Basalt, height 5 feet 8 inches.* A in front view *(Schneider-Lengyel);* b and c, back and side-face. *(Aleppo Museum).*

28. *Assyrian Art. Hadatu (Arslan Tash).* Head of the Genius holding a Box. *8th century B.C. Aleppo Museum. Basalt, total height 5 feet 8 inches. (Schneider-Lengyel).*

29. *Assyrian Art. Kalakh (Nimrud).* Winged Human-headed Lion. *9th century B.C. British Museum. Gypseous alabaster, height 11 1/2 feet. (British Museum).*

30. *Assyrian Art. Dur Sharrukin (Khorsabad).* Gate 'A' of the Citadel, adorned with two human-headed bulls, each followed by a winged genius carrying a situla. *8th century B.C. In situ. Gypseous alabaster, height 12 feet 10 inches. (After G. Loud, II, Pl. 2).*

31. *Assyrian Art. Kalakh (Nimrud).* Guardian Lion. *9th century B.C. British Museum. Gypseous alabaster, height 8 1/2 feet, length 13 feet. (British Museum).*

32. *Assyrian Art. Kalakh (Nimrud).* Winged Human-headed Bull. *9th century B.C. Gypseous alabaster, height 11 feet. (Illustrated London News, July 22, 1950).*

33. *Provincial Assyrian Art. Hadatu (Arslan Tash).* Guardian Lion. *8th century B.C. Aleppo Museum. Basalt, height 8 feet 10 inches, length 12 feet. (Schneider-Lengyel).* Cf. the Bull from the same site, No. 88.

34a. *Assyrian Art. Dur Sharrukin (Khorsabad).* Winged Human-headed Bull. *8th century B.C. Louvre. Gypseous alabaster, height 13 feet 10 inches. (Tel-Vigneau).*
Such a bull figured on each side of the main entrances of the palace.

34b. *Assyrian Art. Dur Sharrukin (Khorsabad).* Winged Human-headed Bull. *8th century B.C. Oriental Institute, Chicago. Gypseous alabaster, height 15 feet. (Oriental Institute).*
Figured in front of the walls of the palace.

35. *Assyrian Art. Dur Sharrukin (Khorsabad).* Winged Human-headed Bull, detail. *8th century B.C. Louvre. Gypseous alabaster, over-all height 13 feet 10 inches. (Tel-Vigneau).*

36. *Assyrian Art. Dur Sharrukin (Khorsabad).* Gilgamesh holding a Lion Cub. *8th century B.C. Louvre. Gypseous alabaster, height 15 1/2 feet. (Tel-Vigneau).*
Placed in front of a wall of the palace, between two bulls carved in side view (of the type of 34b) with the heads full face.

37. *Assyrian Art. Dur Sharrukin (Khorsabad).* Winged Human-headed Genius holding Situla and Pine-cone. *8th century B.C. Louvre. Gypseous alabaster, total height 13 feet. (Tel-Vigneau).*

38. *Assyrian Art. Dur Sharrukin (Khorsabad).* Gilgamesh holding a Lion Cub, detail. *8th century B.C. Louvre. Gypseous alabaster, total height 15 1/2 feet. (Tel-Vigneau).*

39a. *Assyrian Art. Kalakh (Nimrud).* Stele of Assurnasirpal II, detail. *879 B.C. Mosul Museum. Sandstone, height 4 feet 2 1/2 inches.* (Iraq, 1952, *pl. III).*

39b. *Assyrian Art. Kurkh.* Stele of Shalmaneser III. *9th century B.C. British Museum. Limestone, height 7 feet 2 1/2 inches. (British Museum).*

39c. *Assyrian Art. Zinjirli.* Esarhaddon holding on a leash Kings Abdimilkutti and Ushanahuru. *7th century B.C. Berlin Museum. Dolerite, height 10 1/2 feet. (British Museum).*
Cf. this stele with the stele (No. 86) found at Til Barsip, on which the same scene is carved.

40a. *Assyrian Art. Babylon.* Assurbanipal carrying a Basket. *7th century B.C. British Museum. Stone, height 14 1/2 inches. (British Museum).*
Cf. with the Sumerian stele from Telloh (Lagash) representing Ur-Nina (Ur-Nanshe), in André Parrot, *Sumer, p. 130, pl. 159 A and B.*

40b. *Assyrian Art. Kalakh (Nimrud).* 'Obelisk' of Shalmaneser III, also called 'The Black Obelisk.' *9th Century B.C. British Museum. Black alabaster, height 6 feet 7 1/2 inches. (British Museum).*

40c. *Assyrian Art. Nineveh (Kuyunjik).* Incomplete 'Obelisk' of Tiglathpileser I. *12th century B.C. British Museum. Black alabaster, height 15 3/4 inches. (British Museum).*

41. *Assyrian Art. Kalakh (Nimrud).* Assurbanipal seated, cup in hand, with a guardsman and menial with a fly-whisk in attendance. *9th century B.C. British Museum. Gypseous alabaster, height 7 feet 9 inches. (British Museum).*

42. *Assyrian Art. Kalakh (Nimrud).* Assurnasirpal holding a Bow and followed by a Winged Human-headed Genius. *9th century B.C. British Museum. Gypseous alabaster, height 7 feet 8 inches. (British Museum).*

43. *Assyrian Art. Dur Sharrukin (Khorsabad).* Sargon II carrying the Sacrificial Ibex. *8th century B.C. Louvre. Gypseous alabaster, height 8 feet 9 inches. (Louvre).*

44. *Assyrian Art. Dur Sharrukin (Khorsabad).* Carriers of 'Towns.' *8th century B.C. Louvre. Gypseous alabaster, height 5 feet 4 inches. (Tel-Vigneau).*

45. *Assyrian Art. Dur Sharrukin (Khorsabad).* Plumed Horses' Heads. *8th century B.C. Oriental Institute, Chicago. Gypseous alabaster, height 35 1/2 inches. (Oriental Institute).*
Cf. a similar relief in the Louvre (AO 19899) and in the British Museum.

46. *Assyrian Art. Nineveh (Kuyunjik).* Sack of the City of Hamaan. *First millennium B.C. British Museum. Gypseous alabaster, height 35 3/4 inches. (Mansell).*

47. *Assyrian Art. Kalakh (Nimrud).* Fugitives swimming with the aid of Water-skins. *9th century B.C. British Museum. Gypseous alabaster, height 39 inches. (British Museum).*

48. *Assyrian Art. Dur Sharrukin (Khorsabad).* 'Seascape.' Floating Timber on the Phœnician Coast. *8th century B.C. Louvre. Gypseous alabaster, height 9 feet 7 inches.* (*Tel-Vigneau*).

49. *Assyrian Art. Nineveh (Room XXXVI of the Palace of Sennacherib).* Sennacherib at the Siege of Lachish (690 B.C.). *British Museum* (124911). *Gypseous alabaster, height 4 1/2 feet.* (*British Museum*).

50. *Assyrian Art. Nineveh (Kuyunjik).* The Defeat of the Elamites. *7th century B.C. British Museum. Gypseous alabaster, height 4 feet 4 inches.* (*British Museum*).

51. *Assyrian Art. Nineveh (Kuyunjik).* Wild Sow and her young in the Marshlands of Southern Mesopotamia. *7th Century B.C. British Museum. Gypseous alabaster.* (*British Museum*).

52. *Assyrian Art. Nineveh (Kuyunjik).* Warfare in the Marshes. *7th century B.C. Gypseous alabaster, height 5 feet.* (*British Museum*).

53. *Assyrian Art. Nineveh (Kuyunjik).* Townsfolk led into Captivity, detail. *7th century B.C. Louvre. Gypseous alabaster, over-all height 38 inches.* Campaigns of Assurbanipal. (*Tel-Vigneau*).

54. *Assyrian Art. Nineveh (Kuyunjik).* Townsfolk led into Captivity, detail. *7th century B.C. Louvre. Gypseous alabaster, over-all height 47 1/4 inches.* Campaigns of Assurbanipal. (*Tel-Vigneau*).

55. *Assyrian Art. Nineveh (Kuyunjik).* Townsfolk led into Captivity, detail of the Siege of Lachish. *7th century B.C. British Museum. Gypseous alabaster, 39 3/4 by 30 inches.* (*British Museum*).

56. *Assyrian Art. Nineveh (Kuyunjik).* Townsfolk led into Captivity, detail. *7th century B.C. Louvre. Gypseous alabaster, over-all height 5 feet 3 3/4 inches.* (*Tel-Vigneau*).

57. *Assyrian Art. Nineveh (Kuyunjik).* Horseman shouting, detail. *7th century B.C. Louvre. Gypseous alabaster, over-all height 50 3/4 inches.* (*Tel-Vigneau*).

58. *Assyrian Art. Nineveh (Kuyunjik).* Camp Scene: Orderly in a Tent. *7th century B.C. Berlin Museum. Gypseous alabaster, height 15 3/8 inches.* (*Marburg*).

59. *Assyrian Art. Nineveh (Kuyunjik).* Captives resting and eating. *7th century B.C. Louvre. Gypseous alabaster, height 16 inches.* (*Tel-Vigneau*).

60. *Assyrian Art. Nineveh (Kuyunjik).* 'The Feast in a Garden.' *7th century B.C. British Museum. Alabaster, height 4 feet 4 3/4 inches, length 5 feet.* (*British Museum*). Assurbanipal is telling the Queen the story of his campaigns against Elam.

61. *Assyrian Art. Nineveh (Kuyunjik).* Musicians, detail. *7th century B.C. Louvre. Gypseous alabaster, over-all height 5 feet.* (*Tel-Vigneau*).

62. *Assyrian Art. Kalakh (Nimrud).* Assurnasirpal hunting Bulls. *9th century B.C. British Museum. Gypseous alabaster, height 35 1/2 inches.* (*British Museum*).

63. *Assyrian Art. Nineveh (Kuyunjik).* Assurbanipal slaying a Lion. *7th century B.C. British Museum. Gypseous alabaster, width 43 1/4 inches.* (*British Museum*).

64. *Assyrian Art. Kalakh (Nimrud).* Assurnasirpal Lion-hunting. *9th century B.C. British Museum. Gypseous alabaster, height 34 inches.* (*British Museum*).

65. *Assyrian Art. Nineveh (Kuyunjik).* Assurbanipal Lion-hunting. *7th century B.C. British Museum. Alabaster, length 21 feet, height 5 feet 2 inches.* (*British Museum*).

66. *Assyrian Art. Dur Sharrukin (Khorsabad).* Hunting and Hawking. *8th century B.C. Louvre. Basalt, height 5 feet 4 inches.* (*Tel-Vigneau*).
Here undoubtedly we see Sennacherib, then Crown Prince. There is a relief (118829) in the British Museum with a similar scene.

67. *Assyrian Art. Dur Sharrukin (Khorsabad).* Hunting and Hawking, detail. *8th century B.C. Louvre. Basalt, total height 5 feet 4 inches.* (*Tel-Vigneau*).

68. *Assyrian Art. Nineveh (Kuyunjik).* Huntsman holding a Dog in Leash. *7th century B.C. British Museum. Gypseous alabaster, height 13 inches, length 20 inches.* (*British Museum*).
This and the following sculptures form part of the group of Hunting Reliefs of Assurbanipal. Cf. also Nos. 63 and 65.

69. *Assyrian Art. Nineveh (Kuyunjik).* Lion released from its Cage before the Hunt begins. *7th century B.C. British Museum. Gypseous alabaster, 39 by 33 inches.* (*British Museum*).

70. *Assyrian Art. Nineveh (Kuyunjik).* The Dying Lioness. *7th century B.C. British Museum. Gypseous alabaster, height 23 1/2 inches.* (*British Museum*).

71. *Assyrian Art. Nineveh (Kuyunjik).* Lion and Lioness. *7th century B.C. Gypseous alabaster, height 39 inches, length 48 inches.* (*British Museum*).

72. *Assyrian Art. Nineveh (Kuyunjik).* Hunting Wild Asses. *7th century B.C. British Museum. Alabaster, height 20 3/4 inches.* (*British Museum*).

73. *Assyrian Art. Nineveh (Kuyunjik).* Gazelles in Flight. *7th century B.C. British Museum. Alabaster, height 20 3/4 inches.* (*British Museum*).

74. *Assyrian Art. Nineveh (Kuyunjik).* Hunting Scene, detail: Grooms bringing in a Dead Lion. *7th century B.C. Louvre. Gypseous alabaster, height 46 inches.* (*Tel-Vigneau*).

75. *Assyrian Art. Nineveh (Kuyunjik).* Grooms bringing in a Dead Lion. *7th century B.C. British Museum. Gypseous alabaster.* (*British Museum*).

76. *Assyrian Art. Nineveh (Kuyunjik).* Assurbanipal making libation over the Slain Lions. *7th century B.C. British Museum. Alabaster, height 22 inches, length 63 3/4 inches.* (*British Museum*).

77. *Assyrian Art. Dur Sharrukin (Khorsabad).* Winged Human-headed Genius holding Pine-cone and Situla. *8th century B.C. Louvre. Gypseous alabaster, height 10 feet.* (*Tel-Vigneau*).

78. *Assyrian Art. Kalakh (Nimrud).* Winged Genius with Human Body and Eagle's Head performing rite in front of Sacred Tree. *9th century B.C. Louvre. Gypseous alabaster, height 40 1/2 inches.* (*Tel-Vigneau*).

79. *Assyrian Art. Assur (Qalaat Shergat).* Scene of Worship. *First millennium B.C. Glazed bricks, height 22 inches. (After W. Andrae).*
The presence of a locust makes it clear that the rite concerns a plague of locusts. The worshipper (probably the king) is praying the god to spare the land this calamity.

80. *Iraq. Hines Region.* Rock Sculptures of Sennacherib. *7th century B.C. Oriental Institute Publication XXIV, pl. 13. (Oriental Institute, Chicago).*

81. *Assyrian Art. Gomel Gorge, Hines Region.* Relief of Sennacherib, formerly known as the 'Bavian Relief.' *7th century B.C. (Iraq Museum).*
The King in prayer. In front of him the god Assur standing on his animal attribute, passant to the right.

82. *Assyrian Art. Assur (Qalaat Shergat).* Ritual Basin adorned with Deities with the Flowing Vase and Genii with Situlae. *8th-7th centuries B.C. Berlin Museum. Limestone, height 46 inches. (Marburg).*
Found in fragments in the well of the temple of the god Assur.

83. *Assyrian Art. Assur (Qalaat Shergat).* Deity with the Flowing Vase, detail of the Ritual Basin. *8th-7th centuries B.C. Berlin Museum. Total height 46 inches. (Marburg).*

84. *Provincial Assyrian Art. Hadatu (Arslan Tash).* The God Adad holding Lightning-flash and standing on a Bull. *8th century B.C. Louvre. Basalt, height 53 inches. (Louvre).*

85. *Provincial Assyrian Art. Til Barsip (Tell Ahmar).* Ishtar of Arbela standing on a Lion. *8th century B.C. Louvre. Red breccia, height 47 1/2 inches. (Louvre).*

86. *Provincial Assyrian Art. Til Barsip (Tell Ahmar).* Stele of King Esarhaddon, showing him holding on a leash Abdimilkutti, King of Sidon (kneeling), and Ushanahuru, son of Taharqa, King of Nubia and Egypt. *669 B.C. Aleppo Museum. Basalt, height 12 1/2 feet. (Aleppo Museum).*
Cf. the Zinjirli stele, on the same theme (No. 39c).

87. *Hittite Art. Til Barsip (Tell Ahmar).* The God Teshub brandishing Lightning-fork and Axe. The animal attribute was a Bull. *Late 2nd-early 1st millennium B.C. Aleppo Museum. Basalt, height c. 10 feet. (Schneider-Lengyel).*

88. *Provincial Assyrian Art. Hadatu (Arslan Tash).* Bull passant. *8th century, B.C. Louvre. Basalt, height 5 feet 2 inches, length 7 feet 10 inches. (Draeger).*
Cf. Lion from the same site (No. 33).

89. *Hittite Art. Til Barsip (Tell Ahmar).* The God Teshub brandishing Lightning-fork and Axe, standing on a Bull, his animal attribute. *Late 2nd-early 1st millennium B.C. Louvre. Basalt, height 7 feet 10 inches. (Tel-Vigneau).*

90. *Provincial Art of the Khabur Region. Tell Halaf.* Queen (or Goddess). *Early 1st millennium B.C. Aleppo Museum. Basalt, height 9 feet. (Schneider-Lengyel.)*

91. *Provincial Art of the Khabur Region. Tell Halaf.* Scorpion-man. *Early 1st millennium B.C. Aleppo Museum. Basalt, height 5 feet 3 inches, length 6 feet 9 inches. (Schneider-Lengyel).*

92. *Provincial Art of the Khabur Region. Tell Halaf.* Palace of Kapara. Reconstruction of the 'Scorpion Gate.' *Early 1st millennium B.C. (C. Abeille, after Frankfort).*

93. *Provincial Art of the Khabur Region. Tell Halaf.* Plan of the Palace of Kapara. *Early 1st millennium B.C. (C. Abeille, after Frankfort).*

94. *Provincial Art of the Khabur Region. Tell Halaf.* Scorpion-man, detail. *Early 1st millennium B.C. Aleppo Museum. Basalt, total height 5 feet 3 inches. (Schneider-Lengyel).*

95. *Provincial Art of the Khabur Region. Tell Halaf.* Portico of the Palace of Kapara. Reconstruction with the column statues: two gods and a goddess. *Early 1st millennium. Tell Halaf Museum, Berlin. (Marburg).*

96. *Provincial Art of the Khabur Region. Tell Halaf.* Portico of the Palace of Kapara, detail. Gods upon their Animal Attributes. *Early 1st millennium B.C. Tell Halaf Museum, Berlin. (Marburg).*

97a. *Provincial Art of the Khabur Region. Tell Halaf.* Bull-hunt. *Early 1st millennium B.C. Aleppo Museum. Basalt, height 4 feet 7 inches, length 6 feet 7 inches. (Schneider-Lengyel).*
Partially destroyed after excavation. Fragment preserved in the Aleppo Museum.

97b. *Provincial Art of the Khabur Region. Tell Halaf.* Genii and Winged Disk. *Early 1st millennium B.C. Aleppo Museum. Basalt, height 49 1/4 inches. (Schneider-Lengyel).*

97c. *Provincial Art of the Khabur Region. Tell Halaf.* Stag-hunt. *Early 1st millennium B.C. Aleppo Museum. Basalt, height 4 feet 11 inches, length 5 feet 11 inches. (Schneider-Lengyel).*
Partially destroyed after excavation. Fragment preserved in the Aleppo Museum.

98a. *Provincial Art of the Khabur Region. Tell Halaf.* Lion passant. *Early 1st millennium B.C. Tell Halaf Museum, Berlin. Basalt, height 4 feet 11 inches, length 5 feet 10 inches. (Schneider-Lengyel).*

98b. *Provincial Art of the Khabur Region. Tell Halaf.* The God Teshub holding Mace and Boomerang. *Early 1st millennium B.C. Tell Halaf Museum, Berlin. Basalt, height 52 1/4 inches. (Tell Halaf, III, pl. 107).*
Destroyed in 1943 by air-raids.

98c. *Provincial Art of the Khabur Region. Tell Halaf.* Winged Human-headed Bull. *Early 1st millennium B.C. Tell Halaf Museum, Berlin. Basalt, height 5 feet 1 inch, length 6 feet 3 inches. (Tell Halaf, III, pl. 109).*
Destroyed in 1943 by air-raids.

99a. *Provincial Art of the Khabur Region. Tell Halaf.* Archer. *Early 1st millennium B.C. Louvre. Basalt, height 22 inches. (Tel-Vigneau).*

99b. *Provincial Art of the Khabur Region. Tell Halaf.* Lion Erect. *Early 1st millennium B.C. Aleppo Museum. Basalt, height 22 3/4 inches. (Schneider-Lengyel).*

99c. *Provincial Art of the Khabur Region. Tell Halaf.* Winged Genius in the posture of an Atlas. *Early 1st millennium B.C. Louvre. Basalt, height 21 1/2 inches. (Tel-Vigneau).*

99d. *Provincial Art of the Khabur Region. Tell Halaf.* Slaying of a Bearded Giant by two Acolytes. *Early 1st millennium B.C. Walters Art Gallery, Baltimore. Basalt, height 24 3/8 inches.* (Tell Halaf, *III*, Pl. 103a).

100. *Provincial Art of the Khabur Region. Tell Halaf.* Animal Orchestra. *Early 1st millennium B.C. Limestone, height 30 3/4, width 46 inches.* (Tell Halaf, *III*, Pl. 100, Fig. A). Present whereabouts unknown.

101. *Provincial Art of the Khabur Region. Tell Halaf.* Divine (or Royal) Couple. *Early 1st millennium B.C. Aleppo Museum. Basalt, height 31 1/2, width 34 1/2 inches.* (V. Derounian, Aleppo).

102a. *Provincial Art of the Khabur Region. Tell Halaf.* King (or God). *Early 1st millennium B.C. Adana Museum. Basalt, height 39 3/8 inches.* (Marburg).

102b. *Provincial Art of the Khabur Region. Tell Halaf.* Queen (or Goddess). *Early 1st millennium B.C. Aleppo Museum. Basalt, total height 9 feet.* (Marburg).

103. *Provincial Art of the Khabur Region. Tell Halaf.* Goddess with Hanging Braids. *Early 1st millennium B.C. Tell Halaf Museum, Berlin. Basalt, height 6 feet 3 1/2 inches.* (V. Derounian, Aleppo).
From a plaster cast in Aleppo Museum, the original having been destroyed in 1943 by air-raids.

104. *Provincial Art of the Khabur Region. Tell Halaf.* Goddess with Hanging Braids, detail. *Early 1st millennium B.C. Tell Halaf Museum, Berlin. Basalt.* (V. Derounian, Aleppo).
From a plaster cast in Aleppo Museum, the original having been destroyed in 1943 by air-raids.

105. *Provincial Art of the Khabur Region. Tell Halaf.* Bird of Prey on a Capital. *Early 1st millennium B.C. Tell Halaf Museum, Berlin. Basalt, height 6 feet.* (Tell Halaf, *III*, Fig. 138).
Has disappeared following the Russian occupation.

106. *Provincial Art of the Khabur Region. Tell Halaf.* Seated Goddess, detail of her crowned head. *Early 2nd millennium B.C. Aleppo Museum. Basalt, over-all height 4 feet 8 inches.* (Schneider-Lengyel).

107. *Assyrian Art. Dur Sharrukin (Khorsabad).* The 'Harem,' reconstruction of Gate Z, after Victor Place, *Ninive et l'Assyrie,* pl. 24. *8th century B.C. Glazed bricks, length c. 23 feet.*
As a result of the excavations by the Oriental Institute of Chicago, it is now known that the so-called 'Harem' was one of a group of religious edifices.

108. *Assyrian Art. Dur Sharrukin (Khorsabad).* Decoration of Residence K. *8th century B.C. Wall painting, height 44 feet.* (After Loud and Altman, Khorsabad, *II*, pl. 89).

109. *Assyrian Art. Til Barsip (Tell Ahmar).* Wall Painting in the Palace. Winged Genius leading a Bull. *8th century B.C. Copy by L. Cavro, Paris. Height of the fragment, 35 1/2 inches.*
Published in black and white on a smaller scale by Thureau-Dangin, *Til Barsip,* pl. XLVIII.

110. *Assyrian Art. Til Barsip (Tell Ahmar).* Wall Painting in the Palace. Winged Human-headed Bull and Man with a Lotus. *8th century B.C. Copy by L. Cavro, Paris. Height 5 feet 5 inches, length 8 feet 5 inches.*
Published in black and white by Thureau-Dangin, *Til Barsip,* pl. XLVIII.

111. *Assyrian Art. Til Barsip (Tell Ahmar).* Wall Painting in the Palace, detail of No. 113. Two Servants standing behind the Throne. *8th century B.C. Louvre, Paris.* (Draeger).

112. *Assyrian Art. Til Barsip (Tell Ahmar).* Wall Painting in the Palace. King Tiglathpileser III giving Audience. *8th century B.C. Copy by L. Cavro, Paris. In its entirety (not reproduced here) this painting measures some 72 feet in length.*
Published in black and white by Thureau-Dangin, *Til Barsip,* pl. XLIX.

113. *Assyrian Art. Til Barsip (Tell Ahmar).* Wall Painting in the Palace. King Tiglathpileser III giving Audience. *8th century B.C. Copy by L. Cavro, Paris. Length 18 feet.*
Published in black and white by Thureau-Dangin, *Til Barsip,* pl. LII.

114. *Assyrian Art. Til Barsip (Tell Ahmar).* Wall Painting in the Palace, detail of No. 113. Two Court Officials. *8th century B.C. Aleppo Museum. Height 13 3/4 inches.* (Schneider-Lengyel).

115. *Assyrian Art. Til Barsip (Tell Ahmar).* Wall Painting in the Palace, detail of No. 116. Execution of a Prisoner. *8th century B.C. Copy by L. Cavro, Paris. Height 5 feet.*
Published in black and white by Thureau-Dangin, *Til Barsip,* pl. LI.

116. *Assyrian Art. Til Barsip (Tell Ahmar).* Wall Painting in the Palace. Soldier executing a Prisoner before Women and Children. *8th century B.C. Copy by L. Cavro, Paris. Length, 12 feet 2 inches.*
Published in black and white by Thureau-Dangin, *Til Barsip,* pl. LI.

117. *Assyrian Art. Til Barsip (Tell Ahmar).* Wall Painting in the Palace. Prisoners harnessed to a Chariot. *8th century B.C. Copy by L. Cavro, Paris. Length 7 feet 3 1/2 inches.*
Published in black and white by Thureau-Dangin, *Til Barsip,* pl. XLIX.

118. *Assyrian Art. Til Barsip (Tell Ahmar).* Wall Painting in the Palace. The 'White Horses.' *8th or 7th century B.C. Copy by L. Cavro, Paris. Length 35 3/8 inches.*
Reproduced on a smaller scale in black and white by Thureau-Dangin, *Til Barsip,* pl. LIII.

119. *Assyrian Art. Til Barsip (Tell Ahmar).* Wall Painting in the Palace. The 'Brown Horses' and 'Black Horses.' *8th or 7th century B.C. Copy by L. Cavro, Paris. Length 8 feet 2 inches.*
Reproduced on a smaller scale in black and white by Thureau-Dangin, *Til Barsip,* pl. LIII.

120. *Assyrian Art. Til Barsip (Tell Ahmar).* Wall Painting in the Palace. The 'Pink Horse.' *8th or 7th century B.C. Copy by L. Cavro, Paris. Length 32 3/4 inches.*
Reproduced on a smaller scale in black and white by Thureau-Dangin, *Til Barsip,* pl. LII.

121. *Assyrian Art. Imgur Bel (Balawat).* Door Plaque of Shalmaneser III. The Invalid King of Hama, lying on a terrace, surrendering to the Assyrians. Syrian Campaign (849 B.C.). *9th century B.C. British Museum. Bronze, height c. 11 inches.* (British Museum).

122. *Assyrian Art. Imgur Bel (Balawat).* Door Plaque of Shalmaneser III. Boats laden with Tribute from Tyre. Phœnician Campaign (858 B.C.). *9th century B.C. British Museum. Bronze, height c. 11 inches. (British Museum).*

123. *Assyrian Art. Imgur Bel (Balawat).* The Capture of Ashtamaku. The Assyrian Camp. Syrian Campaign (849 B.C.). *9th century B.C. British Museum. Bronze. (British Museum).*

124. *Assyrian Art. Imgur Bel (Balawat).* The Capture of Ashtamaku. Syrian Campaign (849 B.C.). *9th century B.C. British Museum. Bronze. (British Museum).*

125. *Assyrian Art. Imgur Bel (Balawat).* Prisoners Impaled. North Syrian Campaign (858 B.C.). *9th century B.C. British Museum. Bronze. (British Museum).*

126. *Assyrian Art. Imgur Bel (Balawat).* King Shalmaneser receiving the submission of the King of Hama. Syrian Campaign (849 B.C.). *9th century B.C. British Museum. Bronze. (British Museum).*

127. *Assyrian Art. Imgur Bel (Balawat).* The Siege of Dabigu. North Syrian Campaign (858 B.C.). *9th century B.C. British Museum. Bronze. (British Museum).*

128. *Assyrian Art. Imgur Bel (Balawat).* Archers attacking the City of Dabigu. North Syrian Campaign (858 B.C.). *9th century B.C. British Museum. Bronze. (British Museum).*

129. *Assyrian Art. Imgur Bel (Balawat).* Submission of Representatives from the City of Hama. Syrian Campaign (849 B.C.). *9th century B.C. British Museum. Bronze. (British Museum).*

130a and b. *Assyrian Art.* Labartu Plaque. *First half of the 1st millennium B.C. De Clercq-Boisgelin Collection. Bronze, height 5 1/4 inches. (Archives Photographiques).*

131. *Assyrian Art.* The Demon Pazuzu. *First half of the 1st millennium B.C. Louvre, Paris. Bronze, height 5 3/4 inches (Louvre).*

132. *Assyrian Art. Dur Sharrukin (Khorsabad).* Crouching Lion. *8th century B.C. Louvre, Paris. Bronze, height 11 3/8, length 16 1/8 inches. (Tel-Vigneau).*

133. *Assyrian Art.* King Esarhaddon and his Mother Naqia. *7th century B.C. Louvre, Paris. Bronze, height 13 inches. (G. Franceschi).*

134a and b. *Art of Urartu. Lake Urmya Region.* King Assurdan. *10th century B.C. Louvre, Paris. Bronze, height 11 3/4 inches. (Tel-Vigneau).*

135. *Art of Urartu. Erzerum.* God standing on a Horned Lion. *1st millennium B.C. Louvre, Paris. Bronze, height 5 7/8 inches. (Tel-Vigneau).*

136. *Achaemenian Art. Susa.* Detail of a Capital. *5th-4th centuries B.C. Louvre, Paris. Grey stone, over-all length 19 feet. (Tel-Vigneau).*

137. *Art of Urartu.* Bull's Head. *1st millennium B.C. Louvre, Paris. Bronze, height 4 inches. (Louvre).*

138. *Assyrian Art. Imgur Bel (Balawat).* Dedication of a Royal Stele. Armenian Campaign (860 B.C.) *9th century B.C. British Museum. Bronze. (British Museum).*

139. *Assyrian Art. Imgur Bel (Balawat).* Carrying off War Booty after the Armenian Campaign (860 B.C.). *9th century B.C. British Museum. Bronze. (British Museum).*

140. *Assyrian Art. Imgur Bel (Balawat).* Felling Trees in a Conquered City. Armenian Campaign (860 B.C.). *9th century B.C. British Museum. Bronze. (British Museum).*

141. *Assyrian Art. Imgur Bel (Balawat).* Setting Fire to the City of Khazanu. Phœnician Campaign (858 B.C.). *9th century B.C. British Museum. Bronze. (British Museum).*

142. *Assyrian Art. Imgur Bel (Balawat).* Massacre of Prisoners. Phœnician Campaign (858 B.C.). *9th century B.C. British Museum. Bronze. (British Museum).*

143. *Assyrian Art. Imgur Bel (Balawat).* Sacrifices and Erection of a Stele. Campaign at the Sources of the Tigris (853 B.C.). *9th century B.C. British Museum. Bronze. (British Museum).*

144. *Assyrian Art. Imgur Bel (Balawat).* Royal Pavilion. Baking Bread. Armenian Campaign (860 B.C.). *9th century B.C. British Museum. Bronze. (British Museum).*

145. *Assyrian Art. Imgur Bel (Balawat).* Assyrian Army at the Battle of Dabigu. Convoy of Prisoners and Animals. North Syrian Campaign (858 B.C.). *9th century B.C. British Museum. Bronze. (British Museum).*

146. *Assyrian Art. Imgur Bel (Balawat).* Assyrian Army. Prisoners led out of Sugunia. Armenian Campaign (860 B.C.). *9th century B.C. British Museum. Bronze. (British Museum).*

147. *Art of Luristan. Pusht-i Kuh.* Head of a Warrior or God, detail of a complete statue. *Late 2nd - early 1st millennium B.C. Teheran Museum. Bronze, height 15 inches. (Teheran Museum).*

148. *Art of Luristan.* Cheek-piece. *First half of the 1st millennium B.C. Teheran Museum. Bronze. (Teheran Museum).*

149. *Art of Luristan.* Bit with Moufflons. *First half of the 1st millennium B.C. Louvre, Paris. Bronze, height 5 7/8 inches. (Tel-Vigneau).*

150. *Art of Luristan.* Cheek-piece. Winged Moufflon with a Rosette stamped on its Haunch. *First half of the 1st millennium B.C. David-Weill Collection. Bronze, height 4 1/8, width 3 1/4 inches. (David-Weill).*

151. *Art of Luristan.* Pin-head. Heroes and Animals. *First half of the 1st millennium B.C. David-Weill Collection. Bronze, height 4 3/4 inches. (David-Weill).*

152. *Art of Luristan.* Pin-head. Heroes and Animals. *First half of the 1st millennium B.C. David-Weill Collection. Bronze, height 6 5/8 inches. (David-Weill).*

153. *Art of Luristan.* Idol. *First half of the 1st millennium B.C. Louvre, Paris (AO 14024). Bronze, height 7, width 2 3/4 inches. (Louvre).*

154. *Sumerian Art.* Cylinder Seal. *Mid-3rd millennium B.C. Louvre, Paris. Translucent stone, height 2 inches. (Tel-Vigneau).*
Placed here for purposes of comparison, showing the survival of an ancient Mesopotamian theme in the Luristan idol (No. 153).

155. *Art of Luristan.* Axe-head with a Lion Rampant. *First half of the 1st millennium B.C. David-Weill Collection.* Bronbe and iron, height 2 3/4 inches. *(David-Weill).*

156. *Art of Luristan.* Ornamentation of a Standard. Four Men holding Hands and dancing in a Ring. *First half of the 1st millennium B.C. Louvre, Paris. Bronze, height* 13 *inches.* *(Tel-Vigneau).*

157a. *Mesopotamian Art. Mari (Tell-Hariri).* Babylonian Mould: Four Men holding Hands and dancing in a Ring. *18th century B.C. Aleppo Museum. Terracotta, diameter 8 inches.* *(Schneider-Lengyel).*
Placed here for comparison with No. 156, demonstrating the persistence of this theme.

157b. *Syro-Cappadocian Art.* Cylinder Seal. Four Gilgameshes in a Ring holding the Flowing Vase. *First half of the 2nd millennium B.C. E.T. Newell Collection. Haematite, height 7/8 of an inch. (Collection Photo).*

158a. *Art of Luristan.* Situla with Winged Sphinxes, with and without Beards. *First half of the 1st millennium B.C. Louvre, Paris. Bronze, height 5 1/2 inches. (Louvre).*

158b. *Art of Luristan.* Situla with a Banquet Scene. *First half of the 1st millennium B.C. Louvre, Paris. Bronze, height 6 1/4 inches. (Louvre).*

159. *Art of Luristan.* Belt Plaque with Hunting Scene. *First half of the 1st millennium B.C. Louvre, Paris. Bronze, length 20 inches. (Tel-Vigneau).*

160. *Han Art (China).* The 'Red Bird.' *2nd century A.D* *(Musée Guimet-Segalen).*

161. *Shang Art (China).* Ritual Vase. *14th-12th centuries B.C. C.R. Holmes Collection. Bronze. (Musée Roypl d'Art et d'Histoire, Brussels).*

162. *Chinese Art.* T'ao-t'ieh Head (highly stylized face of an animal represented without the lower jaw). *(Musée Guimet).*

163. *Art of Luristan.* Ceremonial Axe. *First half of the 1st millennium B.C. David-Weill Collection. Bronze, éength 6 1/2 inches. (Collection Photo).*

164. *Art of Luristan.* Axe with Toothed Socket. *First half of the 1st millennium B.C. Louvre, Paris (AO 12428). Bronze, length 7 7/8 inches. (Draeger).*

165. *Art of Luristan.* Ceremonial Axe adorned with a Human Figure and an Animal-Muzzle. *First half of the 1st millennium B.C.*

166. *Art of Luristan.* Battle-Axe with Socket decorated with stylized Animal-Muzzles. *First half of the 1st millennium B.C. Louvre, Paris (AO 18954). Bronze, length 7 5/8 inches. (Draeger).*

167. *Mannaean Art. Ziwiyeh.* Pectoral. *First half of the 1st millennium B.C. Teheran Museum. Gold, width 14 1/8 inches. (Teheran Museum).*

168. *Mannaean Art. Ziwiyeh.* Pectoral, detail. *First half of the 1st millennium B.C. Teheran Museum. Gold, over-all width 14 1/8 inches. (Teheran Museum).*

169. *Mannaean Art. Ziwiyeh.* Head of a Griffin. *First half of the 1st millennium B.C. Teheran Museum. Gold, height 3 1/8 inches. (Teheran Museum).*

170a. *Mannaean Art. Ziwiyeh.* Fragment of a Torque. *First half of the 1st millennium B.C. Teheran Museum. Gold. (Teheran Museum).*

170b. *Mannaean Art. Ziwiyeh.* Fragment of a Belt Plaque. *First half of the 1st millennium B.C. Teheran Museum. Gold, length 1 1/2 inches. (Teheran Museum).*

170c. *Mannaean Art. Ziwiyeh.* Bracelet. *First half of the 1st millennium B.C. Metropolitan Museum of Art, New York. Gold. (Metropolitan Museum).*

170d. *Mannaean Art. Ziwiyeh.* Bracelet. *First half of the 1st millennium B.C. Metropolitan Museum of Art, New York. Gold, width 3 1/4 inches. (Metropolitan Museum).*

170e. *Art of the Zagros Mountains.* Bracelet. *Early 1st millennium B.C. Louvre, Paris. Electrum, height 4 inches. (Louvre).*

171. *Mannaean Art. Ziwiyeh.* Ibex. *First half of the 1st millennium B.C. Teheran Museum. Gold, width 6 5/8 inches. (Teheran Museum).*

172. *Art of Mazandaran.* Kalar Dasht. Bowl decorated with Lions. *Early 1st millennium B.C. Teheran Museum. Gold, diameter 4 1/4, height 3 1/2 inches. (Teheran Museum).*

173a. *Mannaean Art. Ziwiyeh.* Decorative Plaque with a Bounding Lion. *First half of the 1st millennium B.C. Teheran Museum. Silver, height 12 1/2 inches. (Teheran Museum).*

173b. *Mannaean Art. Ziwiyeh.* Decorative Plaque with a Bounding Lion, detail. *First half of the 1st millennium B.C. Teheran Museum. Silver, over-all height 12 1/2 inches. (Teheran Museum).*

174. *Mannaean Art. Ziwiyeh.* Lioness and Rabbit, detail of a Pectoral. *First half of the 1st millennium B.C. Teheran Museum. Gold, over-all width 14 1/8 inches. (Teheran Museum).*

175. *Scythian Art. Kelermes (Kuban).* Lioness. *Early 1st millennium B.C. Hermitage, Leningrad. Gold. (After Godard, fig. 35).*

176. *Assyrian Art (?). Ziwiyeh.* Bronze Tub, detail. *9th century B.C.* Fragments preserved in the Teheran Museum. *Bronze. (Teheran Museum).*

177a. *Assyrian Art. Ziwiyeh.* Dignitaries and Bull Hunt. *8th century B.C. Ivory, height 5 7/8 inches. (After Godard, fig. 80).*

177b. *Assyrian Art. Ziwiyeh.* Lion Hunt and Procession of Dignitaries. *9th century B.C. Ivory, height 16 inches. (After Godard, fig. 81).*

178. *Assyrian Art. Ziwiyeh.* Banquet Scene. *8th century B.C. Teheran Museum. Ivory, height 2 3/8 inches. (After Godard, fig. 78).*

179a. *Assyrian Art. Assur (Qalaat Shergat).* Comb with a Ritual Scene. *Late 2nd - early 1st millennium B.C. Ivory, length 2 1/2 inches. (After Arndt Maller, Die Gräber und Grüfte von Assur, fig. 163b).*

179b. *Assyrian Art. Assur (Qalaat Shergat).* Pyx with a Symbolic Scene. *Late 2nd - early 1st millennium B.C. Ivory, height 3 1/4 inches. (After Arndt Maller, Die Gräber und Grüfte von Assur, fig. 161).*

180a. *Syro-Phœnician Art. Dur Sharrukin (Khorsabad).* 'Woman at the Window.' *8th century B.C. Ivory, height 4 inches. (After John Albert Wilson and Thomas George Allen,* Khorsabad, *II, fig. 29).*

180b. *Syro-Phœnician Art. Dur Sharrukin (Khorsabad).* One of the Genii protecting Horus. *8th century B.C. Ivory, height 4 inches. (After John Albert Wilson and Thomas George Allen,* Khorsabad, *II, fig. 38).*

180c. *Syro-Phœnician Art. Dur Sharrukin (Khorsabad).* Sphinx. *8th century B.C. Ivory, height 3 3/8 inches. (After John Albert Wilson and Thomas George Allen,* Khorsabad, *II, fig. 43).*

181. *Syro-Phœnician Art. Hadatu (Arslan Tash).* Cow suckling her Calf. *8th century B.C. Aleppo Museum. Ivory, length 4 1/4 inches. (Schneider-Lengyel).*

182. *North Syrian Art. Kalakh (Nimrud).* Woman with a Crown and Long Braids. *First millennium B.C. British Museum* (118197). *Ivory, height 5 1/8 inches. (British Museum).*

183. *Assyrian Art. Kalakh (Nimrud).* King Assurnasirpal. *9th century B.C. Ivory, height 10 5/8 inches. (After* Iraq, *pl. XIV, Photo Antran, Copyright M.E.L. Mallowan).*

184. *Assyrian Art. Kalakh (Nimrud).* Bull Passant. *9th-8th centuries B.C. Ivory, length 8 5/8 inches. (Illustrated London News, July 7, 1950, p. 151, Copyright M.E.L. Mallowan).*

185. *Assyrian Art. Kalakh (Nimrud).* 'Monna Lisa.' *8th century B.C. Baghdad Museum. Ivory, height 5 feet 5 inches. (Schneider-Lengyel).*

186. *Assyrian Art. Kalakh (Nimrud).* Lioness mauling an Ethiopian (?), detail. *8th century B.C.* Two identical versions, one in the British Museum, another in the Baghdad Museum. *Ivory, gold, coloured paste, polychrome stones; height 2 3/8 inches. (Schneider-Lengyel).*

187. *Assyrian Art. Kalakh (Nimrud).* Lioness mauling an Ethiopian (?). *8th century B.C. Ivory, gold, coloured paste, polychrome stones; height 2 3/8 inches. (Copyright M.E.L. Mallowan).*

188. *Assyrian Art. Kalakh (Nimrud).* Harness Ornament. Winged Sphinx beside a Cartouche inscribed with the name 'Janen' or 'Jejanen.' *8th century B.C. Metropolitan Museum of Art, New York. Ivory, length 7 1/4 inches. (Copyright M.E.L. Mallowan).*

189. *Assyrian Art. Kalakh (Nimrud).* Woman seated on a Throne beneath the Winged Disk. *8th century B.C. Iraq Museum, Baghdad. Ivory, height 4 5/8 inches. (Copyright M.E.L. Mallowan).*

190. *Assyrian Art. Kalakh (Nimrud), Fort Shalmaneser.* Divine Hero vanquishing a Monster. Prototype of 'St. George and the Dragon.' *8th century B.C. Institute of Archaeology, London. Ivory, height 4, width 2 3/8 inches. (Copyright M.E.L. Mallowan).*

191a. *Assyrian Art. Kalakh (Nimrud).* Decoration of a Bed. Palmettes and Figures with the Situla. Winged Disk. *8th century B.C. British Museum. Ivory, length 33, height 22 inches. (Copyright M.E.L. Mallowan).*

191b. *Assyrian Art. Kalakh (Nimrud).* Decoration of a Bed. Rosettes and volutes. *8th century B.C. Metropolitan Museum of Art, New York. Ivory, length 19 1/4 height 13 inches. (Copyright M.E.L. Mallowan).*

192. *Assyrian Art.* Cylinder Seal. Hunter spearing a Lion. *First half of the 1st millennium B.C. British Museum. Black serpentine, height 1 1/2 inches. (British Museum).*

193. *Assyrian Art.* Cylinder Seal. Archer hunting. *First half of the 1st millennium B.C. Pierpont Morgan Library, New York, after E. Porada. Steatite, height 1 1/4 inches. (Morgan Library).*

194. *Assyrian Art.* Cylinder Seal. Mythological Scene. Combat of a Winged Genius with Two Winged Bulls. *First half of the 1st millennium B.C. British Museum. Jasper, height 1 3/8 inches. (British Museum).*

195. *Assyrian Art.* Cylinder Seal. Mythological Scene. *First half of the 1st millennium B.C. Pierpont Morgan Library, New York, after E. Porada. Steatite, height 1 1/2 inches. (Morgan Library).*

196. *Assyrian Art.* Cylinder Seal. Archer Shooting at a Sphinx. *First half of the 1st millennium B.C. Pierpont Morgan Library, New York, after E. Porada. Black serpentine, height 1 3/8 inches. (Morgan Library).*

197. *Assyrian Art.* Cylinder Seal. Hero fighting Two Winged Sphinxes. *First half of the 1st millennium B.C. Louvre, Paris. Brown chalcedony, height 1 3/8 inches. (Tel-Vigneau).*

198. *Assyrian Art.* Cylinder Seal. Hero subduing Ibexes. *First half of the 1st millennium B.C. Louvre, Paris. Carnelian, height 1 inch. (Tel-Vigneau).*

199. *Assyrian Art.* Cylinder Seal. Centaur-lion fighting a Lion. *First half of the 1st millennium B.C. Berlin Museum. Chalcedony, height 1 3/8 inches. (Marburg).*

200. *Assyrian Art.* Cylinder Seal. Combat of a Lion and a Winged Horse. *First half of the 1st millennium B.C. British Museum. Pink agate, height 1 5/8 inches. (British Museum).*

201. *Assyrian Art.* Cylinder Seal. Lion attacking a Bull beside Palm Trees. *First half of the 1st millennium B.C. Louvre, Paris. Brown jasper streaked with black, height 2 inches. (Tel-Vigneau).*

202. *Assyrian Art.* Cylinder Seal. Gazelle in Wooded Country. *First half of the 1st millennium B.C. Pierpont Morgan Library, New York, after E. Porada. Chalcedony, height 1 1/4 inches. (Morgan Library).*

203. *Assyrian Art.* Cylinder Seal. Adoration of the Goddess Ishtar. *First half of the 1st millennium B.C. British Museum. Chalcedony, height 1 1/2 inches. (British Museum).*

204. *Assyrian Art. Kalakh (Nimrud).* Cylinder Seal. Mythological Scene. *8th century B.C. British Museum. Chalcedony, height 1 1/8 inches. (Illustrated London News, July 29, 1950, Copyright M.E.L. Mallowan).*

205. *Assyrian Art.* Cylinder Seal. Adoration of the Sacred Tree, beneath the Winged Disk. *First half of the 1st millennium B.C. Pierpont Morgan Library, New York, after E. Porada. Marble, height 1 1/2 inches. (Morgan Library).*

206. *Assyrian Art. Mari (Tell Hariri).* Cylinder Seal. Banquet Scene. *First half of the 1st millennium B.C. Louvre, Paris. Stone, height 1 3/8 inches. (Louvre).*

207. *Assyrian Art. Dur Sharrukin (Khorsabad).* Threshold of the Palace, with Flower Patterns. *8th century B.C. Louvre, Paris. Gypseous alabaster, height 4 feet 1 1/4 inches, width 6 feet 10 inches. (Draeger).*

208. *Art of Luristan.* Sword with Decorated Openwork Hilt. *First half of the 1st millennium B.C. Louvre, Paris (AO 21069). Bronze, length 20 1/8 inches. (Louvre).*

209. *Art of Luristan.* Pin-head with Mask in high Relief. *First half of the 1st millennium B.C. Louvre, Paris (AO 20553). Bronze, height 6 inches. Formerly in the Coiffard Collection. (Louvre).*

210. *Art of Luristan.* Pin-head with Coil Patterns. *First half of the 1st millennium B.C. Louvre, Paris (AO 20800). Bronze, diameter 1 7/8 inches. Formerly in the Coiffard Collection. (Louvre).*

211. *Art of Luristan.* Pin-head with Animals Fighting. *First half of the 1st millennium B.C. Louvre, Paris (AO 20607). Bronze, diameter 4 1/2 inches. Formerly in the Coiffard Collection. (Louvre).*

212. *Art of Luristan.* Pin-head with Divine Hero Subduing Serpents. *First half of the 1st millennium B.C. Louvre, Paris (AO 20615). Bronze, diameter 3 inches. Formerly in the Coiffard Collection. (Louvre).*

213. *Babylonian Art. Sippar (Abu Habba).* The Sippar Tablet, detail. The God Shamash under a Canopy holding the Ring and Staff. Inscription of Nabu-apal-iddin. *9th century B.C. British Museum. Stone, width 7 inches. (British Museum).*

214. *Assyro-Babylonian Art.* Cylinder Seal. Mythological Scene. Scorpion-Men on either Side of the God Assur (?). *First half of the 1st millennium. Louvre, Paris. Chalcedony, height 1 1/8 inches. (Tel-Vigneau).*

215. *Babylonian Art. Sippar (Abu Habba).* The Sippar Tablet. King Nabu-apal-iddin 'presented' to the God Shamash, whose Emblem stands on a Table in front of the Dais. *9th century B.C. British Museum (91000). Stone, width 7 inches. (British Museum).*

216. *Babylonian Art.* Boundary Stone of Marduk-apal-iddin (called Merodach-Baladan in the Bible). *8th century B.C. Berlin Museum. Black marble, height 18 1/8 inches. (Marburg).*

217. *Babylonian Art.* Boundary Stone of Marduk-zakir-shumi. *9th century B.C. Louvre, Paris. Limestone, height 13 inches. (Tel-Vigneau).*

218. *Neo-Babylonian Art. Babylon.* View of the City and the Ziggurat. Reconstruction by Herbert Anger, from data furnished by Eckhard Unger. *7th-6th centuries B.C. (From Unger,* Babylon, *pl. 5).*

219. *Babylon.* Plan of the City, based on Koldewey's excavations. *7th-6th centuries B.C. (Claude Abeille, after Unger).*

220. *Neo-Babylonian Art. Babylon.* The Ishtar Gate and the Processional Way. Reconstruction by Herbert Anger, from data furnished by Eckhard Unger. *7th-6th centuries B.C.* In the right background, the 'hanging gardens' and the ziggurat. *(From* Babylon, *frontispiece).*

221a. *Neo-Babylonian Art. Babylon.* Lion Passant on the Sacred Way. *7th-6th centuries B.C. Louvre, Paris. Glazed bricks, length 7 feet 5 inches, height 3 feet 5 inches. On deposit from the Berlin Museum. (Draeger).*

221b. *Neo-Babylonian Art. Babylon.* Dragon on the Ishtar Gate. Animal Attribute of Marduk. *7th-6th centuries B.C. Berlin Museum. Glazed bricks, height 3 feet 5 inches.*

221c. *Neo-Babylonian Art. Babylon.* Bull on the Ishtar Gate. Animal Attribute of Adad. *7th-6th centuries B.C. Berlin Museum. Glazed bricks, height 3 feet 5 inches.*

222. *Neo-Babylonian Art. Babylon.* The Ishtar Gate. *7th-6th centuries B.C.* Reconstruction. *Berlin Museum. Glazed bricks, height 47 feet.*

223. *Neo-Babylonian Art. Babylon.* Plan of the Palaces. *7th-6th centuries B.C. (Claude Abeille, after A. Parrot).*

224. *Neo-Babylonian Art. Babylon.* Decoration of the Throne Room of the Palace. *7th-6th centuries. Berlin Museum. Glazed bricks, over-all height 11 feet, 2 inches. (After Wetzel,* Assur und Babylon, *p. 36).*

225. *Neo-Babylonian Art. Babylon.* Plan of the Temple of Ishtar of Akkad. *7th-6th centuries B.C. (Claude Abeille, after A. Parrot).*

226. *Neo-Babylonian Art (?). Babylon.* Lion trampling a Man. *First millennium B.C. In situ. Basalt, length 8 feet 6 inches, width 2 feet 9 1/2 inches, height 5 feet 5 inches. (Schneider-Lengyel).*

227. *Neo-Babylonian Art.* Cylinder Seal. Hero fighting Wild Animals. *7th-6th centuries B.C. Pierpont Morgan Library, New York, after E. Porada. Carnelian, height 1 1/2 inches. (Morgan Library).*

228. *Neo-Babylonian Art.* Cylinder Seal. Hero capturing Birds. *7th-6th centuries B.C. Pierpont Morgan Library, New York, after E. Porada. Chalcedony, height 15/16 of an inch. (Morgan Library).*

229. *Neo-Babylonian Art.* Adoration of the Goat-Fish. *7th-6th centuries B.C. Pierpont Morgan Library, New York, after E. Porada. Lapis-lazuli, height 1 5/8 inches. (Morgan Library).*

230. *Neo-Babylonian Art.* Head of a Dragon, Animal Attribute of Marduk. *7th-6th centuries B.C. Louvre, Paris. Bronze, height 5 7/8 inches. (Draeger).*

231. *Neo-Babylonian Art.* Cylinder Seal. Adoration of the Sacred Tree dominated by the Winged Disk. *7th-6th centuries B.C. Pierpont Morgan Library, New York, after E. Porada. Chalcedony, height 1 5/8 inches. (Morgan Library).*

232. *Assyro-Babylonian Art.* Cylinder Seal. Archer shooting a Winged Quadruped. *First millennium B.C. Louvre, Paris. White chalcedony, height 1 3/8 inches. (Tel-Vigneau).*

233. *Assyro-Babylonian Art.* Cylinder Seal. Two Kneeling Men worshipping the Sacred Tree, dominated by the Winged Disk. *First millennium B.C. Louvre, Paris. White sardonyx, height 1 1/4 inches. (Tel-Vigneau).*

234. *Neo-Babylonian Art.* Cylinder Seal. Winged Centaur shooting a Roaring Lion. *7th-6th centuries B.C. Pierpont Morgan Library, New York, after E. Porada. Agate, height 1 3/16 inches. (Morgan Library).*

235. *Neo-Babylonian Art.* Cylinder Seal. Winged Hero subduing Two Ostriches. *7th-6th centuries B.C. Pierpont Morgan Library, New York, after E. Porada. Yellow chert, height* 1 1/4 *inches. (Morgan Library).*

236. *Assyro-Babylonian Art.* Cylinder Seal. Detail, Fleeing Ostrich. *First millennium B.C. Pierpont Morgan Library, New York, after E. Porada. Grey marble, height* 1 1/4 *inches. (Morgan Library).*

237. *Achaemenian Art. Persepolis.* Head of a Mede. *5th-4th centuries B.C. Louvre, Paris. Grey limestone, height* 9 *inches. (Tel-Vigneau).*

238. *Achaemenian Art. Persepolis.* Babylonian Tributaries bringing Gifts. *6th-5th centuries B.C. In situ. Limestone. (After E. Schmidt, 1953).*
To provide a better lay-out, this relief has been reproduced in reverse.

239. *Achaemenian Art. Susa.* View of the Palace. *6th-4th centuries B.C. (Aerial Survey Photo, Oriental Institute, Chicago).*

240. *Achaemenian Art. Pasargadae.* View of the Palace. *6th century B.C. (Oriental Institute, Chicago).*

241. *Achaemenian Art. Pasargadae.* Winged Genius decorating a Gate of the Palace. *6th century B.C. In situ. Stone. (Oriental Institute, Chicago).*

242. *Achaemenian Art. Persepolis.* Aerial View of the Ruins. *6th-5th centuries B.C. (Aerial Survey Photo, Oriental Institute, Chicago).*

243. *Achaemenian Art. Persepolis.* Monumental Stairway on the East Side of the Apadana. *6th-5th centuries B.C. Stone. (Oriental Institute, Chicago).*

244. *Achaemenian Art. Persepolis.* King or Hero mastering a Lion Cub. *6th-5th centuries B.C. Stone, height* 5 *feet* 7 *inches. (After Ernst Herzfeld, Iran in the Ancient East, pl.* 70*).*

245. *Achaemenian Art. Persepolis.* Servant of the Palace of Darius. *6th-5th centuries B.C. Stone, height* 5 *feet* 5 *inches. (After Ernst Herzfeld, Iran in the Ancient East, pl.* 82*).*

246a. *Neo-Babylonian Art. Babylon.* Plan of the Neo-Babylonian Palaces. *7th-6th centuries B.C. (Claude Abeille, after A. Parrot).*
Shown here so as to enable comparison with Nos. 246b and c.

246b. *Achaemenian Art. Susa.* Plan of the Palace. *6th-7th centuries B.C. (Claude Abeille, after A. Parrot).*

246c. *Achaemenian Art. Persepolis.* Plan of the Palaces. *6th-5th centuries B.C. (Claude Abeille, after A. Parrot).*

247. *Achaemenian Art. Susa.* Archer of the Royal Guard. *5th century B.C. Louvre, Paris. Glazed bricks, height of the archer* 4 *feet* 10 *inches. (Draeger).*

248. *Achaemenian Art. Naksh-i-Rustam.* Tomb of Darius I. *5th century B.C. (Oriental Institute, Chicago).*

249. *Achaemenian Art. Persepolis.* Portrait of a Prince (? Xerxes). *5th century B.C. Teheran Museum. Lapis lazuli paste, height* 2 1/2 *inches.*

250. *Achaemenian Art.* Cylinder Seal. The King, standing on Two Sphinxes, grappling with Two Lions. *First millennium B.C. Pierpont Morgan Library, after E. Porada. Eyestone, height* 1 1/4 *inches. (Morgan Library).*

251. *Achaemenian Art. Susa.* Torque. *5th-4th centuries B.C. Louvre, Paris. Gold with inlays of turquoise, lapis lazuli and mother of pearl; diameter* 7 7/8 *inches. (Draeger).*

252. *Achaemenian Art.* Bowl with an Ostrich Hunt. *6th-4th centuries B.C. Louvre, Paris (AO* 20115*). Bronze, diameter* 8 5/8 *inches. (Draeger).*

253. *Achaemenian Art. Susa.* Capital with foreparts of Bulls. Apadana of the Palace of Artaxerxes II. *5th-4th centuries B.C. Louvre, Paris. Grey marble, height* 19 *feet. (Tel-Vigneau).*

254. *Achaemenian Art. Samsun or Armenia (?).* Vase-Handle in the form of a Winged Ibex. *5th-4th centuries B.C. Louvre, Paris. Silver inlaid with gold, height* 10 3/8 *inches. (Draeger).*
An identical vase-handle is in the Berlin Museum. Both belonged to the same vase.

255. *Romanesque Art. Chartres.* Tympanum of the Royal Portal. *12th century A.D. Cathedral of Chartres. Stone. (Tel-Vigneau).*

256. *Achaemenian Art. Gordion.* Cylinder Seal. Scene of Worship. *6th-4th centuries B.C. Ankara Museum. (Ankara Museum).*

257. *Achaemenian Art.* Cylinder Seal. Scene of Combat. *6th-4th centuries B.C. Bibliothèque Nationale, Paris. Chalcedony, height* 1 1/2 *inches. (Bibliothèque Nationale).*

258. *Achaemenian Art.* Cylinder Seal. Bull Passant. *6th-4th centuries B.C. Pierpont Morgan Library, New York, after E. Porada. Chalcedony, height* 1 *inch. (Morgan Library).*

259. *Achaemenian Art.* Cylinder Seal. Scene of Worship. *6th-4th centuries B.C. Bibliothèque Nationale, Paris. Chalcedony, height* 1 1/4 *inches. (Bibliothèque Nationale).*

260. *Achaemenian Art.* Cylinder Seal. Ritual Scene. *6th-4th centuries B.C. Private Collection. (Collection Photo).*

261. *Achaemenian Art. Thebes.* Cylinder Seal of Darius. *6th-5th centuries B.C. British Museum. Agate, height* 1 1/4 *inches. (British Museum).*

262. *Achaemenian Art.* Cylinder Seal. Hero fighting a Winged Lion. *Boston Museum of Fine Arts. (Museum of Fine Arts).*

263. *Achaemenian Art.* Cylinder Seal. Homage to a Queen (?). *6th-4th centuries B.C. De Clercq-Boisgelin Collection. Agate, height* 1 1/4 *inches. (Collection Photo).*

264. *Achaemenian Art.* Cylinder Seal. Two Warriors on either side of Ahuramazda, beneath the Winged Disk. *6th-4th centuries B.C. Berlin Museum (VA* 3022*). Chalcedony, height* 1 1/4 *inches. (Marburg).*

265. *Mesopotamian Art.* Craftsman at Work. *Early 3rd millennium B.C. Louvre, Paris. Terracotta, height* 3 1/8 *inches. (Louvre).*

266. *Assyrian Art. Til Barsip (Tell Ahmar).* Wall Painting in the Palace. King Tiglathpileser III giving Audience. Detail of No. 113. *8th century B.C. Copy by L. Cavro, Paris.*

267. *Assyrian Art. Dur Sharrukin (Khorsabad).* Seascape, detail. Floating Wood along the Phœnician Coast. *8th century B.C. Louvre, Paris. Gypseous alabaster, overall height 9 feet 7 inches. (Tel-Vigneau).*

268. *Sumerian Art.* Cattle about to quit a Stable. *Early 3rd millennium B.C. Louvre, Paris. Limestone, height 9 5/8 inches. (Louvre).*
Possibly the cattle are not actually moving. This may be a conventional design intended to show the interior of the stable, with a partial view of the animals. The emblems surmounting the structure indicate its sacred character.

269. *Lagash (Telloh), Iraq.* Construction of a Zarifeh (reed hut), 1930. *(André Parrot).*
Type of dwelling built on the same lines as in early times. Made of rush-mats laid over a reed framework.

270. *Mesopotamian Art. Kish (al 'Oheimir).* Plano-convex Bricks. *3rd millennium B.C. Terracotta or unbaked clay. (André Parrot).*

271. *Sumerian Art. Lagash (Telloh).* Well of Eannatum. Herring-bone Work. *First half of the 3rd millennium B.C. Terracotta. (André Parrot).*

272. *Sumerian Art. Lagash (Telloh).* Bricks inscribed with the Name of Gudea, Patesi of Lagash. *22nd century B.C. Private Collection. Terracotta, 11 3/4 by 11 3/4 inches. (André Parrot).*
With a dedication to Ningirsu, the city god.

273. *Mesopotamian Art. Larsa (Senkereh).* Palace of Nur-Adad. *Early 2nd millennium B.C. Baked ana unbaked bricks. (André Parrot).*
Excavations of André Parrot, 1933.

274. *Sumerian Art. Ur (Muqayyar).* Tomb 1054. Domed Vault. *First half of the 3rd millennium B.C. Bricks. Funerary chamber, 8 feet 6 inches by 7 feet 2 inches, height 5 feet 7 inches. (Claude Abeille, after André Parrot).*

275. *Assyrian Art. Dur Sharrukin (Khorsabad).* Column Base. *8th century B.C. Basalt, diameter 5 feet 9 inches. (After E. Schmidt).*

276. *Assyrian Art. Dur Sharrukin (Khorsabad).* Plan and Reconstruction of the 'Bit-Hilani.' *8th century B.C. (Claude Abeille, after André Parrot).*

277. *Sumerian Art. Al 'Ubaid.* Dairy Scene. *First half of the 3rd millennium B.C. Iraq Museum, Baghdad. Limestone, copper and schist; height 8 5/8, length 45 1/4 inches. (Schneider-Lengyel).*

278. *Sumerian Art. Al 'Ubaid.* Nail-heads with a Flower Pattern. *First half of the 3rd millennium B.C. Iraq Museum, Baghdad; University Museum, Philadelphia; British Museum, London. Terracotta, white limestone, pink stone, black stone, bitumen; varying in length from 9 7/8 to 14 1/2 inches; average diameter 4 1/2 inches. (Museum Photos).*

279. *Mesopotamian Art. Tell Brak.* Frieze decorating a Podium. *First half of the 3rd millennium B.C. Aleppo Museum. Gold, blue limestone, white marble, blue-green schist; length 44 1/2 inches. (After Mallowan, Iraq, IX, pl. III).*

280a. *Sumerian Art. Lagash (Telloh).* Toadstone inscribed with Gudea's Name. *Second half of the 3rd*

millennium B.C. Louvre, Paris. Diorite, length 24 3/8, width 13 3/8, height 11 inches. (André Parrot).

280b. *Mesopotamian Art. Ashnunnak (Tell Asmar).* Window. *Sargonid Period. 25th-23rd centuries B.C. Terracotta, height 19 inches.*

281. *Sumerian Art. Lagash (Telloh).* Plan of a House. *Late 3rd millennium B.C. (Claude Abeille, after André Parrot).*

282. *Assyrian Art. Assur (Qalaat Shergat).* The God Assur surrounded by his Aura. *9th century B.C. British Museum. Glazed brick, height 11 inches. (British Museum).*

283. *Neo-Babylonian Art. Babylon.* The Ziggurat E-temen-an-ki. Reconstruction by Eckhard Unger. *7th-6th centuries B.C. Model.*

284. *Assyrian Art. Jerwan (Iraq).* Aqueduct of Sennacherib. *7th century B.C. Stone. (Oriental Institute, Chicago).*

285. *Sumerian Art. Lagash (Telloh).* Human-headed Bull. *Second half of the 3rd millennium B.C. Louvre, Paris. Black steatite, originally inlaid; height 4 3/4 inches. (Tel-Vigneau).*

286. *Art of Urartu. Toprak Kale.* Centaur. *First millennium B.C. British Museum. Bronze (the inlays on the face are missing), height 7 7/8 inches. (British Museum).*

287a. *Sumerian Art. Lagash (Telloh).* Cylinder Seal and its Impression. Friezes of Crouching Animals. *Late 4th - early 3rd millennium B.C. Louvre, Paris. Pink marble, height 1 1/2 inches. (Tel-Vigneau).*

287b. *Sumerian Art. Lagash (Telloh)* (?). Stamp Seal with Decorated Reverse Side. *Late 4th - early 3rd millennium B.C. Jasper. (Tel-Vigneau).*

288. *Sumerian Art. Lagash (Telloh).* Impression of a Stamp Seal. Two Men Walking. *Late 4th - early 3rd millennium B.C. Louvre, Paris. Brick-red stone, 1 9/16 by 1 5/8 inches. (Tel-Vigneau).*

289. *Mesopotamian Art. Tepe Gawra.* Mould. *Mid-3rd millennium B.C. Sandstone, 11 3/4 by 9 by 4 1/4 inches.* Eight different instruments could be cast with this mould: three on one side, four on the other, and one on the edge.

290. *Mesopotamian Art. Mari (Tell Hariri).* Adze. *Early 2nd millennium B.C. Louvre, Paris. Bronze, length 6 1/4, width 2 inches.*

291a. *Sumerian Art. Ur (Muqayyar).* Rein-ring with an Onager. *First half of the 3rd millennium B.C. British Museum. Silver and electrum, height 5 1/4 inches. (British Museum).*

291b. *Sumerian Art. Ur (Muqayyar).* Helmet of Meskalamdug. *3rd millennium B.C. Baghdad Museum. Electrum, height 9 inches. (Schneider-Lengyel).*

291c. *Sumerian Art. Ur (Muqayyar).* Dagger in its Sheath. *First half of the 3rd millennium B.C. Baghdad Museum. Electrum, length 14 1/2 inches. (Baghdad Museum).*

291d. *Achaemenian Art. Susa.* Earring. *7th-6th centuries B.C. Louvre, Paris. Gold and coloured stones, diameter 1 3/4 inches. (Louvre).*

292a. *Iranian Art. Susa.* Decorated Bowl. *4th millennium B.C. Louvre, Paris. Painted terracotta, diameter 5 1/8, height 2 1/2 inches. (Draeger).*

292b. *Iranian Art. Susa.* Decorated Bowl. *4th millennium B.C. Louvre, Paris. Painted terracotta, diameter 4 3/4, height 3 1/2 inches. (Draeger).*

293a. *Mesopotamian Art. Hassuna.* Decorated Pottery. *4th millennium B.C. Iraq Museum, Baghdad. Terracotta. (Claude Abeille, after A. Parrot).*

293b. *Mesopotamian Art. Hassuna.* Decorated Pottery. *4th millennium B.C. Iraq Museum, Baghdad. Terracotta. (Claude Abeille, after A. Parrot).*

294. *Iranian Art. Sialk and Tepe Giyan.* Pottery Designs with Human Figures. *Late 4th millennium B.C. Louvre, Paris, and Teheran Museum. Terracotta. (Claude Abeille, after A. Parrot).*

295a. *Mesopotamian Art. Arpatchiya.* Plate decorated with the Maltese Cross. *Second half of 4th millennium B.C. Iraq Museum, Baghdad. Painted terracotta, diameter 9 inches. (Schneider-Lengyel)*

295b. *Mesopotamian Art. Arpatchiya.* Plate decorated with a Rosette and dotted with small Crosses. *Second half of the 4th millennium B.C. Iraq Museum, Baghdad. Painted terracotta, diameter 12 5/8 inches. (Schneider-Lengyel).*

296. *Mesopotamian Art. Eridu (Abu Shahrein).* Painted Pottery. *Second half of the 4th millennium B.C. Iraq Museum, Baghdad. Terracotta with geometric designs. (Claude Abeille, after André Parrot).*

297. *Mesopotamian Art. Jemdet Nasr.* Painted Pottery. *Late 4th - early 3rd millennium B.C. Terracotta, diameter 9 1/4, height 8 1/4 inches. (After Ernest Mackay,* Anthropology Memoirs, *Vol. I, 87, 1).*

298a. *Mesopotamian Art. Mari (Tell Hariri).* Flat-handled Jar with Engraved Designs. *First half of the 3rd millennium B.C. Louvre, Paris. Terracotta, diameter 9 3/4, height 13 1/8 inches. (Draeger).*

298b. *Iranian Art. Susa.* Vase with Engraved Designs inlaid with White Slip. A Bird pecking at a Fish. *Early 2nd millennium B.C. Louvre, Paris. Terracotta, height 7 1/2 inches. (Draeger).*

299. *Mesopotamian (? Hurrian) Art. Tell Billa.* Goblet with Geometric and Animal Designs. *Mid-2nd millennium B.C. Terracotta, with part of the design in reserve slip. (Claude Abeille, after André Parrot).*

300. *Assyrian Art. Assur (Qalaat Shergat).* Decorated Vase. *First millennium B.C. Berlin Museum. Glazed terracotta, height 11 5/8 inches. (Berlin Museum).*

301. *Iranian Art. Sialk, Cemetery B.* Vase with Long Spout, decorated with Geometric and Animal Designs. *Early 1st millennium B.C. Louvre, Paris (AO 17719). Terracotta, height 5 7/8, width 12 3/4 inches. (Draeger).*

302. *Mesopotamian Art. Larsa (Senkereh).* Tub-shaped Burial Vessel. *Early 2nd millennium B.C. Terracotta. (André Parrot).*

303. *Sumerian Art. Lagash (Telloh).* Cloche-shaped Burial Jar. *Late 3rd millennium B.C. Terracotta. (André Parrot).*

304. *Sumerian Art. Lagash (Telloh).* Twin-vessel Burial Jar. *Late 3rd - early 2nd millennium B.C. Terracotta. (André Parrot).*

305. *Sumerian Art. Ur (Muqayyar).* View of the 'Royal' Cemetery. *First half of the 3rd millennium B.C. Tombs of brick and stone. (British Museum).*

306. *Sumerian Art. Lagash (Telloh).* Modelled Figurine. *First half of the 3rd millennium B.C. Louvre, Paris. Terracotta, height 3 3/4 inches. (André Parrot).*

307. *Mesopotamian Art. Larsa (Senkereh).* Figurine of a Nude Woman. *Early 2nd millennium B.Ct Louvre, Paris. Terracotta, made from a mould; heigh. 4 1/8 inches. (André Parrot).*

308. *Mesopotamian Art of the Upper Khabur. Tell Halaf.* 'Mother-Goddess.' *4th millennium B.C. Terracotta, height 3 inches. (After Oppenheim,* Tell Halaf, *I, pl. 105).* Meant perhaps to suggest the position of a woman in childbirth.

309a. *Mesopotamian Art. Ur (Muqayyar).* Figurine of a Nude Snake-headed Woman. *4th millennium B.C. British Museum. Terracotta and bitumen, modelled, incised and inlaid; height 5 7/8 inches. (British Museum).*
Such figurines as this may well represent demons rather than divinities.

309b. *Mesopotamian Art. Eridu (Abu Shahrein).* Male Figurine. *4th millennium B.C. Iraq Museum, Baghdad. Terracotta, modelled and inlaid; height 5 1/2 inches. (Iraq Museum).*
The only known example of a male figurine of this type.

310a. *Mesopotamian Art. Lagash (Telloh).* Headless Figurine of a Nude Woman, with Touches of Black Paint. *4th millennium B.C. Louvre, Paris. Terracotta, modelled and painted; height 2 1/2 inches. (Chuzeville).*

310b. *Mesopotamian Art. Lagash (Telloh).* Male Figurine with Touches of Black Paint. *4th millennium B.C. Louvre, Paris. Terracotta, modelled and painted; height 1 7/8 inches. (Chuzeville).*

310c. *Sumerian Art. Lagash (Telloh).* Figurine of a Nude Woman. *Mid-3rd millennium B.C. Louvre, Paris. Terracotta, modelled, incised and inlaid; height 4 1/4 inches. (Chuzeville).*

311a. *Mesopotamian Art. Larsa (Senkereh).* Small Figure-Plaque. Turbaned Figure holding a Cup. *Late 3rd - early 2nd millennium B.C. Louvre, Paris. Terracotta, made in a mould; height 4 1/2 inches. (Chuzeville).*

311b. *Mesopotamian Art. Lagash (Telloh).* Small Figure-Plaque. Worshipper in Front View. *Late 3rd - early 2nd millennium B.C. Louvre, Paris. Terracotta, made in a mould; height 4 3/4 inches. (Chuzeville).*

311c. *Mesopotamian Art. Lagash (Telloh).* Small Figure-Plaque. Worshipper in Side View. *Late 3rd - early 2nd millennium B.C. Louvre, Paris. Terracotta, made in a mould; height 3 3/8 inches. (Chuzeville).*

312. *Sumerian Art. Lagash (Telloh).* Figurine. Demon clutching a Bird with its Paws. *Second half of the 3rd millennium B.C. Louvre, Paris. Terracotta, modelled with hollow body; height 5 1/8 inches. (Tel-Vigneau).*

313. *Sumerian Art. Lagash (Telloh).* Figurine. Warrior with an Adze. *Second half of the 3rd millennium B.C. Iraq Museum, Baghdad, Terracotta, modelled, incised and inlaid; height 7 1/2 inches. (André Parrot).*

314. *Assyrian Art.* Winged Eagle-headed Genius holding a Staff. *First half of the 1st millennium B.C. Louvre, Paris. Terracotta, height 5 1/4 inches. (Louvre).*

315. *Assyrian Art. Dur Sharrukin (Khorsabad).* Gilgamesh holding a Staff. *8th century B.C. Louvre, Paris. Clay, height 9 1/2 inches. (Draeger).*

316. *Neo-Babylonian Art. Larsa (Senkereh).* Mother nursing a Child. *7th-6th centuries B.C. Louvre, Paris (AO 16966-16967). Terracotta, height 3 5/8 inches. (Louvre).*

317. *Sumerian Art. Ur (Muqayyar).* Decoration of a Box, detail. Animal Passant. *First half of the 3rd millennium B.C. University Museum, Philadelphia. Shell and bitumen, height 1 1/4 inches. (University Museum).*

318. *Sumerian Art. Ur (Muqayyar).* Decorative Inlay, detail of No. 322. Gilgamesh grappling with two Human-headed Bulls. *First half of the 3rd millennium B.C. University Museum, Philadelphia. Shell (incised and painted) and lapis-lazuli, height 2 1/2 inches. (British Museum).*

319. *Sumerian Art. Ur (Muqayyar).* The 'Standard' of Ur, detail. Servant and Guest at a Banquet. *First half of the 3rd millennium B.C. British Museum. Inlay of shell, lapis-lazuli and red stone; over-all height 7 7/8 inches; over-all length 18 1/2 inches. (British Museum).*

320a. *Sumerian Art. Ur (Muqayyar).* The 'Standard' of Ur, side representing 'Peace.' *First half of the 3rd millennium B.C. British Museum. Inlay of shell, lapis-lazuli and red stone; height 7 7/8, length 18 1/2 inches. (British Museum).*

320b. *Sumerian Art. Ur (Muqayyar).* The 'Standard' of Ur, side representing 'War.' *First half of the 3rd millennium B.C. British Museum. Inlay of shell, lapis-lazuli and red stone; height 7 7/8 inches, length 18 1/2 inches (British Museum).*

321. *Sumerian Art. Ur (Muqayyar).* Gaming Board. *First half of the 3rd millennium B.C. British Museum. Inlay of shell, bone, red limestone and lapis-lazuli set in bitumen; length 10 5/8 inches. (British Museum).*

322. *Sumerian Art. Ur (Muqayyar).* Decorated Sound-box Panel of a Harp. Gilgamesh, Animals at a Banquet Animal musicians, and Scorpion-Man. *First half of the 3rd millennium B.C. University Museum, Philadelphia. Shell inlay set in bitumen; height 8 5/8 inches. (British Museum).* Cf. No. 318.

323. *Sumerian Art. Ur (Muqayyar).* Decoration of a Box. *First half of the 3rd millennium B.C. Iraq Museum, Baghdad. Shell and lapis-lazuli, over-all height 13 3/4 inches. (Iraq Museum).*

324. *Mesopotamian Art. Mari (Tell Hariri).* 'Standard.' Aftermath of War and Numbering of Captives. *First half of the 3rd millennium B.C. Aleppo Museum. Louvre, Paris. Inlay of shell and red stone set in bitumen and wood. (Tel-Vigneau).* It is impossible to determine the over-all dimensions of the work, owing to its fragmentary state. The average height of the figures is 4 inches.

325. *Mesopotamian Art. Mari (Tell Hariri).* Warrior with an Adze. *First half of the 3rd millennium B.C. Louvre, Paris. Shell, height 3 7/8 inches. (Tel-Vigneau).*

326. *Syro-Phœnician Art. Hadatu (Arslan Tash).* Winged Ram-headed Sphinxes. *8th century B.C. Aleppo Museum. Ivory, height 3 1/4, length 7 3/4 inches. (After Thureau-Dangin, Arslan-Tash, pl. 27, p. 22).*

327. *Assyrian Art (?). Kalakh (Nimrud).* Fragment of the Head of a Woman wearing a Diadem decorated with Rosettes. *9th-8th centuries B.C. Ivory and gold, height 3 1/8 inches. (Illustrated London News, July 22, 1950, p. 17).*

328a. *Sumerian Art. Lagash (Telloh).* Decorative Motif. Bull attacked by a Lion. *First half of the 3rd millennium B.C. Louvre, Paris. Shell, height 2 3/4 inches. (Tel-Vigneau).*

328b. *Sumerian Art. Lagash (Telloh).* Decorative Motif. Ibex leaning against a Shrub. *First half of the 3rd millennium B.C. Louvre, Paris. Shell, height 2 3/8 inches. (Tel-Vigneau).*

329. *Assyrian Art. Assur (Qalaat Shergat).* Palace of Tukulti-Ninurta I. Mountain-God with the Flowing Vase. *13th century B.C. Berlin Museum. Ivory, height 4 1/8, length 6 3/4 inches. (Berlin Museum).*

330. *Assyrian Art. Kalakh (Nimrud).* Lilith. *First half of the 1st millennium B.C. Ivory, height 4 5/8 inches. (Illustrated London News, August 22, 1953).*

331. *Assyrian Art.* Lions and Antelope on a wooded Hillside. *First half of the 1st millennium B.C. Louvre, Paris. Silver and ivory, height 2 1/2, length 12 5/8 inches. (Chuzeville).*

332. *Mesopotamian Art. Tell 'Uqair.* Altar Decoration. *Late 4th - early 3rd millennium B.C. Painting. (After Seton Lloyd and Fuad Safar, Journal of Near Eastern Studies, II, 1943, pl. XI).*

333. *Mesopotamian Art. Mari (Tell Hariri).* Sacrificial Scene, detail. Officiant directing the Sacrifice. *18th century B.C. Louvre, Paris. Painting on plaster, from Court 106 of the Palace. Height 31 1/2, length 53 inches. (Draeger).*

334. *Mesopotamian Art. Mari (Tell Hariri).* 'The Investiture of the King,' detail. Goddess with the Flowing Vase. *18th century B.C. Louvre, Paris. Painting on mud plaster, height 13 3/4 inches, length 8 feet 2 inches. (Draeger).*

335. *Kassite Art. Aqar Quf (Dur Kurigalzu).* Wall Painting. Procession of Dignitaries, detail. *14th century B.C. (After Taha Baqir, Iraq, VIII, 1946, pl. XII).*

336. *Assyrian Art. Til Barsip (Tell Ahmar).* Wall Painting in the Palace. Ibex. *8th-7th centuries B.C. Aleppo Museum. (Schneider-Lengyel).* The museum authorities have varnished the painting; this accounts for its being darker in tone than the painting in the Louvre (No. 337).

337. *Assyrian Art. Til Barsip (Tell Ahmar).* Wall Painting in the Palace. Ibex. *8th-7th centuries B.C. Louvre, Paris. Height 19 1/2 inches, width 24 1/2 inches. (Draeger).* No varnish having been added to this painting, it is lighter in tone than No. 336.

338. *Assyrian Art. Til Barsip (Tell Ahmar).* Wall Painting in the Palace. Archer. *8th century B.C. Aleppo Museum. (Schneider-Lengyel).*
This painting too has been varnished and is therefore darker than No. 337.

339. *Assyrian Art. Til Barsip (Tell Ahmar).* Wall Painting in the Palace. Galloping Horseman. *7th century B.C. Copy by L. Cavro, Paris.*
Published in black and white by Thureau-Dangin, *Til Barsip,* p. 70.

340. *Assyrian Art. Til Barsip (Tell Ahmar).* Wall Painting in the Palace. Roaring Lion. *8th or 7th century B.C. Copy by L. Cavro, Paris. Height 13 3/4 inches.*
Published in black and white on a smaller scale by Thureau-Dangin, *Til Barsip,* pl. L, upper right.

341. *Assyrian Art. Dur Sharrukin (Khorsabad).* Wall Decoration in the Palace of Sargon. Geometric and Animal Designs. *8th century B.C. Length 10 feet. (After Loud and Altman, Khorsabad, II, pl. 90).*

342. *Assyrian Art. Til Barsip (Tell Ahmar).* Wall Decoration in the Palace. Geometric and Animal Designs. *8th century B.C. Copy by L. Cavro, Paris. Height 4 feet, length 6 1/2 feet.*
Published in black and white on a smaller scale by Thureau-Dangin, *Til Barsip,* pl. XLVII (XXI).

343. *Assyrian Art. Til Barsip (Tell Ahmar).* Wall Painting in the Palace. Panels with Geometric and Animal Designs. *8th century B.C. Copy by L. Cavro, Paris. Height 8 feet 10 inches.*
Published in black and white on a smaller scale by Thureau-Dangin, *Til Barsip,* pl. XLV.

344. *Assyrian Art. Til Barsip (Tell Ahmar).* Wall Painting in the Palace. Anatolians (?) led into Captivity. *8th century B.C. Copy by L. Cavro, Paris. Height 45 1/4 inches.*
Published in black and white on a smaller scale by Thureau-Dangin, *Til Barsip,* pl. XLIX (XXIVa, b, c).

345. *Assyrian Art. Til Barsip (Tell Ahmar).* Wall Painting in the Palace. Large Hunting Scene with Chariots. *7th century B.C. Copy by L. Cavro, Paris. Length 21 feet.*
Published in black and white on a smaller scale by Thureau-Dangin, *Til Barsip,* pl. LIII (XXVIIe).

346. *Assyrian Art. Til Barsip (Tell Ahmar).* Wall Painting in the Palace. Head of a Dignitary. *8th century B.C. Aleppo Museum. (Schneider-Lengyel).*
Published in black and white on a smaller scale by Thureau-Dangin, *Til Barsip,* pl. XLIV, 1. The painting is here reproduced in reverse.

347. *Assyrian Art. Til Barsip (Tell Ahmar).* Wall Painting in the Palace. Horses and Lancer. *8th century B.C. Copy by L. Cavro, Paris. Length 6 1/2 feet.*
Published in black and white on a smaller scale by Thureau-Dangin, *Til Barsip,* pl. XLIX, upper left.

348. *Assyrian Art. Til Barsip (Tell Ahmar).* Scribes at Work, one on a Papyrus Sheet (?), the other on a Clay Tablet. *8th century B.C. Wall painting in Room 24 of the palace, height 4 feet 7 inches. Copy by L. Cavro, Paris.*

349. *Sumerian Art.* Tablet with 'Archaic' Pictographic Script. *Late 4th - early 3rd millennium B.C. Louvre, Paris. Clay, height 1 5/8, width 2 inches. (Arthaud).*

The early characters of Mesopotamian writing were based on the familiar sights of daily life: men, cattle, dwelling houses, plant forms, implements, etc.

350. The French Assyriologist François Thureau-Dangin (1872-1944). *Photograph taken in 1943. (Pestre).*

351. The American Assyriologist Samuel Noah Kramer (b. 1897).

352. *Sumerian Art.* Tablet with a Catalogue of Literary Works. *2nd millennium B.C. Louvre, Paris (AO 5393). Clay, 37 1/2 by 21 inches. (Draeger).*

353. *Neo-Sumerian Art. Lagash (Telloh).* Gudea, the so-called 'Architect with a Plan.' *22nd century B.C. Louvre, Paris. Diorite, height 36 1/2 inches. (Roger Parry).*
The inscription is a dedication of the statue to Ningirsu, followed by an enumeration of the countries supplying materials for the construction of the shrine of the *eninnu* and its chapel, the *gigunu*; and ending with maledictions against anyone removing or tampering with the statue.

354a. *Neo-Sumerian Art. Lagash (Telloh).* Cylinder Seal 'A' of Gudea. *22nd century B.C. Louvre, Paris. Terracotta, height 22 3/4, diameter 12 1/4 inches. (Chuzeville).*
Cylinders 'A' (30 inscribed columns) and 'B' (No. 354b) tell us a great deal about Sumerian religious beliefs and practices in the time of Gudea.

354b. *Neo-Sumerian Art. Lagash (Telloh).* Cylinder Seal 'B' of Gudea. *22nd century B.C. Louvre, Paris. Terracotta, height 21 1/4, diameter 13 inches. (Chuzeville).*
Though a little shorter (24 columns) than that of Cylinder 'A,' the inscription on this cylinder is equally important for the information it gives us.

355. *Mesopotamian Art. Mari (Tell Hariri).* Inscription on the Statue of Lamgi-Mari, King of Mari. *First half of the 3rd millennium B.C. Aleppo Museum. White Stone, height 10 3/4 inches. (André Parrot).*
As usual, the inscription gives the name of the personage represented, his office, and the name of the divinity (here, 'virile' Ishtar) to whom his statue is dedicated.

356. *Mesopotamian Art. Mari (Tell Hariri).* Inscription on the Statue of Idi-Narum the 'Miller.' *First half of the 3rd millennium B.C. Aleppo Museum. Stone, pink breccia; height 8 inches (with the head, not shown here). (André Parrot).*

357. *Mesopotamian Art. Diyala Region.* Inscription on the Statue of Gin-Ak. *First half of the 3rd millennium B.C. Louvre, Paris (AO 20146). Gypsum, height 10 1/4 inches. (André Parrot).*
As this work was acquired from a dealer, its exact provenance is unknown, but the style is that of the Diyala region.

358. *Babylonian Art.* Nude Winged Goddess on the Burney Plaque. *Early 2nd millennium B.C. Norman Colville Collection. Terracotta, height 19 5/8 inches. (Warburg Institute).*
Though it has been questioned, the authenticity of this work seems to us undeniable.

359. *Akkadian Art.* Seal Impression: Etana. *Second half of the 3rd millennium B.C. Berlin Museum (VA 3456). Serpentine, height 1 3/4 inches. (Marburg).*
The Louvre owns an almost identical cylinder seal from Telloh (MNB 1348), carved in shell, height 1 1/2 inches.

360. *Akkadian Art.* Seal Impression: the Bird-God Zu. *Second half of the 3rd millennium B.C. Louvre, Paris (AO 2129). Green and yellow serpentine, height 1 1/2 inches. (Marc Foucault).*

361. *Akkadian Art.* Cylinder Seal of the Bird-God Zu, detail. *Second half of the 3rd millennium B.C. Louvre, Paris (AO 2129). Green and yellow serpentine. (Marc Foucault).*
The god Zu has the torso of a man combined with the body of a bird. He was led in chains before the water god Ea (Enki).

362. *Babylonian Art.* Tablet of 'The Righteous Sufferer.' *Early 2nd millennium B.C. Louvre, Paris (AO 4462). Clay, 7 by 3 5/8 inches. (Draeger).*

363. *Babylonian Art. Susa.* Code of Hammurabi, detail. *18th century B.C. Louvre, Paris. Basalt, over-all height 7 feet 4 1/2 inches. (Chuzeville).*

364. *Assyrian Art. Assur (Qalaat Shergat) (?).* Tablet narrating Sargon's Eighth Campaign. *8th century B.C. Louvre, Paris. Terracotta, 14 3/4 by 9 5/8 inches. (Chuzeville).*
The text is engraved in three columns on both sides, numbering 430 lines in all. Purchased from a dealer, whose information as to its provenance seems to be reliable.

365. *Babylonian Art. Mari (Tell Hariri).* A Schoolroom in the Palace. *18th century B.C. Unbaked bricks. (André Parrot).*
Room 24 in the palace, measuring 43 1/2 by 24 feet, with forty benches of different sizes. On or between these benches were clay receptacles containing 'school furniture.' A smaller schoolroom in the same palace (Room 25) had twenty benches.

366. *Sumerian Art. Ur (Muqayyar).* Musician on the 'Standard' of Ur. *First half of the 3rd millennium B.C. British Museum. Inlay of shell, lapis lazuli and red limestone; over-all length 18 1/2 inches, over-all height 7 7/8 inches. (British Museum).*

367. *Neo-Sumerian Art. Lagash (Telloh).* Vase. Musicians with a Drum. *22nd century B.C. Louvre, Paris. Dark stone, height 4 3/4 inches. (Giraudon).*

368a and b. *Babylonian Art. Tell Harmal.* Terracotta Cylinder with Musical Notation (?). *Early 2nd millennium B.C. Iraq Museum, Baghdad. Clay. (Illustrated London News).*

369. *Sumerian Art. Ur (Muqayyar).* Harp from the Tomb of 'Queen' Shubad. *First half of the 3rd millennium. British Museum (121198). Wood inlaid with shell, lapis lazuli and red stone; height 42 inches. Eleven strings. (After Woolley, Ur, pl. 109).*

370. *Sumerian Art. Ur (Muqayyar).* Lyre from Tomb 1237, the so-called 'Death Pit.' *First half of the 3rd millennium B.C. University Museum, Philadelphia. Wood overlaid with silver, height 45 3/4 inches. (After Woolley Ur, pl. 112).*

371. *Sumerian Art. Ur (Muqayyar).* Lyre from the 'Royal' Tomb 1151. *First half of the 3rd millennium B.C. Iraq Museum, Baghdad. Wood, height 35 1/2, length 39 3/8 inches. (After Woolley, Ur, pl. 118b).*

372a. *Sumerian Art. Ur (Muqayyar).* Soundbox panel of the Lyre from the 'Royal' Tomb 789. Animal playing Harp. *First half of the 3rd millennium B.C. University Museum, Philadelphia. Shell inlay set in bitumen, height 2 inches. (British Museum).*

372b. *Sumerian Art. Ur (Muqayyar).* Cylinder Seal. Banquet Scene with Musical Entertainment. *First half of the 3rd millennium B.C. University Museum, Philadelphia. Lapis lazuli, height 1 1/2 inches. (After Woolley, Ur, pl. 193, fig. 18; U 10872).*

372c. *Sumerian Art. Ur (Muqayyar).* Cylinder Seal. Banquet Scene with Musical Entertainment. *First half of the 3rd millennium B.C. Lapis lazuli, height 1 5/8 inches. Tomb 1237. (After Woolley, Ur, pl. 194, fig. 22; U 12374).*

372d. *Sumerian Art. Ur (Muqayyar).* Cylinder Seal. Banquet Scene with Musical Entertainment. *First half of the 3rd millennium B.C. Iraq Museum, Baghdad (14597). Gold leaf over an unspecified core, height 1 5/8 inches. (After Woolley, Ur, pl. 193, fig. 21; U 11904).*

373a. *Sumerian Art. Ur (Muqayyar).* The 'Standard' of Ur, side representing 'Peace.' Banquet with Musical Entertainment, detail. *First half of the 3rd millennium B.C. British Museum. Inlay of shell, lapis lazuli and red limestone, height 7 7/8 inches. (British Museum).*

373b. *Mesopotamian Art. Khafaje.* Votive Plaque. Banquet Scene with Musical Entertainment. *First half of the 3rd millennium B.C. Oriental Institute, Chicago. Stone, length 7 7/8, width 7 7/8 inches. (After Frankfort, pl. 105, fig. 185).*

374. *Sumerian Art. Adad (Bismaya).* Procession with Two Harpists. *First half of the 3rd millennium B.C. Oriental Institute, Chicago. Steatite, diameter of the vase 8 5/8 inches (?). (Oriental Institute).*

375. *Neo-Sumerian Art. Lagash (Telloh).* Stele of Gudea with Musical Scene. *22nd century B.C. Louvre, Paris (AO 52). Stone, height 49 1/4 inches. (Draeger).*

376. *Babylonian Art. Larsa (Senkereh).* Potsherd with a Harpist. *Early 2nd millennium B.C. Iraq Museum, Baghdad. Terracotta, 6 by 5 1/4 inches. (André Parrot).*

377. *Babylonian Art. Ashnunnak (Tell Asmar).* Small Figure-Plaque. Harpist. *Early 2nd millennium B.C. Louvre, Paris (AO 12453). Terracotta, height 4 3/4, width 2 3/4 inches. (Draeger).*

378. *Babylonian Art. Ashnunnak (Tell Asmar).* Small Figure-Plaque. Harpist. *Early 2nd millennium B.C. Louvre, Paris (AO 12455). Terracotta, height 4 1/8, width 2 3/8 inches. (Draeger).*

379. *Babylonian Art. Ashnunnak (Tell Asmar).* Small Figure-Plaque. Harpist. *Early 2nd millennium B.C. Louvre, Paris (AO 12454). Terracotta, height 3 1/2, width 2 7/8 inches. (Draeger).*

380. *Babylonian Art.* Small Figure-Plaque. Lute Player. *Early 2nd millennium B.C. Louvre, Paris. Terracotta. (Draeger).*

381. *Mesopotamian Art. Mari (Tell Hariri).* Fragment of 'Ur-Nina,' hand with musical instrument. *First half 3rd millennium B.C. Damascus Museum. Gypsum, height 5 inches. (André Parrot).*

382a. *Sumerian Art. Ur (Muqayyar).* Seal Impression. Banquet with Musical Entertainment. *First half of the 3rd millennium B.C. University Museum, Philadelphia. Lapis-lazuli, height 1 1/2 inches. Drawing by Claude Abeille, after Woolley.* Cf. No. 372b.

382b. *Sumerian Art. Ur (Muqayyar).* Seal Impression. Banquet with Musical Entertainment. *First half of the 3rd millennium B.C. Iraq Museum, Baghdad (14597). Gold, height 1 5/8 inches. Drawing by Claude Abeille. after Woolley.* Cf. 372d.

382c. *Sumerian Art. Ur (Muqayyar).* Seal Impression. Banquet with Musical Entertainment. *First half of the 3rd millennium B.C. Lapis lazuli, height 1 5/8 inches. Drawing by Claude Abeille, after Woolley.* Cf. 372c.

383. *Neo-Sumerian Art. Lagash (Telloh).* Small Figure-Plaque. Woman with a Tabor. *22nd-21st centuries B.C. Louvre, Paris. Terracotta, 6 5/8 inches. (André Parrot).*

384. *Babylonian Art. Mari (Tell Hariri).* Rattle. *21st-20th centuries B.C. Louvre, Paris (AO 19511). Terracotta, diameter 4 1/4, height 1 7/8 inches. (Draeger).*

385. *Neo-Sumerian Art. Lagash (Telloh).* 'Bass Drum' with Studded Rim. *22nd century B.C. Louvre, Paris. Stone, height 11 3/4, width 14 1/4 inches. (Draeger).*

386. *Sumerian Art. Ur (Muqayyar).* Cylinder Seal. Mythological Scene with a Monkey playing the Flute. *First half of the 3rd millennium B.C. Iraq Museum, Baghdad (14314). Lapis-lazuli, height 1 3/8 inches. (After Woolley, Ur, pl. 192, fig. 12; U 11734).*

387. *Babylonian Art. Larsa (Senkereh).* Monkey playing the Flute. *Early 2nd millennium B.C. Louvre, Paris (AO 16932). Terracotta, height 3 3/4 inches. (Draeger).*

388. *Seleucid Art. Larsa (Senkereh).* Woman with a Pan-Pipe. *3rd-2nd centuries B.C. Louvre, Paris (AO 16957). Terracotta, height 3 1/2 inches. (Draeger).*

389. *Babylonian Art. Mari (Tell Hariri).* Wall Painting in the Palace. Horn Player. *18th century B.C. Painting on plaster, height 15 3/4, width 21 1/4 inches. Copy by Pierre Hamelin. (André Parrot).*

390. *Mesopotamian Art. Mari (Tell Hariri).* Two Horn-players ('The Clowns'). *First half of the 3rd millennium B.C. Louvre, Paris (AO 17568). Gypsum, height 8 7/8, width 5 1/2 inches. (Monuments Historiques, Archives Photographiques).*

391. *Assyrian Art. Nineveh (Kuyunjik).* Musicians on a Relief of Assurbanipal. *7th century B.C. Louvre, Paris. Gypseous alabaster, height 15 inches. (Tel-Vigneau).*

392. *Assyrian Art. Nineveh (Kuyunjik).* Relief of Assurbanipal. Military Band celebrating the Victory over Teuman, King of the Elamites. *7th century B.C. British Museum. Gypseous alabaster, length 57, height 15 3/8 inches. (British Museum).*

393. *Assyrian Art. Nineveh (Kuyunjik).* Captives playing Lyres. *7th century B.C. British Museum. Gypseous alabaster, width 39 3/4, height 38 3/4 inches. Palace of Sennacherib. (British Museum).*

394. *North Syrian Art. Kalakh (Nimrud).* Pyx (reconstructed) Banquet Scene with Musical Entertainment. *9th century B.C. British Museum (118179). Ivory, height 2 1/2 inches. (After Barnett, Ivories, pl. XVI, S, 3).*

395. *North Syrian Art. Kalakh (Nimrud).* Pyx (reconstructed). Banquet Scene with Musical Entertainment, detail. *9th century B.C. British Museum (118179). Ivory, height 2 1/2 inches. (British Museum).*

396. *Maps.* Mesopotamian Sites from the 18th to the 4th century B.C. Zones of Influence.

397. *Map.* Mesopotamian Sites.

398. General Map of the Anciant Near East.

Drawings by Claude ABEILLE
from original documents or reproductions in André PARROT, *Archéologie mésopotamienne*, I and II.
Maps by Henri JACQUINET,
Marius CAGNON and Roger GRAINDORGE.

MAPS

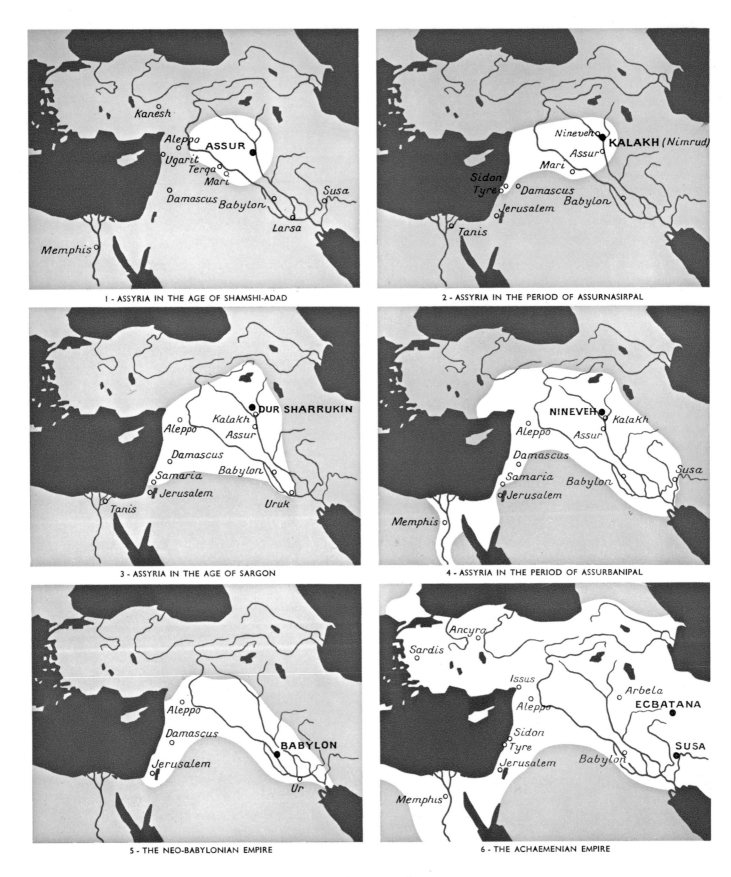

1 - ASSYRIA IN THE AGE OF SHAMSHI-ADAD

2 - ASSYRIA IN THE PERIOD OF ASSURNASIRPAL

3 - ASSYRIA IN THE AGE OF SARGON

4 - ASSYRIA IN THE PERIOD OF ASSURBANIPAL

5 - THE NEO-BABYLONIAN EMPIRE

6 - THE ACHAEMENIAN EMPIRE

396 - MESOPOTAMIAN SITES FROM THE 18th TO THE 4th CENTURY B.C. - ZONES OF INFLUENCE

380

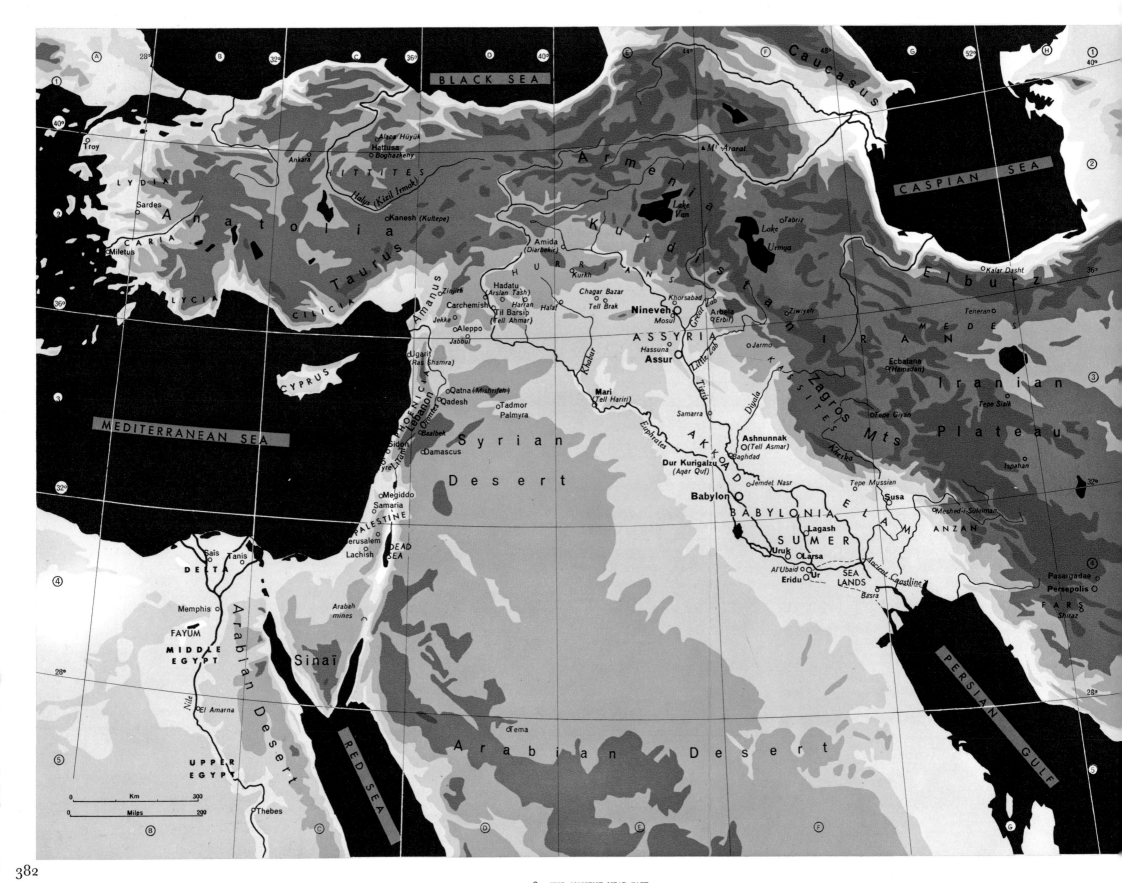

BLACK SEA

CASPIAN SEA

Caucasus

Armenia

Kurdistan

MEDES

IRAN

Elburz

Iranian

Plateau

Anatolia

LYDIA

CARIA

LYCIA

CILICIA

Taurus

Amanus

Lebanon

Anti-Lebanon

PHOENICIA

PALESTINE

DEAD SEA

Syrian

Desert

ASSYRIA

Zagros Mts

KASSITES

AKKAD

ELAM

ANZAN

BABYLONIA

SUMER

SEA LANDS

FARS

MEDITERRANEAN SEA

DELTA

MIDDLE EGYPT

FAYUM

UPPER EGYPT

Arabian Desert

Sinaï

RED SEA

Arabian Desert

PERSIAN GULF

Troy
Ankara
Alaca Hüyük
Hattusa
Boghazkeny
HITTITES
Halys (Kizil Irmak)
Sardes
Kanesh (Kultepe)
Miletus
Zinjirli
Hadatu (Arslan Tash)
Carchemish
Harran
Til Barsip (Tell Ahmar)
Halaf
Jekke
Aleppo
Jabbul
Ugarit (Ras Shamra)
Qatna (Mishrifeh)
Qadesh
Qadesh
Tadmor
Palmyra
Orontes
Baalbek
Damascus
Sidon
Tyre
Litani
Megiddo
Samaria
Jerusalem
Lachish
Saïs
Tanis
Memphis
El Amarna
Thebes
Tema
Arabah mines

Mt Ararat
Lake Van
Tabriz
Lake Urmia
Amida (Diarbekir)
Kurkh
HURRIANS
Chagar Bazar
Tell Brak
Khorsabad
Nineveh
Mosul
Hassuna
Assur
Mari (Tell Hariri)
Samarra
Khabur
Tigris
Euphrates
Diyala
Ashnunnak (Tell Asmar)
Baghdad
Dur Kurigalzu (Aqar Quf)
Jemdet Nasr
Babylon
Lagash
Uruk
Larsa
Al'Ubaid
Ur
Eridu
Basra
Ancient Coastline

Arbela (Erbil)
Great Zab
Little Zab
Ziwiyeh
Jarmo
Kerkha
Tepe Mussian
Susa
Meshed-i-Suleiman

Kalar Dasht
Teheran
Ecbatana (Hamadan)
Tepe Giyan
Tepe Siak
Ispahan
Pasargadae
Persepolis
Shiraz

CYPRUS

Km 300
Miles 290

382
383

ALPHABETICAL LISTS OF THE SITES

Opposite : Modern Names - Ancient Names
Below : Ancient Names - Modern Names
Reference Maps : A. The Mesopotamian Sites
B. The Ancient Near East

Some of the modern names designate sites whose ancient names have not yet been identified.

Ancient Names	Modern Names	A	B
Adab	Bismaya	d 7	
Agade	Deir (?)	c 6	
Aleppo	Aleppo		D 2
Amida	Diarbekir		E 2
Arbela	Erbil	c 2	F 2
Ashnunnak	Tell Asmar	c 5	F 3
Assur	Qalaat Shergat	b 3	E 3
Babylon	Babil	c 6	F 3
Barsip (Til)	Tell Ahmar		D 3
Borsippa	Birs Nimrud	c 6	
Byblos	Jebail		C 3
Carchemish	Jerablus		D 2
Damascus	Esh Sham		D 3
Dur Kurigalzu	Aqar Quf	c 5	F 3
Dur Sharrukin	Khorsabad	b 2	E 2
Dur Untashi	Choga Zambil	g 6	
Ecbatana	Hamadan	g 4	G 3
Eridu	Abu Shahrein	e 8	F 4
Guzana	Tell Halaf		E 2
Hadatu	Arslan Tash		
Harran	Harran		D 2
Hattusa	Boghazkeuy		C 2
Imgur Bel	Balawat	b 2	
Isin	Ishan Bahriyat	d 7	
Jericho	Er Riba		C 4
Jerusalem	Jerusalem or El Quds		C 4
Kalakh	Nimrud	b 2	
Kanesh	Kultepe		C 2
Kish	al 'Oheimir	c 6	
Lagash	Telloh	c 7	F 4
Larsa	Senkereh	d 7	F 4
Mari	Tell Hariri	a 4	E 3
Megiddo	Tell Mutesellim		C 3
Nerab	Neirab		
Nineveh	Kuyunjik	b 2	E 2
Nippur	Niffer	d 6	
Nuzi	Yorgan Tepe	c 3	
Palmyra	Tadmor		D 3
Pasargadae	Pasargade		H 4
Persepolis	Persepolis		H 4
Qadesh	Tell Nebi Mend		D 3
Qatna	Mishrifeh		D 3
Samarra	Samarra	b 4	F 3
Shaduppum	Tell Harmal		
Shuruppak	Fara	d 7	
Sidon	Saida		C 3
Sippar	Abu Habba	c 5	
Susa	Shushan	g 6	G 3
Terqa	Asharah		
Tutub	Khafaje (?)	c 5	
Troy	Hissarlik		A 2
Tyre	Sur		C 3
Ugarit	Ras Shamra		C 3
Umma	Jokha	d 7	
Ur	Muqayyar	e 8	F 4
Uruk	Warka	d 7	F 4
Washshukani	Fecherieh (?)		

Modern Names	Ancient Names	A	B
Abu Habba	Sippar	c 5	
Abu Shahrein	Eridu	e 8	F 4
Agrab (Tell)		d 5	
Ahmar (Tell)	Til Barsip		D 3
Akshak		c 6	
Aleppo	Aleppo		D 2
Ankara	Ancyra		C 2
Aqar Quf	Dur Kurigalzu	c 5	F 3
Arpatchiya		b 2	
Arslan Tash	Hadatu		D 2
Asharah	Terqa		
Asmar (Tell)	Ashnunnak	c 5	F 3
Baalbek	Heliopolis		D 3
Babil	Babylon	c 6	F 3
Baghdad		c 5	F 3
Balawat	Imgur Bel	b 2	
Basra		f 8	F 4
Bavian		b 2	
Billa (Tell)		b 2	
Birs Nimrud	Borsippa	c 6	
Bismaya	Adab	d 7	
Boghazkeuy	Hattusa		C 2
Brak (Tell)			E 2
Chagar Bazar	Shubat Enlil (?)		E 2
Chemchemal		c 3	
Choga Zambil	Dur Untashi	g 6	
Deir	Agade (?)	c 6	
Diarbekir	Amida		E 2
Dizful		g 6	
Djowi		g 6	
Erbil	Arbela	c 2	F 2
Er Riba	Jericho		C 4
Esh Sham	Damascus		D 3
Fara	Shuruppak	d 7	
Fecherieh	Washshukani (?)		
Gawra (Tepe)		b 2	
Giyan (Tepe)		g 5	G 3
Halaf (Tell)	Guzana		E 2
Hamadan	Ecbatana	g 4	G 3
Hariri (Tell)	Mari	a 4	E 3
Harmal (Tell)	Shadupum		
Harran	Harran		D 2
Hassuna		b 3	E 3
Hilleh			
Hines		b 2	
Hissarlik	Troy		A 2
Hit		a 5	
Ishan Bahriyat	Isin	d 7	
Ischali	Dur Rimush (?)	c 5	
Ischali	Neribtum (?)	c 5	
Ischali	Shatlash (?)	c 5	
Jarmo		c 3	F 5

Modern Names	Ancient Names	A	B
Jebail	Byblos		C 3
Jemdet Nasr		c 6	F 3
Jerablus	Carchemish		D 2
Jerusalem or El Quds	Jerusalem		C 4
Jezireh		a 1	
Jighan			
Jokha	Umma	d 7	
Kalar Dasht			H 2
Khafaje	Tutub (?)	c 5	
Khorsabad	Dur Sharrukin	b 2	E 2
Kirkuk		c 3	
Kultepe	Kanesh		C 2
Kuyunjik	Nineveh	b 2	E 2
Lahm (Tell el)		e 8	F 4
Maltai		b 2	
Meshed-i-Suleiman			G 3
Mishrifeh	Qatna		D 3
Mosul		b 2	E 2
Muallafat		b 2	
Muqayyar	Ur	e 8	F 4
Mutesellim (Tell)	Megiddo		C 3
Nakshi Rustam			
Nebi Mend (Tell)	Qadesh		D 5
Neirab	Nerab		
Niffer	Nippur	d 6	
Nimrud	Kalakh	b 2	
'Oheimir (al)	Kish	c 6	
Pasargadae	Pasargade		H 4
Persepolis	Persepolis		H 4
Qalaat Shergat	Assur	b 3	E 3
Ras Shamra	Ugarit		C 3
Saida	Sidon		C 3
Samarra	Samarra	b 4	F 3
Senkereh	Larsa	d 7	F 4
Shanidar		c 2	F 2
Shemshara			
Shushan	Susa	g 6	G 3
Sialk			
Suleimaniya		d 3	
Sur	Tyre		C 3
Surkh Dum			
Tadmor	Palmyra		D 3
Telloh	Lagash	e 7	F 4
Tepe Mussian		f 6	F 3
Tepe Sialk			G 3
'Ubaid (al)		d 8	F 4
'Uqair (Tell)		c 6	
Warka	Uruk	d 7	F 4
Yorgan Tepe	Nuzi	c 3	
Zarzi		d 3	
Ziwiyeh		e 3	F 2

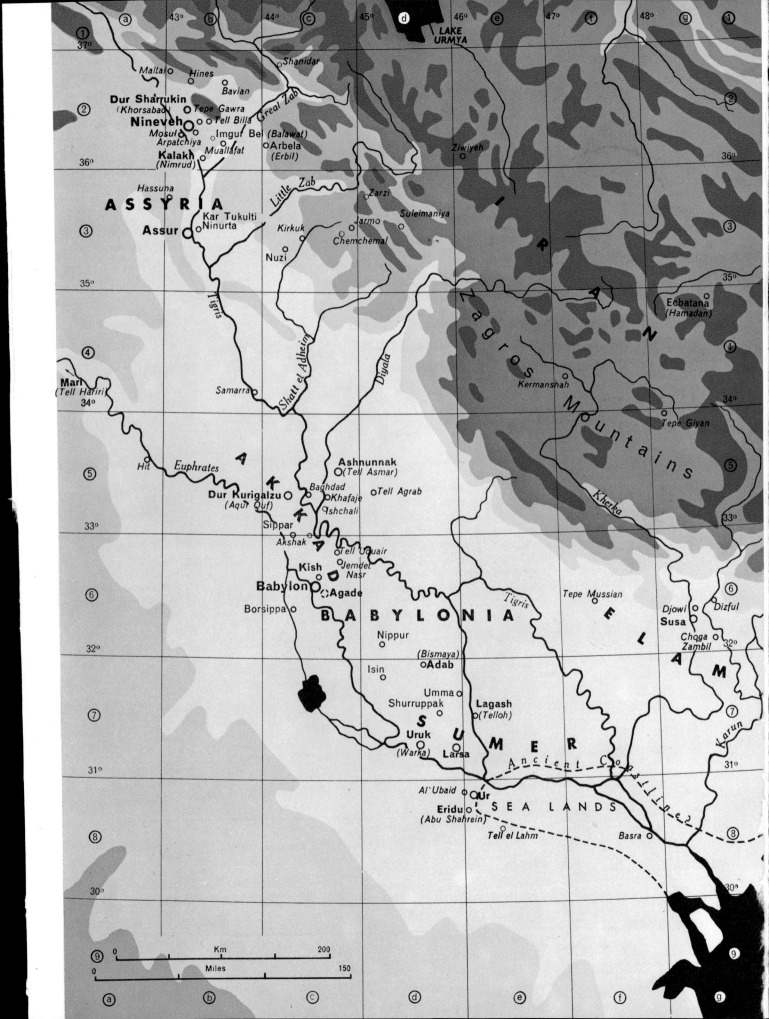

THIS, THE SECOND VOLUME OF THE SERIES 'THE ARTS OF MANKIND,'
EDITED BY ANDRÉ MALRAUX AND GEORGES SALLES, HAS BEEN
PRODUCED UNDER THE SUPERVISION OF ALBERT BEURET, EDITOR-
IN-CHARGE OF THE SERIES. THE BOOK WAS DESIGNED BY ROGER
PARRY. THE TEXT AND PLATES IN BLACK AND WHITE AND IN
IVORY WERE PRINTED BY L'IMPRIMERIE GEORGES LANG, PARIS;
PLATES IN SEPIA, GREY, METALLIC INKS AND COLOUR BY
L'IMPRIMERIE DRAEGER, MONTROUGE. DESIGNED BY MASSIN, THE
BINDING WAS EXECUTED BY BABOUOT, GENTILLY.

PRINTED IN FRANCE